THE OFFICIAL®
PRICE GUIDE TO
CARNIVAL GLASS

FROM THE EDITORS OF
THE HOUSE OF COLLECTIBLES

CONSULTING EDITORS
CHARLES AND DONNA JORDAN

SECOND EDITION

THE HOUSE OF COLLECTIBLES
NEW YORK, NEW YORK 10022

Important Notice. The format of *The Official Price Guide Series,* published by *The House of Collectibles,* is based on the following proprietary features: *All facts and prices are compiled through a nationwide sampling of information* obtained from noteworthy experts, auction houses, and specialized dealers. *Detailed "indexed" format* enables quick retrieval of information for positive identification. *Encapsulated histories* precede each category to acquaint the collector with the specific traits that are peculiar to that area of collecting. *Valuable collecting information* is provided for both the novice as well as the seasoned collector. How to begin a collection; how to buy, sell, and trade; care and storage techniques; tips on restoration; grading guidelines; lists of periodicals, clubs, museums, auction houses, dealers, etc. *An average price range* takes geographic location and condition into consideration when reporting collector value. *An inventory checklist system* is provided for cataloging a collection.

All of the information, including valuations, in this book has been compiled from the most reliable sources, and every effort has been made to eliminate errors and questionable data. Nevertheless the possibility of error, in a work of such immense scope, always exists. The publisher will not be held responsible for losses which may occur in the purchase, sale, or other transaction of items because of information contained herein. Readers who feel they have discovered errors are invited to *write* and inform us, so they may be corrected in subsequent editions. Those seeking further information on the topics covered in this book are advised to refer to the complete line of Official Price Guides published by The House of Collectibles.

Published by: The House of Collectibles
201 East 50th Street
New York, New York 10022

Distributed by Ballantine Books, a division of Random House, Inc., New York and simultaneously in Canada by Random House of Canada Limited, Toronto.

Manufactured in the United States of America

Library of Congress Catalog Card Number: 85-646239

ISBN: 0-87637-532-8

10 9 8 7 6 5 4 3

TABLE OF CONTENTS

ACKNOWLEDGMENT

The editors to the *Official Price Guide to Carnival Glass* would like to extend their appreciation to Lee Markley, secretary of the International Carnival Glass Association, for his extensive work on this edition. Mr. Markley provided a fresh new look to the book by adding many new patterns, colors, and prices on carnival glass.

The editors would also like to thank Galina Kolev for assisting in the production of this book.

Note to Readers

MARKET REVIEW

Intense collector interest has already driven the price of Carnival glass into the astronomical range. An amethyst Carnival Farmyard Plate sold for $8,000 just this past year. The tables have turned over the years as this originally cheap imitation of art glass now far exceeds in value the high quality glass it sought to imitate. Long regarded with disdain by many dealers, collectors, and auction houses, Carnival glass is now turning up on the most prestigious auction blocks in the country.

The Carnival glass scene is a healthy one with prices continuing to be strong, especially for rarities. However, there hasn't been a great deal of change in the market for more plentiful pieces. Some of the prices realized at a Carnival glass auction held in Missouri included: square, purple Farmyard bowl, $2200; purple Garden Path chop plate, $900; blue opalescent Vintage bowl, $750; Millersburg green Trout and Fly bowl, $350.

Absentee bidding played a major role in a very successful Midwestern auction. A sampling of prices realized are as follows: marigold Stag and Holly 12″ footed plate, $450; pair of aqua opalescent Hearts and Flowers compotes, $440; amethyst Millersburg Diamonds pitcher, $210; marigold Nuart Homestead plate, $475; and cobalt Fenton Makodo with Cherries, 10″ compote, $235.

When assessing the Carnival glass market it is very important to remember that there can be vast differences in Carnival prices from one part of the country to another. It also seems that more large collections are being auctioned off which could mean that some rarities may actually come down in price slightly. One thing is for sure, collectors are willing to spend a great deal of money on rare pieces.

Another interesting trend in all fields of collecting is the number of collectors who prefer to acquire all types of glass rather than one specific type. These collectors seem to look for the interesting and unique color, shape, or type of glass. Consequently, many of the old established collecting modes are changing as dealers discover the new demand for the eclectic in glass. This trend is hardly new to the Carnival field, however, as its collectors have always been drawn to the more unusual and unlikely subject matter. Who would have thought that the Farmyard pattern would end up being the most expensive Carnival glass in the world?

INTRODUCTION

The development of glass is certainly one of the most important of man's contributions to civilization. Glass has given us very practical solutions to our need for eating utensils and safe storage of foodstuffs, providing very decorative and aesthetic works of art in the process. Through glass we have been able to combine function with beauty, sometimes inexpensively (pattern glass, Carnival glass, and Depression glass), and sometimes at greater expense (cut glass and art glass). Regardless of cost, however, we all enjoy the benefits of glass daily.

We do not know the exact date of the discovery of glass but we do know that it predates the time of Christ, anywhere from 5,000 to 12,000 years. The first use of glass was probably as a glaze for stone beads which were worn as jewelry in Western Asia. Eventually the beads themselves were made of glass, which was thought to have magical properties.

The Egyptians and Syrians developed glassmaking considerably. Indeed, small blue glass vases from the Egyptian 18th Dynasty have been excavated near Thebes, and they reveal the great glassmaking skill which had been attained by the Egyptians. The most significant development in the history of glass was the blowing of glass which some experts feel was developed by the Syrians around 50 B.C. They originated mold-blown glass and later, free-blown glass.

The expansion of the Roman Empire dispersed glassmaking widely. Glass was made all over Persia and Europe, but it was in Venice, Italy that glass really achieved its most glorious application to date. Venetian glass was at its height in the 15th and 16th centuries. Despite every attempt to keep Venetian techniques a secret, these methods gradually made their way across Europe. Giacomo Verzelini of Venice managed a glass factory in London in 1575 and glass production flourished all over England. The next great refinement came when George Ravenscroft of England developed lead crystal in 1675. This new heavy glass permitted cutting, engraving, and decoration and was preferred over the paper thin Venetian-style glass. By the 19th century colored glass, especially Bohemian glass, was enjoying great popularity.

In the United States, around 1825, molds were developed which pressed patterns into glass imitating the expensive cut glass of Europe. At last decorative glass tableware was within the reach of the middle classes.

By the 1870s American craftsmen were producing ornate cut glass for the wealthy upper classes in America. The years from 1876 to 1914 are referred to as the brilliant period of cut glass. Heavy lead crystal was deeply cut, faceted, and polished by hand, resulting in pieces which were prismatic and intricate beyond belief.

Art glass came into being during the last half of the 19th century as part of the Victorian preoccupation with the fussy and elaborate. But it was as a result of the worldwide Art Nouveau movement that the beautiful art glass of Tiffany, Galle, Lalique, and others was created. It captured the attention of all with its natural sensual lines and incredible color, shading, and iridescence.

In 1905, taffeta, or Carnival glass as it has come to be known, was born out of the craze for iridescent art glass. Using mass production and new chemical techniques, Carnival glass was widely produced toward the end of the Art Nouveau period. Tastes changed, however, ushering in the streamlined Art Deco period. Even though it continued to be produced until 1930, by 1925 Carnival glass was on the way out. With a dwindling market, this glass was sold by the trainload to fairs and carnivals to be given away as prizes. Hence, it has come to be called Carnival glass.

With the Wall Street Crash of 1929, the United States economy collapsed, and the era of Great Depression was ushered in. At this time tank glass production was developed, which allowed for the machine molding of huge quantities of glass tableware in just one step. This mass produced tableware has come to be known as Depression glass. It was usually made of colored glass with green, blue, amber, pink, cobalt, red, amethyst, and opaque white being the predominant colors. There was some clear glass produced as well. The patterns were often lacy and elaborate as much to hide the imperfections in the glass itself as for decoration. This glass was often made in complete sets of tableware and given as a premium at gas stations, stores, movie theaters, and in cereal boxes. The prices were incredibly cheap and it was common for a complete service for four to cost a mere $1.99.

The shimmering, dazzling colors which capture the flamboyant variations of the fire opal and the abalone shell characterize the most unusual glass ever produced in the history of America. Once known as Taffeta glass for its glossy, shiny appearance, Carnival glass is easily recognizable because of its bright iridescence. The chameleon colors flash different exotic shades as the viewer observes it from different angles and in different light. This trait attracts the most attention.

The unusual use of colors, the ornate patterns, and the elaborate shapes—some borrowed and some original—emerged from an intermingling of styles from the past as well as ones contemporary with the period when Carnival glass was first produced. The further development of industrial mechanisms and production know-how provided the means for creating something new and different. Handcrafting combined with mass production added a distinctive flair.

During the 1800s, Americans invented practical methods for producing pressed pattern glass. By the end of the century, refinements engendered greater efficiency, thus allowing for inexpensive glass to be produced in larger quantities with a more extensive range in shapes and patterns. Eventually, pressed glass fused the geometric designs of cut glass with naturalistic motifs, culminating in an intricacy impossible fifty years earlier.

Tradition, conventionality, inhibitions, and social restraints in all areas of life were challenged and discarded at the turn of the century. A newly mechanized society with the means of providing widespread news revealed the fashions and tastes of the rich, the famous, and the avant–garde to the view of the middle class more readily than ever before. The exotic, sensuous artifacts of Art Nouveau with their sinuous lines and undulating colors fascinated the middle class, but these works were too expensive for them. As the popularity of pattern glass faded, a small group of glass producers offered a different type of glassware that was in the average person's price range, yet satisfied their desire for articles which reflected the new style so popular with the wealthy. These manufacturers devised inexpensive methods for treating intricately designed pressed glass which resulted in a surface iridescence imitative of the highly favored Tiffany glass. The masses gratefully bought this glass which displayed a boldness and innovation in color and design indicative of the new era.

When first produced, Carnival glass provided a combination of the old coupled with an exotic originality. At times, Carnival displays the purity and perfect balance of line associated with classical pieces, such as the Buttermilk Goblet made by Fenton; or the naturalistic, free-flowing forms representative of the Art Nouveau style, such as the Ripple Vase made by Imperial. The patterns typical of cut glass in glittering green, such as the Potpourri

Punch Bowl and Near–Cut Wreath Bowl by Millersburg, offer a startling difference compared to the starkness of cut glass. Plus, the profusion of motifs common in pattern glass—floral, fruit, and animals—were freely utilized. Although the Carnival patterns and basic shapes were formed by the same methods used in pressed pattern—the molten glass was forced into a mold by being pressed with a plunger—many Carnival pieces were further worked on by hand. Craftsmen often shaped articles by ruffling, crimping, or inverting the rim of a bowl, pulling a vase into an elongated form which modified the pattern designs, or shaping some portion of an object into an asymmetric mode. Even with this handwork, manufacturers were able to keep their production costs down. Carnival also differed from pressed in that it was opaque, making raised patterns on the inside and the outside of objects possible, though the inside surface was usually left plain when the piece was made to hold liquids. Despite the borrowing of styles and motifs, and attempts to imitate art glass, Carnival glass offered the consumer a new dramatic look.

While Carnival was being produced, the manufacturers merely referred to it as iridescent pressed glass. Some advertised it as taffeta or rhodium glass. Others used names such as Etruscan or Pompeiian, associating it with ancient glass, which often forms a sort of iridescence from aging. During the late 1920s, Depression glass supplanted Carnival glass in popularity, which led to massive amounts of the iridescent glass being sold at even lower prices to carnivals and dime stores. These businesses used the glass for promotions, prizes, and giveaways. The name Carnival evolved from any of the earlier collectors recalling how they had won a piece of this glass playing a game of chance at a carnival.

The feature of most importance to Carnival glass collectors is probably color. Color determines the value of a piece to a great extent. Rare colors, such as red, pastel yellow-green, and amber, are sought after by many collectors, commanding high prices because so few of them were made. Sometimes particular shapes and patterns often drive their prices very high. The rarest, most valuable pieces are red. Few of these were made because of the cost. Gold, copper, and selenium were necessary for producing a clear, strong red shade. Although bright colors, except for marigold, were more expensive to produce, these bright pieces were extremely popular with their original owners as well as with today's collectors.

While recent trends have indicated a continued interest in red, it isn't completely accurate to characterize it as the most valuable color. The pastel colors of ice blue and ice green, as well as aqua opalescent, often bring prices that are higher.

Production and sales for marigold surpassed all other colors, partially because the orangish-yellow color set off the dark furniture common in homes during the earlier part of the century, but mostly because it was the least expensive to produce. Certain inexpensive metallic salts applied to clear glass produce iridescent marigold; whereas, agents which produced red, amethyst, blue, and green were more expensive.

Intensive experimentation by a few glass manufacturers resulted in the development methods for mass-producing colored, opaque glass imitative of art glass. Frank Fenton and Harry Northwood probably pioneered the majority of this experimentation. They devised a method of applying different acids and salt solutions to clear or colored pressed glass which became iridized when reheated.

The reheating process melded the various colors, allowing each color to show through in varying degrees in a wavering rainbow. Greater variety in colors and shades were possible on one piece if the base glass was colored. The base glass could be either very bright or pastel, though the vivid base colors created more popular pieces.

A wide range of hues exist under each color category. For example, marigold is usually described as orange. Orange derives from the two primary colors, yellow and red. Consequently, marigold appears in shades which include the entire spectrum range of pale yellow to the deepest red; and sometimes, the entire range of colors is seen on just one piece.

Once in a while, the alert collector finds bargains for pastel Carnival pieces sheerly because these pieces are not generally recognized as being Carnival. The most desirable of the pastels is white Carnival which has a clear base with a frosty iridescence. The iridescence gives articles a pearl-like lustre with a mellow glimmer of pink, yellow, blue, and green.

Peach opalescent has milky-white edges that extend down into the piece. It has been sprayed with the marigold spray and is, in effect, white or clear opalescent pattern glass, given the Carnival glass treatment. Dugan, Fenton, Northwood, and Westmoreland made most of the peach opalescent.

Carnival was made not only in a great many colors, but the number of shades is immense, also. For example, the very popular blue pieces can be light blue, dark blue, or a stunning cobalt blue which has the sheen of peacock feathers. Purple pieces come in the lightest lavenders to a black purple. Many of the colors were also produced with a frosted iridized surface.

Experience in looking at and handling Carnival glass will enable you to distinguish the subtle differences in shades. By holding a piece close to a bright light, the base glass will be discernible from surface iridized color. When examining rare amber pieces in such a manner, you would be able to determine that the base glass is amber with the iridized surface being brown.

The iridescence on amber is likely to be any color, but most often the marigold spray was used. The brown color is due to the amber or brown of the base glass, not the iridescence.

High relief and ornateness distinguish Carnival patterns from other types of glass, also. For the most part, Carnival glass designs were made for display, and these profusive designs intensify the luminosity of hues as the numerous planes refract the light. Although color and shape attract the most collector interest, pattern designs provide the best means of identifying different Carnival pieces. But for the beginner, identification can be confusing in that there are more than a thousand patterns.

The patterns can be categorized as: near-cut or geometric patterns (many of these derived from early pressed pattern glass which attempted to imitate cut glass); Art Nouveau motifs of flowers, leaves, foliage, fruit, birds, butterflies, and dragonflies; and scenic designs.

Manufacturers produced some patterns, such as Grape and Cable, and Orange Tree, in a large number of different pieces. Yet, the most impressive patterns are those which were designed for one particular piece only. For example, Leaf Swirl and Small Flowers, made in a compote only, displays esthetic, graceful lines not always present in more prolific patterns.

To add to the collector's confusion, some patterns have more than one name, because most pieces were named by the earlier collectors, not by the manufacturers. By reading and examining a large number of glass pieces, you'll become adept at recognizing the majority of patterns by their most descriptive name.

The grape motif appears on numerous glass pieces. All of the major manufacturers created their own versions of the grape motif: the collector can learn to distinguish each of these versions from the others. Popular with the original buyers, grape designs interest more collectors than any other motif; in fact, many collectors specialize in collecting grape patterns. The most common pattern, the Grape and Cable, was produced by Northwood with some fifty different types of objects having this design. New patterns continue to be discovered every once in awhile, and these new finds are invariably rarities.

Even though the shape of an object is less important than color or pattern, it can greatly influence desirability and value either due to rarity or esthetic appeal. For the most part, utility was secondary to decorativeness. So, objects suitable for display dominated. Consequently, large dinner or luncheon tableware sets were never made until after the 1920s when Depression glass table sets garnered most of the middle income buyers. During the initial popularity of Carnival glass, manufacturers created small sets. A table set included a sugar bowl, creamer, butter dish, spooner, and possibly a large pitcher. Water sets, the most sought after of the sets today, consisted of a pitcher and six or eight tumblers; wine sets were made up of a decanter and four or six stemmed glasses. The berry sets—one serving bowl with six small bowls—are the easiest sets to find, because large numbers were made.

Surprisingly, few plates were made in comparison to other common objects. The flat surface of a place does not lend itself to the decorativeness of Carnival in that only one surface is normally visible; and, of course, a decorative plate was impractical for serving food. Rarity combined with the ease of displaying plates has made these articles popular with collectors.

Don't be fooled into thinking that you have found a rare plate when you really have a low bowl in that it doesn't have the bowl's rimmed sides, and the edges of the plate are less than an inch and a quarter above the surface it sits on.

The opaqueness of Carnival glass made it highly suitable for flower vases—the ties holding the arrangements together and the brackish water were not visible, and florists found the glass inexpensive enough to use regularly. The rose bowl, an object produced widely in pottery and porcelain, also became quite popular.

Many other types of objects were made in Carnival glass, some which are common today, and some which are very rare. Hats and baskets, popular items in Victorian times, offer the collector with a limited budget tremendous opportunities.

Today, Carnival glass remains as concrete evidence of the yearning for change and freedom from the heavy, overbearing Victorian era. The vibrant, pulsating colors, and the daring designs stand as a watermark of the entry of 20th century man into a new age.

THE MAJOR MANUFACTURERS

Until just recently, only four glass companies were credited with the majority of Carnival glass productions, but now two more manufacturers also are recognized as being prolific producers of Carnival. At this time, the information as to how much these two companies produced and which pieces can be attributed to them is still not definitive.

The major manufacturers include Northwood, Fenton, Millersburg, Imperial, Dugan/Diamond, and Westmoreland. Other glass manufacturers, such as U.S. Glass, Cambridge, and Indiana Glass and Consolidated, produced some Carnival; but they never made the extensive amount attributed to the six major glass companies.

The founder of the Northwood Glass Company, Harry Northwood, receives most of the credit for first developing a mechanized method for making iridized glass. Northwood worked in the glass industry starting in 1880 when he joined the venerable glass company of Hobbs, Brockunier and Company of Wheeling, West Virginia. After years of refining his skills, Northwood opened his own company, locating it in Indiana, Pennsylvania. Three years later, he affiliated his company with National Glass but broke off in 1901.

At that time, he bought the deserted plant of Hobbs, Brockunier and Company, and kept plants operating in Wheeling and Indiana, Pennsylvania. In 1904, he leased the Indiana plant to Thomas E. Dugan and W. G. Minnemeyer, who had been the managers of the plant. They immediately changed the name to the Dugan Glass Company.

As to when Northwood first made iridized glass remains unknown, but he first sold iridized glass in 1908 after his former apprentice, Frank Fenton, had successfully made and sold iridized glass. It is believed that Fenton learned the secret of creating the imitation art glass while working with Norwood and possibly learned something about making it inexpensively.

Northwood's company went on to produce a large number of Carnival pieces up until the founder's death in 1921 just as the popularity for the new glass began to subside.

Frank Fenton began organizing the Fenton Glass Company in 1905, the year after leaving the Northwood Company. He located his operation at Martin's Ferry, Ohio. Starting in 1908, he introduced the first Carnival glass to the public which was received with great enthusiasm. Although the Fenton company offered a full line of decorative wares, the Carnival glass dominated in production and popularity with almost 150 different patterns attributed to them. The company made an extensive line for fifteen years.

The year after Fenton's Carnival glass had made such a splash, Frank Fenton's two brothers, John and Robert, left the company to start their own operation, the Millersburg Glass Company. Robert returned to the Fenton company in 1910.

At first, the Millersburg company produced crystal and Carnival, using the process developed by Frank Fenton. After many experiments, John Fenton developed a unique method for iridizing inexpensive glassware that is referred to as a radium finish. Shortly after offering this new glass, it was judged at a glass exposition as being the most outstanding entry at the exposition.

Although the glass was very popular and was shipped to Europe and Australia, the company was forced to declare bankruptcy in 1911, due to John Fenton's extravagance and financial mismanagement.

The Millersburg Company was bought by Samuel B. Fair and renamed the Radium Glass Company, with John Fenton retained as vice-president. Six months later, the company closed down, unable to recoup after the loss of reputation and skilled workers. Today collectors covet any and all of the Millersburg pieces—fewer specimens were produced due to the company's short existence, and the radium process resulted in an appealing, brilliant Carnival.

The Dugan/Diamond Company produced Carnival glass as a subcontractor for Northwood and finally, as an independent operation. Apparently, Dugan and Minnemeyer leased Northwood's Indiana, Pennsylvania, plant from 1904 to 1913. It is still unclear as to how long the Dugan glass was produced for Northwood, but the plant's name was changed to Diamond in 1913; and it kept making iridized glass until 1931, when it burned down. Some glass researchers feel that Dugan produced more than eighty different patterns; others feel this estimate to be too high.

The Imperial Glass Company of Bellaire, Ohio, started with inexpensive pressed pattern tableware. Edward Muhleman, the founder, devised his own methods for producing iridized glass and sold these wares widely by 1910. In 1920, Imperial modified its iridized glass, making what is now referred to as late Carnival.

In the early 1960s, Imperial joined the nostalgic movement for making Carnival reproductions.

The Westmoreland Specialty Company of Grapeville, Pennsylvania, issued more than thirty-five patterns and novelties, almost as many as Millersburg. The company began operating in 1889, creating novelties and packaging glass. It appears that Carnival was made from 1909 to 1912. The short duration may be related to the loss of their sales manager, Ed Minnemeyer, in 1912. While working at Westmoreland, Ed Minnemeyer apparently was influenced by his brother, W. G. Minnemeyer, who was co-founder of the Dugan/Diamond Glass Company. As the sales manager, his views on glass were reflected in the lines which were chosen for production. It is not known if some Carnival was made after Ed Minnemeyer left to join his brother at Dugan. The Westmoreland pieces have often been attributed to Millersburg due to their similarities. The short period of production and its aesthetic appeal should make these pieces highly sought after in the near future.

Unfortunately, Northwood was the only Carnival glass manufacturer to emboss their glass with their mark, and only about half of their pieces bear one of the four marks. The marked pieces with an N inside two circles appear to have been made before 1910. Three other marks include an N inside one circle, an N underlined, and a circle.

For their more recent reproductions, Imperial and Fenton both emboss the bases. Imperial places an *I* superimposed over a *G* on its remakes, while Fenton's name is inside a circle.

FENTON ART GLASS COMPANY
CARNIVAL GLASS CATALOG REPRINT

This catalog is reprinted through the courtesy of the Fenton Art Glass Company, Williamstown, West Virginia.

THE FENTON ART GLASS COMPANY
WILLIAMSTOWN, W. VA.

Cover of an early Fenton Art Glass Company Carnival Glass catalog. An exact date cannot be attributed to this catalog as none of the Fenton catalogs were dated prior to 1932.

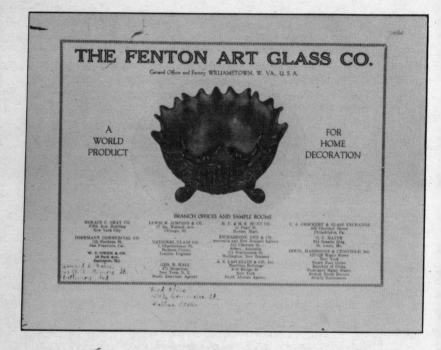

THE FENTON ART GLASS COMPANY

General Offices and Factory

WILLIAMSTOWN, W. VA., U. S. A.

SPANISH

"Tenemos suma gusto en presentar junto con esta, nuestro catalogo general, demostrando á lo mejor de nuestra habilidad una porción del gran surtido de cristalería iridescente y otras novedades las cuales nosotros fabricamos. Aquellos de Uds. quienes ya han comerciado en cristalería iridescente, saben que es imposible el demostrar por medio de la ilustración los hermosos colores del arco iris y sus efectos; por lo tanto, este catalogo no tiene otra objeto que el dar una idea de las formas y dibujos en esta clase de artículo. Nosotros fabricamos cristalería iridescente en los siguientes colores: Oro, Azul Regio, Violeta, Verde y Perla, para el mayor número de ventas se efectuan en los colores Oro y Azul Regio. El efecto de todos los diferentes colores es muy hermoso, porque las rayos de luz al reflejarse en el cristal demuestran con todos los diferentes colores; las diversas tintas del arco iris. Nosotros somos los originadores de las cristalería iridescente, y fabricamos el mas grande y variado surtido que se fabrica en cualquier parte. Nuestras listas de precios dan el precio neto de cada artículo, y toda la mercancía se envía puesta en la fábrica con los gastos de transporte desde esta hasta su destino por cuenta del consignador. Sus tarifas, por cuenta del cliente, el precio de los tarros y catalogo.

Esperando vernos favorecidos con una parte de su clientela, quedamos de Uds.

Attos. y S. S. S.

THE FENTON ART GLASS COMPANY

THE FENTON ART GLASS COMPANY

General Offices and Factory

WILLIAMSTOWN, W. VA., U. S. A.

FRENCH

"Nous avons le plaisir de vous présenter notre catalogue général demontrant notre habilité dans la fabrication de la cristallerie iridescente, ainsi que plusieurs nouveautés de notre fabrication. Ceux qui connaissent la cristallerie iridescente savent qu' il est impossible de demontrer par l'illustration les belles couleurs de l'arc-en-ciel et leurs effets. Pourtant, notre catalogue n'a d'autre but que de donner les formes et les dessins de cet article.

Nous fabriquons de la cristallerie iridescente dans les couleurs suivant: Or, Bleu royal, Violet, Vert et Perle. Les plus recherchés sont les couleurs Or et Bleu royal combinés. L'effet de tous les différents couleurs est très joli, ils reflètent sur le cristal les couleurs de l'arc-en-ciel. Nous sommes les originateurs de la cristallerie iridescente, et nous fabriquons les plus grand assortiments variés que vous ne pourez trouver autre part.

Notre catalogue donne le prix net de toute marchandise prise a la fabrique, avec le prix pour les paquets extra.

Esperant que vous me favoriserez avec votre patronage, nous vous presentons, Messieurs, la expression de notre salutations les plus distinguées.

THE FENTON ART GLASS COMPANY

TO THE TRADE

We take pleasure in presenting herewith our general catalogue showing to the best of our ability a portion of the large line of Iridescent and other novelties which we manufacture. Those of you who have handled Iridescent glassware are aware that it is impossible to show the beautiful rainbow effects by any manner of illustration, therefore, this book is intended merely to give you an idea of shapes and designs. We are making Iridescent goods in the following colors: Golden, Royal Blue, Violet, Green and Pearl, but the largest sales are on the golden and royal blue. The effect of all the different colors is very beautiful as rays of light reflected on the glass show, (on all the different colors) the varying tints of the rainbow. We are the originators of Iridescent ware and make the largest and best-line made anywhere. Our price list gives net prices on all items and all goods are sold F. O. B. factory, with regular package charge extra. Hoping you will favor us with a share of your patronage, we are

Yours very truly,
THE FENTON ART GLASS COMPANY.

This page features a variety of tableware in the Butterfly and Berry pattern.

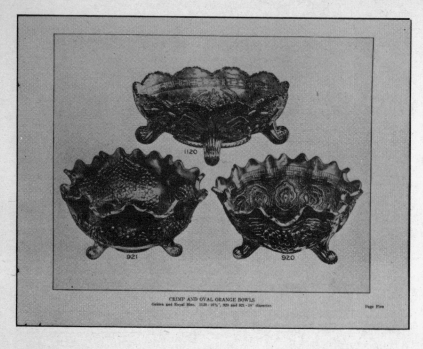

CRIMP AND OVAL ORANGE BOWLS
Golden and Royal Blue. 1120 - 10½", 920 and 921 - 10" diameter.

Page Five

*Patterns illustrated are: **1120,** Fenton Thistle interior with Water Lily and Cattail exterior; **921,** Orange Tree; **920,** Persian Medallion interior with Grape and Cable exterior.*

Patterns illustrated are: **32**, Panelled Diamond & Bows; **1124**, Butterfly and Berry; **916**, Fenton Rib; **504**, Diamond and Rib; **517**, Rustic; **412**, April Showers; **507**, Rustic.

These three bowl variations feature *Mikado* interiors and Fenton Cherry exteriors.

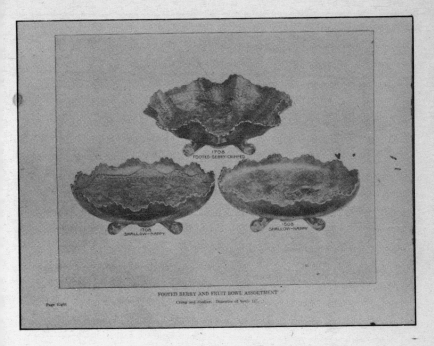

Patterns illustrated are: **1708,** Two Flowers; **1608,** Stag and Holly.

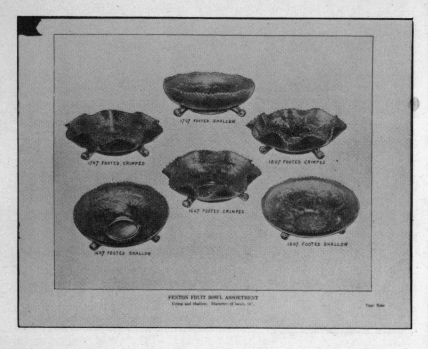

*Patterns illustrated are: **1707**, Two Flowers; **1607**, Little Fishes; **1807**, Water Lily.*

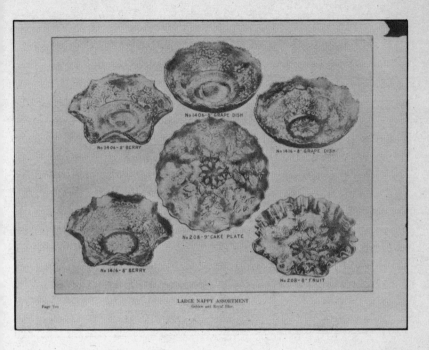

*Patterns illustrated are: **1406**, Orange Tree; **1416**, Leaf Chain; **208**, Carnival Holly.*

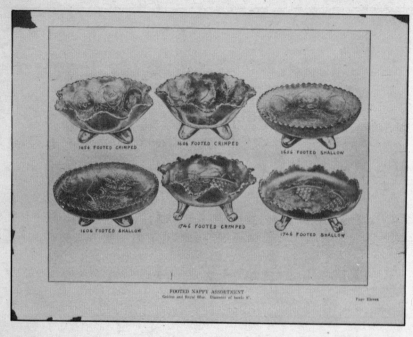

FOOTED NAPPY ASSORTMENT
Golden and Royal Blue. Diameter of bowls 8".

Page Eleven

Patterns illustrated are: **1656,** Dragon and Lotus; **1606,** Stag and Holly; **1746,** Grape and Cable.

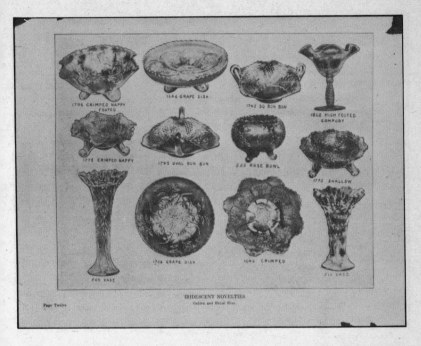

IRIDESCENT NOVELTIES
Golden and Royal Blue.

Patterns illustrated are: Top; row: **1706**, *Stag and Holly;* **1646**, *Peacock and Grape;* **1745**, *Lotus and Grape;* **1802**, *Sailboats. Middle row:* **1775** *and* **1745**, *Lotus and Grape;* **525**, *Garlands. Bottom row:* **509**, *Knotted Beads;* **1706**, *Stag and Holly;* **1646**, *Peacock and Grape,* **510**, *Rustic.*

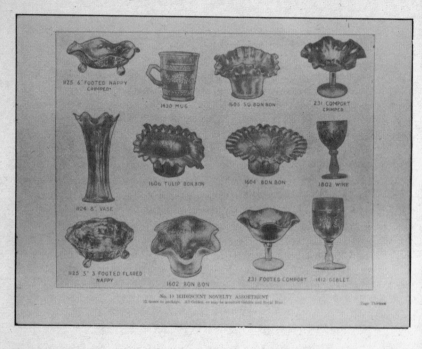

Patterns illustrated are: Top row: **1125,** *Butterfly and Berry;* **1430,** *Orange Tree;* **1605,** *Flowering Dill;* **231,** *Rib and Holly Sprig. Middle row:* **1124,** *Butterfly and Berry;* **1606** *and* **1604,** *Flowering Dill;* **1802,** *Sailboats. Bottom row:* **1125,** *Butterfly and Berry;* **1602,** *Flowering Dill;* **231,** *Rib and Holly Sprig,* **1412,** *Orange Tree.*

Patterns illustrated are: Top row: **1695**, Two Fruits; **1802**, Sailboats; **47**, Daisy Cut; **1401**, Orange Tree. Bottom row: **1416**, Orange Tree; **1192**, Basket with Blackberry interior; **922**, Vintage; **1124**, Butterfly and Berry.

AMERICAN IRIDESCENT WATER AND LEMONADE SETS

Patterns illustrated are: **1583**, Lattice and Grape; **1561**, Apple Tree; **1562**, Blueberry.

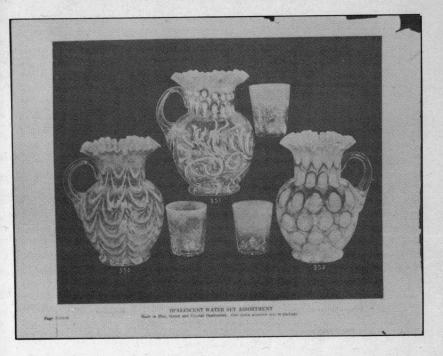

OPALESCENT WATER SET ASSORTMENT
Made in Blue, Green and Crystal Opalescent. One dozen assorted only in package.

Patterns illustrated are: **350,** *Fenton Drapery;* **351,** *Buttons and Braids;* **352,** *Coinspot.*

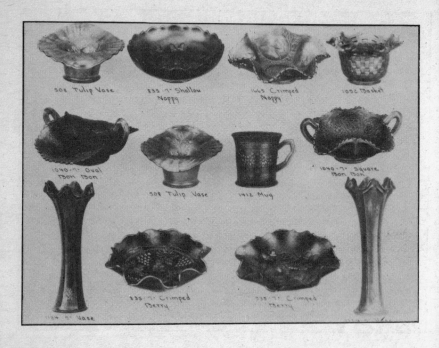

MISCELLANEOUS FENTON CATALOG SHEET REPRINTS

Patterns illustrated are: Top row: 508, Carnival Holly; 835, Acorn; 1665, Horses' Heads. Middle row: 1040, Persian Medallion; 508, Carnival Holly; 1412, Orange Tree; 1040, Persian Medallion. Bottom row: Swirled Flute vase; 835, Grape and Cable; 935, Acorn: Swirled Flute Vase.

Fenton catalog sheet reprints courtesy of the Fenton Art Glass Company, Williamstown, West Virginia.

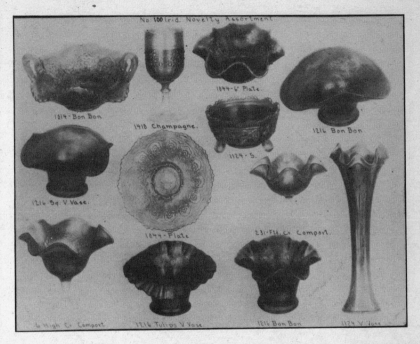

Patterns illustrated are: **1014,** Persian Medallion; **1410,** Orange Tree; **1044,** Sailboats; **1216,** Carnival Holly; **1044,** Persian Medallion; **1124** and **1125,** Butterfly and Berry; **1216,** Blackberry Spray.

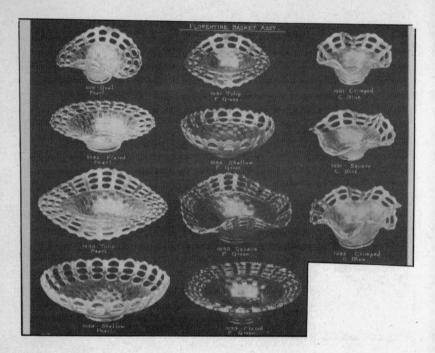

Assorted open-edge baskets.

Patterns illustrated are: **504**, *Diamond and Rib;* **1047**, *Persian Medallion;* **303**, *Blackberry Bramble;* **427**, *Little Flowers;* **916**, *Fenton Rib;* **408**, *Peacock Tail;* **1057**, *Ten Mums;* **1075**, *Birds and Cherries;* **1092**, *Basket;* **407**, *Peacock Tail;* **922**, *Vintage;* **437**, *Feathered Serpent,* **466**, *Vintage;* **411**, *Peacock Tail;* **409**, *Peacock Tail;* **231**, *Rib and Holly Sprig;* **1036**, *Concord;* **920**, *Grape and Cable;* **467**, *Vintage.*

Patterns illustrated are: **1216**, Blackberry Spray; **1902**, Fenton's Basket; **74**, Strawberry; **212**, Stippled Rays interior/Scale Band exterior; **1430**, Orange Tree; **835**, Acorn; **1126**, Fenton Rib vase; **231**, Carnival Holly; **1216**, Blackberry Spray; **1804**, Water Lily; **212**, Rib and Holly Sprig.

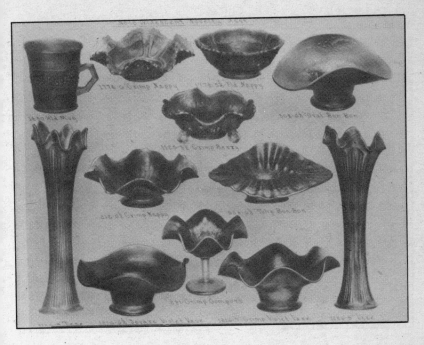

Patterns illustrated are: **1430**, *Orange Tree;* **1774**, *Sailboats;* **508**, *Carnival Holly;* **1125**, *Butterfly and Berry exterior/Hearts and Trees interior;* **508**, *Carnival Holly;* **1126**, *Fenton Rib;* **1216**, *Blackberry Spray;* **231**, *Rib and Holly Sprig.*

Patterns illustrated are: **1607**, Little Fishes; **1707**, Two Flowers; **1807**, Water Lily; **920**, Grape and Cable exterior/Persian Medallion interior; **1120**, Fenton Thistle; **921**; Orange Tree.

The above bowls illustrate variations of Carnival Holly (208) and Vintage (466).

Patterns illustrated are: **1411, 1403, 1405, 413, 1406; 406** and **410,** Orange Tree; **1414,** Water Lily; **410,** Rustic; **548,** Persian Medallion.

Patterns illustrated are: **1109,** Fluffy Peacock; **910,** Butterfly and Fern; **1012,** Floral and Grape.

Decorated patterns illustrated are: **1014**, Prism Band; **1015**, Zig Zag; **1016**, Banded Drape.

BUILDING A COLLECTION

Many beginners feel overwhelmed when they read about some of the rarities of Carnival glass selling for thousands of dollars. Regardless, this is a collecting field that everyone can enjoy and still adhere to their budget. Many pieces, particularly the more common ones, sell for under $50 or $60. The newcomer needs to read and study about Carnival glass in order to develop an understanding of what characteristics influence value. Generally, supply and demand control prices. If the demand for a particular piece surpasses the supply, its value will usually soar; but, if the supply exceeds the demand, the price will stagnate or even drop in price. The production level of certain patterns, colors, and objects was low. Low production in itself does not drive up prices—numerous collectors must want these particular pieces. Some pieces that are plentiful are very popular, but their availability keeps the prices from rising very much.

For the most part, collectors are not interested in late Carnival glass. Whether you are or not, you need to learn how to recognize it and know how its values compare to other Carnival glass. Since the quality of these pieces is considerably less, you should never pay the same prices you would pay for the earlier pieces. Once you have compared the late Carnival with the earlier pieces, you will easily distinguish one from the other. The shapes and patterns are more typical of the 1930s—more simplistic, less busy; the patterns often lack the ornateness associated with Carnival. The iridescence on these pieces was sprayed on. These flashed-on surfaces don't match the sheen of the earlier articles, partially because the finish is not as durable. Often, the iridescence has started to wear off.

Even though the popularity for iridized pieces dissipated quickly during the late 1920s, manufacturers continued to produce some of these wares, because there was still some demand for them. Manufacturers already had molds for the earlier pieces; and since most of their cost was for designing and making molds, they could afford to produce the same old articles and still profit when selling them at exceedingly low prices. Even so, few people could afford to buy glass sheerly for decorative purposes during the Depression; besides, the popularity of Art Nouveau waned, and the public wearied of the brash, fanciful imitations.

As the Depression tableware sets became popular, table sets made of Carnival were produced. These sets are considered to be iridized Depression glass by some collectors, and late Carnival by others. Usually, the same sets are known by different names. For instance, the Carnival set called Bouquet and Lattice is known to Depression glass collectors as Normandie. Also, there have been several iridized sets produced in the last 30 years which further confuses hobbyists.

During the Depression, the time and skill necessary for producing new Carnival pieces cost the manufacturers too much. For the most part, Carnival glass production ceased until the revival of reproductions in the 1960s.

The collecting of Carnival glass has increased tremendously over the last 20 years. Even though a large number of Carnival pieces were made, their survival rate has been low. We know that advertising pieces were made in fairly large numbers, yet out of every thousand pieces made only a half dozen exist today. These figures give us an idea of how few pieces of the Carnival has actually been saved or kept. With the increasing demand, the supply continues to dwindle.

Since the hobbyist will discover few bargains, he needs to protect himself from spending too much for an item by developing an understanding of values. You should know which colors, patterns, or articles are rare and popular, because these items will sell for thousands of dollars. For example, two-piece articles usually carry higher price tags, since it is difficult to find two pieces intact.

By studying this price guide and comparing its values for articles sold at auctions, flea markets, shops, and bazaars, you'll develop a sense or feeling as to how much a piece should sell for. You'll learn to calculate the value of a piece by weighing its rarity, popularity, esthetic appeal, and condition. If you should stumble across a piece of iridescent glass at an estate sale or a small local auction, your knowledge will enable you to spot an authentic Carnival piece and allow you to grab it up for a bargain.

Of course, no one should purchase collectibles purely as an investment, because too many unpredictable variables can affect the values adversely. You will be happiest buying what you like, so that at the very least you will have the pleasure of owning something that you enjoy. Still, anyone would be foolish to make substantial purchases without some consideration to the investment potential. The rarest pieces probably have excellent investment potential if the owner keeps them for more than five years. Most Carnival, except the most common pieces, will most likely appreciate enough to offset inflation, and any possible loss of income if the money had been invested in something else.

Although the high-priced rarities would be the best investment, even moderately scarce pieces could be profitable if the collector pays attention to quality. You should try to buy only pieces in excellent condition. The better the condition, the better chance you have for a good investment. Also, pay attention to the intensity of the iridescence, the variations in shading, esthetic appeal of the shape, the ornateness of the pattern, and any historical significance—any or all of these attributes will affect a piece's future value.

If your budget is limited, you might be wise to collect a few articles at moderately high prices. Wealthy collectors compete for the scarce objects, often driving their values out of range for most hobbyists, but the pieces just above average may be affordable for you.

As you gain more know-how, you'll become more confident about how much you should pay. You'll be able to gauge the importance of a piece to you, its suitability to your collection and how much other collectors would be willing to pay for it.

Collectors often narrow their collections by purchasing pieces by the type of object, by the manufacturers, or by the pattern. For instance, some collectors restrict their accumulations to just tumblers, or collect only marigold. But most collectors can't resist selecting pieces that include the entire range of colors available in Carnival glass.

In developing your collection, you should remain cognizant that a hodgepodge collection will have a total worth much less than that of a comparable collection that has continuity. This is true for a number of reasons. A collection is often sold en masse with the selling price being based mostly on the scarce or popular pieces. Miscellaneous, common, or poor specimens can be picked up by most avid collectors. But a collection of one motif, or all the pieces of one pattern offer the buyer something unique—something it takes time and diligence to accumulate. So, it is well worth the effort to decide on a specialized direction for your collection. Besides, a collection of all cobalt blue or all hats and baskets makes for a much more impressive visual impact.

When new Carnival pieces are made from old original molds or from molds made from old pieces, they are considered to be reproductions. Of course, there is nothing wrong with reproductions as long as they are marked appropriately, so that unsuspecting buyers don't pay prices suitable for original pieces. The Imperial Glass Company embosses an I superimposed over a G on all its reproductions; the Fenton Glass Company embosses its name within a circle. Unfortunately, other manufacturers have only placed a paper label on the base. Obviously, these labels can be easily removed, allowing pieces to be passed off as originals. Sometimes reputable dealers and collectors sell such items as originals, unaware that the labels were removed. Even the embossed pieces can be sold as originals if someone grinds the mark off. So be wary of any articles which look like the base has been tampered with.

All collectors should read the various periodicals and books about Carnival. Many of these will catalog those pieces which have been reproduced. Of the more than 1,000 original patterns, less than 50 have been reproduced, and most of these are pieces that require very little handwork or none. So this knowledge could aid you tremendously. Also, reproduced pieces feel different when handled, plus the iridescence has a gaudy appearance in that it lacks the subtle nuance of original Carnival.

An original piece will normally show at least minute scratches or other signs of being old. Still, scratches and dirt are sometimes added to a reproduction in order to make it look more authentic. Also, there are a number of original pieces of iridized glass that have been produced recently—not as reproductions—but as new glass with an old look.

When reproductions are first made, the prices for the originals will often decrease slightly, because a small portion of collector demand will be satisfied with these items. But, staunch collectors will insist on purchasing the original pieces, and their persistence usually brings those prices back up.

The more know-how the collector gathers and the more he handles good specimens, the more adept he'll become at spotting bogus items. Of course, buying from reputable dealers will diminish the possibility of buying reproductions.

Experience handling Carnival glass, picking up information from other collectors, reading about new developments in research—and a generous dash of your own creativity will allow you to develop an interesting, valuable collection that can bring pleasure to your family and friends as well as yourself.

CARE AND REPAIR

The condition of a piece of glass affects its value immensely. A cracked or badly damaged specimen will have very little value unless a piece is very rare. Minor flaws will diminish the value depending on the extent of the damage. Obviously, you should expect a higher level of condition for objects created only for decorative purposes. Articles that were used to serve food and beverages in can be expected to show more wear, chips, scratches, and other imperfections. So, you should take your time and examine a piece carefully before you decide to purchase it.

Take the piece in your hand. Inspect the entire surface in a good light carefully running your hand over it. Repaired cracks or deep scratches are not always discernible to the eye, but you should be able to feel any irregularities or roughness that indicate damage or repair. The edges and rims are the most likely spots, so pay special attention to those areas.

Next, hold the piece up to the light. Since Carnival glass is opaque, mended cracks and chips are not easy to spot, particularly if they were clean breaks.

Obviously, perfect condition is ideal, but not always possible. After you've examined many pieces of glass, you'll learn to judge how many minor flaws are acceptable. Often, collectors become panicky when they find a hard-to-find item in poor condition. They're afraid they'll not get the chance to purchase it again. Just remember: numerous pieces of Carnival were produced; and there are bound to be pieces sitting forgotten in musty corners, their owners unaware of their value. Another piece will probably show up. If you do buy a damaged piece, don't pay much and keep in mind that it is merely a show piece.

Quite often, bubbles and other impurities will be visible in Carnival glass. This is nothing to be concerned with as it does not affect the value. This type of glass was made quickly and with low-quality ingredients—internal flaws are to be expected; and besides, these flaws are visible only when held up in a very strong light. In many hobbies, errors or freaks sell for much more than common specimens. This is true with Carnival collectors. In fact, many hobbyists enthusiastically snatch up any oddities which were misshapen or flawed during the manufacturing process. These are favored by some collectors not only because they're unique, but because they exemplify the difficulties faced by the glass makers.

Sometimes you will discover a piece of Carnival at a garage sale or a charity bazaar which will be very dirty from being stored away in an attic or basement. The late Carnival should be cleaned with extreme care, but the earlier pieces can be cleaned with less trepidation. The earlier pieces can be cleaned with powdered ammoniated cleaner dissolved in warm water. A soaking should remove most of the grime. If not, you could use a soft toothbrush dipped in the cleaning solution and lightly brush around the crevices of the designs. If you avoid hot water and any other strong cleaners, the iridescence will be unaffected. The late Carnival should be cleaned only in warm soapy water as the flashed-on surfaces do not hold up well to harsh or frequent washings.

If your glass is not particularly dirty, you will need only to clean it periodically with either a soap and water bath or a spray glass cleaner. Be sure to dry each piece with a lint-free towel. The earlier pieces can be rubbed lightly in order to give them an extra shine.

The earlier pieces can be displayed where the sun hits them and not suffer any fading or cracking; but the late Carnival should be kept out of the sun as they can lose their coloring.

Although most advanced collectors do not advocate buying damaged pieces, don't hesitate to fix a piece that becomes damaged after you own it. It can still be used as a display piece if repaired. Special agents for gluing glass are available. Check your glass publications and local hobby and handyman shops. You'll need to devise a means of clamping the broken pieces together tight so it mends properly. Try using elastic bands, rubber bands and heavy string to secure the pieces while they dry.

Also, carefully consider the location you choose to store or display your Carnival. Try to keep them where they are in a light traffic area in your house. Placing them on a shelf that could be accidently brushed by anyone who walks in is an invitation to trouble. An enclosed cabinet with special lighting is ideal—it provides a safe, clean place to keep your glass pieces where they are visible to any visitors.

A WORD TO THE WISE

Unfortunately, forging of marks and signatures is not uncommon in the glass world. Similarly, reproductions and reissues are passed off on the novice collector as the original item. There are several important steps the collector may take to protect against these possible pitfalls.

1. ALWAYS deal with a knowledgeable and reputable dealer. Get a written description of the piece along with a certificate of authenticity. Honest dealers will always make good on any piece they sell which turns out to be a fake or reproduction.

2. Study the type of glass you are collecting and learn about its characteristics by seeing as much of it as possible at museums, fine art galleries and antique shops. Reproductions will always differ from the original even if only slightly.

3. Look for the unmistakable signs of age such as random scratches on the bottom of the base which appear after many years of standing. Glass that is 50–100 years old will not look brand new.

4. Beware of very low prices on an item you know should bring considerably more. Use common sense. Do you really expect to find a genuine signed Tiffany favrile vase worth several thousand dollars at a flea market for $75.00? As you become more knowledgeable you may indeed spot some real treasures in dusty junk stores. Until then, don't expect to find incredible bargains and when you do, beware.

5. Color is crucial in collectible glassware of all kinds. A number of reissues in pattern, Carnival, and Depression glass have been done in recent years. The colors are different even if slightly and are a giveaway that the piece is not original. It is only by seeing a great deal of Depression glass that one

learns the true colors of the original. New reissues tend to be in strange tints and hues, and they have a muddy look when compared with the pristine colors of the original.

PERIODICALS

Carnival Glass News and Views, P.O. Box 5421, Kansas City, MO 64131. Reports on auctions, collectors, and Carnival glass.

Carnival Glass Tumbler and Mug News, P.O. Box 5421, Kansas City, MO 64131. Provides information about patterns and new discoveries.

Encore, Dorothy Taylor, editor, P.O. Box 11734, Kansas City, MO 64138. A bimonthly for Carnival glass collectors.

Depression Glass Daze, P.O. Box 57, Otisville, MI 48463. A monthly newspaper with articles and ads.

The Glass Collector, P.O. Box 27037, Columbus, OH 43227. A quarterly magazine on late 19th century and 20th century American glassware.

Glass Review, P.O. Box 542, Marietta, OH 45750. A monthly magazine on 20th century glassware with articles, pictures, and ads.

Heisey Glass Newscaster, P.O. Box 102, Plymouth, OH 44865. A quarterly pamphlet on identification and research.

The Paden City Partyline, 13325 Danvers Way, Westminster, CA 92683. A quarterly newsletter about Paden glass on new discoveries and pricing.

CLUBS

American Carnival Glass Association
P.O. Box 273
Gnadenhutten, OH 44629
Publishes *American Carnival Glass News* with club activities, auction results, and information.

American Custard Glass Collectors
P.O. Box 5421
Kansas City, MO 64131
Publishes *Partyline* with sales, and news about rarities and the market.

American Cut Glass Association
P.O. Box 7095
Shreveport, LA 71107
Publishes *Hobstar* monthly, which provides information about cut glass, shows, and sales.

Antique And Historical Glass Foundation
P.O. Box 7413
Toledo, OH 43615

Fenton Art Glass Collectors Of America, Inc.
P.O. Box 2441
Appleton, WI 54911
Publishes *Butterfly Net,* a newsletter about club activities and discoveries in Fenton glass.

Fostoria Glass Society of America, Inc.
P.O. Box 826
Moundsville, WV 26041
Publishes *Facets of Fostoria*, a 12-page newsletter.

Glass Art Society
c/o Tom McGlauchin
Toledo Museum of Art
Toledo, OH 43609
Publishes the *Glass Art Society Newsletter* annually.

Glass Collectors' Club of Toledo
P.O. Box 2695
Toledo, OH 43606

Happy Hunters Carnival Glass Club
Bernice Allen, Secretary
3316 Boston Street
Hopewell, VA 23860

Heart of America Carnival Glass Association
3048 Tamarak Drive
Manhattan, KS 66502
Publishes *The H.O.A.C.G.A. Bulletin* monthly with articles about Carnival glass and information about shows.

Heisey Collectors of America, Inc.
P.O.Box 27
Newark, OH 43055
Publishes *The Heisey News*, a newsletter with information on patterns, history of Heisey, and advertisements.

Imperial Glass Collectors' Society
P.O. Box 4012
Silver Spring, MD 20904
Publishes the *Imperial Collectors Glasszette* quarterly.

International Carnival Glass Association
R.R. #1
Mentone, IN 46539
Publishes the *Carnival Town Pump* newsletter.

Land of Lincoln Carnival Glass Association
5113 North Nordica
Chicago, IL 60656

National Cambridge Collectors, Inc.
P.O. Box 416
Cambridge, OH 43725
Publishes the *Cambridge Crystal Ball* monthly with information about patterns, factory history, and other facts.

National Depression Glass Association, Inc.
8337 Santa Fe Lane
Shawnee Mission, KS 66212
Publishes the *News & Views* monthly, reporting club business and meetings.

The National Duncan Glass Society
P.O. Box 965
Washington, PA 15301
Publishes the *National Duncan Glass Journal* with reprints of early ads for Duncan glass, articles, and club news.

The National Early American Glass Club
c/o Mrs. Shirley Pope
9 Commonwealth Avenue, Apt. 4 A
Boston, MA 02116
Publishes the *Glass Club Bulletin* with articles about old glass and the *National Early American Glass Club Newsletter* which lists events.

National Greentown Glass Association
1807 West Madison
Kokomo, IN 46901
Publishes the *N.G.G.A. Newsletter* quarterly.

New Bedford Glass Society
P.O. Box F 655
65 N. Second Street
New Bedford, MA 02740

Northern California Carnival Glass Club
630 North Lower Sacramento Road
Lodi, CA 95240

Ohio Candlewick Collectors' Club
613 South Patterson Street
Gibsonburg, OH 43431

Pacific Northwest Carnival Glass Club
48900 Middle Fork Road
North Bend, WA 98045

Pairpoint Cup Plate Collectors of America, Inc.
9308 Brandywine Road
Clinton, MD 20735
Publishes *The Thistle* quarterly with news about members, meetings, and information about old glass.

Stained Glass Association of America
1125 Wilmington Avenue
St. Louis, MO 63111
Publishes *Stained Glass Magazine* quarterly.

MUSEUMS

Allen Art Museum
Oberlin College, Oberlin, OH

Art Institute of Chicago
Chicago, IL 60603

Bennington Museum
Bennington, VT 05201

John Nelson Bergstrom Art Center and Museum
Neenah, WI 54956

Cambridge Glass Museum, The
Cambridge, OH 43725

Carnegie Institute Museum of Art
Pittsburgh, PA 15213

Chrysler Museum at Norfolk
Norfolk, VA 23510

Corning Museum of Glass and Glass Center
Corning, NY 14830

Currier Gallery of Art
Manchester, NH 03104

Degenhart Paperweight And Glass Museum, Inc.
Cambridge, OH 43725

Edison Museum
Milan, OH

Fenton Art Glass Company
Williamstown, WV 26187

Greentown Glass Museum, Inc.
Greentown, IN 46936

Henry Ford Museum
Dearborn, MI 48121

Historical Society of Western Pennsylvania
Pittsburgh, PA 15213

Jones Gallery of Glass and Ceramics
Sebago, ME 04075

Judy's Museum
Mountain View, MO

Lightner Museum
St. Augustine, FL 32084

Marathon County Historical Society
Wausau, WI 54401

Metropolitan Museum of Art
New York, NY 10028

Morse Gallery
Winter Park, FL

National Heisey Glass Museum
Newark, OH 43055

New York Historical Society
New York, NY 10024

New Bedford Glass Museum
New Bedford, MA 12742

Old Sturbridge Village
Sturbridge, MA 01566

Oglebay Institute-Mansion Museum
Wheeling, WV 26003

Philadelphia Museum of Art
Philadelphia, PA 19101

Portland Art Museum
Portland, ME

Sandwich Glass Museum
Sandwich, MA 02563

Smithsonian Institution Museum of History and Technology
Washington, D.C. 20560

Study Gallery
A Center for Glass & Ceramics
Douglas Hill, ME 04024

Toledo Museum of Art
Toledo, OH 43697

Wadsworth Atheneum
Hartford, CT 06103

GLOSSARY

ACID ETCHING

A process in decorative glassmaking, whereby the glass is first coated with a resistant wax into which a pattern is drawn. When hydrofluoric acid is applied, it cuts a pattern into the areas not protected by the wax. It is most often found on cased glass as it is less expensive than wheel engraving.

AGATA GLASS

Art glassware produced by the New England Glass Company in the late 19th century. It is characterized by brown or purple mottled finish patterns which was achieved by sprinkling alcohol on the color.

AIR TWIST GLASS

A glassmaking process developed and popularized in England during the mid-1700s. Air bubbles were injected into the base of a glass bowl. The base was then pulled down and twisted into a stem, thus the elongated bubbles formed spiralling threads of air.

AKRO AGATE

Founded in 1911 in Akron, Ohio, this company manufactured marbles, moving to Clarksburg, West Virginia, several years later. In the early 1930s they added a line of novelty items including ashtrays, planters, vases, flowerpots, and children's toy dishes. These items were made in solid and marbleized opaque glass.

ALABASTER WARE

Glassware which resembles alabaster in its appearance.

ALBANY GLASS

Albany, New York, was the site of a glass factory that achieved some importance in the late 18th and early 19th centuries. It was established in the 1780s, temporarily ceased operations about 1790 and resumed in 1792, continuing into the 1820s. Though not noted for remarkable artistry this firm was versatile and its products are eagerly sought by collectors. It manufactured a general line of wares including window glass. It was at one time known as the Hamilton Manufacturing Society.

ALBERTINE

Albertine glass was made by the Mt. Washington Glass Company. It features moderately lavish decor against an opaque ground. Subsequently Albertine became known as Crown Milano. Vases are most abundant. Exceptional specimens can be costly. Albertine was a favorite "parlor glass" of the late Victorian era.

ALEXANDRITE GLASS

A type of English art glass made in the late 19th century by Thomas Webb. This translucent glass was skillfully shaded from blue, through rose, to yellow by reheating it at various temperatures.

AMBER

Yellowish brown color of glass.

AMBERETTE

Amberette is technically pressed glass but by nature of its characteristics and workmanship is generally classified as art glass. Pieces are frosted and stained, the basic color being a velvety yellow. Amberette is still in the modest range of price, perhaps because the attraction common to much art glass—a manufacturer's signature—is not present. It is nevertheless handsome and has attracted increased collecting interest in recent years.

AMBERINA

An American art glass produced in New England during the late 19th century. It was patented by Joseph Locke in 1883. It was a clear, translucent, flint glass with shading from light amber at the base to ruby red at the top. It was usually molded into tableware as well as ornamental objects.

AMELUNG GLASS

A German glassmaker, John Frederick Amelung, established the New Bremen Glassware Factory in Maryland in 1784. The factory operated for only ten years, yet his pieces are considered the finest glass produced in America.

AMERICAN FLINT GLASS WORKS

The American Flint Glass Works, also known by the name of its proprietor, Southwick & Co., was established at Wheeling in what is now West Virginia but then was Virginia in the 1840s. The firm was innovative and maintained a quality standard somewhat above the normal for that period. Its products included blown-mold and pressed wares as well as free-blown flint and various colored glass.

AMETHYST

Shades of purple from very light to extremely dark. See BLACK AMETHYST.

ANIMAL DISHES

Covered glass dishes in the shapes of animals came into vogue during the latter part of the 19th century. They were made by a number of firms, and specimens representing dozens of animals, both domesticated and wild, can be found. At first, animal dishes were regarded strictly as novelties. Their era of greatest popularity was 1890–1910. Except for scattered exceptions they ceased to be made during the Depression years.

ANNEALING

The tempering of glass immediately following manufacture, whether made by hand or machine, by controlled gradual cooling. This process strengthens the glass, thus making it more practical. See also ANNEALING CRACK; LEER.

ANNEALING CRACK

A crack or fissure in the glass due to its improper cooling.

APPLICATION

Applying hot rods of glass to blown or pressed blanks to form pedestals, handles, etc.

APPLIED STEM

The stem is applied to a piece rather than blown when making the object.

APRICOT

Deep yellow color.

A O P

Abbreviation for "all over pattern."

ART GLASS

Various kinds of late-19th-century American decorative glassware in the Victorian style. It was ornamental glass that was fabricated into free-blown, pressed tableware, and decorative glassware. Ornate designs and various color effects were employed to achieve many successful varieties.

ART NOUVEAU (1885–1925)

An artistic movement which literally translated means "new art." Breaking away from past historic academic styles, it was a style of architecture and decoration which used bolder colors, free-flowing designs, asymmetrical shapes, celestial figures, tall swirling plant forms, and whiplash curves. It was strongly influenced by Gothic and Japanese art forms. Realism was rejected as it was an inspired return to nature. Its rich linear rhythm was found not only in architecture and art, but it also decorated every kind of furnishings, jewelry, and glass. Ornament became so profuse as the movement advanced that construction of a piece was sometimes concealed.

AURENE GLASS

A brightly colored iridescent ornamental glass created by Frederick Carder, manager of the Steuben Glass Works, New York, in 1905. Although inspired by Tiffany, it has a far greater variety. See ART GLASS.

AVENTURINE

A type of lustrous Venetian glass that combined small flakes of gold and copper, in suspended state, with colored glass. Although an ancient technique, this decorative process was revived during the 19th century.

BACCARAT GLASS

Fine-quality glassware for tableware and decorative glass, especially paperweights. Glassworks in France and Belgium manufactured this quality glass from the late 18th century and throughout the 19th century.

BALTIMORE GLASS

Products of any one of several glassworks in Baltimore, Maryland, including Amelung glass and Baltimore flint glass.

BANANA DISH

A glass dish with two highly curved sides and two ends left open on a pedestal base.

BASKET

Basket-shaped glass piece used for decoration, food service, or vase.

BELL

Novelty item made in every type of glass, often ringable. Used at the dinner table as a signal to the servants that it was time to serve.

BERRY BOWL

Small round bowl.

BITTERS BOTTLE

Small decanter used for holding Angostura bitters which is used in making mixed alcoholic drinks.

BLACK AMETHYST

Purple glass so dark it appears almost black.

BLANK

Uncut glass objects which were cut or decorated into the finished product.

BLOWN-MOLDED GLASS

A method of glassmaking in which hot glass was blown through a blowpipe into a pre-formed metal mold. The mold was used for giving shape to a glass vessel and for impressing a design on its surface. It was used as a means of quick and inexpensive glass production. It is easily discernible from pressed glass since the pattern undulations are also on the inside of the vessel. See FREE-BLOWN GLASS.

BLOWN MOLDED

Glass is blown into a mold to reproduce the design of the inner mold.

BLOWPIPE

A long metal tube used in blowing glass.

BLUE, ELECTRIC

Royal blue.

BLUERINA

Bluerina was named for Amberina and shares its characteristic of embodying tones which meld from one distinct color into another, in this case blue to amber. Guidelines on classification are not firm, as the name may be applied to the glassware of any manufacturer that exhibits such coloring, even if known better by a product designation; for example, some Alexandrite glass falls into the realm of Bluerina.

BOHEMIAN GLASS

An ornamental glass manufactured during the latter part of the 17th century in an attempt to imitate Venetian glass. Coming from one of the chief European glassmaking regions, Bohemian glass was especially suitable for ornate engraved and cut decorations. It was renowned for its rich colors, such as bright yellow, ruby red, etc.

BON BON

Small, uncovered candy dish.

BREAD AND BUTTER PLATE

Six-inch plate.

BRIDES' BASKET

Glass bowl held in a silverplated frame. Very often the bowl has a delicately ruffled, fluted, or crimped edge. Although made in all sizes, most ranged from 9 to 14 inches in diameter and 9 to 16 inches in height. Brides' baskets were made of every type of glass and first captured the imagination of the public at the World's Columbian Exposition in Chicago in 1893. These bowls were a favorite wedding gift from the 1890s to 1920, hence the term "brides' basket." This term surfaced in the 1960s.

BRILLIANT PERIOD

The term given to cut glass of the golden age of its manufacture, the second half of the 19th century, when great energy was spent in creating intricate, luxurious patterns. This ware was deeply cut and highly polished. The best American examples date from about 1870 to 1895. Brilliant period cut glass is considered the most desirable variety of its species by collectors and has gained considerably in value over the years, enhanced by the fact that production ceased more than half a century ago.

BRISTOL GLASS

An English decorated clear and colored glassware produced in Bristol factories during the 17th and 18th centuries. Dark blue, red, and green were used to create snuffboxes, candlesticks, vases, decanters, jars, mugs, etc. They were noted for their fine production of small articles in white opaque milk glass, which was an imitation of porcelain and painted with enamel colors.

BRISTOL-TYPE GLASS

A plentiful Victorian art glass sold by a number of manufacturers in the 19th century. Its name is taken from the city of Bristol in Great Britain, which at one time served as headquarters for numerous glassmakers. After being imported to and becoming popular in the U.S., domestic factories began producing it and it was sold commonly in variety shops and other outlets for many years. The pieces were generally opaque, with enameled hand painting. Originally it was regarded as a better-than-nothing substitute for those who could not afford the more expensive varieties of fine glass. Passage of time and heightened collector interest has resulted in increased prices.

BURMESE GLASS

Burmese glass was introduced late in the 19th century by the Mt. Washington Co., then subsequently produced by Webb of England. Uranium was added to the fabric, producing pleasing tonal effects shading from pink to pastel yellow. So-called Gunderson Burmese is of much later manufacture than the Mt. Washington and Webb varieties but is nevertheless collectible and can be a worthy alternative for those unable to afford the high prices often obtained for "old Burmese."

BUTTERBALL OR CONFECTION DISH

Shallow glass dish which has long center pole with closed handle at top. Butterballs or tidbits are arranged on the dish around the center pole.

BUTTER PLATE, INDIVIDUAL

Tiny glass plate used for serving individual portions of butter.

BUTTER TUB

Small pail-shaped glass holder used to hold butter balls or pats.

CAKE PLATE

Large flat plate with three short legs.

CALCITE GLASS

A glass resembling, but not manufactured from, the mineral calcite, having a rich cream white color. The most notable examples were the work of Frederick Carder at the Steuben company, who pioneered their manufacture. The method of decoration varied. Calcite glass is frequently termed "Aurene."

CAMBRIDGE GLASS CO.

The Cambridge Glass Co., located in the Ohio town of that name, was chiefly a producer of cut glass, though it sold other types as well. Its operations were very extensive and for many years, especially during the 1920s and 1930s, it maintained a near monopoly on the manufacture of cut glass tableware. Some of its designs were most creative.

CAMEO GLASS

Ornamental glassware made from layers of different colors, often white on blue, in which the outer opaque layer was cut away so that the background color showed. It could also be made in three or more layers. Although a rare and difficult technique developed by the Romans in the first century, it was almost unknown until the 19th century.

CAMPHOR GLASS

A white American pressed glass, that was semiopaque blown molded glass.

CANARY

Yellow glass or crystal.

CANDELABRUM

A candlestick lampstand or chandelier with two or more branches.

CANDLESTICK

A movable candle holder from the mid-16th century. It is a simple tube with a socketed glass holder at one end and a flattened base at the other.

CARAFE

A bottle used for serving wine or water. Their era of most extensive use was from about 1760 to 1820, when the water carafe (or, more likely, a series of them) could not be omitted from a well-appointed dining table without causing comment. Crushed or cubed ice could be included in the carafe to keep water at lower than room temperature; this was looked upon as a novelty, and the beverage as a welcome refreshment, in the days before electrical refrigerators. Carafes again came into vogue in the late Victorian age, when a number of American manufacturers produced them.

CARDER, FREDERICK

Founder of the Steuben Glass Co. (1903). Products of Steuben from that year until 1932 are sometimes, though confusingly, referred to as "Carder glass." Frederick Carder lived to the age of 100; he died in 1963.

CARNIVAL GLASS

An inexpensive glass produced from 1908 to 1930 and later used as prizes awarded at a carnival or fair. It consisted of fruit bowls, sugar bowls, pitchers, creamers, etc. with molded decorations in iridescent colored glass. It was manufactured in both Europe and America in red, blue, green, mauve, marigold, white, and more.

CASED GLASS

A blown glass in two to five layers of different colors, including clear glass and opaque white. The layers were fused one inside the other while the glass was hot. It was blown into decanters, glasses, etc. and decorated by cutting away parts of each layer, which offered many diverse decorative effects. It was produced mainly in the 19th century.

CASTOR SET

Glass condiments held in a silver-plated metal frame with handle. There were breakfast, lunch, and dinner castor sets which held the different condiments required for each specific meal. For example, the breakfast castor set would contain salt and pepper shakers, syrup pitcher, and jelly or marmalade jar. Dinner castor sets would contain salt and pepper shakers and oil and vinegar cruets, etc. They were used during the Victorian period.

CELERY

Either a tall cylindrical vessel or a long, flat, narrow dish for serving celery.

CHAIN

Guilloche, trailed circuit. Heavy glass threads are applied in a chain design.

CHAMPAGNE GLASS

The classic or traditional shape of champagne glass—a wide shallow bowl surmounting a stem, with circular base—evolved in the second quarter of the 19th century.

CHARTREUSE

Opaque glass of yellow-green.

CHECKERED DIAMOND

Motif featuring a large diamond with four small diamonds cut in each.

CHEESE AND CRACKER DISH

Two-tiered glass serving dish for cheese and crackers.

CHEESE DISH

Round dome-shaped cover with flat-bottom dish.

CHERRY JAR

Glass jar with large mouth and lid for holding maraschino cherries.

CHIGGER BITE

Term used by the glass trade and auctioneers to describe small chips on a piece of glass.

CHOP PLATE

Salver; large serving plate.

CHUNKED

Damaged glass in very poor condition.

CIGAR JAR

Large-mouthed glass humidor or canister with lid for storing cigars or tobacco.

CLAM BROTH

Semiopaque grayish glass.

CLARET

Stemmed glass for serving claret wine.

CLOSED HANDLED

Solid tab handles.

COASTER

Small round object with shallow rim, used under glassware to protect the furniture.

COBALT BLUE

Dark, rich, deep shade of blue glass, highly prized. It was produced by mixing cobalt and aluminum oxides.

COMPORT

Compote. Usually stemmed, open shallow dish or bowl.

CONCENTRIC RINGS

Design motif of circles within circles.

CONSOLE BOWL

Centerpiece bowl, often accompanied by matching candlesticks as a set.

CORAL

Opaque glass covered with heat-sensitive glass resulting in yellow-to-red shading. See Wheeling Peach Blow.

CORALENE GLASS

A type of art glass that was introduced in America but popular in Europe. It was ornamented with raised branches that looked like coral. They were formed from enamel to which drops of clear or opalescent glass were applied.

CORNING GLASS WORKS

An important American glass factory, established in the 19th century and still flourishing at the present. For more than 100 years it has been in the control of successive generations of the Houghton family. Today the firm, which has long operated Steuben Glass, maintains a museum of glass at its headquarters in Corning, New York, in which are displayed various examples of important ancient and modern glass. Its first year of operation at the present location was 1868, at which time it was known as the Corning Flint Glass Co. In 1875 the name was changed to Corning Glass Works.

COSMOS

Milk Glass (pressed) decorated by staining. Sold extensively in the early years of this century, Cosmos glass was traditionally of little regard in the collecting fraternity. It has now gained a moderate following, with prices in triple digits being not uncommon.

CORDIAL

Small goblet used to serve liqueurs and after-dinner drinks.

COVERED BON BON

Covered candy dish.

COVERED BUTTER DISH

Round dome-shaped glass cover over flat-bottom glass dish. Smaller than covered cheese dish.

CRANBERRY GLASS

A type of Victorian blown-molded glass with a light bright-red tint. It was made into vases or bowls with fluted rims. The color was light so as to mask the imperfections in the glass itself. An inexpensive glass, it was easily discernible from the better-quality ruby glass.

CRAQUELLE GLASS

Very rough texture which is produced by rolling in crushed glass and reheating and reblowing or by dipping hot glass into cold water.

CREAM SOUP

Small two-handled dish.

CROWN MILANO

See ALBERTINE.

CRUET

Small decanter, often handled, used in tandem to serve oil and vinegar.

CRYSTAL GLASS

A brilliant colorless glass which contains a high amount of lead oxide. Originally it was the *cristallo* glass developed in Venice in the mid-15th century. It derived its name from its resemblance to rock crystal. See FLINT GLASS: LEAD GLASS.

CULLETS

Scraps of broken glass which were remelted and added during glassmaking to encourage fusion.

CUSTARD GLASS

A creamy or yellowish milk glass popular in the early 20th century.

CUT GLASS

Glass decorated with faceted designs. The glass was carved or ground into deep sparkling facets by revolving wheels layered with an abrasive. It developed during the 16th century in Bohemia and was very popular until the invention of molded pressed glass in America about 1825, which was an inexpensive imitation of cut glass. It enjoyed a revival during the Brilliant period of cut glass in America which dated from 1876 to 1916.

DAISY-IN-HEXAGON

Motif which features a flower enclosed in a hexagon.

DAUM

A French glassworks, noted for its production of Art Glass. As a result of its location in the town of Nancy, the ware is often referred to as Nancy Daum—suggesting the existence of a glassmaker named Nancy Daum. The firm has had a distinguished history, for more than 100 years, and continues in operation today, though the word *Daum* has now been deleted from its title: the new name is Cristalleries de Nancy. Its beginnings date to 1875 when an already existing factory was acquired by Jean Daum. The era of its most noteworthy achievements was from about 1895 to the outbreak of World War I, when it was a leader in the production of Art Nouveau glass and was influential in setting styles followed or imitated by other manufacturers, notably in America.

DELPHITE

Blue milk glass. It is opaque and a pale blue in color.

DENNIS GLASSWORKS

English factory, near Stourbridge, run by the Webb family. It was founded in 1855 and is still in operation; the era of greatest achievement was in the later 1800s, when it produced much fashionable art glass.

DEPRESSION GLASS

Colored glassware which was produced in America primarily from the late 1920s through the 1930s. Inexpensively made, this glassware was turned out in quantity and sold at dime stores or given away as promotions or inducements to buy other products.

DIAMOND-DAISY

Diamond-shaped squares containing a daisy pattern.

DIAMOND POINT

Design which features faceted diamond projections which come to a point.

DIP MOLD

One-piece mold used for imprinting a decoration; has open top.

DISPENSERS

Glass container with a spigot for dispensing cold water from the refrigerator. Also includes the juice dispensers found in drugstore soda fountains.

DOMINO TRAY

Tray for holding creamer and sugar cubes. Has built in container for creamer.

DORFLINGER GLASS WORKS

The Dorflinger Glass Works was established at White Mills, Pennsylvania, by Christian Dorflinger, a German immigrant. He came to the U.S. in 1846 and six years later was operating the Long Island Flint Glass Works of Brooklyn, New York. The Pennsylvania factory was shut down in 1921. It specialized in high grade tableware.

DRESSER SET

Glass accessories with glass tray for dressing table. Includes items such as hair receiver, puff box, glove box, hatpin holder, hairpin tray or box, perfume and cologne bottles, etc.

DRESSER TRAY

Large glass tray which holds dressing table accoutrements such as hair receiver, cologne bottles, glove box, puff box, ointment jars, etc.

EDINBURGH CRYSTAL GLASS CO.

Important producer of cut glass, from the later 19th century to the present. The factory is now located outside Edinburgh in the Scottish village of Penicuik.

EBONY

Black-colored glass.

EMBOSSING

Patterns are in bas-relief; that is, they project slightly from the ground of the piece.

ENAMEL

A glass coating colored with pigments derived from metallic oxides. It was applied to glassware by firing to fuse the enamel to the original glaze.

ENGRAVED GLASS

A design is cut in the glass surface by small wheels coated with an abrasive, such as emery or diamond-point.

EPERGNE

An ornamental centerpiece for a dining table, it incorporated a number of small dishes around a central bowl.

ETCHED GLASS

An inexpensive substitute for hand-cutting on Victorian cased glass. Patterns are scratched in acid-resistant wax and acid is then applied.

FAVRILE

The trade name for the American Art glass marketed by Louis Tiffany, in the Art Nouveau style.

FENTON ART GLASS COMPANY

Founded in Martin Ferry, Ohio, this company has been producing fine glassware since 1907. In the early years they made Carnival, custard, opalescent, and a variety of other pressed and molded wares. Over the years they added hobnail, stretch, slag, and overlay pieces to their line. Famous for the hand decoration work, Fenton is still producing quality glassware in Williamstown, West Virginia, today.

FERN BOWL

Glass container for holding potted ferns. It has a liner and is tri-footed.

FINGERBOWL

This table convenience is of earlier origin than might be imagined and has a long history, encompassing many styles, shapes, sizes, and motifs. Silver or pewter fingerbowls were at times favored over glass. Nevertheless, a great number were made of glass, in both Europe and America. Their time of chief vogue was the Victorian era and the early 20th century.

FIRED-ON

Baked-on color.

FIRE POLISHING

A detail work on glass of a final firing to give added glaze and smooth finish to pressed glass.

FLASHED GLASS

A glass, popular in Victorian America, with a thin coat of colored glass over a clear base.

FLINT GLASS

The name by which English lead glass was known in the 17th and 18th century and occasionally afterward. So entrenched did this terminology become that, even to this day, English glass of that era is called "flint glass." A small quantity of pulverized flint was used as an ingredient, later replaced by sand.

FLOWER BOWL

Large shallow bowl used for floating flowers with short stems.

FLUX

Chemicals or metals such as oxide of lead, carbonate of soda, and potash which, when added to silica, cause it to fuse into glass.

FLUTED

Scalloped edge.

FOSTORIA GLASS COMPANY

Founded in Fostoria, Ohio, in 1887, Fostoria continues in production at their Moundsville, West Virginia, factory today. Many of their lovely glassware lines are considered to be "elegant" Depression era glass, and these patterns are avidly sought by collectors today.

FREE-BLOWN GLASS

Hand-maneuvered glass blowing without a mold, an ancient technique of high-quality craftsmen.

FROG

Round, domed, heavy glass object with holes drilled for placing in vases to hold flowers in place.

FROSTED GLASS

Glass with an opaque outer surface made by exposing the surface to the vapor of hydrofluoric acid.

FRY, H.C.

American manufacturer, born 1840, founded the Rochester Tumbler Co. in 1872 and the H.C. Fry Glass Co. in 1901, both located at Rochester, Pennsylvania. "Fry glass" includes Art glass and other varieties. Fry died at the age of 89 in 1929, and the business succumbed to the Depression several years later.

FUSION

The melting point of glass, which occurs at 2500° Fahrenheit. At this point glass is blown or pressed into the desired shape.

GADROON

A border trim of reeds and flutes, sometimes referred to as knurling.

GAFFER

Master glass blower and shop foreman.

GALLÈ, ÉMILE

Pioneer in the French Art Nouveau movement who gained fame for his Cameo glass in the late 1880s. His art glass featured floral designs in natural colors, and an oriental style was often followed.

GILDING

Application of gold to an object for decoration.

GLASSBORO

The Glassboro Glassworks was established at Glassboro, New Jersey, early in 1781 by Jacob Stanger. It was New Jersey's second glass manufacturing establishment. Successful in enduring many hardships and periods of economic uncertainty, the factory continued into the 20th century—one of very few American business enterprises, glass or otherwise, to span three centuries. Positive identification of its early products is difficult.

GLOVE BOX

Glass rectangular box used on dressing table or vanity to hold gloves.

GOBLET

Stemmed glass.

GONE WITH THE WIND LAMP

Parlor lamp, either kerosene or electric, consisting of a glass base and round globe glass shade.

GRAVY BOAT

Oval-shaped spouted bowl, often with pedestal.

GREEN, APPLE

Light green glass.

GREEN, EMERALD

Deep green, the shade of an emerald.

GREEN GLASS

The natural color of alkaline- or lime-based glass.

GREGORY, MARY

Designation for a particular variety of 19th-century glassware, painted with white or pastel pink enamel, featuring a likeness of a boy, a girl, or boy and girl. Traditional legend holds that "Mary Gregory" was an enameler for the Boston & Sandwich Glass Co. in the 1870s, where this type of ware was once believed to have originated.

GRILL PLATE

Plate divided into three sections by means of raised ridges.

GROUND

The name given to the background on which decoration is imposed.

HAIRPIN BOX

Small box, part of dresser set, used to hold hairpins on a dressing table.

HAIR RECEIVER

Small round box with lid which has a large hole in the middle. Used on Victorian dressing tables to hold hair which accumulated in hair brush.

HAMMONTON

The Hammonton Glassworks was established at the New Jersey town of that name by William Coffin and Jonathan Haines in 1817. It remained in operation for a number of years under the name Coffin & Haines. Its products are classified as South Jersey–type glassware.

HAND BLOWN

See FREE BLOWN.

HANDEL, PHILIP J.

An American glassmaker who established the Handel Company in 1885 in Meriden, Connecticut; a branch factory was later started in New York City. Popular products included acid-cut-back cameo vases in the Art Nouveau style and lamps similar to Tiffany lamps but less expensive.

HATPIN HOLDER

Tall cylindrically shaped glass Victorian dressing table accessory, used to hold hatpins.

HAZEL ATLAS GLASS COMPANY

This large company produced pressed wares from 1902 to 1956. Factories were located in Pennsylvania, Ohio, and West Virginia.

HEISEY

The A.H. Heisey Glass Co. was established in the 1860s at Newark, Ohio, by a partnership which included George Duncan and Daniel C. Ripley. It manufactured cut and pressed wares.

HIGHBALL OR BEER GLASS

Tall tumbler used for serving highballs or beer.

HOBNAIL

A manner of decorating glassware, either by pressing or cutting, with an overall pattern of small raised knobs known technically as prunts. The pattern became popular in Britain as early as 1800 but not in the U.S. until after the Civil War.

HOCKING GLASS COMPANY—ANCHOR HOCKING CORPORATION

The history of Anchor Hocking Corporation is the story of a company that started small but grew through initiative and desire on the part of its founders and employees. In the years that have passed since the Hocking Glass Company was founded in 1905 in Lancaster, Ohio, by I. J. Collins, it has grown into the Anchor Hocking Corporation worldwide. The company is a leading manufacturer of glass and ceramic tableware, glass and plastic containers, plastic and metal closures, plastic dinnerware, decorative hardware, and plastic- and glass-forming equipment. Manufacturing facilities and sales offices are located in the United States, Canada and the Netherlands, and the company has licensing agreements with a number of other companies.

HONESDALE

The Honesdale Decorating Co. was founded at Honesdale, Pennsylvania, in 1901 by the Dorflingers. It was active until 1932. Some of its ware was gold-decorated and is highly regarded by collectors.

HORSERADISH JAR

Glass jar with lid used to serve horseradish.

HOT PLATE

Glass plate used to sit under hot items in order to protect surface beneath.

ICE BLUE

Light crystal blue.

ICE BUCKET OR TUB

Deep pail-shaped container usually with closed handles for holding ice.

ICE CREAM PLATE

Small glass plate.

ICE CREAM TRAY

Large glass tray with shallow rim, usually made of cut glass, for serving ice cream.

ICE LIP

A rim which prevents ice from spilling out of the spout of a pitcher.

IMPERIAL

The Imperial Glass Co., a major producer of Carnival ware, was established at Bellaire, Ohio, in 1901. After enjoying great success, the company went bankrupt during the Depression but was reorganized and saved.

INCISING

The decorative technique of engraving or cutting into a surface of glass, as opposed to relief decoration.

INDIANA TUMBLER & GOBLET CO.

Firm noted for its manufacture of pressed glass in the late 19th/early 20th centuries. It was also the producer of Carmel Slag glass, a bizarre ware featuring striations of color that suggest medieval German glass. Holly Amber was another of its lines. In general its articles are not expensive and have been receiving increased attention.

INKWELL

Small heavy glass bottle for holding ink.

INTAGLIO

A design cut underneath a surface leaving a reverse relief.

INTARSIA

A variety of glass produced during the 1920s by Steuben when under directorship of Frederick Carder. It consisted of a core of colored glass sandwiched between layers of clear, decorated by etching. Painstaking and costly to manufacture, intarsia ware was never circulated in large numbers and is quite scarce today. The designs are sometimes said to be suggestive of patterns in ancient glassware; this was probably more accidental than intentional.

IRIDESCENT GLASS

An American art glass with a shimmering quality, used by Tiffany in the early 20th century.

IVORY

Term used to describe custard glass in the Vermont and Delaware patterns.

IVRENE

Opaque white glass by Steuben with an iridescent pearlized quality.

JADEITE

Pale green opaque glass color.

JAM JAR

Small jar with lid which usually has opening for spoon handle. Used to hold jams, jellies, and preserves.

JARVES, DEMING

Founder of the New England Glass Co. (1818), and the Boston & Sandwich Glass Co. (1825). In 1837 he set up the Mt. Washington Glass Works, though he played no role in its operations; its directorship was assigned to George Jarves, his son. The last company he established was the Cape Cod Glass Co. in 1858. Jarves died at age 79 in 1869, by all odds the most influential and financially successful American glass executive of the middle 19th century.

JELLY TRAY

Small shallow tray with rim for serving sliced cranberry jelly or jellied consomme.

JEANNETTE GLASS COMPANY

This company has been producing glassware in Jeannette, Pennsylvania, since around the turn of the century.

JENNYWARE

Kitchenware items made by Jeannette are called Jennyware by collectors. The aquamarine pieces are the most sought after and the most common.

JERSEY GLASS CO.

The Jersey Glass Co. was founded at Jersey City, New Jersey, in 1824 by George Drummer. It manufactured chiefly tableware, both cut and pressed.

KEW BLAS

An iridescent variety of art glass, introduced by the Union Glass Co. in the 1890s. The chief color is brown, shading into various hues and intermixed with green.

KNIFE REST

Small, glass, barbell-shaped table accessory used to hold knife blade off table while eating.

KNOP

A ball-shaped swelling on the stem of a wine glass.

LACE GLASS

See-through Venetian glass with a glassy, threadlike motif. Layered on either side in clear glass. Popular in the mid-16th century.

LACY PRESSED GLASS

An American variety of pressed glass distinguished by motifs of angular and round compositions, encompassing a complete surface. Popular in the mid-19th century.

LALIQUE

A leader of the Art Nouveau movement in glassware, Rene Lalique was for many years one of the more influential designers and manufacturers. His factory was located at Combs, France, and supplied the Parisian market as well as exporting heavily to the U.S. Unlike many of his contemporaries he continued to enjoy success after Art Nouveau had waned, following World War I, and in fact some of his greatest successes came in the 1920s and 1930s. He died in 1945 at the age of 85, having spent more than 60 years in the glass industry.

LATTICINO

Refers to solid, Venetian glass from the 16th century, with white opaque threadwork contrasting with the clear glass.

LAVA GLASS

Tiffany glass of dark blue hue with tendrils or coated decorations in gold or silver.

LEAD GLASS

In the 17th century, George Ravenscroft, an English glassmaker, invented a type of glass of extreme brilliance, fused with an oxide of lead.

LEER

Lehr glassmaker's oven for gradually toughening ware. Improved designs led to more ornate glass from the mid to late 18th century.

LIBBEY GLASS

Late 19th century glassworks from Toledo, Ohio, known for cut and pressed glasswares of high quality.

LIBERTY WORKS

This glass company was located in Egg Harbor, New Jersey, and produced glassware from 1903 to 1932.

LILY-PAD

The name given to an applied decoration in American glass. The lily-pad motif was shaped from a superimposed layer of glass, and varied in design. One typical motif had a curving stem which supported a flat leaflike ovoid pad.

LIME GLASS

Discovered in 1864 as a substitute for lead glass by William Leighton, a chemist employed by a glass works at Wheeling, West Virginia. It was cheaper than lead glass, cooled quicker and was lighter in weight, even though its appearance was inferior. Employed for glass or domestic utility, later became more widely used.

LOCKE, JOSEPH

English glassmaker and designer, active in the United States in the late 19th and 20th centuries. Pioneer of a number of varieties of art glass, including Agata. Locke died in 1936 at age 90.

LÖTZ GLASS OR LOETZ GLASS

Austrian Art Nouveau glass from the factory of Johann Lötz. Influenced by Tiffany glass.

LOVING CUP

Large footed tri-handled glass cup.

LUNCHEON PLATE

Eight-to-nine inch plate, smaller than a dinner plate, larger than a salad plate.

LUTZ GLASS

A thin, clear glass striped with colored twists in the Venetian style. Introduced at the Boston and Sandwich Glass Works by Nicholas Lutz. Sometimes referred to as "candy stripe glass."

MACBETH EVANS GLASS COMPANY

With several locations in Indiana, Macbeth Evans has produced glassware since 1899.

MARVER

A marble plate on which blown glass is shaped.

MAYONNAISE

Open compote often with underplate. Used for serving mayonnaise.

McKEE

Involved in United States glassmaking since the 1840s, the McKee Glass Company was organized in the late 1800s in Jeannette, Virginia. In 1961, it was bought by the Jeannette Corporation.

MERCURY GLASS

Two layers of glass sandwiching a coating of mercury or silver nitrate between.

MERESE

Pediment of glass bridging the bowl and stem.

METAL

When referring to glassmaking, the molten material from which it is made.

MILK GLASS

An opaque glass, handblown and decorated like porcelain, in the 17th and 18th century, popular for pressed glass.

MORGANTOWN GLASS WORKS

Located in Morgantown, West Virginia, Morgantown Glass Works produced glassware from the 1800s to 1972.

MILLEFIORI

A paperweight with a stylized floral motif achieved by using several different-colored glass rods together in a pattern and covering them with a thick glass metal, popular in the 18th century.

MILLERSBURG

An important producer of Carnival glass, though short-lived. The Millersburg Glass Co. was founded by John Fenton of the Fenton Art Glass Co. in 1909. It pioneered a variety of ware featuring so-called radium finish (which did, indeed, carry measurable traces of radiation; this was overlooked at the time, but after World War II, when the public became radiation-conscious, some persons disposed of their Millersburg wares out of fear of radium poisoning. It has since been demonstrated that the quantities are far too minute to cause harm.)

MOLD PRESSED

Another name for pressed glass: ware manufactured by pressing into a mold, rather than by blowing. It was made extensively in the U.S. from the second quarter of the 19th century onward.

MONART GLASS

A Spanish glass oxidized with marbling effects.

MONAX

Thin white glass produced by Macbeth Evans.

MOSS AGATE

A variety of Art glass manufactured by Steuben, featuring a marbleized overall effect worked up from the use of powdered glass and injection of cold water. The normal colors are red or brown.

MOTHER-OF-PEARL

Layered glass with air trapped in between.

MOTIF

Design or pattern of glass.

MOUNT VERNON GLASS

American art glass from the 19th century, blown-molded vases and novelties.

MOUNT WASHINGTON GLASS WORKS

An American art glass manufacturer famous for Cameo glass and other fine glass such as Burmese and Crown Milano.

MUFFINEER

See SUGAR SHAKER.

MURANO GLASS

The finest of Venetian glasses produced on a small island in southern Italy.

MUSTARD JAR

Small glass jar with lid which has indention for spoon. Used to serve mustard.

NAPOLI

Object is covered with enamel and gilt all over outside and inside.

NAPPY

Refers to a bowl. Old English term. Often found with one or two handles.

NASH

Prominent family of Anglo-American glass designers and manufacturers, founders of the A. Douglas Nash Corporation, noted for its art glass in the Tiffany manner. Unlike cheap imitators of Tiffany, who were plentiful in the World War I era, Nash worked in the Tiffany manner because of the family's close association with that firm, and produced wares of high quality.

NEW BREMEN

One of the most influential factories in America in the Federal period. The New Bremen Glass Manufactory was located at New Bremen (from Bremen, a town in Germany), Maryland, founded by Johann F. Amelung in 1784. Unlike most makers of that era it signed and even dated some of its work. New Bremen or "Amelung" glass is scarce and eagerly sought; most recorded examples are found in museums.

NEW ENGLAND GLASS COMPANY

A leading glassmaking company established at Cambridge, Massachusetts, by Deming Jarves and associates in 1818 and which remained active until c. 1880; known for all kinds of glassware, including pressed and cut glass and a variety of art glasses, such as Agata, Amberina, Pomona, and Wild Rose Peachblow.

NEW GENEVA

Glass works established 1797 in Fayette County, Pennsylvania, by Albert Gallatin. This was the farthest west that a glassworks was set up prior to the 19th century. Gallatin later gained notoriety by serving twelve years as U.S. Secretary of the Treasury, under John Adams and Jefferson. Its chief output was household ware of modest design, and it made some sheet glass for windows. The name "New Geneva" was chosen because of the preponderence of Swiss immigrants in the area.

NEW MARTINSVILLE GLASS COMPANY

Starting in 1901, New Martinsville Glass Company produced art glass for many years. The company later produced pressed pattern glass, novelty items and Depression glass. In 1944, New Martinsville was bought by another company and became The Viking Glass Company.

NIPT DIAMOND WAVES

A diamond pattern on glassware produced by pinching together thick vertical threads of applied glass.

"OFF-HAND" GLASS

The curiosity glassware the craftsmen made from the leftover glass at factories, some works of art, some utilitarian, some vulgar.

OGIVAL–VENETIAN DIAMOND

Diamond formation pattern in pattern glass. Also called reticulated or expanded diamond.

"OLD GOLD"

Deep amber stain.

OLIVE DISH

Small shallow relish dish.

OLIVE JAR

Glass container with wide mouth and lid used to serve olives.

OPAL GLASS

Milk glass.

OPALESCENT GLASS

Iridescent glass made by adding heat-sensitive chemicals to the batch and refiring. Bluish milky color.

OPALINE GLASS

A luxurious variety of glass, employed in the manufacture of pressed and art wares. It seems to have been introduced or at any rate popularized by Baccarat in the 1820s, but they in no way held any monopoly on its manufacture.

OPAQUE GLASS

A glass with little or no translucency and highly colored.

OPAQUE-WHITE GLASS

A porcelain-like glass with a milky quality.

OVERLAY GLASS

A glass molding technique of placing one colored glass over another, with designs cut through one layer only.

OVERSHOT GLASS

Novelty glass of Sandwich and Reading which has rough icy finish which is acquired by rolling molten wares in crushed glass.

PADEN CITY GLASS COMPANY

Known primarily for the glass it produced, Paden City also produced pottery. Started in 1916 in Paden City, West Virginia, the company closed in 1951. Many of the depression glass elegant patterns were made by Paden City.

PAIRPOINT

The Pairpoint Manufacturing Co. was established in 1865 at New Bedford, Massachusetts. Eventually it acquired the prestigious Mt. Washington Glass Co. The firm, with various changes of name, operated until 1958.

PARISON

Mass of molten glass which is gathered on the end of the blowpipe.

PARFAIT

Tall, footed ice cream dish in which sundaes are served.

PATE DE VERRE

"Paste of glass" or "glass paste." Made from powdered glass, melted and colored, pate de verre is of ancient origin and has been used in the manufacture of various articles. It is sometimes carved.

PATTERN GLASS

A kind of pressed glass, popular in the 1830s when it was imitative of the design and appearance of cut glass. In time the patterns became more complex, including circular, oval and elliptical patterns. In the 1860s the New England Glasshouse developed a way to press soda-lime glass, which was of inferior quality and did not make a bell-like ring when struck, as did the formerly used flint glass. To compensate for such imperfections, the entire surface was covered with more ornate designs. This type of glass was extensively produced in the second half of the 19th century.

PATTERN-MOLDED GLASS

A blown-molded glass in which the pattern is first impressed in a small mold before the glass is blown to full size.

PEACH BLOW GLASS

An American art glass of the late 19th century, characterized as a partially opaque glass shaded from cream or bluish-white to pink or violet-red.

PEARL ORNAMENTS

Molded allover patterns of ogivals or diamonds.

PEARLINE GLASS

Late 19th century art glass, varying from deep to pale opaline blue in the same piece.

PHILADELPHIA GLASS

A term usually applied to glassware from an 18th-century glassworks in Kensington, near Philadelphia, of which no examples can be certifiably identified.

PHOENIX GLASS

A term especially applied to a cased milk glass known as mother-of-pearl glass, produced by the Phoenix Glassworks Company in Pittsburgh, late 19th century.

PICKLE CASTOR

Glass jar held in a silver-plated metal frame with handle and spoon. Used during the Victorian period for serving pickles.

PICKLE DISH

Oblong tray smaller than a celery dish.

PIGEON BLOOD

Brown highlighted ruby glass.

PITTSBURGH FLINT GLASS WORKS

In American glass, the formal name for Bakewell's glassworks, established in 1808.

PITTSBURGH GLASS

Late-18th-century and 19th-century American glass, especially known for high-quality pressed glass.

PLATED GLASS

Layered glass made by dipping blown glass into different colored glass.

PLATINUM BAND

Ornamental silver-colored rim.

PLATONITE

Heat-resistant white glass by Hazel Atlas.

POKAL

A large standing cup with a cover, especially one featuring fine decoration and artistic merit.

POMONA GLASS

A variety of late-19th-century art glass originated by the New England Glass Company, characterized by two separate surfaces, one frosted and etched and the other tinted amber.

PONTIL, PUNTEE, OR PUNTY ROD

Long iron bar which holds vessel after it has been detached from the blow-pipe while the final touches are being done.

PRESERVE DISH

Footed candy dish.

PRESSED GLASS

An inexpensive substitute for free-blown cut glass, thicker and heavier and formed in a mold by mechanical pressure rather than by blowing. It was developed in the early 19th century and soon was in general use in American glasshouses.

PRUNTS

A glass-drop ornament attached to some early drinking vessels, notably used by the Germans on such glasses as the Krautstrunk and Roemer.

PUFF BOX

Small lidded box used for powder and powder puff, found on Victorian dressing tables.

PUMICE

Volcanic rock which has been ground into a powder and is used for polishing.

PURLED GLASS

Ribbing added around the base of a vessel.

QUARTZ GLASS

An Art glass introduced by Steuben, designed to imitate the appearance of quartz. It was produced in a variety of colors and shades.

QUATREFOIL

A form based on four leaves or a four-petaled flower, a gothic motif in architecture and window tracery.

QUEZAL GLASS

An iridescent semiopaque imitation of Tiffany's Favrille glass which is sometimes molded. It was made in Brooklyn about 1917.

QUILLING

On glass, a wavy ornament worked into a pattern by nips with the pincers at regular intervals.

RANGE SETS

Also called grease sets or drip sets for range tops that include a large salt and pepper and a drippings jar. Other items in a range set could include a flour jar, sugar jar, or spice shaker. Found in Depression era glass.

RAVENSCROFT

George Ravenscroft (1632–1683) is commonly regarded as the first commercially successful glassmaker in England and responsible for popularizing lead glass. He in fact may be credited with a larger accomplishment; as the result of his efforts, glass for use in tableware gradually began to replace pewter and other materials. Pieces proved beyond doubt to be his work are rare (not for lack of output but breakage over the years) and sell for high prices. Much research has been done into his life.

RAYED

Design of sunburst cuts on bottom of glassware.

REAMER

Juice extractors, reamers consist of a handled, high-sided saucer with a pouring lip. In the center of the saucer is a pointed cone reaming section. The citrus half is seated on the reaming section and turned to produce juice.

REFRIGERATOR CONTAINERS

Refrigerator containers are glass kitchenware items made for use in the refrigerator. Some are made to hold butter, vegetables, or leftovers, and some are made for easy stacking in the refrigerator.

RELISH

Pickle dish; oblong tray, sometimes with one or two handles.

RETICULATION

See OGIVAL.

REVERSE PAINTING

Designs are painted on the back of glass, appearing in proper perspective when viewed from the front.

RIGAREE

Applied decoration of glass with close-set, narrow, vertical bands, sometimes in different colors.

ROLLED EDGE

Curved lip or edge which may roll either toward the center or away.

ROPE EDGE

Ropelike design around the edge of a piece of glass ware.

ROSE

Deep red cranberry stain flashing.

ROSE BOWL

Small, round, often tri-footed bowl having small opening in center.

ROYAL FLEMISH GLASS

Type of Art glass made by the Mount Washington Glass Works decorated with thin surface staining and raised gilding.

RUBINA

Crystal which gradually goes from rich cranberry at top to clear at the bottom.

RUBINA VERDE

Crystal which gradually goes from rich cranberry at top to yellow-green at the bottom.

RUBY GLASS

Popularized by Carder of Steuben, ruby glass was a kind of handsome art glass with delicate impressive coloring, either of pastel pink or strong red.

SALAD PLATE

Seven-to-7½-inch plate.

SALT CELLAR

A bowl for holding salt at the table, common prior to the use of shakers and even for awhile thereafter. It was open at the top so that users could take pinches of salt between the fingers and sprinkle them on food. Salt cellars vary considerably in size. There are also individual salt cellars used with tiny spoons. Salt cellars were sometimes footed.

SALTS BOTTLE

Small glass bottles with silver tops carried by Victorian ladies and containing smelling salts should they feel faint.

SALVE BOX

Small lidded jar used to hold salves, ointments, creams, etc., found on Victorian dressing tables.

SALVER

Large platter, 11 to 12 inches.

SANDWICH GLASS

An American pressed glass, popular in America and Europe as a substitute for cut glass, produced in Massachusetts during the 19th century.

SANDWICH SERVER

Center-handled salver.

SASE

Abbreviation for self-addressed stamped envelope. Used in mail order advertisements in glass and antique publications.

SATIN GLASS

An American art glass consisting of layers of colored glass covered with square indentations, then given an acid-vapor bath to produce a satin finish.

SHERBET

Small, footed dessert dish.

SICK GLASS

Poor-quality glass which either has been damaged by external factors or was simply made from inferior materials and with inferior processes.

SIGNATURE

Mark of the maker and/or manufacturer.

SILVER DEPOSIT

Silver decoration on glassware often in floral motif.

SILVERIA GLASS

A technique of rolling a thin layer of silver over glass, sealing it, and then blowing, which shatters the foil into glittering flecks.

SILVERINA

A variety of art glass pioneered by Steuben in the 1920s, using flakes of mica.

SILVER ONYX GLASS

Pressed opaline glass decorated by staining parts of the pattern with platinum lustre.

SLAG GLASS

A leaded glass first produced in England in the middle 19th century. It employs slag, which is the refuse from steel works. The glass could be molded in many forms.

SODA GLASS

A light, easily worked glass from the Renaissance on in Venice.

SOUTH BOSTON GLASS

Associated with the Boston Glass Co., the originators of the three-mold glass.

SOUTH JERSEY GLASS

Eighteenth-century tableware produced by the glassworks of Caspar Wistar and other factories in the New Jersey area. First made for the workers' private use and local markets, the pieces are characterized by bold, almost crude form. The style gradually spread throughout New England and New York.

SOWERBY'S ELLISON GLASS WORKS

Founded by George Sowerby, this glasshouse has specialized in pressed glass, which it began to produce in the 1880s. Its output has included slag glass, opalescent glass, and an opaque glass called vitro-porcelain used for imitating porcelain services.

SPANGLED GLASS

A late-19th-century American art glass principally made into glass baskets with fancy decorated handles and rims. Flakes of mica were incorporated in the clear glass inner layer, and an overlay of clear tinted glass of various colors was applied.

SPATTER GLASS

Type of opaque white or colored glass in both England and America. The English color version usually has a white lining. The exterior is mottled with large spots of different colored glass.

SPOON DISH

Rectangular or oval shallow glass dish used for holding dessert spoons.

SPOON HOLDER OR SPOONER

Tall, cylindrical holder with or without handles, used to hold dessert spoons.

STAINED GLASS

Imitation colored glass achieved by painting clear glass with metallic stain.

STEUBEN

Manufacturer of Art glass, noted today for figurines and elaborate decorative pieces created as objets d'art rather than for utilitarian purpose. The firm was begun by Frederick Carder at Corning, New York, in 1903 and soon became an influential style-setter whose products were copied by others. It was absorbed (though still under Carder) by the Corning Glass Works in 1918.

STRIPED GLASS

An American art glass from the late 19th century, characterized by wavy bands of contrasting color on a background.

SUGAR AND LEMON TRAY OR DISH

Two-tiered serving dish. Cut lemons were placed on the bottom tier and sugar was held by bowl which made up the top tier.

SUGAR SHAKER

Resembles salt shaker except that it is larger in size with bigger holes in the lid, used for sprinkling sugar. It is also called a muffineer.

SUNSET-GLOW GLASS

A glass evolving in the late 18th century which was milky white and opalescent.

SUPERIMPOSED DECORATION

Decorations and designs are tooled in glass and applied on the original surface.

SYRUP PITCHER

Small pitcher with hinged metal lid for serving syrup.

TAZZA

A decorative drinking vessel, usually mounted on a stem and made of glass; especially valued are the beautifully wrought pieces of the 16th century.

TEA CADDY

Large wide-mouth glass canister with lid used for storing loose tea.

TEAL

Blue-green glass.

TEAR

Bubble of air trapped in glass. Sometimes purposely blown in stem for decoration.

THREAD CIRCUIT

A decorative motif on glass, applying threads of twisted glass on the bowl or neck of a vessel. Sometimes the appliques are of different-colored glass in concentric circles or symmetrical patterns. It had its beginnings in Venetian glass during the Renaissance.

TIDBIT TRAY

Tiered dish for serving hors d'oeuvres. Generally a metal pole runs through the center of each tier, which is largest on the bottom, becoming smaller as they go up.

TIFFANY

Louis Comfort Tiffany, the most celebrated of American glassmakers, was born in 1848. He traveled abroad as a youth, studied painting, and became introduced to the beginnings of the Art Nouveau movement, at that time unknown in the U.S. By 1885 he had set up a glass factory at Long Island in New York. As the result of vast publicity achieved through the exhibition of his products at world's fairs and their popularity among the social elite, he soon gained an unrivaled reputation. The business was expanded to include not only glassware but decorative household objects, furniture, jewelry and miscellaneous lines, as well as interior decoration service. Tiffany pioneered a number of varieties of art glass, sold in the studios he established and in fashionable shops. Of these, Favrile was undoubtedly the foremost, and the style with which he came to be best identified. Every piece of Tiffany glass is now in the rank of prime collector's item, with prices for some of them, such as lamps, going into five figures. Tiffany died at age 85 in 1933.

TIFFIN GLASS COMPANY

Based in Tiffin, Ohio, the Tiffin Glass Company was a subsidiary of U.S. Glass Company. It closed in 1980.

TOILET WATER BOTTLE

Bottle which is larger than cologne bottle used for holding toilet water on dressing table.

TOOLS

In glassmaking these include: block, blowpipe, caliper, compass, crimper, punty rod, and pucellas.

TOOTHBRUSH BOTTLE

Tall cylindrical glass bottle with cap, used to store toothbrush.

TOOTHPICK HOLDER

Small glass container found in novelty shapes and sizes used to hold toothpicks.

TOOTHPOWDER JAR

Small lidded jar for holding toothpowder.

TOPAZ

Bright yellow glassware.

TRANSLUCENT

Glass which diffuses light in such a way that objects cannot be clearly seen through it.

TRANSPARENT

Glass which permits light to pass through, which makes it easy to see through.

TRIVET

Footed hotplate.

TUMBLER

A glass vessel, not having a stem or handle, resting on a base rather than a foot or other support. The normal shape is cylindrical; capacity varies.

TUMBLE UP

Water bottle and inverted glass set which is intended for a nightstand.

ULTRAMARINE

Blue-green by Jeannette.

VASA MURRHINA

An art glass with an inner layer of colored glass that has various colored metals in flake or dust form used in it. Produced in Boston during the late 19th century.

VASELINE BOX

Small lidded ointment box; part of Victorian dressing table accoutrements.

VASELINE GLASS

A decorative glass originally from France. Produced during the second half of the 19th century in England and America, it is characterized by its greenish-yellow tone resembling the ointment. Often referred to as yellow opaline.

VERRE-DE-SOIE

Art glass produced by Steuben, among others, which is distinguished by its translucent silky iridescence.

WAFER DISH

Small square or rectangular glass dish used for serving wafers and crackers.

WATERFORD

Irish glass produced in Ireland from the 18th century onward associated with deep-cut glass of a bluish tint, avidly collected.

WESTMORELAND GLASS

An American glass in the 19th century imitating earlier styles.

WHEELING GLASS

Table glass from Virginia in the 19th century.

WHISKEY JUG
Whiskey decanter shaped like a jug, with or without handle.

WHISKEY TUMBLER
Small flat-bottom glass for serving whiskey.

WHITNEY GLASS
An American glass from the 18th century producing bottles and flasks.

WINE GLASS
Stemmed glass for serving wine.

WINE SET
Decanter and wine glasses usually on a matching tray.

WRYTHING ORNAMENTATION
Fluting and/or swirled ribbing.

ZANESVILLE GLASS
An American art glass, produced in the early 19th century in Ohio.

ZWISCHENGOLDGLAS
A form of glass, popular in 18th century Bohemia, which was gilded and inlaid in another straight-sided glass.

GLASS ARTICLES

Goblet

Champagne

Claret

Sherry

Wine

Cordial

Comport

Basket

Creamer
and
Sugar

Cruet

Decanter

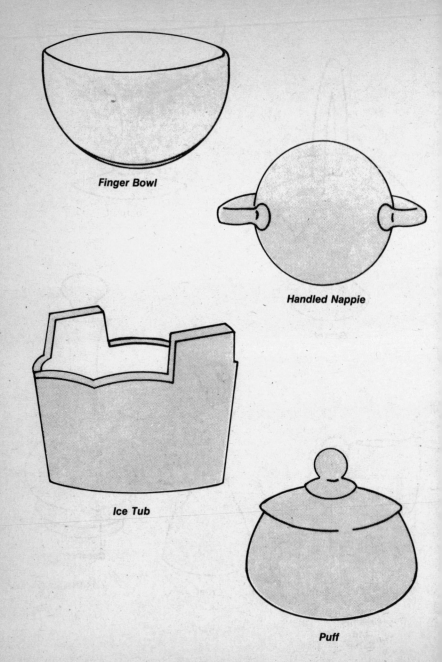

Finger Bowl

Handled Nappie

Ice Tub

Puff

Rose Bowl

Punch Bowl

Tumbler

Water Bottle

Whiskey Bottle

CUT GLASS MOTIFS APPEARING IN CARNIVAL GLASS

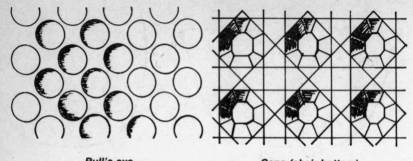

Bull's-eye

Cane (chair bottom)

Buzz Star

Cross Hatching

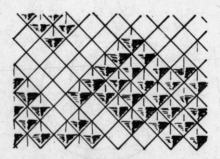

Diamond Point

Fan-Feathered Fan

Flashed Rosette

Flashed Fan

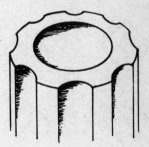

Fluting

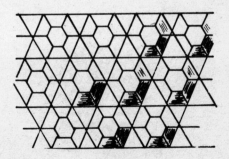

Hobnail

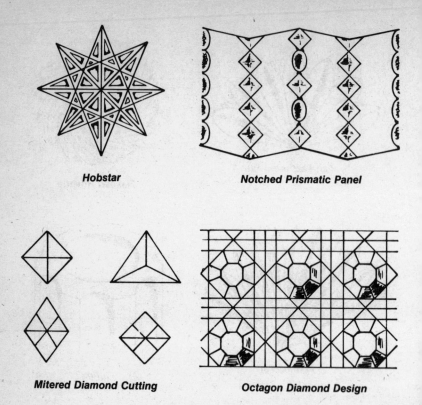

Hobstar

Notched Prismatic Panel

Mitered Diamond Cutting

Octagon Diamond Design

Rosette

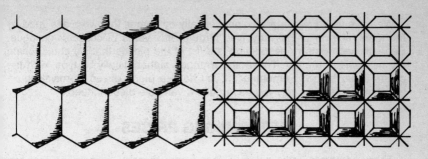

St. Louis

Square Block

Single Star

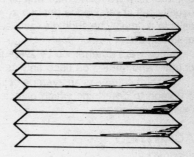

Step or Prism Fluting

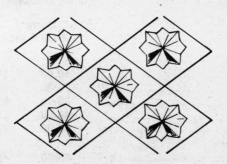

Strawberry Diamond

HOW TO USE THIS BOOK

We have listed all patterns alphabetically by names that were assigned by the manufacturer or have evolved through fifty years of collector dialogue. Beneath each pattern description is a list of the pieces that we could locate on the dealer's market. These are arranged alphabetically by type, with the colors listed below. Remember, if you have a piece of red Carnival glass, whether we list it or not, you have quite a valuable piece indeed.

DETERMINING PRICES

There are three price columns found next to each listing. The first two columns create a price range. The range shows the lowest and highest retail selling price for each piece. These prices reflect the geographical differences of the glassware market, as well as the laws of supply and demand. Dealers usually sell at retail price but buy at wholesale value. Therefore, if a collector sells to a dealer, he should expect a lower price than if he sold at an auction or flea market.

Values were determined by averaging the prices of actual sales across the country and should be used only as a guideline.

The third column is an average of last year's prices for the item. This allows a person to determine which objects have decreased or increased in value over the last year.

ACANTHUS
Imperial

An iridescent molded glass, heavy and well detailed with a flowing swill design. The pattern has the look of a water whirlpool suddenly frozen. Most common in smoke and marigold, it can be found in several other colors.

	Current Price Range		Prior Year Average
Bowl, diameter 8″			
☐ purple	50.00	60.00	52.00
☐ green	70.00	80.00	72.00
☐ blue	70.00	80.00	72.00
☐ marigold	45.00	55.00	47.00
☐ smoke	60.00	70.00	62.00
Bowl, diameter 9½″			
☐ purple	36.50	45.00	40.00
☐ green	36.50	45.00	40.00
☐ blue	36.50	45.00	40.00
☐ marigold	35.00	40.00	30.00
☐ smoke	48.00	60.00	50.00

	Current Price Range		Prior Year Average
Plate, diameter 9½"			
☐ marigold	125.00	1450.00	128.00
☐ green	120.00	150.00	125.00
☐ smoke	120.00	150.00	125.00
☐ clambroth	125.00	155.00	125.00

ACORN
Fenton

A naturalistic design of three tiers of acorns in a round, flowing group. The branches reliefed oak leaves. Known in the widest range of colors available to Carnival glass.

Bowl, diameter 7"			
☐ marigold	20.00	30.00	25.00
☐ purple	50.00	60.00	52.00
☐ green	25.00	35.00	27.00
☐ blue	35.00	45.00	37.00
☐ amethyst	28.50	50.00	30.00
☐ peach opalescent	120.00	135.00	125.00
☐ vaseline	110.00	125.00	115.00
☐ red	370.00	400.00	375.00
Bowl, diameter 8"–9"			
☐ marigold	18.00	28.00	20.00
☐ green	30.00	40.00	32.00
☐ blue	55.00	65.00	57.00
Plate, diameter 9"			
☐ purple	285.00	340.00	300.00
☐ green	285.00	340.00	300.00
☐ blue	285.00	340.00	300.00
☐ amethyst	285.00	340.00	300.00

ACORN
Millersburg

Alternating stems with acorns and leaves, the round pattern rotates vertically from the interior center. The edges of the piece are generally fluted in a petal design and fine stem and base follow the bowl's shape. A molded heavy glass, the colors are equally green or amethyst. Acorn is rare and highly prized.

	Current Price Range		Prior Year Average
Compote			
☐ purple	325.00	375.00	330.00
☐ green	325.00	375.00	330.00
☐ amethyst..	325.00	375.00	350.00
☐ vaseline...	2250.00	3250.00	2500.00

ACORN AND FILE

	Current Price Range		Prior Year Average
Compote			
☐ vaseline...	900.00	1100.00	950.00

ACORN BURRS
Northwood

Oak leaves and acorns adorn the piece in an overall design of finely ridged bark. The foliage is raised in relief giving the piece an interesting shape and a natural appearance. The mold is good and clean; the design is sharply engraved. Found in the full range of colors, the opalescent varieties are unusual and costly.

Acorn Burrs

	Current Price Range		Prior Year Average
Berry, bowl diameter 5″			
☐ marigold	17.00	22.00	18.00
☐ purple	30.00	33.00	32.00
☐ blue	30.00	33.00	32.00
☐ green	30.00	33.00	32.00
☐ amethyst	30.00	33.00	32.00
☐ ices	55.00	70.00	58.00
Berry, bowl diameter 10″			
☐ marigold	60.00	72.00	54.00
☐ purple	130.00	140.00	132.00
☐ blue	115.00	120.00	117.50
☐ green	115.00	120.00	117.50
☐ amethyst	115.00	120.00	117.00
☐ ices	295.00	320.00	310.00
Covered Butter			
☐ marigold	130.00	150.00	135.00
☐ purple	190.00	210.00	200.00
☐ blue	190.00	210.00	200.00
☐ green	190.00	210.00	200.00
☐ amethyst	190.00	210.00	200.00
☐ white	260.00	275.00	205.00
☐ ices	260.00	275.00	205.00
Spooner			
☐ marigold	60.00	90.00	65.00
☐ purple	95.00	110.00	98.00
☐ blue	110.00	145.00	115.00
☐ green	110.00	145.00	115.00
☐ amethyst	110.00	145.00	115.00
☐ white	150.00	200.00	160.00
☐ ice blue	150.00	200.00	175.00
☐ ice green	150.00	200.00	175.00
Tumbler			
☐ marigold	40.00	50.00	42.00
☐ purple	45.00	55.00	47.00
☐ green	55.00	65.00	57.00
☐ amethyst	40.00	60.00	50.00
Pitcher			
☐ marigold	360.00	390.00	370.00
☐ purple	475.00	525.00	485.00
☐ green	475.00	525.00	485.00
☐ amethyst	475.00	525.00	485.00

	Current Price Range		Prior Year Average

Punch Bowl, two-piece set

☐ marigold	250.00	335.00	250.00
☐ purple	360.00	435.00	375.00
☐ blue..	360.00	435.00	375.00
☐ green	360.00	435.00	375.00
☐ amethyst...	360.00	435.00	375.00
☐ white..	1000.00	1300.00	1100.00
☐ ice blue	1000.00	1300.00	1100.00
☐ ice green	1500.00	2000.00	1700.00
☐ aqua opalescent	7000.00	10000.00	7400.00

Punch Cup

☐ marigold	15.00	25.00	17.00
☐ purple	20.00	30.00	22.00
☐ blue..	30.00	35.00	32.00
☐ green	30.00	40.00	32.00
☐ amethyst...	40.00	60.00	50.00
☐ white..	35.00	45.00	37.00
☐ ices...	70.00	80.00	72.00
☐ aqua opalescent	240.00	260.00	250.00

Sugar Bowl and Creamer

☐ marigold	60.00	90.00	65.00
☐ purple	110.00	145.00	115.00
☐ blue..	110.00	145.00	115.00
☐ green	110.00	145.00	115.00
☐ amethyst...	110.00	145.00	115.00
☐ white..	150.00	200.00	160.00
☐ ice blue	150.00	200.00	160.00
☐ ice green	150.00	200.00	160.00

A DOZEN ROSES
Imperial

Bowl, diameter 8½"–10"

☐ purple	135.00	155.00	140.00
☐ green	135.00	155.00	140.00
☐ marigold	135.00	155.00	140.00
☐ amethyst...	135.00	155.00	140.00

AFRICAN SHIELD

An oddly symmetrical design with a handcrafted look highlights these pieces. Two ridged shields appear in a mirror image motif with connecting ribbons of long loops radiating out of an eightpoint star. The rims of the pieces are jagged in a sawtooth motif. The entire design rings of a medieval era, crude but distinctly well crafted.

	Current Price Range		Prior Year Average

Toothpick Holder
☐ marigold 40.00 60.00 45.00

AGE HERALD
Fenton

An advertising item from the Birmingham newspaper, the plate or bowl depicts the Age Herald Building. The detail of the bricks and windows is good, and the inscription is in flowing script writing. Only in amethyst, the color is rainbowlike. The rim is a modified sawtooth.

Bowl
☐ amethyst...................................... 950.00 1050.00 1000.00
Plate
☐ amethyst...................................... 950.00 1050.00 1000.00

AMARYLLIS
Northwood

A pattern of three full-blown poppies and several buds adorn the expanded triangular bowl. The colors are cobalt, marigold, and purple, and the glass is nicely iridescent.

Compote
☐ marigold 35.00 55.00 40.00
☐ purple 57.50 75.00 62.00
☐ blue 57.50 75.00 62.00
☐ amethyst...................................... 57.50 75.00 62.00

AMERICAN
Fostoria

Apothecary Jar (small)
☐ marigold .... 50.00 — —
Tumbler
☐ marigold 450.00 525.00 475.00

APPLE AND PEAR INTAGLIO
Northwood

The technique of decorating by intaglio is achieved by impressing the design into the piece, as opposed to relief patterns which are raised off the surface. This pattern shows swirls of stylized pears and apples with stems and leaves deeply molded into heavy, thick glass. The colors are clear or red, unusual in other tints.

	Current Price Range		Prior Year Average
Bowl, diameter 10″ (5″ berry)			
☐ marigold	75.00	90.00	78.50

APPLE BLOSSOMS
Dugan

A prolific pattern, produced for mass distribution at carnivals and fairs, Apple Blossom pieces can be readily obtained. The central flower is surrounded by four smaller blossoms in a circular pattern. The bowls and plates have an irregular shell-shaped rim. The colors are marigold, peach, and other pastels. Occasionally the glass is white and the brighter colors are also in existence.

	Current Price Range		Prior Year Average
Bowl, diameter 7″–9″			
☐ marigold	35.00	45.00	37.50
☐ purple	40.00	50.00	42.00
☐ blue	40.00	50.00	42.00
☐ amethyst	40.00	50.00	42.00
☐ white	60.00	80.00	65.00
☐ peach opalescent	40.00	50.00	42.00
Plate, diameter 8½″			
☐ marigold	45.00	57.50	48.50
☐ purple	65.00	85.00	70.00
☐ blue	65.00	85.00	70.00
☐ amethyst	65.00	85.00	70.00
☐ white	85.00	110.00	90.00
☐ peach opalescent	85.00	110.00	90.00

APPLE BLOSSOM TWIGS
Dugan

The exterior pattern on pieces with the Apple Blossom Twig design is the basket-weave motif. The interior is a square of flowers and stems, sharply molded in relief, surrounding a central blossom. The edges of the piece are fluted and the colors are marigold, purple, and peach.

	Current Price Range		Prior Year Average
Bowl, diameter 9″			
☐ marigold	27.00	53.00	30.00
☐ purple	100.00	120.00	110.00
☐ amethyst	55.00	65.00	57.00
☐ white	55.00	65.00	57.00
☐ peach opalescent	120.00	140.00	125.00
Plate, diameter 9¼″			
☐ marigold	45.00	67.50	48.00
☐ purple	85.00	110.00	90.00
☐ blue	85.00	110.00	90.00
☐ amethyst	85.00	110.00	90.00
☐ white	110.00	140.00	120.00
☐ peach opalescent	160.00	190.00	165.00

APPLE PANELS
Sowerby

An intaglio design of apples and leaves is set into the piece with ridged panels. Found only in sugar and creamers, the shape is simple with classic lines reminiscent of Greek urns. The glass is iridescent, colors usually green and marigold.

Creamer			
☐ marigold	22.00	27.00	25.00
☐ blue	32.00	37.00	34.00
Sugar Bowl			
☐ marigold	22.00	27.00	24.00
☐ blue	32.00	37.00	35.00

APPLE TREE
Fenton

The all-over design of reliefed apples, twigs, and leaves is naturalistic and sharply formed. The pattern is busy and dominates the piece. The upper border is a stylized fence top. Found in water pitchers and tumblers, the shape is rather typical, but the top rim of the pitcher has an interesting, closely fluted design.

Pitcher			
☐ marigold	125.00	145.00	128.00
☐ blue	200.00	275.00	215.00
☐ white	500.00	600.00	525.00
Tumbler			
☐ marigold	20.00	40.00	22.00
☐ blue	40.00	50.00	42.00
☐ white	50.00	60.00	52.00

APRIL SHOWERS
Fenton

Like beads of rain streaming down a glass pane, the pattern has the look of frozen motion. The glass is heavy and iridescent, the colors, usually blue, white, marigold, green, and purple, have the rainbow when caught by the light. The vased rim is ruffled in a wavy manner and the base is solid and thick.

	Current Price Range		Prior Year Average
Vase			
☐ marigold	30.00	40.00	35.00
☐ purple	30.00	40.00	35.00
☐ green	30.00	40.00	35.00
☐ blue	30.00	40.00	35.00
☐ white	30.00	40.00	35.00

ARCADIA BASKETS

Plate, diameter 8″			
☐ marigold	35.00	50.00	37.50

ARCHED FLEUR-DE-LIS
Higbee

Mug			
☐ marigold	100.00	120.00	105.00

ARCHED PANELS

Tumbler			
☐ marigold	45.00	60.00	48.50

ARCS
Imperial

Radiating half-circles emanate from the circular medallion in a rather symmetrical design. Each group of arc consists of four patterns, alternating bubbly glass with shiny, smooth glass. The colors are amethyst and marigold, and less commonly green or smoke.

	Current Price Range		Prior Year Average

Bowl
☐ marigold	15.00	20.00	17.00
☐ green	22.50	27.50	24.00
☐ purple	22.50	27.00	24.00
☐ amethyst	22.50	27.00	24.00
☐ smoke	37.00	42.50	39.00

Compote
☐ marigold	15.00	20.00	18.00
☐ purple	22.50	27.50	24.00
☐ amethyst	22.50	27.50	24.00
☐ smoke	22.50	27.50	24.00

ART DECO
Sowerby

Bowl
☐ marigold	22.00	28.00	24.00

ASTERS

Bowl, 6"
☐ marigold	20.00	28.00	22.00

ASTRAL

Bowl
☐ marigold	45.00	—	—

AUGUST FLOWERS

Bowl
☐ marigold	35.00	—	—

AURORA

Bowl, 8½"
☐ marigold	45.00	55.00	47.00
☐ white	65.00	75.00	67.00

AUSTRALIAN FLOWER SET

A vase for flower arrangements, the piece is shallow bowl with a center device for holding stems. The design is simple—a three-tiered threading along a gentle scalloped edge. The color is green, and the iridescent glass is very bright and clear.

	Current Price Range		Prior Year Average

Flower Set
☐ ice green 47.00   55.00   49.00

AUSTRALIAN GRAPE

A vertical grape pattern adorns the long side of the piece, dropping down from the vine which circles right below the upper border. The grapes are formed by reliefed ridges within the interior of the fruit flat on the glass. The color is clearer and weaker than typical Carnival glass but is of the same tone.

Tumbler
☐ marigold 22.50   27.00   34.00

AUSTRALIAN SWAN

The graceful swan literally floats among the ripples of the central medallion. The perspective is good; the outward band is a wreath of holly-like foliage. The glass is transparent, the iridescence bright.

Bowl, diameter 5½″–9½″
☐ marigold 47.50   55.00   50.00
☐ purple 95.00   110.00   100.00
Miniature
☐ white .... 75.00   —   —

AUTUMN ACORNS
Fenton

Acorns, although, only sparsely sprinkled over the piece are still the main attraction on these bowls and rare plates. The rim is bravely fluted in a vertical band, forming a frame for the sharply detailed leaves that are bunched around the interior.

Autumn Acorns

	Current Price Range		Prior Year Average
Bowl			
☐ marigold	35.00	45.00	37.00
☐ purple	45.00	55.00	46.00
☐ green	35.00	45.00	37.00
☐ blue	40.00	50.00	42.00
☐ amethyst	45.00	55.00	47.00
☐ red	45.00	55.00	47.00
Plate, diameter 7½″			
☐ purple	60.00	75.00	62.00
☐ green	60.00	75.00	62.00
☐ blue	60.00	75.00	62.00
☐ amethyst	60.00	75.00	62.00

AUTUMN OAK

	Current Price Range		Prior Year Average
Lamp Shade			
☐ marigold	22.50	30.00	25.00

AZTEC
McKee

	Current Price Range		Prior Year Average
Creamer and Sugar			
☐ marigold	95.00	105.00	97.00
☐ clambroth	145.00	155.00	147.00
Pitcher			
☐ marigold	1200.00	1400.00	1250.00
Rosebowl			
☐ clambroth	225.00	275.00	245.00
Tumbler			
☐ marigold	50.00	60.00	55.00

BABY'S BOUQUET

	Current Price Range		Prior Year Average
Child's Plate			
☐ marigold	90.00	—	—

BAKER'S ROSETTE

Ornament			
☐ marigold	65.00	—	—
☐ amethyst	80.00	—	—

BALL AND SWIRL

Mug			
☐ marigold	90.00	—	—

BALLOONS
Imperial

A simple design on absolutely beautiful iridescence makes pieces of this pattern intriguing. The band of balloons that crosses the middle waist is anchored down with diagonal etchings. The rest of the piece is smooth, glossy, and devoid of design.

Cake Plate, center handle			
☐ marigold	90.00	110.00	92.00
☐ smoke	90.00	110.00	92.00
Compote			
☐ marigold	82.50	95.00	85.00
☐ smoke	87.50	100.00	88.00
Perfume Atomizer			
☐ marigold	50.00	70.00	60.00
☐ smoke	85.00	95.00	80.00
Vase			
☐ marigold	85.00	90.00	87.00
☐ smoke	90.00	100.00	92.00

BAMBOO BIRD JAR

Jar			
☐ amethyst	485.00	510.00	490.00

BANDED DIAMOND
Crystal Glass Works (Australia)

The interest is in the shape of these pieces, created by a band of geometrically divided diamonds in an indented triangular form. The glass has a radium finish, the iridescence is mirror-like.

Banded Diamond

	Current Price Range		Prior Year Average
Tumbler			
☐ marigold	350.00	450.00	400.00
☐ purple	250.00	350.00	300.00
☐ amethyst..	250.00	350.00	300.00
Water Pitcher			
☐ marigold	750.00	850.00	800.00
☐ purple	1200.00	1400.00	1300.00
☐ amethyst..	1200.00	1400.00	1300.00

BANDED DIAMOND AND FANS
English Manufacturer

Toothpick Holder			
☐ marigold	60.00	70.00	62.00

BANDED DRAPE
Fenton

A neat, centrally located band of ridging runs the diagonal on these water sets. The design is an enameled lily stemming from the engraved band with its painted foliage below.

	Current Price Range		Prior Year Average

Tumbler
☐ marigold	18.00	28.00	20.00
☐ blue	28.00	32.00	29.00
☐ amethyst	28.00	32.00	29.00
☐ green	35.00	41.00	37.00
☐ white	35.00	41.00	37.00

Water Pitcher
☐ marigold	70.00	85.00	72.00
☐ blue	185.00	200.00	190.00
☐ amethyst	185.00	200.00	190.00
☐ green	450.00	500.00	475.00
☐ white	240.00	275.00	245.00

BANDED GRAPE AND LEAF
English Manufacturer

A rare water pitcher and glass set, the design is busy and encompasses most of the pieces. A swirling band of grape vines curves up and down, encircling grape clusters and leaves. The color is marigold and exceedingly bright.

Tumbler
| ☐ marigold | 95.00 | 100.00 | 97.00 |

Water Pitcher
| ☐ marigold | 375.00 | 425.00 | 380.00 |

BANDED PANELS

Sugar Bowl
| ☐ marigold | 30.00 | 40.00 | 32.00 |
| ☐ amethyst | 40.00 | 50.00 | 45.00 |

BANDED PORTLAND
U.S. Glass

Puff Box
| ☐ marigold | 55.00 | 65.00 | 57.00 |

BARBER BOTTLE
Cambridge

☐ marigold	370.00	380.00	372.00
☐ green	415.00	425.00	417.00
☐ amethyst	445.00	455.00	447.00

BASKET
Northwood

A popular pattern and shape for novelty Carnival glass items, the design is woven ridges with a cane or wicker appearance. The baskets have sturdy, pudgy feet and rounded handles stemming from the upper rim. The wide range of colors include purple, cobalt, ice blue, green, aqua, white, and marigold.

	Current Price Range		Prior Year Average
Basket, flared top			
☐ marigold	60.00	70.00	62.00
☐ purple	75.00	85.00	78.00
☐ green	225.00	245.00	230.00
☐ ices..	200.00	350.00	220.00
☐ aqua opalescent	250.00	270.00	255.00
☐ white...	135.00	155.00	140.00
Basket, straight edge			
☐ marigold	60.00	70.00	62.00
☐ purple	75.00	85.00	78.00
☐ green	225.00	245.00	230.00
☐ ices..	200.00	350.00	220.00
☐ aqua opalescent	250.00	270.00	255.00
☐ white...	135.00	155.00	140.00

BASKETWEAVE
Fenton

This popular pattern, woven wicker-like ridges, is used on many pieces that have different interior motifs as the exterior design. The pattern is in high relief with the three-tiered ridges over and under bamboo-like poles. The sculpture catches the light and the iridescence is good. The colors are blue, peach, white, amethyst, and marigold.

Candy Dish

☐ marigold	22.50	30.00	25.00
☐ purple	32.50	40.00	35.00
☐ green	32.50	40.00	35.00
☐ blue	32.50	40.00	35.00
☐ amethyst..	32.50	40.00	35.00
☐ white...	50.00	65.00	35.00
☐ ice blue	50.00	65.00	35.00
☐ ice green	50.00	65.00	35.00

	Current Price Range		Prior Year Average

Hat Shape, plain or blackberry

☐ marigold	20.00	30.00	22.00
☐ purple	28.00	35.00	30.00
☐ green	28.00	35.00	30.00
☐ blue	28.00	35.00	30.00
☐ amethyst	28.00	55.00	30.00
☐ red	160.00	175.00	165.00

Vase

☐ marigold	250.00	300.00	275.00
☐ blue	325.00	425.00	375.00

BASKETWEAVE AND CABLE
Westmoreland

A rare pattern, these pieces probably were limited editions. The design is a bold panel of woven threads circling the middle of the piece, with a series of triangular shapes on the rim. The pedestal is waisted with a flaring foot and the handle is attached from the rim to the waist band. The colors are amethyst, green, pale marigold, and green, rare in white.

Creamer

☐ marigold	22.50	30.00	25.00

Sugar Bowl

☐ marigold	22.50	30.00	25.00

BATHTUB
U.S. Glass

Miniature Figural

☐ white	70.00	80.00	72.00

BEADED
Northwood

The combination of patterns connected by ribbons of beads makes this an interesting and beautiful design. The flowers, blooms, and daisies interconnected with the pearly beads are well balanced and tiered.

Bowl, diameter 8″

☐ marigold	30.00	35.00	32.00
☐ blue	37.00	42.00	40.00
☐ green	37.00	42.00	40.00
☐ purple	37.00	42.00	40.00

	Current Price Range		Prior Year Average

Bowl, diameter 9″

☐ marigold	30.00	25.00	32.00
☐ blue	37.00	42.00	35.00
☐ green	37.00	42.00	35.00
☐ purple	37.00	42.00	35.00

BEADED ACANTHUS
Imperial

The swirls of the acanthus pattern are molded into an all-over diamond shape surrounded by pearly beads. It is found on a water pitcher with a modified scalloped rim and pronounced lip for pouring. The handle is attached in the upper middle of the piece, below the rim and above the base. Existing colors are marigold, smoke, green and probably amethyst.

Milk Pitcher

☐ marigold	40.00	55.00	42.00
☐ green	120.00	135.00	125.00
☐ smoke	60.00	75.00	62.00

BEADED BAND AND OCTAGON

Kerosene Lamp

☐ marigold	85.00	95.00	90.00

BEADED BASKETS
Dugan

A combination of the basket weaves adorn these novelty pieces, alternating a diagonally spliced weave with a parallel one. The mold work is sharp and the craftsmanship is excellent. The basket's handles rise vertically from a thumbprint rim and the base is plain and thick. The colors come in marigold, smoke, and purple; blue and green exist but are very unusual.

Basket

☐ marigold	48.00	55.00	50.00
☐ blue	70.00	82.50	72.00
☐ green	70.00	85.00	72.00
☐ purple	60.00	70.00	62.00
☐ smoke	100.00	105.00	102.00

BEADED BULL'S-EYE
Imperial

A delicate pattern seen on vases, the long, pulled look of the body is topped by a circular series of six "bull's-eyes" or medallion-like imprints encapsulated by beads. The color is usually marigold; other tints are more rare.

	Current Price Range		Prior Year Average
Vase			
☐ marigold	20.00	30.00	25.00
☐ purple	32.50	37.50	35.00
☐ green	32.50	37.50	35.00
☐ blue	32.50	37.50	35.00
☐ amethyst	32.50	37.50	35.00

BEADED CABLE
Northwood

Found mostly on bowls used for rose arrangements, this is a very popular pattern with designers. Interlocking ribbons of bold glass move in a wavy design across the middle of the piece. The swirls are decorated with pearly beads of different sizes. The bowl's shape is interesting and different. It stands on pudgy round feet and the rim is rippled inward, almost closing the top. The colors are seen in the widest range of Northwood tints.

Beaded Cable

	Current Price Range		Prior Year Average

Candy Dish
☐ marigold	25.00	35.00	27.00
☐ purple	45.00	55.00	47.00
☐ green	40.00	50.00	42.00
☐ blue	32.50	40.00	35.00
☐ amethyst	32.50	40.00	35.00

Rose Bowl
☐ marigold	45.00	55.00	47.00
☐ purple	60.00	85.00	65.00
☐ green	80.00	90.00	82.00
☐ blue	85.00	95.00	87.00
☐ amethyst	50.00	62.50	52.00
☐ aqua opalescent	215.00	230.00	220.00
☐ ice green	650.00	725.00	675.00

BEADED HEARTS
Northwood

Bowl
☐ marigold	45.00	55.00	46.00
☐ amethyst	55.00	65.00	57.00
☐ green	55.00	65.00	57.00

BEADED PANELS
Westmoreland

On a compote dish with a footed stem, perched on a wide, convex base, this pattern contains beads radiating upward to form the fluted edges. The stem is a series of larger beads seemingly welded together in three curved strands. Seen in marigold and peach opalescent, the iridescence is excellent.

Compote
☐ marigold	42.50	45.00	43.00
☐ purple	50.00	60.00	52.00
☐ peach opalescence	50.00	60.00	52.00

Powder Jar
| ☐ marigold | 50.00 | 60.00 | 52.00 |

BEADED SHELL
Dugan

The shell motif is treated with strands of beads to form large nautical panels. The upper rims of the pieces are styled by the top of the shell and the base is a group of ridged shells pointing outward. The colors are blue, green, purple, marigold, and white.

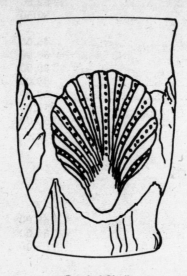

Beaded Shell

	Current Price Range		Prior Year Average
Berry Bowl, footed, diameter 6½"			
☐ marigold	20.00	25.00	22.00
☐ purple	35.00	42.50	37.00
☐ amethyst	35.00	42.50	37.00
Berry Bowl, footed, diameter 9"			
☐ marigold	40.00	55.00	42.00
☐ purple	60.00	75.00	62.00
☐ amethyst	60.00	75.00	62.00
Butter Dish, lidded			
☐ marigold	100.00	125.00	110.00
☐ purple	200.00	250.00	205.00
☐ amethyst	200.00	250.00	205.00
Creamer, covered			
☐ marigold	55.00	65.00	60.00
☐ purple	55.00	75.00	60.00
☐ amethyst	85.00	110.00	90.00

	Current Price Range		Prior Year Average

Mug

☐ marigold	130.00	150.00	135.00
☐ purple	75.00	95.00	85.00
☐ blue	80.00	90.00	82.00
☐ amethyst	60.00	75.00	62.00
☐ white	300.00	375.00	310.00

Water Pitcher

☐ marigold	275.00	325.00	295.00
☐ purple	350.00	425.00	375.00
☐ blue	350.00	425.00	375.00
☐ amethyst	350.00	425.00	375.00

Spooner

☐ marigold	50.00	60.00	55.00
☐ purple	85.00	110.00	90.00
☐ amethyst	85.00	110.00	90.00

Sugar Bowl, covered

☐ marigold	40.00	50.00	42.00
☐ purple	85.00	110.00	90.00
☐ amethyst	85.00	110.00	90.00

Tumbler

☐ marigold	40.00	52.50	42.00
☐ purple	60.00	75.00	62.00
☐ blue	60.00	75.00	62.00
☐ amethyst	60.00	75.00	62.00

BEADED SPEARS
Australian Manufacturer

A delicate and beautiful design of faceted beads ranging from perfectly round to geometrically angular. The pointed shape circles the piece with clear smooth glass between each pattern. The upper rim of the pitcher and most of the body of the water glass is a neat pattern of beads in parallel rows.

Tumbler

☐ marigold	70.00	85.00	72.00
☐ purple	85.00	95.00	87.00
☐ amethyst	85.00	95.00	87.00

Water Pitcher

☐ marigold	165.00	185.00	170.00
☐ purple	225.00	250.00	240.00
☐ amethyst	225.00	250.00	240.00

BEADED STARS AND VARIANTS
Fenton

	Current Price Range		Prior Year Average
Bowl			
☐ marigold	30.00	40.00	32.00
☐ peach opalescent...........................	50.00	60.00	52.00
Plate, 9″			
☐ marigold	85.00	95.00	87.00
Rose Bowl			
☐ marigold	40.00	50.00	42.00

BEADED SWIRL
Davison

As the name implies, the pattern is one of motion and diagonal direction, with panels of clear glass alternating with ribbons of beads in a reverse diagonal set up. The upper rim is gently rounded in wide flutes; the footed base is a simple ridged design. Often seen in marigold, other colors probably exist.

	Current Price Range		Prior Year Average
Butter Dish, covered			
☐ marigold	40.00	50.00	45.00
Compote			
☐ marigold	20.00	30.00	22.50
Milk Pitcher			
☐ marigold	60.00	80.00	65.00
Sugar Bowl covered			
☐ marigold	40.00	50.00	45.00

BEADS
Northwood

	Current Price Range		Prior Year Average
Bowl, 8″–9″			
☐ marigold	35.00	45.00	37.00
☐ amethyst..	50.00	60.00	52.00

BEADS AND BARS
U.S. Glass

	Current Price Range		Prior Year Average
Spooner			
☐ marigold	45.00	55.00	47.00

BEAUTY BUD
Dugan

The long slender bud vase is delightfully plain, showing off an excellent color iridescence. The base and stem are stylized into a twiggy tree root on top of a round flat platform. Colors range from marigold to purple, and this pattern is avidly sought by collectors.

	Current Price Range		Prior Year Average
Vase, twig size			
□ marigold	140.00	—	—
□ purple	160.00	—	—
Vase, without twig feet			
□ marigold	30.00	—	—
□ smoke	32.00	—	—
Vase			
□ marigold	22.50	27.50	25.00
□ purple	37.50	45.00	40.00
□ white	55.00	65.00	60.00
□ amethyst	37.50	45.00	40.00

BEETLE ASHTRAY

Ashtray			
□ blue	485.00	515.00	490.00

BEETLE HATPIN

Hatpin			
□ amethyst	25.00	35.00	27.00

BELLAIRE
Imperial

A souvenir piece with the inscription ''Bellaire; Good Will Talk'' on the inside of the shallow bowl. The outside pattern is outwardly emanating ribs. The iridescence is fine and the color a clear marigold.

	Current Price Range		Prior Year Average
Bowl, diameter 7″			
☐ marigold	60.00	72.50	62.00

BELLS AND BEADS
Dugan

A finely decorated piece with swirls of bell-like flowers on stylized beaded stems. The shape has a swooping fluted edge, rolling up and down with the interior design. The colors are blue, amethyst, green, peach opalescent, and of course, marigold.

Compote			
☐ marigold	12.50	18.00	14.00
☐ purple	22.50	27.50	24.00
☐ amethyst...	22.50	27.50	24.00
Plate, diameter 6¾″			
☐ purple	40.00	50.00	42.00
☐ amethyst...	40.00	50.00	42.00
Bowl, 7½″			
☐ marigold	35.00	—	—
☐ purple	45.00	—	—
☐ green	50.00	—	—
☐ blue	55.00	—	—
☐ peach opalescent............................	60.00	—	—
Nappy			
☐ marigold	40.00	—	—
☐ purple	65.00	—	—
☐ peach opalescent............................	70.00	—	—
Hat Shape			
☐ marigold	35.00	—	—
☐ purple	45.00	—	—
Gravy Boat, handled			
☐ marigold	45.00	—	—
☐ purple	60.00	—	—
☐ peach opalescent............................	80.00	—	—

BERNHEIMER BOWL
Millersburg

An advertising product of great quality, the pattern is over six-pointed stars of bubbly glass in varying sizes surrounding a central medallion containing the logo of the company. The rim is triangularly fluted with a beaded edge. It is blue iridescent in color.

	Current Price Range		Prior Year Average
Bowl			
☐ blue	500.00	600.00	525.00
Berry Basket			
☐ marigold	45.00	—	—
Salt and Pepper Shakers			
☐ marigold	65.00	—	—

BIG BASKETWEAVE
Dugan

	Current Price Range		Prior Year Average
Basket, small			
☐ marigold	35.00	—	—
☐ purple	40.00	—	—
Vase, 6″–14″			
☐ marigold	25.00	—	—
☐ purple	40.00	—	—
☐ peach opal	50.00	—	—
☐ aqua opal	80.00	—	—
☐ white..............................	70.00	—	—

BIG FISH
Millersburg

The interior design of pieces with a big fish pattern is of the finest craftsmanship. The relief molded fish, twisting in an athletic jump, leaps into a spray of petals and leaves. The pond is depicted in the background with excellent perspective. The colors and bowl shapes range widely.

	Current Price Range		Prior Year Average
Bowl, diameter 9″			
☐ marigold	175.00	200.00	190.00
☐ green.............................	175.00	200.00	190.00
☐ purple	175.00	200.00	190.00

	Current Price Range		Prior Year Average
Bowl, diameter 9¾"			
☐ marigold	200.00	225.00	210.00
☐ green	225.00	240.00	230.00
Rose Bowl			
☐ vaseline...	5,500.00	—	—

BIG THISTLE
Millersburg

A bold, tall punchbowl on a stemmed foot. The base curves gently in wide-panel ridges from the edge to the base. The color is superlative; it is considered to be among the finest of the Carnival glass, and the price it commands proves it.

Punchbowl with base			
☐ purple	5000.00	6500.00	5200.00
☐ amethyst.......................................	5000.00	6500.00	5200.00

BIRD OF PARADISE
Northwood

Advertising Bowl			
☐ amethyst.......................................	190.00	200.00	192.00
Advertising Plate			
☐ amethyst.......................................	215.00	230.00	217.00

BIRD WITH GRAPES
Dugan

A wall vase of triangular shape with an all-over matte finish and the design is smooth. The bird resembles a heron, with elongated legs and a stylized body. The grapes are of high relief and refract the light iridescently. It is marigold and amber.

Wall Vase			
☐ marigold	45.00	55.00	47.00

BIRDS AND CHERRIES
Fenton

Five birds rest among the cherry branches in the interior design of this pattern. The style is realistic and uses the technique of high relief. The colors are amethyst, blue, green, vaseline, ice blue, and green.

	Current Price Range		Prior Year Average
Bon Bon			
☐ amethyst...........................	32.50	37.50	34.00
☐ blue.................................	55.00	65.00	57.00
☐ green...............................	45.00	52.50	49.00
Bowl, diameter 5″			
☐ amethyst...........................	225.00	250.00	230.00
☐ blue.................................	380.00	420.00	385.00
☐ marigold	400.00	435.00	410.00
Bowl, diameter 9″			
☐ amethyst...........................	450.00	600.00	460.00
☐ blue.................................	600.00	750.00	625.00
☐ marigold	600.00	750.00	625.00
Compote			
☐ amethyst...........................	50.00	60.00	52.00
☐ blue.................................	60.00	70.00	62.00
☐ green...............................	35.00	45.00	38.00
☐ marigold	60.00	75.00	63.00
Plate, diameter 10″			
☐ blue.................................	600.00	750.00	625.00
☐ green...............................	600.00	1000.00	625.00

BLACKBERRY
Fenton

An interior pattern on many basketweave pieces, the blackberries appear on the bottom of the bowl. The colors are marigold, cobalt, amethyst, green, and red.

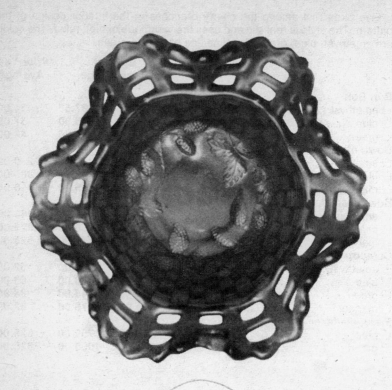

Blackberry

	Current Price Range		Prior Year Average
Bowl			
☐ marigold	25.00	30.00	27.00
☐ green	32.00	37.00	33.00
☐ amethyst	32.00	37.00	33.00
☐ cobalt	32.00	37.00	33.00
☐ green	32.00	37.00	33.00

	Current Price Range		Prior Year Average
Hat Shape			
☐ marigold	28.00	30.00	29.00
☐ green	32.50	35.00	33.00
☐ amethyst	32.50	35.00	33.00
☐ cobalt blue	32.50	35.00	33.00
☐ green	32.50	35.00	33.00
☐ ice blue	55.00	60.00	58.00
☐ red	170.00	190.00	175.00
Plate			
☐ marigold	275.00	—	—
☐ blue	375.00	—	—
☐ white	400.00	—	—
Spittoon			
☐ marigold	2500.00	—	—
☐ blue	2700.00	—	—

BLACKBERRY
Northwood

An overall pattern of berries and foliage radiate out from a central medallion. The undecorated glass is clearer than most Carnival glass and usually marigold, purple, green, blue, and white.

Bowl, three-footed			
☐ marigold	45.00	—	—
☐ purple	60.00	—	—
Compote			
☐ marigold	22.00	24.00	23.00
☐ purple	40.00	60.00	50.00
☐ green	32.00	34.00	33.00

BLACKBERRY MINIATURE

Compote			
☐ marigold	50.00	60.00	52.00
☐ purple	63.00	70.00	64.00
☐ green	45.00	65.00	55.00
☐ white	275.00	300.00	280.00

BLACKBERRY BANDED
Fenton

Hat-shaped pieces are decorated with this circular pattern of foliage and berries alternating with finely ridged vertical bands on the interior wall. The top band edge is ruffled in a large flowing rim. The colors are marigold or blue, unusual in green or smoke.

	Current Price Range		Prior Year Average
Hat Shape			
☐ marigold	17.50	21.00	20.00
☐ blue	25.00	30.00	26.00
☐ green	25.00	30.00	26.00
☐ peach opalescent	—	—	60.00
☐ cobalt blue	25.00	30.00	26.00

BLACKBERRY BARK

Vase			
☐ amethyst	1450.00	1550.00	1475.00

BLACKBERRY BLOCK
Fenton

This piece reflects light like a mirror rainbow. The pattern is busy, in checkerboard squares up the side like a trellis with fruit and foliage. The shape is Victorian, the handle attached in the lower middle. The colors are marigold, green, and cobalt blue.

Blackberry Block

	Current Price Range		Prior Year Average
Pitcher			
☐ marigold	250.00	300.00	275.00
☐ purple	300.00	365.00	310.00
☐ green	300.00	365.00	310.00
☐ blue	300.00	365.00	310.00
☐ amethyst	300.00	365.00	310.00
☐ white	800.00	1000.00	850.00
☐ cobalt blue	350.00	425.00	375.00
Tumbler			
☐ marigold	35.00	45.00	37.00
☐ purple	70.00	80.00	72.00
☐ green	90.00	110.00	95.00
☐ blue	60.00	72.50	62.00
☐ amethyst	60.00	72.50	62.00
☐ white	75.00	95.00	77.00
☐ cobalt blue	60.00	72.50	62.00

BLACKBERRY BRAMBLE
Fenton

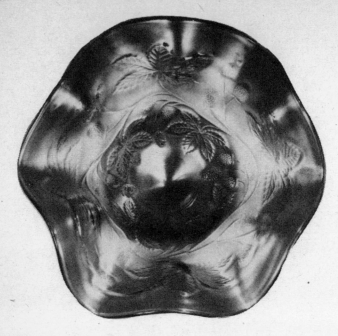

Blackberry Bramble

	Current Price Range		Prior Year Average
Bowl			
☐ blue	45.00	55.00	47.00
Compote			
☐ marigold	35.00	42.00	37.00
☐ blue	45.00	55.00	47.00
☐ green	55.00	65.00	57.00
☐ purple	—	—	25.00

BLACKBERRY SPRAY

Four groups of branches are clumped around the modified square body. The fruit is small and in light relief. It comes in a variety of shapes and the colors are amethyst, green, cobalt, aqua, red, and marigold.

	Current Price Range		Prior Year Average

Bon Bon

☐ marigold	22.00	25.00	23.00
☐ purple	22.00	25.00	23.00
☐ green	22.00	25.00	23.00
☐ blue	22.00	25.00	23.00
☐ amethyst	22.00	25.00	23.00

Compote

☐ marigold	17.50	22.50	20.00
☐ purple	18.00	23.00	19.00
☐ green	18.00	23.00	19.00
☐ blue	18.00	23.00	19.00
☐ amethyst	18.00	23.00	19.00

Hat Shape

☐ marigold	22.00	25.00	20.00
☐ purple	22.00	25.00	20.00
☐ green	22.00	25.00	20.00
☐ blue	22.00	25.00	20.00
☐ amethyst	22.00	25.00	20.00
☐ aqua opalescent	125.00	160.00	130.00
☐ white	—	—	50.00
☐ red	—	—	250.00

BLACKBERRY WHIMSY VASE
Fenton

The blackberry interior pattern complements the elongated ridge weaved exterior of this iridescent vase. The top panel resembles arched windows of clear glass. The upper rim has the sawtooth motif. The color is cobalt blue.

Vase

☐ cobalt blue	1000.00	1500.00	1100.00

BLACKBERRY WREATH
Millersburg

The stems of the blackberry branch curve together to form a wreath, surrounding a bunch of fruit and foliage. The rim is gently scalloped and the base has a rayed-star motif used on many Millersburg patterns. The exterior has wide panels of smooth glass and the colors range widely.

	Current Price Range		Prior Year Average
Bowl, diameter 5″			
☐ marigold	20.00	30.00	22.00
☐ purple	30.00	40.00	32.00
☐ green	35.00	45.00	37.00
Bowl, diameter 7″			
☐ marigold	40.00	50.00	45.00
☐ purple	35.00	45.00	38.00
☐ blue	200.00	225.00	210.00
☐ green	40.00	60.00	42.00
Bowl, diameter 9″			
☐ marigold	45.00	55.00	47.00
☐ purple	60.00	70.00	62.00
☐ blue	78.00	83.00	80.00
☐ green	78.00	83.00	80.00
Ice Cream Bowl, diameter 10″			
☐ marigold	90.00	120.00	95.00
☐ blue	135.00	140.00	188.00
☐ purple	135.00	140.00	188.00
Plate, diameter 6″			
☐ marigold	460.00	490.00	470.00
☐ green (8″)	575.00	625.00	580.00
☐ purple	575.00	625.00	580.00
Plate, diameter 10″, very rare			
☐ marigold	1500.00	2000.00	1750.00
☐ purple	2000.00	2500.00	2200.00
Spittoon Whimsy			
☐ green	700.00	900.00	750.00

BLOCKS AND ARCHES

Pitcher			
☐ marigold	145.00	155.00	147.00
☐ amethyst.......................................	195.00	210.00	197.00
Tumbler			
☐ marigold	65.00	75.00	67.00
☐ amethyst.......................................	80.00	90.00	82.00

BLOSSOMS AND BAND
Imperial

The slender vases that are decorated with this pattern have long faceted prisms branded with thumbprints and a band of straightforward poppy-like flowers and foliage. The color is transparent with pinkish iridescence.

	Current Price Range		Prior Year Average
Berry Bowl, diameter 6½″			
☐ marigold	10.00	14.00	12.00
Berry Bowl, diameter 9″			
☐ marigold	20.00	25.00	22.00
Car Vase			
☐ marigold	20.00	25.00	22.00

BLOSSOMS AND SPEARS

Plate, 8″			
☐ marigold	40.00	50.00	42.00

BLOSSOMTIME
Northwood

Thorny branch stems and stylized flowers roam in an overall pattern on the interior of these compotes. The rim is unevenly fluted, resembling a cut section of logs, and the stem is geometrically ringed down to a plain, smooth circular base. It is a scarce pattern, available in many colors.

Compote			
☐ marigold	35.00	42.00	37.00
☐ purple	46.00	55.00	48.00
☐ green	46.00	55.00	48.00
☐ amethyst..	46.00	55.00	48.00
☐ white..	65.00	85.00	68.00

BLUEBERRY
Fenton

A fabulously iridescent glass molded in a lovely design makes these pieces the favorite of many. Its gold mirror iridescence is sharp and clear; the pattern is simple and classical with a raised ridge band surrounding a bunch of pearly fruit on elongated stems.

Blueberry

	Current Price Range		Prior Year Average
Pitcher			
☐ marigold	350.00	425.00	375.00
☐ blue	325.00	385.00	330.00
☐ white..	375.00	440.00	390.00
Tumbler			
☐ marigold	27.50	35.00	30.00
☐ blue	80.00	90.00	82.00
☐ white..	50.00	65.00	58.00

BOGGY BAYOU
Fenton

The ribboned edge on the upper ridge is the distinctive feature on these geometrical vases. The wide panels are rough and angular, ending with a starburst motif at the base. The colors are green, blue, amethyst, marigold, and white.

Vase			
☐ green	75.00	100.00	40.00
☐ blue	75.00	100.00	40.00
☐ amethyst..	75.00	100.00	40.00
☐ marigold	50.00	65.00	52.00
☐ white..	100.00	125.00	110.00

BOOT

	Current Price Range		Prior Year Average
Boot Shape			
☐ marigold	70.00	80.00	72.00

BO PEEP
Fenton

This delightful pattern on children's ware is avidly collected because of its clear marigold color and pearly iridescence. The alphabet adorns the outside rim, surrounding Little Bo Peep with her staff and sheep.

Bowl			
☐ marigold	—	—	300.00
Mug			
☐ marigold	100.00	125.00	110.00
Plate			
☐ marigold	—	—	450.00

BORDER PLANTS
Dugan

A shell motif is used to adorn this wildly patterned article. The rim follows up and down in a wavy scallop reminiscent of conch shells. The interior design resembles an eight-point starfish. The colors are the darks as well as peach opalescent.

Bowl, flat			
☐ purple	45.00	55.00	47.50
☐ amethyst........................	45.00	55.00	47.50
☐ peach opalescent.............	65.00	75.00	67.50
Plate, handgrip			
☐ purple	—	—	125.00
☐ peach opalescent.............	—	—	125.00
Bowl, footed			
☐ purple	55.00	65.00	57.00
☐ amethyst........................	55.00	65.00	57.00
☐ peach opalescent.............	80.00	90.00	82.00

BOUQUET
Fenton

This water set's pattern encompasses all of the available space; daisies, embroidery, ribbons, and bows are arranged over all. The iridescence is mirror-like, the glass heavy.

	Current Price Range		Prior Year Average
Tumbler			
☐ marigold	40.00	55.00	42.00
☐ purple	70.00	85.00	78.00
☐ white	—	—	65.00
☐ blue	70.00	85.00	78.00
☐ amethyst	70.00	85.00	78.00
Water Pitcher			
☐ marigold	175.00	220.00	200.00
☐ white	350.00	425.00	375.00
☐ blue	325.00	380.00	330.00

BOUQUET AND LATTICE

These table sets were made for mass production on the carnival circuit. The blossoms are superimposed over a trellis work in low relief. The iridescence is fair, the mold work average, the color marigold.

	Current Price Range		Prior Year Average
Creamer			
☐ marigold	4.00	6.00	5.00
Cup and Saucer			
☐ marigold	4.00	6.00	5.00
Dinner Plate			
☐ marigold	5.00	7.00	6.00
Sugar Bowl			
☐ marigold	4.00	6.00	7.00

BOUTONNIERE
Millersburg

This is an interesting and well-conceived pattern of a central poinsettia-type flower folded in the middle, each petal emanating a stippled ray which extends to the rim.

	Current Price Range		Prior Year Average
Compote			
☐ marigold	35.00	45.00	37.00
☐ purple	40.00	50.00	42.00
☐ green	40.00	50.00	42.00
☐ clambroth	—	—	90.00
☐ amethyst	40.00	50.00	42.00

BOW AND ENGLISH HOBNAIL

	Current Price Range		Prior Year Average
Nut Bowl			
☐ marigold	45.00	55.00	47.00
☐ blue	50.00	60.00	52.00

BOXED STAR

	Current Price Range		Prior Year Average
☐ pastel	100.00	—	—

BRIAR PATCH

Hat Shape

	Current Price Range		Prior Year Average
☐ marigold	30.00	40.00	35.00
☐ amethyst	40.00	50.00	42.00

BRIDAL ROSETTE

☐ marigold	80.00	—	—
☐ purple	100.00	—	—

BROCADED ACORNS
Fostoria

These are beautifully decorated pieces, achieving the look of a satin party dress in glowing iridescence. The design is foliage and acorns; the edge is an interesting gilded rim.

Cake Tray

☐ white	45.00	55.00	47.00
☐ ice green	45.00	55.00	47.00
☐ ice blue	45.00	55.00	47.00

Ice Bucket

☐ white	27.50	35.00	30.00
☐ ice blue	27.50	35.00	30.00
☐ ice green	27.50	35.00	30.00

BROCADED DAFFODILS
Fostoria

Another satin-like pattern, these pieces have an intricate floral design of daffodils with foliage and stars. The motif is in low relief; the finish is perfection.

Bon Bon

☐ ice blue	35.00	45.00	37.00
☐ ice green	35.00	45.00	37.00
☐ white	35.00	45.00	37.00

	Current Price Range		Prior Year Average
Cake Tray, handled			
☐ ice blue	60.00	70.00	62.00
☐ ice green	60.00	70.00	62.00
☐ white..	60.00	70.00	62.00
Flower Set, three pieces			
☐ ice blue	90.00	110.00	92.00
☐ ice green	90.00	110.00	92.00
☐ white..	90.00	110.00	92.00
Tray			
☐ ice blue	60.00	80.00	62.00
☐ ice green	60.00	80.00	62.00
☐ white..	60.00	80.00	62.00
Vase			
☐ ice blue	60.00	80.00	62.00
☐ ice green	60.00	80.00	62.00
☐ white..	60.00	80.00	62.00

BROCADED PALMS
Fostoria

Like its predecessors, this fabric-like pattern has a sheen and beauty typical of Fostoria productions. The palm tree tops are placed in a wide band, bending toward each other flirtatiously.

	Current Price Range		Prior Year Average
Bread Tray			
☐ white..	40.00	50.00	42.00
☐ ice blue	40.00	50.00	42.00
☐ ice green	40.00	50.00	42.00
Cake Plate			
☐ white..	45.00	55.00	47.00
☐ ice blue	45.00	55.00	47.00
☐ ice green	45.00	55.00	47.00

BROCADED ROSES

These are all found in various pastels.

	Current Price Range		Prior Year Average
Bon Bon			
☐ ices..	35.00	45.00	38.00
Bowl			
☐ ices..	50.00	60.00	52.00

	Current Price Range		Prior Year Average
Bowl, large, footed			
☐ ices...............................	95.00	110.00	98.00
Box, with lid			
☐ ices...............................	70.00	80.00	75.00
Ice Bucket			
☐ ices...............................	85.00	95.00	87.00
Rose Bowl			
☐ ices...............................	65.00	75.00	68.00
Tidbit Server, with center handle			
☐ ices...............................	70.00	80.00	72.00
Tray			
☐ ices...............................	75.00	85.00	77.00
Vase			
☐ ices...............................	85.00	95.00	87.00
Wine Goblet			
☐ ices...............................	40.00	50.00	42.00

BROCADED SUMMER GARDENS

These are all found in various pastels and are very similar to pieces found in the Brocaded Roses pattern.

Bon Bon			
☐ ices...............................	35.00	45.00	38.00
Bowl, large, footed			
☐ ices...............................	95.00	110.00	98.00
Box, with lid			
☐ ices...............................	70.00	80.00	75.00
Ice Bucket			
☐ ices...............................	85.00	95.00	87.00
Rose Bowl			
☐ ices...............................	65.00	75.00	68.00
Tidbit Server, with center handle			
☐ ices...............................	70.00	80.00	72.00
Tray			
☐ ices...............................	75.00	85.00	77.00
Vase			
☐ ices...............................	85.00	95.00	87.00
Wine Goblet			
☐ ices...............................	40.00	50.00	42.00

BROKEN ARCHES
Imperial

This geometrical pattern illustrates the best of the near-cut achievements. The large rounded arches are divided into upwardly flaring squares, each with a thumbprint in the center. Alternating with tiny devices is a half-arch decorated with rows of vertical beadwork.

	Current Price Range		Prior Year Average
Bowl, diameter 8″			
☐ purple	45.00	55.00	47.00
☐ green	45.00	55.00	47.00
☐ marigold	40.00	—	—
☐ amethyst	45.00	55.00	47.00
Punch Bowl, with base			
☐ marigold	250.00	350.00	270.00
☐ purple	325.00	375.00	335.00
☐ amethyst	325.00	375.00	335.00
Punch Cup			
☐ marigold	13.00	17.00	14.00
☐ purple	22.50	27.50	25.00
☐ amethyst	22.50	27.50	25.00

BROOKLYN

Bottle, with stopper			
☐ marigold	65.00	75.00	67.00
☐ amethyst	85.00	95.00	87.00

BROOKLYN BRIDGE
Dugan

Bowl			
☐ marigold	310.00	340.00	315.00

BUBBLE BERRY

Lamp Shade			
☐ white	60.00	—	—

BUBBLES

Hatpin			
☐ purple	35.00	—	—

	Current Price Range		Prior Year Average

Lamp Chimney (shade)
☐ white... 45.00 — —

BUDDHA

Figurine of Buddha
☐ marigold .... 600.00 — —
☐ blue .... 500.00 — —
☐ ice blue .... 700.00 — —
☐ white.. 700.00 — —

BULLDOG

Paperweight
☐ marigold .... 250.00 — —

BULL'S-EYE

Oil Lamp
☐ marigold .... 185.00 — —

BULL'S-EYE AND BEADS (different pattern from Beaded Bull's-Eye)
Imperial

Vase
☐ marigold .... 35.00 — —
☐ green .... 50.00 — —
☐ purple .... 50.00 — —
☐ smoke .... 55.00 — —

BULL'S-EYE AND LEAVES
Northwood

Bowl, 8½"
☐ marigold 35.00 45.00 37.00
☐ green 45.00 55.00 47.00
☐ amethyst...................................... 45.00 55.00 47.00

BULL'S-EYE AND LOOP
Millersburg

Vase
☐ amethyst...................................... 170.00 180.00 172.00

BULL'S-EYE AND SPEARHEAD

Wine
☐ marigold .... 45.00 — —

BUMBLEBEES

	Current Price Range		Prior Year Average

Hatpin

☐ purple	25.00	—	—

BUNNY

Bank

☐ marigold	30.00	—	—

BUTTERFLIES
Fenton

Bon Bon

☐ marigold	35.00	45.00	37.00
☐ blue	45.00	55.00	47.00
☐ green	60.00	70.00	62.00
☐ white	65.00	75.00	67.00
☐ purple	55.00	—	—

Tray, small

☐ blue	55.00	65.00	57.00
☐ marigold	35.00	—	—

BUTTERFLIES AND BELLS
Australian Manufacturer

Compote

☐ marigold	120.00	130.00	122.00
☐ purple	125.00	—	—

BUTTERFLIES AND WARATAH
Australian Manufacturer

Compote

☐ marigold	115.00	130.00	120.00
☐ amethyst	245.00	255.00	247.00

BUTTERFLY
Northwood

The butterfly rests in the center of the bowl, its wings fluttering rays of stipled ridges. The shape of the piece is usually a modified square with a fluted edge. The colors are usually amethyst, marigold, and other pastels. There are two exteriors—smooth and ribbed. The latter has been only in purple and ice blue.

	Current Price Range		Prior Year Average
Bon Bon			
☐ white...	27.50	32.00	25.00
☐ ice green	27.50	32.00	25.00
☐ ice blue (ribbed only)	27.50	32.00	25.00
☐ marigold	27.50	32.00	25.00
☐ amethyst (regular)	27.50	32.00	25.00
☐ amethyst (ribbed)	260.00	—	—
☐ green..	22.50	27.50	24.00
☐ blue...	22.50	27.50	24.00
Pin Tray			
☐ marigold	35.00	—	—

BUTTERFLY AND BERRY
Fenton

The butterfly and berry is a pleasing all-over pattern, the exterior being dominated with wide panels of each motif. The berries are in a triangular shape with the stem and leaves below; the butterfly is a large Monarch in high relief. The rim is sawtoothed, and the foot has a porcelain look. The colors are cobalt, green, white, and amethyst, unusual in red.

Butterfly and Berry

	Current Price Range		Prior Year Average
Berry Bowl, 5″			
☐ marigold	25.00	—	—
☐ purple	40.00	—	—
☐ blue	40.00	—	—
☐ green	50.00	—	—
☐ white	80.00	—	—
☐ red	750.00	—	—
Berry Bowl, footed, diameter 10″			
☐ marigold	55.00	65.00	57.00
☐ purple	80.00	90.00	82.00
☐ green	80.00	90.00	82.00
☐ blue	85.00	95.00	87.00
☐ amethyst	85.00	95.00	87.00
☐ white	175.00	—	—
Butter Dish, lidded			
☐ marigold	90.00	105.00	95.00
☐ purple	220.00	280.00	230.00
☐ green	220.00	280.00	230.00
☐ blue	220.00	280.00	230.00
☐ amethyst	220.00	280.00	230.00
Cuspidor			
☐ purple	650.00	850.00	660.00
☐ blue	650.00	850.00	660.00
☐ amethyst	650.00	850.00	660.00
Hatpin Holder			
☐ marigold	675.00	725.00	685.00
☐ blue	500.00	650.00	525.00
Pitcher			
☐ marigold	150.00	200.00	160.00
☐ purple	350.00	400.00	365.00
☐ green	425.00	500.00	450.00
☐ blue	350.00	400.00	365.00
☐ amethyst	350.00	400.00	365.00
Tumbler			
☐ marigold	25.00	35.00	27.00
☐ purple	120.00	130.00	122.00
☐ green	65.00	75.00	67.00
☐ blue	30.00	35.00	31.00
☐ amethyst	45.00	55.00	47.00
Vase			
☐ marigold	50.00	60.00	52.00
☐ blue	32.50	40.00	33.00
☐ red	375.00	425.00	385.00
☐ white	400.00	—	—

BUTTERFLY AND CORN
Northwood

   This delightful vase is shaped like a half cob of corn in its husk on a short stem and foot. A butterfly is lighting on one of the jutting leaves. The molding is very sharp and realistic; the color is vaseline with a marigold tint.

	Current Price Range		Prior Year Average
Vase			
☐ marigold on vaseline......................	750.00	800.00	775.00

BUTTERFLY AND FERN
Fenton

   A mirror iridescent molded pattern that refracts light in all the hues. Wide butterfly panels decorate the long sides with wreaths of foliage around them. The rim is an unusual shape of irregular flutes; the handles are sunk low past the middle. Colors are gold, amethyst, cobalt, and green.

Butterfly and Fern

	Current Price Range		Prior Year Average
Pitcher			
☐ marigold	180.00	215.00	190.00
☐ purple	375.00	450.00	400.00
☐ green	425.00	500.00	440.00
☐ blue	375.00	450.00	400.00
☐ amethyst	375.00	450.00	400.00
Tumbler			
☐ marigold	30.00	40.00	32.00
☐ purple	35.00	47.50	37.00
☐ green	35.00	47.50	37.00
☐ blue	50.00	60.00	57.00
☐ amethyst	35.00	47.50	37.00

BUTTERFLY AND TULIP
Dugan

A heavy glass with a sharp, succinct mold of a butterfly among the flora. The style is naturalistic and well proportioned. Available in marigold and purple.

Bowl, round			
☐ marigold	250.00	300.00	375.00
☐ purple	750.00	900.00	800.00
Bowl, square			
☐ marigold	475.00	500.00	480.00
☐ purple	850.00	925.00	860.00

BUTTERFLY BOWER
Australian Manufacturer

A central butterfly motif is the distinct feature of this bowl, with a trellis design with interwoven flowers and branches surrounding. The exterior design is a ridged serpentine pattern with a jagged edge. The colors are marigold and purple.

Cake Plate			
☐ marigold	125.00	140.00	130.00
☐ purple	125.00	140.00	130.00
Compote			
☐ marigold	80.00	100.00	90.00
☐ purple	80.00	100.00	90.00

BUTTERFLY BUSH

	Current Price Range		Prior Year Average
Compote			
☐ marigold	105.00	115.00	110.00
☐ amethyst	145.00	155.00	147.00

BUTTERFLY ORNAMENT
Fenton

A small giveaway for visitors to the Fenton factory, the novelty is shaped like a moth butterfly, simple in line with beaded decoration. The colors are marigold, ice blue, cobalt, white, green, and amethyst.

Butterfly Shaper			
☐ marigold	45.00	60.00	50.00
☐ cobalt blue	50.00	70.00	65.00
☐ green	50.00	70.00	65.00
☐ amethyst	50.00	70.00	65.00
☐ white	50.00	70.00	65.00
☐ ice blue	50.00	70.00	65.00

BUTTERFLY TUMBLER
U.S. Glass

An exquisite design and all-over pattern helps to make this piece one of the most sought after pieces in the world of Carnival glass collecting. Beautifully molded butterflies are the central motif on the band of the tumbler with stippled diamonds and upside down leaves directly under the rim. The design on the base of the glass, matching the upper rim, is molded circles in relief.

Butterfly Tumbler

	Current Price Range		Prior Year Average
Tumbler			
☐ marigold	4000.00	6000.00	4500.00
☐ olive green	1150.00	—	—

BUTTERMILK GOBLET
Fenton

A very plain and simple glass on a long stem and pedestal foot. The mark that makes it Carnival glass is its glowing iridescence on the interior. Colors are in a wide range, especially in green and amethyst.

Goblet			
☐ marigold	37.00	43.00	40.00
☐ green	45.00	50.00	48.00
☐ purple	45.00	50.00	48.00
☐ blue	45.00	50.00	48.00
☐ amethyst	45.00	50.00	48.00

BUTTON AND DAISY

The top hat shape and the iridescent faceted glass make this novelty a top collectible. The pattern is all over and almost resembles cut glass. The daises are geometrically stylized and alternate with round medallion shapes. The wide range of colors is available.

	Current Price Range		Prior Year Average

Hat
☐ ice blue	62.00	70.00	64.00
☐ ice green	62.00	70.00	64.00
☐ aqua	62.00	70.00	64.00
☐ vaseline...	62.00	70.00	64.00
☐ clambroth	62.00	70.00	64.00

Slipper
☐ ice blue	72.00	80.00	76.00
☐ ice green	72.00	80.00	76.00
☐ aqua	72.00	80.00	76.00
☐ vaseline...	72.00	80.00	76.00
☐ clambroth	72.00	80.00	76.00

BUTTON AND FAN

Hatpin
☐ amethyst.......................................	50.00	60.00	52.00

BUTTRESS
U.S. Glass

Pitcher
☐ marigold	290.00	315.00	295.00

BUZZ SAW CRUET
Cambridge

The novelty, whose mold is sharp and pattern is interesting, is distinctive because it is indicated on the bottom that it is blown into its mold by a pontil mark. The style is angular ridges and geometric medallions. Colors are green and marigold.

Cruet, height 6″, 4″
☐ marigold	250.00	325.00	260.00
☐ green	265.00	325.00	275.00

Lamp Shade
☐ marigold	40.00	—	—

CACTUS
Millersburg

Found only as a complementing pattern on the exterior of bowls, Cactus is a series of vertical bands of stippled glass. The iridescence is usually carried on the inside.

	Current Price Range		Prior Year Average
Bowl, diameter 8¼"			
☐ marigold	22.50	27.50	24.00
☐ purple	30.00	40.00	32.00
☐ green	30.00	40.00	32.00
☐ blue	30.00	40.00	32.00
☐ amethyst	30.00	40.00	32.00
Bowl, diameter 9½"			
☐ marigold	22.50	27.50	24.00
☐ purple	30.00	40.00	32.00
☐ green	30.00	40.00	32.00
☐ blue	30.00	40.00	32.00
☐ amethyst	30.00	40.00	32.00

CANADA DRY

Bottle

☐ marigold	15.00	—	—
☐ white	20.00	—	—

CANE
Imperial

The same cane pattern seen on chair backs and seats is repeated here with a molded band around the center of the bowl interior. The outer rim resembles a full-blown blossom. The colors are clear, usually marigold and seen in smoke and amethyst.

Bowl, diameter 7½"			
☐ marigold	27.00	33.00	30.00
☐ smoke	35.00	40.00	38.00
Bowl, diameter 10"			
☐ marigold	27.00	33.00	30.00
☐ smoke	35.00	40.00	36.00
Dish, oval			
☐ marigold	27.00	30.00	29.00
☐ smoke	35.00	40.00	37.00
Wine Goblet			
☐ marigold	22.00	27.00	24.00
☐ amethyst	22.00	27.00	24.00

CANE AND DAISY
Jenkins

	Current Price Range		Prior Year Average
Basket			
☐ marigold	170.00	180.00	172.00
☐ smoke	185.00	195.00	187.00
Vase			
☐ marigold	85.00	95.00	87.00

CANE AND SCROLL

A creamer pitcher with a classical flair. Four different patterns work well together, covering the piece. Diagonals, bird's feet, beadwork, and interesting scrolls complement the angular shape of the handle and spout. The color is clear with a rosy tint.

Creamer, Sugar			
☐ marigold	40.00	45.00	42.00
Rose Bowl			
☐ marigold	55.00	—	—
☐ blue	70.00	—	—

CANNON BALL
Fenton

A rare enameled design on a water pitcher and tumblers. The glass is opaque but wonderfully iridescent. The dogwood blossom is wide and dominant and flanked by foliage. Found only in marigold.

Pitcher			
☐ marigold	300.00	350.00	315.00
Tumbler			
☐ marigold	75.00	100.00	80.00

CANOE
U.S. Glass

☐ marigold	75.00	—	—

CAPITOL
Westmoreland

Bowl			
☐ purple	65.00	—	—
☐ blue	65.00	—	—
Mug			
☐ marigold	75.00	—	—

CAPTIVE ROSE
Fenton

An extremely busy pattern covers the entire surface of the shallow bowl. Tiers of diamonds, circles, and scales encircle a wide ribbon of carefully spaced roses in full bloom. The colors are cobalt, green, amethyst, and marigold.

	Current Price Range		Prior Year Average
Bon Bon			
☐ marigold	40.00	—	—
☐ green	60.00	—	—
☐ blue	55.00	—	—
Bowl, diameter 8⅝"			
☐ marigold	22.50	27.50	24.00
☐ purple	32.50	40.00	34.00
☐ green	32.50	40.00	34.00
☐ blue	32.50	40.00	34.00
☐ amethyst	32.50	40.00	34.00
Compote			
☐ marigold	22.50	27.50	24.00
☐ purple	32.50	40.00	34.00
☐ green	50.00	60.00	55.00
☐ blue	32.50	40.00	34.00
☐ amethyst	32.50	40.00	34.00
☐ white	55.00	—	—
Plate, diameter 6½"			
☐ marigold	27.50	35.00	29.00
☐ purple	35.00	47.50	38.00
☐ green	35.00	47.50	38.00
☐ blue	35.00	47.50	38.00
☐ amethyst	35.00	47.50	38.00
Plate, diameter 8"			
☐ marigold	45.00	60.00	48.00
☐ purple	70.00	95.00	72.00
☐ green	70.00	95.00	72.00
☐ blue	70.00	95.00	72.00
☐ amethyst	70.00	95.00	72.00

CARNATION
New Martinsville

Punch Cup			
☐ marigold	45.00	—	—

CARNIVAL BELL

☐ marigold	350.00	—	—

CARNIVAL HONEYCOMB
Imperial

	Current Price Range		Prior Year Average
Bon Bon			
☐ marigold	35.00	—	—
☐ purple	40.00	—	—
☐ green	40.00	—	—
Bowl, 6″, handled			
☐ marigold	30.00	—	—
Creamer and Sugar			
☐ marigold	25.00	—	—
Plate, 7″			
☐ purple	80.00	—	—

CAROLINA DOGWOOD
Westmoreland

A smooth opaque pattern with dogwood blossoms, suggested all over the piece. Six sprays radiate from the central single bloom. Colors are varied.

Bowl, diameter 8½″			
☐ amethyst	90.00	—	—
☐ marigold	65.00	—	—
☐ purple	40.00	45.00	42.00
☐ blue	40.00	45.00	42.00
☐ peach opalescent	75.00	100.00	78.00
☐ aqua opalescent	—	—	250.00

CAROLINE
Dugan

Banana Bowl			
☐ peach opalescent	290.00	310.00	295.00
Basket			
☐ peach opalescent	390.00	410.00	395.00
Bowl			
☐ marigold	45.00	55.00	47.00
☐ blue	80.00	90.00	82.00

CARTWHEEL
Heisey

A simple, plain design in excellent taste makes this compote distinctive. The stubby wide-paneled stem ends with a disk pedestal. The short-walled tray has a series of ridged triangles radiating from a central medallion.

	Current Price Range		Prior Year Average

Compote
| ☐ marigold .... | 70.00 | 90.00 | 72.00 |

CATHEDRAL
Davisons of Gateshead

A beautiful pattern with many motifs that complement each other. The base is simple, but working upward, the first panel of ridged studs starts the busy design. Next going up is diamonds containing flowers, then a flying "V" form surrounding a crown motif. The colors are blue, amethyst, and marigold.

Butter, diameter 10″
☐ marigold	33.50	37.00	35.00
☐ amethyst.....................................	45.00	52.00	46.00
☐ blue ,...	45.00	52.00	46.00

Butter Dish
| ☐ marigold .... | 135.00 | 150.00 | 140.00 |

Chalice, height 7″
☐ marigold	67.50	80.00	70.00
☐ amethyst.....................................	75.00	90.00	80.00
☐ blue	75.00	90.00	80.00

Compote
☐ marigold	38.50	42.00	40.00
☐ amethyst.....................................	45.00	55.00	47.00
☐ blue	45.00	55.00	47.00

Creamer
| ☐ marigold .... | 38.50 | 45.00 | 40.00 |

Epergne
| ☐ marigold .... | 435.00 | 450.00 | 440.00 |

Flower Holder
| ☐ marigold .... | 55.00 | 75.00 | 60.00 |

CATTAILS AND WATER LILIES
Fenton, Northwood

A nice simple pattern highlights the iridescence on the many pieces of this design. Along the bottom is a hint of a basketweave forming the soil for the well-molded cattails and the pretty water lilies. The glass is heavy and nearly opaque.

Berry Bowl, diameter 9″
| ☐ marigold .... | 22.50 | 27.50 | 24.00 |

	Current Price Range		Prior Year Average

Bon Bon
☐ marigold	60.00	—	—
☐ purple	70.00	—	—
☐ blue	75.00	—	—
☐ red	350.00	—	—

Bowl, oval, footed (this four-footed banana bowl is known by the interior pattern, Fenton's Thistle)
☐ marigold	60.00	75.00	62.00
☐ purple	85.00	110.00	90.00
☐ green	85.00	110.00	90.00
☐ blue	85.00	110.00	90.00
☐ amethyst	85.00	110.00	90.00

Creamer
☐ marigold	30.00	40.00	32.00

Spooner
☐ marigold	30.00	40.00	32.00

Tumbler
☐ marigold	12.50	18.00	15.00

Water Pitcher
☐ marigold	65.00	85.00	70.00

Whimsey Toothpick (although called this, it is shown as a jelly dish in Fenton catalogs)
☐ marigold	32.50	40.00	33.00

CENTRAL SHOE STORE
Northwood

Bowl
☐ amethyst	200.00	220.00	205.00

CHAIN AND STAR
Fostoria

Butter Dish, covered
☐ marigold	890.00	920.00	895.00

Tumbler
☐ marigold	740.00	760.00	745.00

CHATELAINE
Imperial

The design is tasteful and executed beautifully. The mold is sharp; the color vibrant and iridescent to the maximum degree. This water pitcher commands a staggering price when it changes hands, which is rarely. The central motif is a beaded cascade reminiscent of April showers. The wide panels just off center are made up of two angular medallions topped by a ridged fan design. The shape is classical, with a bullet rim and beaded handle. The detail is magnificent. Deep purple is the only existent color.

Chatelaine

	Current Price Range		Prior Year Average
Pitcher			
□ purple	1100.00	1450.00	1200.00
Tumbler			
□ purple	200.00	265.00	220.00
## CHATHAM			
U.S. Glass			
Candlesticks, pair			
□ marigold	70.00	80.00	72.00
Compote			
□ marigold	60.00	70.00	62.00

CHECKERBOARD
Westmoreland

A diagonal checkerboard pattern is the central motif on this water set. The deep-cut etchings surround a medallion of stippled glass. The rim is fan scalloped and the handle and spout angular. Colors are dark cobalt and green.

	Current Price Range		Prior Year Average

Cruet
☐ clambroth	500.00	—	—

Goblet
☐ marigold	250.00	—	—
☐ purple	300.00	—	—

Pitcher
☐ purple	3000.00	—	—

Punch Cup
☐ marigold	75.00	—	—
☐ purple	90.00	—	—

Tumbler
☐ marigold	600.00	—	—
☐ purple	450.00	—	—

Wine
☐ marigold	250.00	—	—

CHECKERBOARD BOUQUET

Plate, 8″
☐ purple	50.00	—	—

CHECKERS

Butter Dish
☐ marigold	130.00	150.00	135.00

Plate, 7″
☐ marigold	45.00	55.00	47.00

CHERRY

Bowl, 5″
☐ marigold	25.00	35.00	27.00
☐ amethyst	35.00	45.00	37.00

Bowl, 8″
☐ marigold	45.00	55.00	47.00
☐ amethyst	55.00	65.00	57.00
☐ peach opalescent	145.00	155.00	147.00

Bowl, footed, 8½″
☐ marigold	60.00	70.00	62.00
☐ amethyst	70.00	80.00	72.00
☐ peach opalescent	180.00	200.00	185.00

Plate, 6″
☐ amethyst	180.00	200.00	185.00
☐ peach opalescent	350.00	—	—

CHERRY
Millersburg

The cherries among intricate foliage form the exterior panels on many shapes of Millersburg products. The relief is high and the moldwork is excellent. The branches and leaves are stippled and the cherries are round, glossy glass. The iridescence is mirror-like and the colors found in a wide range.

	Current Price Range		Prior Year Average
Bowl, diameter 5½″			
☐ marigold	18.00	23.00	20.00
☐ purple	26.00	32.00	28.00
☐ green	26.00	32.00	28.00
☐ blue	50.00	65.00	52.00
☐ amethyst	26.00	32.00	28.00
Bowl, diameter 9¼″			
☐ marigold	40.00	60.00	45.00
☐ purple	60.00	75.00	62.00
☐ green	60.00	75.00	62.00
☐ blue	120.00	150.00	125.00
☐ amethyst	60.00	75.00	62.00
Compote			
☐ marigold	450.00	525.00	475.00
☐ purple	460.00	535.00	485.00
☐ green	460.00	535.00	485.00
☐ blue	850.00	1000.00	870.00
☐ amethyst	460.00	535.00	485.00
Creamer			
☐ marigold	40.00	50.00	42.00
☐ purple	85.00	110.00	90.00
☐ green	85.00	110.00	90.00
☐ amethyst	85.00	110.00	90.00
Pitcher, Milk			
☐ marigold	180.00	215.00	190.00
☐ purple	360.00	430.00	375.00
☐ green	360.00	430.00	375.00
☐ amethyst	360.00	430.00	375.00
Plate, diameter 6″			
☐ marigold	225.00	275.00	232.00
Plate, diameter 7½″			
☐ purple	57.50	75.00	62.00
☐ green	57.50	75.00	62.00
☐ amethyst	57.50	75.00	62.00
Powder Jar			
☐ green	425.00	500.00	450.00

	Current Price Range		Prior Year Average
Spooner			
☐ marigold	40.00	50.00	42.00
☐ purple	85.00	110.00	90.00
☐ green	85.00	110.00	90.00
☐ amethyst	85.00	110.00	90.00
Sugar Bowl			
☐ marigold	40.00	50.00	45.00
☐ purple	85.00	110.00	90.00
☐ green	85.00	110.00	90.00
☐ amethyst	85.00	110.00	90.00
Tumbler			
☐ marigold	100.00	130.00	120.00
☐ purple	130.00	160.00	140.00
☐ green	180.00	200.00	190.00
☐ amethyst	130.00	160.00	140.00
Water Pitcher			
☐ marigold	375.00	450.00	400.00
☐ purple	575.00	675.00	600.00
☐ green	575.00	675.00	600.00
☐ amethyst	575.00	675.00	600.00

CHERRY
Dugan

A circular spray of cherries on branches adorns the interior of bowls, the fruit forming the center medallion. The rims of the bowls are ruffled in wide waves, the base can be flat or footed. The colors are often deep and dark but pieces can be found in almost all the Carnival colors.

Cherry (Dugan)

	Current Price Range		Prior Year Average
Bowl, flat, diameter 6″			
☐ marigold	16.00	19.00	17.00
☐ purple	23.00	28.00	24.00
☐ green	23.00	28.00	24.00
☐ blue	23.00	28.00	24.00
☐ amethyst	23.00	28.00	24.00
Bowl, footed, diameter 8″			
☐ marigold	25.00	32.00	24.00
☐ purple	37.00	45.00	38.00
☐ green	37.00	45.00	38.00

CHERRY AND CABLE
Northwood

Architectural panels frame the background, with symmetrical bunches of cherries dropping from a stylized leave bow. This pattern repeats, giving the pieces an octagonal shape. The color is a deep marigold with opaque iridescence.

Cherry and Cable

Berry Bowl, 9″			
☐ marigold	55.00	75.00	60.00
Butter Dish, lidded			
☐ marigold	175.00	225.00	180.00

	Current Price Range		Prior Year Average
Creamer			
☐ marigold	70.00	90.00	75.00
Pitcher			
☐ marigold	550.00	675.00	560.00
Sugar Bowl, lidded			
☐ marigold	100.00	125.00	120.00
Spooner			
☐ marigold	70.00	90.00	75.00
Tumbler			
☐ marigold	75.00	95.00	80.00

CHERRY AND CABLE INTAGLIO
Northwood

Bowl, 5″			
☐ marigold	30.00	—	—
Bowl, 10″			
☐ marigold	50.00	—	—

CHERRY AND DAISIES
Fenton

Banana Boat			
☐ marigold	650.00	750.00	675.00
☐ blue	850.00	950.00	875.00

CHERRY BLOSSOMS
Fenton

Pitcher			
☐ blue	90.00	100.00	95.00
Tumbler			
☐ blue	25.00	32.00	27.00

CHERRY CHAIN

The pattern is busy and covers the entire bowl, the central motif being five bunches of cherries connected by an ornate chain. One single bunch forms the central medallion with a hint of the intricate chain network used as a round frame. The colors are blue, green, white, marigold, and amethyst.

	Current Price Range		Prior Year Average
Bon Bon			
☐ marigold	20.00	25.00	22.00
☐ purple	25.00	30.00	27.00
☐ green	25.00	30.00	27.00
☐ red	1200.00	—	—
☐ blue	25.00	30.00	27.00
☐ white	35.00	40.00	27.00
☐ amethyst	35.00	40.00	27.00
Bowl, diameter 8⅞"			
☐ marigold	30.00	40.00	35.00
☐ purple	40.00	55.00	45.00
☐ green	40.00	55.00	45.00
☐ blue	40.00	55.00	45.00
☐ amethyst	40.00	55.00	45.00
☐ white	42.50	55.00	45.00
☐ red	1000.00	—	—
Chop Plate, 10"			
☐ marigold	110.00	—	—
☐ clambroth	200.00	—	—
Plate, 7"–9"			
☐ marigold	85.00	—	—
☐ blue	110.00	—	—
☐ white	150.00	—	—

CHERRY CIRCLES
Fenton

An all-over pattern with dropping cherries in groups of three forming a wide central band, surrounded by wreaths of foliage. The central medallion is ornate fish scales; the outer rim has a houndstooth ridging. Colors are marigold, white, amethyst, green, and cobalt.

Bon Bon			
☐ marigold	30.00	40.00	35.00
☐ amethyst	25.00	30.00	27.00
☐ cobalt blue	25.00	30.00	27.00
☐ red	235.00	250.00	240.00
Bowl			
☐ marigold	35.00	45.00	37.50
☐ amethyst	42.00	50.00	43.00
☐ green	42.00	50.00	43.00
☐ cobalt blue	42.00	50.00	43.00
Chop Plate, 10"			
☐ clambroth	195.00	—	—

	Current Price Range		Prior Year Average
Compote			
☐ marigold	78.00	82.00	80.00
☐ amethyst..	85.00	92.00	87.00
☐ green	85.00	92.00	87.00
☐ blue	85.00	92.00	87.00
Plate, 9″			
☐ marigold	95.00	—	—
☐ blue	120.00	—	—
☐ white...	175.00	—	—

CHERRY SMASH
U.S. Glass

Bowl, 8″			
☐ marigold	45.00	55.00	47.00
Butter Dish			
☐ marigold	100.00	120.00	105.00
Tumbler			
☐ marigold	120.00	150.00	125.00

CHERRY WREATH
Dugan

Butter Dish, lidded			
☐ marigold, cherries	65.00	85.00	70.00
☐ marigold, red cherries.....................	75.00	97.50	80.00
☐ purple	135.00	170.00	140.00
☐ purple, red cherries	150.00	190.00	155.00
☐ green	135.00	170.00	140.00
☐ green, red cherries..........................	150.00	190.00	160.00
☐ blue	135.00	170.00	140.00
☐ blue, red cherries............................	150.00	190.00	155.00
☐ amethyst..	135.00	170.00	140.00
☐ amethyst, red cherries	150.00	190.00	160.00
☐ white...	210.00	265.00	220.00
Cherub Lamp			
☐ white...	425.00	—	—
Creamer			
☐ marigold	50.00	60.00	52.00
☐ marigold, red cherries.....................	57.50	70.00	56.00
☐ purple	85.00	110.00	86.00
☐ purple, red cherries	100.00	135.00	110.00
☐ green	85.00	110.00	86.00
☐ green, red cherries..........................	100.00	135.00	110.00
☐ blue	85.00	110.00	86.00

	Current Price Range		Prior Year Average
☐ blue, red cherries............................	100.00	135.00	110.00
☐ amethyst...	85.00	110.00	86.00
☐ amethyst, red cherries	100.00	135.00	110.00
☐ white...	130.00	175.00	140.00
Cuspidor			
☐ marigold	875.00	1000.00	900.00
Pitcher			
☐ marigold	110.00	140.00	115.00
☐ purple	200.00	250.00	225.00
☐ green	200.00	250.00	225.00
☐ blue	200.00	250.00	225.00
☐ amethyst...	200.00	250.00	225.00
☐ white...	370.00	440.00	375.00
Sugar Bowl			
☐ marigold	50.00	60.00	55.00
☐ marigold, red cherries.....................	57.50	70.00	60.00
☐ purple	85.00	110.00	80.00
☐ purple, red cherries	100.00	135.00	110.00
☐ green	85.00	110.00	90.00
☐ green, red cherries..........................	100.00	135.00	110.00
☐ blue	85.00	110.00	90.00
☐ blue, red cherries............................	100.00	135.00	110.00
☐ amethyst...	85.00	110.00	90.00
☐ amethyst, red cherries	100.00	135.00	110.00
Spooner			
☐ marigold	50.00	60.00	55.00
☐ marigold, red cherries.....................	57.50	70.00	60.00
☐ purple	85.00	110.00	90.00
☐ purple, red cherries	100.00	135.00	110.00
☐ green	85.00	110.00	90.00
☐ green, red cherries..........................	100.00	135.00	110.00
☐ blue	85.00	110.00	90.00
☐ blue, red cherries............................	100.00	135.00	110.00
☐ amethyst...	85.00	110.00	90.00
☐ amethyst, red cherries	100.00	135.00	110.00
☐ white...	130.00	175.00	140.00
Tumbler			
☐ marigold	27.50	35.00	30.00
☐ purple	40.00	50.00	42.00
☐ green	40.00	50.00	42.00
☐ blue	40.00	50.00	42.00
☐ amethyst...	40.00	50.00	42.00
☐ white...	75.00	100.00	80.00

CHESTERFIELD

	Current Price Range		Prior Year Average

Water Pitcher
	Current Price Range		Prior Year Average
☐ clambroth	85.00	—	—

CHIPPENDALE SOUVENIR

Creamer
☐ marigold	60.00	70.00	62.00
☐ amethyst	75.00	85.00	77.00

Sugar Bowl
☐ marigold	60.00	70.00	62.00
☐ amethyst	75.00	85.00	77.00

CHRISTMAS COMPOTE
Northwood

Large half poinsettias form the wide band just under the quickly turned rim of this large compote. They are intricately molded with many pointed petals and they alternate with bunches of cherries. This pattern repeats all over the piece, the interior design filled with bunches of cherries. Colors exist in marigold and deep purple.

Compote
☐ marigold	2000.00	2550.00	2200.00
☐ purple	2250.00	2750.00	3500.00
☐ amethyst	2250.00	2750.00	2400.00

CHRYSANTHEMUM
Fenton

A busy pattern with boats, buildings, and blossoms covers the interior of the pieces. Four sprays of chrysanthemums form across that frames the scenes. The large bowls have ruffled rims and can be flat or footed. Colors are red, ice green, white, marigold, and blue.

Bowl, flat, diameter 10″
☐ marigold	33.00	37.00	35.00
☐ blue	47.00	55.00	50.00
☐ green	47.00	55.00	50.00
☐ purple	55.00	—	—
☐ ice green (vaseline)	95.00	110.00	100.00
☐ white	95.00	110.00	100.00
☐ red	500.00	600.00	550.00

	Current Price Range		Prior Year Average
Bowl, footed, diameter 10″			
☐ marigold	70.00	90.00	80.00
☐ blue	47.00	55.00	50.00
☐ green	47.00	55.00	50.00
☐ ice green (vaseline)	95.00	110.00	100.00
☐ white	95.00	110.00	100.00
☐ red	500.00	600.00	525.00

CHRYSANTHEMUM DRAPE

Lamp

☐ white	900.00	—	—

CIRCLE SCROLL
Dugan

A rather modernistic pattern containing broad ridges all of a sudden swirled in an elongated circular motion. The top rim is gently scalloped. The colors are marigold, purple, and others.

Circle Scroll

	Current Price Range		Prior Year Average
Bowl			
☐ marigold	17.50	22.50	19.00
☐ purple	27.50	32.50	30.00
☐ amethyst	27.50	32.50	30.00
Butter Dish, lidded			
☐ marigold	60.00	72.50	62.00
☐ purple	85.00	110.00	90.00
☐ amethyst	85.00	110.00	90.00
Creamer			
☐ marigold	22.50	27.50	25.00
☐ purple	30.00	40.00	32.00
☐ amethyst	30.00	40.00	32.00
Pitcher			
☐ marigold	360.00	450.00	375.00
☐ purple	540.00	675.00	560.00
☐ amethyst	540.00	675.00	560.00
Spooner			
☐ marigold	22.50	27.50	24.00
☐ purple	30.00	40.00	32.00
☐ amethyst	30.00	40.00	32.00
Sugar Bowl			
☐ marigold	22.50	27.50	25.00
☐ purple	30.00	40.00	32.00
☐ amethyst	30.00	40.00	32.00
Tumbler			
☐ marigold	50.00	60.00	55.00
☐ purple	75.00	95.00	80.00
☐ amethyst	75.00	95.00	80.00
Vase			
☐ marigold	27.50	32.50	30.00
☐ purple	40.00	50.00	42.00
☐ amethyst	40.00	50.00	42.00

CLASSIC ARTS
Davisons of Gateshead

The influence of a Grecian urn can be seen in this pattern. The body is quite simple, until the wide band just beneath the rim which is decorated like a frieze on a Greek ruin. Human figures in various activities are well molded and in sharp contrast to the stippled background. The glass is an iridescent marigold with a green overlay enamel.

Powder Jar			
☐ marigold	125.00	130.00	127.00

	Current Price Range		Prior Year Average

Rose Bowl
□ marigold 125.00 130.00 127.00
Vase, height 7″
□ marigold 140.00 160.00 145.00
Vase, height 10″
□ marigold 180.00 200.00 185.00

CLEOPATRA

Bottle
□ marigold 95.00 115.00 98.00

CLEVELAND MEMORIAL TRAY
Millersburg

Cleveland celebrated its centennial and gave away these four corner plates to commemorate it. The central medallion shows the soldiers and sailors monument with four radiating panels depicting Garfield in statue, his tomb, the great viaduct, and the Chamber of Commerce building. The colors are amethyst and marigold.

Tray
□ amethyst 1300.00 1500.00 1400.00
□ marigold 1700.00 2000.00 1900.00

COAL BUCKET
U.S. Glass

Figural
□ marigold 85.00 95.00 87.00

COBBLESTONE
Imperial

The pattern is simple but covers the piece with a rippled stonelike effect. The iridescence is mirror-like and the indented cobblestones refract the light beautifully. The colors are green, blue, amber, amethyst, and marigold.

Bon Bon
□ marigold 33.00 40.00 35.00
□ green 47.00 52.00 50.00
□ amber 47.00 52.00 50.00
□ amethyst 47.00 52.00 50.00

	Current Price Range		Prior Year Average

Bowl, diameter 5"
☐ marigold	33.00	40.00	35.00
☐ green	47.00	52.00	50.00
☐ amethyst	47.00	52.00	50.00

Bowl, diameter 8⅞"
☐ marigold	32.50	37.50	34.00
☐ purple	40.00	50.00	42.00
☐ green	40.00	50.00	42.00
☐ amethyst	40.00	50.00	42.00

COBBLESTONES
Dugan

Bowl, 5"
| ☐ marigold | 35.00 | 45.00 | 37.00 |
| ☐ amethyst | 35.00 | 45.00 | 37.00 |

Bowl, 9"
| ☐ marigold | 50.00 | 60.00 | 52.00 |
| ☐ amethyst | 65.00 | 75.00 | 68.00 |

COIN DOT
Fenton

A straightforward pattern of radiating coin forms of various sizes adorns the entire piece. The round shapes are stippled and the wavy ruffled rim adds interest to the piece. Colors are marigold, cobalt, red, green, and amethyst.

Bowl, diameter 6"
☐ marigold	22.00	26.00	24.00
☐ purple	32.00	40.00	38.00
☐ green	32.00	40.00	38.00
☐ blue	32.00	40.00	38.00
☐ aqua opalescent	160.00	190.00	165.00

Bowl, diameter 9"
☐ marigold	22.50	27.50	24.00
☐ purple	30.00	40.00	32.00
☐ green	30.00	40.00	32.00
☐ blue	30.00	40.00	32.00
☐ amethyst	30.00	40.00	32.00
☐ aqua opalescent	200.00	250.00	225.00

Pitcher
| ☐ marigold | 110.00 | 160.00 | 115.00 |

	Current Price Range		Prior Year Average
Rose Bowl			
☐ marigold	25.00	30.00	26.00
☐ purple	32.50	40.00	34.00
☐ green	32.50	40.00	34.00
☐ blue	32.50	40.00	34.00
☐ amethyst	32.50	40.00	34.00
Tumbler			
☐ marigold	27.50	35.00	30.00
☐ purple	27.50	35.00	30.00
☐ green	27.50	35.00	30.00
☐ blue	27.50	35.00	30.00
☐ amethyst	27.50	35.00	30.00

COIN DOT VARIANT
Westmoreland

	Current Price Range		Prior Year Average
Basket			
☐ marigold	42.00	50.00	46.00
☐ blue	48.00	60.00	49.00
Bowl			
☐ marigold	35.00	45.00	38.00
☐ amethyst	50.00	60.00	52.00
☐ blue	75.00	85.00	78.00
☐ peach opalescent	90.00	100.00	92.00
Compote			
☐ marigold	55.00	65.00	57.00
☐ peach opalescent	120.00	130.00	122.00
Rose Bowl			
☐ marigold	60.00	70.00	62.00
☐ amethyst	70.00	80.00	72.00

COIN SPOT
Dugan

The exterior pattern of this wide rimmed compote is a series of stippled ovals alternating with flat panels. The rim is opened all the way with a wavy ruffled shape. The base is a plain disk, while the stem is ornate with a balloon waist. Colors come in the wide range of Carnival iridescent.

	Current Price Range		Prior Year Average

Compote

☐ marigold	20.00	24.00	22.00
☐ purple	32.00	40.00	34.00
☐ green	32.00	40.00	34.00
☐ blue	32.00	40.00	34.00
☐ amethyst..	32.00	40.00	34.00
☐ peach opalescent...........................	37.00	45.00	40.00
☐ white...	45.00	57.50	46.00
☐ aqua opalescent	300.00	—	—
☐ ice green	45.00	57.50	46.00

Goblet

☐ ice green	150.00	—	—

COLONIAL
Imperial

A simple pattern formed more by the shape of the piece than the decoration, the architectural style of the pieces is distinguished by wide arched panels. The colors are marigold, purple, and green with a clear iridescence.

Candlesticks

☐ marigold	80.00	95.00	82.00

Creamer

☐ marigold	32.00	37.00	34.00
☐ green	38.00	42.00	40.00
☐ red...	85.00	95.00	57.00

Sugar Bowl

☐ marigold	32.00	37.00	34.00
☐ green	38.00	42.00	40.00
☐ red...	85.00	95.00	87.00

Tumbler

☐ red...	160.00	200.00	185.00

Vase

☐ marigold	35.00	45.00	37.00
☐ green	35.00	45.00	37.00

Water Pitcher

☐ red...	2000.00	3000.00	2200.00

COLONIAL LADY
Imperial

Again, the pattern is simple, but the distinctive feature is the incredible iridescence achieved by the excellent color. The wide panels are resolved by a ruffled rim, the base formed by flutes. The colors are deep, rich purple and marigold.

	Current Price Range		Prior Year Average

Vase
☐ marigold	50.00	60.00	52.00
☐ purple	55.00	65.00	57.00

COLUMBIA
Imperial

Wide panels are treated to a different twist in these pieces, each two that make up the base resolved in a wide blossoming rim. The iridescence is wonderful and the colors are amethyst, marigold, and green.

Compote
☐ amethyst..	14.00	17.00	16.00
☐ marigold	14.00	17.00	16.00
☐ green	14.00	17.00	16.00

Rose Bowl
☐ marigold	100.00	—	—

Vase, height 4″
☐ amethyst..	14.00	17.00	16.00
☐ marigold	14.00	17.00	16.00
☐ green	14.00	17.00	16.00

COLUMBUS

Plate
☐ marigold	35.00	45.00	37.00

COMET

Bowl, diameter 8½″
☐ marigold	27.50	35.00	30.00
☐ purple	37.50	45.00	39.00
☐ green	37.50	45.00	39.00
☐ blue	37.50	45.00	39.00
☐ amethyst..	37.50	45.00	39.00

Compote Vase
☐ marigold	50.00	—	—
☐ purple	55.00	—	—
☐ green	55.00	—	—
☐ blue	60.00	—	—
☐ amber	50.00	—	—

	Current Price Range		Prior Year Average

Plate, diameter 9″

☐ marigold	60.00	75.00	62.00
☐ purple	80.00	110.00	82.00
☐ green	80.00	110.00	82.00
☐ blue	80.00	110.00	82.00
☐ amethyst	80.00	110.00	82.00

CONCAVE DIAMOND
Dugan

A diagonal checkerboard is handled with intaglio imprinting to form the all-over design on these pieces. The colors are marigold and the ices.

Coaster (not iridized)

☐ ice blue	20.00	—	—
☐ vaseline	25.00	—	—

Pickle Caster

☐ marigold	450.00	—	—

Pitcher

☐ ice blue	225.00	275.00	250.00
☐ russet green	450.00	—	—

Pitcher, lidded

☐ vaseline	225.00	275.00	250.00

Tumbler

☐ ice blue	25.00	35.00	28.00
☐ vaseline	25.00	35.00	28.00
☐ russet green	400.00	—	—

Tumble-Up

☐ russet green	375.00	—	—
☐ ice blue	350.00	—	—

CONCORD
Fenton

A netting effect covers the entire surface of these pieces, providing the background for reliefed grapes and stippled leaves. The body is ruffled from the center, and the rim is formed by a sawtooth edging. Colors are blue, amethyst, amber, marigold, and green.

Bowl, diameter 8″

☐ marigold	57.50	70.00	60.00
☐ purple	87.50	100.00	90.00
☐ green	87.50	100.00	90.00
☐ blue	87.50	100.00	90.00
☐ amethyst	87.50	100.00	90.00

	Current Price Range		Prior Year Average

Plate, diameter 9″
☐ marigold	225.00	275.00	250.00
☐ purple	330.00	380.00	350.00
☐ green	330.00	380.00	350.00
☐ amethyst	330.00	380.00	350.00

CONCAVE FLUTE
Westmoreland

Rose Bowl
☐ marigold	45.00	55.00	47.00
☐ green	60.00	70.00	62.00

Vase
☐ marigold	35.00	45.00	37.00
☐ amethyst	55.00	65.00	58.00
☐ green	60.00	70.00	62.00

CONE AND TIE
Imperial

A straightforward pattern of spearlike cones ending in a flat band and un-fluted rim is distinguished by the deep purple color and rainbow iridescence.

Tumbler
☐ purple	460.00	485.00	475.00

CONSTELLATION
Dugan

The form of this compote is its unique feature—the rim is pulled from the center, creating a ruffle and ridges. The exterior pattern is a stippled swirling design, and the interior is glossy, smooth glass. Colors also include white and peach opalescence.

Compote
☐ marigold	20.00	25.00	22.00
☐ purple	30.00	38.00	32.00
☐ vaseline	85.00	—	—
☐ white	70.00	90.00	80.00
☐ peach opalescence	37.00	45.00	40.00

COOLEEMEE ADVERTISING PLATE
Fenton

Plate
☐ marigold	800.00	900.00	825.00

CORAL
Fenton

A floral and fruitful wide band decorates the interior of this piece, radiating all the way out to the irregularly fluted edge. The glass is clear, and the colors are varied.

	Current Price Range		Prior Year Average
Bowl, diameter 8¾″			
☐ marigold	45.00	55.00	47.00
☐ green	70.00	100.00	75.00
☐ blue	70.00	100.00	75.00
☐ amethyst	70.00	100.00	75.00
Compote			
☐ marigold	30.00	40.00	32.00
☐ green	50.00	65.00	52.00
☐ white	125.00	—	—
Plate, diameter 8¼″			
☐ marigold	160.00	200.00	180.00
☐ green	275.00	325.00	300.00
☐ blue	275.00	325.00	300.00

CORINTH
Dugan

Long, broad ridges, resembling reaching fingers form the shape of these pieces. The base is indented and the glass is smooth and glossy, iridized on the inside only. The colors are green, marigold, amethyst, and peach opalescent.

	Current Price Range		Prior Year Average
Bowl, diameter 8″			
☐ marigold	22.50	27.50	25.00
☐ aqua opalescent	85.00	110.00	89.00
Banana Plate			
☐ marigold	27.00	34.00	30.00
☐ purple	40.00	50.00	42.00
☐ amethyst	40.00	50.00	42.00
☐ peach opalescent	32.00	39.00	36.00
Vase, height 7″			
☐ marigold	16.00	20.00	18.00
☐ purple	25.00	30.00	27.00
☐ green	25.00	30.00	27.00
☐ blue	25.00	30.00	27.00
☐ peach opalescent	28.00	35.00	30.00
☐ white	35.00	45.00	37.00
☐ ice blue	35.00	45.00	37.00
☐ ice green	35.00	45.00	37.00

CORINTH
Westmoreland

	Current Price Range		Prior Year Average
Bowl			
☐ marigold	35.00	45.00	37.00
☐ amethyst	45.00	55.00	47.00
☐ teal	55.00	65.00	57.00
☐ peach opalescent	60.00	—	—
Vase			
☐ marigold	25.00	35.00	27.00
☐ amethyst	40.00	55.00	42.00
☐ teal	45.00	55.00	47.00
☐ smoke	55.00	65.00	57.00
☐ peach opalescent	35.00	—	—

CORN BOTTLE
Imperial

The corn husk motif is used again in this bottle with a cork stopper. The individual niblets are sharply molded, the glass has a mirror-like quality. Colors exist in green, amethyst, smoke, and marigold.

	Current Price Range		Prior Year Average
Bottle			
☐ marigold	160.00	180.00	165.00
☐ green	190.00	210.00	200.00
☐ amethyst	190.00	210.00	200.00
☐ smoke	190.00	210.00	200.00

CORN VASE
Northwood

A half an ear of corn with its husk forms the body of this vase, stuck into a rather simple pedestal foot. The geometrical niblets are sharply molded; the lines on the husk are slightly stylized with wavy lines. The colors are ice green and blue, white, and marigold.

Corn Vase

	Current Price Range		Prior Year Average
Vase			
☐ marigold	450.00	500.00	475.00
☐ green	230.00	300.00	250.00
☐ blue	230.00	300.00	250.00
☐ white	200.00	250.00	225.00
☑ aqua opalescent	60.00	—	—
☐ ice blue	750.00	—	—
☐ ice green	275.00	—	—
☐ purple	300.00	—	—
Vase, pulled husk base			
☐ purple	1500.00	3000.00	1600.00
☐ green	1500.00	3000.00	1600.00

CORNUCOPIA

	Current Price Range		Prior Year Average
Candlestick			
☐ marigold	70.00	90.00	74.00
☐ white	70.00	90.00	74.00
Vase, height 5″			
☐ marigold	27.50	32.50	30.00
☐ white	50.00	60.00	55.00

COSMOS
Millersburg

One huge poppy-like flower adorns the entire surface of the interior of this piece, resolving in a rippled rim that follows the petal of the flower. The center of the flower, which is the base of the piece, is stippled in high relief. Green is the usual color with a sharp radium finish.

	Current Price Range		Prior Year Average
Plate, diameter 9″			
☐ green	70.00	100.00	74.00

COSMOS AND CANE
Imperial

A prolific pattern found on many pieces, the combination of different motifs complement each other in a satisfying, balanced way. Along the long side, ferns reach up toward a bond of flowers directly below the rim. The central long panel on each side is stylized crystals in a diagonal trelliswork. The colors are white, marigold.

Cosmos and Cane

	Current Price Range		Prior Year Average
Advertising Tumbler			
☐ marigold	225.00	—	—
Berry Bowl, diameter 8″			
☐ marigold	25.00	30.00	28.00
☐ white	60.00	70.00	65.00
Butter Dish, covered			
☐ marigold	100.00	125.00	110.00
☐ white	160.00	190.00	170.00
Chop Plate			
☐ marigold	375.00	—	—
☐ white	475.00	—	—
Compote			
☐ marigold	60.00	75.00	62.00
☐ white	80.00	100.00	84.00
Creamer			
☐ marigold	40.00	50.00	42.00
☐ white	75.00	100.00	77.00
Pitcher			
☐ marigold	450.00	550.00	475.00
☐ white	675.00	825.00	700.00
Rose Bowl			
☐ marigold	95.00	—	—
☐ amethyst	150.00	—	—
☐ amber	165.00	—	—
☐ white	625.00	—	—
Spittoon			
☐ marigold	3200.00	—	—
☐ white	3200.00	—	—
Spooner			
☐ marigold	40.00	50.00	46.00
☐ white	75.00	100.00	80.00
Sugar Bowl			
☐ marigold	40.00	50.00	42.00
☐ white	75.00	100.00	80.00
Tumbler			
☐ marigold	45.00	55.00	47.00
☐ white	85.00	110.00	90.00

COSMOS VARIANT
Fenton

The central medallion is the cosmos, a poppy-like flower with ridged petals, surrounded by a crisp foliage wreath. The opaque glass is radized with wonderful iridescence and the rim has the sawtooth edge. Colors are purple, marigold, blue, white, and milk glass.

	Current Price Range		Prior Year Average
Bowl, diameter 9″			
☐ marigold	30.00	38.00	32.00
☐ purple	49.00	52.00	50.00
☐ white	50.00	55.00	52.00
Bowl, diameter 10″			
☐ marigold	30.00	38.00	32.00
☐ purple	49.00	52.00	50.00
☐ white	49.00	52.00	50.00
☐ blue	49.00	52.00	50.00
☐ red	200.00	—	—
Plate, diameter 10″			
☐ peach opalescent	270.00	—	—

COUNTRY KITCHEN
Millersburg

An exterior pattern of faceted flowers, triangular ridges, and the fanlike bands adorns these pieces. The emphasis is on the sharp molding that has the look of cut glass. The rims are sawtoothed. The pieces are available in the wide range of Millersburg tints.

	Current Price Range		Prior Year Average
Bowl, 5″			
☐ berry	150.00	—	—
Bowl, 9″			
☐ marigold	40.00	50.00	42.00
Butter Dish, lidded			
☐ marigold	250.00	320.00	275.00
☐ purple	275.00	325.00	300.00
☐ amethyst	275.00	325.00	300.00
Creamer			
☐ marigold	125.00	165.00	140.00
☐ purple	160.00	195.00	170.00
☐ green	160.00	195.00	170.00
☐ amethyst	160.00	195.00	170.00
Cuspidor			
☐ purple	2500.00	2900.00	2600.00
☐ amethyst	2500.00	2900.00	2600.00
Spittoon			
☐ purple	2200.00	2900.00	2250.00
☐ amethyst	2200.00	2900.00	2250.00
Spooner			
☐ marigold	125.00	165.00	130.00
☐ purple	160.00	195.00	165.00
☐ green	160.00	195.00	165.00
☐ amethyst	160.00	195.00	165.00

	Current Price Range		Prior Year Average
Sugar Bowl			
□ marigold	65.00	85.00	70.00
□ purple	100.00	125.00	110.00
□ green	100.00	125.00	110.00
□ amethyst	100.00	125.00	110.00

COURTHOUSE
Millersburg

A souvenir piece of high quality, the Courthouse is depicted with startling clarity. The detail is excellent, down to the panes in the windows. There seems to be perspective in the piece, with the background receding in the distance. The plate is in two styles, ruffled edge or plain. The radized finish makes the opaque iridescence have a glossy mirror-like quality.

Plate, lettered			
□ purple	400.00	450.00	425.00
Plate, unlettered			
□ purple	600.00	700.00	650.00

COVERED FROG
Heisey

Frog			
□ marigold	375.00	—	—
□ white	300.00	—	—
□ ice blue	300.00	—	—
□ ice green	300.00	—	—

COVERED HEN
Sowerby

A nesting hen sits atop a flowery foliage wreath, looking intently into the distance. The detail work is good, the hen's feathers represented by flowing ridges. The piece has the look of an ice sculpture in marigold.

Hen, covered, full size			
□ marigold	45.00	60.00	47.00
Hen, covered, miniature			
□ marigold	125.00	175.00	130.00

COVERED HEN
English Manufacturer

	Current Price Range	Prior Year Average
Hen		
☐ marigold	90.00	— —
☐ blue	110.00	— —

COVERED LITTLE HEN

Hen, miniature		
☐ clambroth	90.00	— —

COVERED MALLARD
U.S. Glass

Mallard		
☐ clambroth	450.00	— —

COVERED SWAN

The amazing feature about this piece is the fact that the swan's long serpentine neck, folding back over its body, is not anchored by its wings. It stands freely, millimeters off the body, an incredible piece of craftsmanship. The detail is simplified but gives the illusion of the smooth, velvety swan. Colors are seen in amethyst.

Swan			
☐ amethyst	45.00	60.00	48.00
☐ marigold	45.00	60.00	48.00

COVERED SWAN
English Manufacturer

Swan		
☐ marigold	150.00	— —
☐ purple	200.00	— —

COVERED TURKEY

Turkey		
☐ purple	375.00	— —

COVERED TURTLE
Heisey

	Current Price Range		Prior Year Average
Turtle			
☐ green	300.00	—	—
☐ pink	300.00	—	—

CRAB CLAW
Imperial

An interlocking pattern of various motifs, including beadwork, hexagons, diamonds and crystals, give these pieces a cut glass appearance. The design is all over and busy with a saw toothed, scalloped rim. The color is seen in marigold, amethyst, and green.

	Current Price Range		Prior Year Average
Berry Bowl, diameter 5″			
☐ marigold	13.50	18.00	15.00
☐ purple	22.50	30.00	24.00
☐ green	22.50	30.00	24.00
☐ amethyst	22.50	30.00	24.00
Berry Bowl, diameter 8¼″			
☐ marigold	20.00	25.00	22.00
☐ purple	40.00	47.50	42.00
☐ green	40.00	47.50	42.00
☐ smoke	40.00	—	—
☐ amethyst	40.00	47.50	42.00
Compote			
☐ marigold	22.50	—	—
Pitcher			
☐ marigold	200.00	250.00	225.00
Tumbler			
☐ marigold	75.00	85.00	77.00

CRACKLE

A flat pattern resembling cracked ice, this design is found on thousands of pieces and on all shapes of Carnival glass. It was mass produced for premium giveaways so it is easy to find on the collector's market. The colors run the full gamut of Carnival tints.

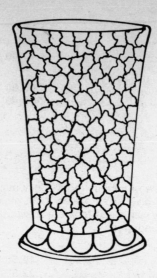

Crackle

	Current Price Range		Prior Year Average
Auto Vase			
☐ marigold	14.00	16.00	15.00
☐ purple	18.00	22.00	19.00
☐ green	18.00	22.00	19.00
Berry Bowl, diameter 5″			
☐ marigold	7.00	10.00	8.00
☐ purple	11.00	13.00	12.00
☐ green	11.00	13.00	12.00
Candlesticks			
☐ marigold	25.00	—	—
Candy Jar, covered			
☐ marigold	22.50	27.00	25.00
Plate, diameter 7″			
☐ marigold	20.00	25.00	22.00
Punch Bowl			
☐ marigold	40.00	60.00	42.00
☐ purple	60.00	70.00	63.00
☐ green	60.00	70.00	63.00
Punch Cup			
☐ marigold	12.00	16.00	14.00
☐ purple	12.00	16.00	14.00
☐ green	12.00	16.00	14.00

	Current Price Range		Prior Year Average

Tumbler
☐ marigold	9.00	11.50	10.00
☐ purple	9.00	11.50	10.00
☐ green	9.00	11.50	10.00

CRUCIFIX
Imperial

Heavy, sculptured glass depicting the death of Christ forms these rare pieces. The style is architectural, on a solid, massive base and resolving in a doorknob-shaped filial above Christ's head. The iridescence is good; the color is clear marigold.

Crucifix
☐ marigold	610.00	750.00	625.00

CURVED STARS

A ruffled edge turned upward distinguishes this pattern. The cut glass band just under the rim is reminiscent of country kitchen and other styles utilizing sunburst and curved spear motifs. The colors that exist are blue, green, marigold, and purple.

Bowl, diameter 4½″
☐ marigold	22.50	27.50	24.00
☐ purple	30.00	40.00	32.00
☐ green	30.00	40.00	32.00
☐ blue	30.00	40.00	32.00
☐ amethyst	30.00	40.00	32.00

Candlestick
☐ marigold	32.50	40.00	35.00

Chalice
☐ marigold	110.00	120.00	115.00
☐ purple	140.00	160.00	145.00
☐ green	140.00	160.00	145.00
☐ blue	140.00	160.00	145.00
☐ amethyst	140.00	160.00	145.00

Creamer
☐ marigold	40.00	45.00	42.00
☐ purple	65.00	70.00	67.00
☐ green	65.00	70.00	67.00
☐ blue	65.00	70.00	67.00
☐ amethyst	65.00	70.00	67.00

Flower Holder
☐ marigold	69.00	80.00	75.00

CUT ARCS
Fenton

	Current Price Range		Prior Year Average
Bowl, diameter 7″–10″			
☐ marigold	30.00	—	—
Compote			
☐ marigold	40.00	—	—
☐ purple	45.00	—	—
☐ blue	45.00	—	—
Vase			
☐ marigold	35.00	—	—
☐ purple	45.00	—	—
☐ blue	40.00	—	—
☐ white	50.00	—	—

CUT COSMOS

An arched panel is the background for this floral and vine design. The moldwork is sharp and the pattern is pleasing because of its restraint. The rim and edge are plain, smooth glass. The color is marigold and iridescent.

Tumbler			
☐ marigold	40.00	50.00	42.00

CUT CRYSTAL
U.S. Glass

A cut glass fan design is the central motif on this pattern. There are a variety of motifs interwoven, including beadwork ferns and stylized flowers. The upper rim is ruffled and the base is a simple pedestal and stem. Marigold is the usual color.

Carafe			
☐ marigold	130.00	160.00	135.00
Compote			
☐ marigold	90.00	—	—

CUT FLOWERS
Jenkins

An intaglio design of dogwood flowers on stalks and leaves. The pattern is deeply cut into the long straight sides and the stang shapes that make up the ridge band catch the light beneath the surface. Colors are generally marigold or smoke.

	Current Price Range		Prior Year Average

Vase

☐ marigold	32.00	38.00	34.00
☐ smoke	39.00	52.00	40.00

CUT OVALS
Fenton

Incised ovals in intaglio and iridescence make the pattern on these pieces. They follow a geometrical line up the long sides of the piece, creating a simple and classic effect. The colors are clearly iridescent.

Candlestick, pair

☐ marigold	32.00	38.00	34.00
☐ ice blue	40.00	45.00	42.00
☐ ice green	40.00	45.00	42.00
☐ red	500.00	—	—

Console Bowl

☐ marigold	50.00	—	—
☐ ice blue	90.00	—	—
☐ ice green	90.00	—	—
☐ red	375.00	—	—

CUT SPRAYS

Vase

☐ marigold	35.00	—	—
☐ peach opalescent	60.00	—	—

DAHLIA
Dugan

Large stylized flowers almost resembling sunbursts are spaced widely around the pieces. They are in high relief and enameled off the rest of the body. The shape is classical with patterned flutes on the rims and convex feet with the same delicate enameling. Colors exist in marigold, white, and purple.

Berry Bowl

☐ marigold	45.00	55.00	46.00
☐ purple	80.00	110.00	82.00
☐ amethyst	80.00	110.00	82.00
☐ white	110.00	140.00	115.00

	Current Price Range		Prior Year Average
Butter Dish, lidded			
☐ marigold	80.00	100.00	85.00
☐ purple	125.00	175.00	130.00
☐ amethyst	125.00	175.00	130.00
☐ white	150.00	200.00	175.00
Creamer			
☐ marigold	45.00	55.00	47.00
☐ purple	70.00	90.00	72.00
☐ amethyst	70.00	90.00	72.00
☐ white	80.00	100.00	84.00
Pitcher			
☐ marigold	400.00	525.00	425.00
☐ purple	600.00	725.00	625.00
☐ amethyst	600.00	725.00	625.00
☐ white	650.00	750.00	675.00
Spooner			
☐ marigold	45.00	55.00	50.00
☐ purple	70.00	90.00	72.00
☐ amethyst	70.00	90.00	72.00
☐ white	80.00	182.00	82.00
Sugar Bowl			
☐ marigold	55.00	67.00	56.00
☐ purple	80.00	100.00	82.00
☐ amethyst	80.00	100.00	82.00
☐ white	90.00	110.00	92.00
Tumbler			
☐ marigold	60.00	70.00	62.00
☐ purple	70.00	90.00	72.00
☐ amethyst	70.00	90.00	72.00
☐ white	85.00	110.00	87.00

DAHLIA AND DRAPE
Fenton

	Current Price Range		Prior Year Average
Tumble-Up			
☐ marigold	145.00	155.00	147.00
☐ ice blue	180.00	190.00	182.00

DAHLIA TWIST
Fenton

	Current Price Range		Prior Year Average
Epergne			
☐ marigold	250.00	—	—
☐ white	300.00	—	—

DAINTY BUD

	Current Price Range		Prior Year Average

Vase
| ☐ marigold .... | 50.00 | — | — |

DAISY
Fenton

Sprays of daisies on stems jet diagonally around a central bloom. The edge is a small saw tooth and bowls are usually footed. Blue is the color most often found.

Bon Bon
☐ marigold	30.00	35.00	32.00
☐ purple	45.00	55.00	47.00
☐ blue	45.00	55.00	47.00

DAISY AND CANE
Sowerly

Geometrical daisies are surrounded by beadwork rows in a diagonal trelliswork. The long thin neck is flanked by rows of short ridges ending in four chunky wedge shapes that rim the upper edge. The color is pale marigold.

Carafe
| ☐ marigold .... | 70.00 | 90.00 | 72.00 |

Compote
| ☐ marigold .... | 25.00 | — | — |

Spittoon
| ☐ blue .... | 185.00 | — | — |

DAISY AND DRAPE
Northwood

An interesting downward swooping motion accompanies this pattern, as the curved ridges radiate toward the footed base. The upper band directly under the moderately ruffled rim is a line of realistic daisies. The colors range widely and the iridescence is excellent.

Vase
☐ marigold	85.00	110.00	86.00
☐ purple	130.00	170.00	135.00
☐ green	130.00	170.00	135.00
☐ blue	130.00	170.00	135.00
☐ aqua opalescent	175.00	225.00	180.00
☐ white...	100.00	125.00	110.00
☐ ice blue	750.00	—	—
☐ ice green	750.00	—	—

DAISY AND PLUME
Northwood

Wide panels of relief daisies with beadwork framing them tightly on either side of this main motif. Long branches with fern-like leaves appear to grow from the base. The upper rim is pushed inward in a tight flute. The colors are generally in the dark iridescent range, yet white is known to exist.

Daisy and Plume

	Current Price Range		Prior Year Average
Candy Dish			
☐ marigold	17.00	23.00	18.00
☐ purple	28.00	35.00	30.00
☐ green	28.00	35.00	30.00
☐ blue	28.00	35.00	30.00
☐ amethyst	28.00	35.00	30.00
☐ white	50.00	60.00	52.00
☐ peach opalescent	90.00	—	—
Compote			
☐ marigold	50.00	—	—
☐ purple	60.00	—	—
☐ green	70.00	—	—
☐ blue	75.00	—	—
☐ peach opalescent	110.00	—	—

	Current Price Range		Prior Year Average

Rose Bowl
☐ marigold	25.00	32.00	26.00
☐ purple	40.00	50.00	42.00
☐ green	55.00	75.00	60.00
☐ blue	40.00	50.00	42.00
☐ amethyst	40.00	50.00	42.00
☐ white	50.00	70.00	52.00
☐ ice blue	50.00	70.00	52.00
☐ ice green	50.00	70.00	52.00
☐ aqua opalescent	1500.00	—	—
☐ peach opalescent	125.00	—	—

DAISY BASKET
Imperial

The elongated basket shape with a tall upright handle is decorated with plenty of blossoms, covering the piece. The relief is high and the mold work is sharp. It was produced in marigold and smoke only.

Basket
☐ marigold	20.00	25.00	22.00
☐ smoke	30.00	35.00	32.00

DAISY BLOCK ROWBOAT
Sowerby

A stationery piece for holding writing implements, the interior pattern is vertical ridges in a simple line meeting at the pointed bottom of the piece. The exterior motif is blocked daisies formed by beadwork. The overall shape suggests a thin rowboat such as the kind men court their ladies in. Marigold, amethyst, and aqua are the colors.

Rowboat
☐ marigold	200.00	255.00	240.00
☐ amethyst	200.00	255.00	240.00
☐ aqua	295.00	350.00	315.00

DAISY CHAIN

Lamp Shade
☐ marigold	45.00	—	—

DAISY CUT BELL
Fenton

The diamond trellis frames the well-molded daisy in this close design. The pattern is intaglio with the sharp cuts all achieved under the surface of the bell. The handle of the bell is decorated with curvy beadwork. Marigold is the standard color.

	Current Price Range		Prior Year Average
Bell			
☐ marigold	465.00	500.00	475.00

DAISY IN OVAL PANELS
U.S. Glass

Creamer			
☐ marigold	50.00	—	—
☐ sugar	50.00	—	—

DAISY SQUARES
Millersburg

Squared-off flowers of low relief form an all-over pattern on these rose bowls and compotes. The upper edge is tightly banded, then flared out in an irregular ruffle. The base is plain for the ornateness of the body. The colors are green, amethyst, gold, and marigold.

Rose Bowl			
☐ marigold	225.00	250.00	230.00
☐ green	225.00	250.00	230.00
☐ amethyst	225.00	250.00	230.00
☐ gold	250.00	300.00	260.00

DAISY WEB
Dugan

Hat			
☐ marigold	35.00	45.00	37.00
☐ amethyst	50.00	60.00	52.00
☐ peach opalescent	65.00	75.00	67.00

DAISY WREATH
Westmoreland

A star-shaped bowl is decorated with shadowy, elongated daisies in a circular design. The central medallion is a lone large daisy overlapping the circular base. The color marigold is over milk glass.

	Current Price Range		Prior Year Average
Bowl, diameter 9″			
☐ marigold	22.00	28.00	24.00
☐ peach opalescent............................	285.00	—	—
☐ aqua opalescent	180.00	220.00	190.00

DANCE OF THE VEILS
Fenton

A dancing spirit in a flowing gown trips around each wide panel. The rest of the body is simply decorated with a glossy sheen. The upper rim flares outward in ruffled flutes. The iridescence is excellent and the color is marigold.

Vase

☐ marigold	1000.00	1500.00	1100.00

DANDELION
Northwood

A bold dandelion and foliage is the central motif on pieces of this design. The background is an arched panel design with a plain upper rim. The colors come in the full range of Northwood colors.

Dandelion

	Current Price Range		Prior Year Average
Mug, lettered			
☐ marigold	200.00	250.00	225.00
Mug, unlettered			
☐ marigold	60.00	75.00	65.00
☐ purple	75.00	100.00	80.00
☐ green	75.00	100.00	80.00
☐ blue	75.00	100.00	80.00
☐ aqua opalescent	250.00	300.00	275.00
Pitcher, tankard style			
☐ marigold	140.00	165.00	145.00
☐ purple	325.00	375.00	330.00
☐ green	325.00	375.00	330.00
☐ blue	325.00	375.00	330.00
☐ ice blue	500.00	600.00	525.00
☐ ice green	500.00	600.00	525.00
Tumbler			
☐ marigold	40.00	50.00	45.00
☐ purple	50.00	70.00	60.00
☐ green	60.00	75.00	62.00
☐ blue	60.00	75.00	62.00
☐ ice blue	90.00	120.00	95.00
☐ ice green	90.00	120.00	95.00

DEEP GRAPE COMPOTE
Millersburg

Bunches of grapes tumble in high relief covering the convex exterior with the fruit and foliage. The stem is plain with base and the upper rim gently scalloped. It was produced in marigold, amethyst, vaseline, and green.

Compote			
☐ blue	2000.00	—	—
☐ marigold	650.00	750.00	675.00
☐ vaseline	2500.00	3000.00	2600.00
☐ green	950.00	1100.00	100.00
☐ amethyst	950.00	1100.00	1000.00

DIAMOND AND DAISY CUT
Jenkins

A swirling band of diamond trellising sweeps along the tops of these pieces. Just below, shadowy daisies decorate the rest of the body. The shape is modern and clean with long lines. Colors are amethyst and marigold.

	Current Price Range		Prior Year Average

Compote
| ☐ marigold | 32.00 | 38.00 | 36.00 |

Pitcher
| ☐ marigold | 135.00 | 170.00 | 140.00 |

Pitcher
| ☐ marigold | 37.00 | 44.00 | 40.00 |

Vase
| ☐ marigold | 85.00 | — | — |

DIAMOND AND FILE

Bowl, 7″
| ☐ marigold | 30.00 | 40.00 | 32.00 |
| ☐ ices | 35.00 | 45.00 | 37.00 |

Bowl, 9″
| ☐ marigold | 30.00 | 40.00 | 32.00 |
| ☐ ices | 35.00 | 45.00 | 37.00 |

DIAMOND AND RIB
Fenton

An interesting and different pattern. The intaglio ovals are made up of elongated ridges in intaglio. Surrounding these forms is shiny smooth glass down the long sides of the vase. The upper edge is ruffled. The colors are green, blue, smoke, amethyst, and marigold.

Jardiniere
☐ marigold	300.00	—	—
☐ purple	500.00	—	—
☐ green	500.00	—	—
☐ blue	450.00	—	—

Vase, 7–12″
☐ marigold	18.00	23.00	20.00
☐ blue	35.00	—	—
☐ purple	30.00	—	—
☐ green	30.00	—	—
☐ smoke	40.00	—	—

DIAMOND AND SUNBURST
Imperial

A diamond frame surround a stylized sunburst, closely decorating the entire body of the piece. The shape of the different pieces is angular to follow the geometric shapes of the diamonds. Colors are purple, amber, green, and marigold.

	Current Price Range		Prior Year Average
Bowl			
☐ marigold	22.00	28.00	24.00
☐ purple	50.00	—	—
☐ green	50.00	—	—
Decanter			
☐ marigold	110.00	140.00	115.00
☐ purple	160.00	190.00	170.00
☐ green	160.00	190.00	170.00
Wine Glass			
☐ marigold	14.00	17.00	16.00
☐ purple	40.00	50.00	42.00
☐ green	40.00	50.00	42.00

DIAMOND CHECKERBOARD

	Current Price Range		Prior Year Average
Bowl, 5″			
☐ marigold	20.00	30.00	22.00
Bowl, 9″			
☐ marigold	30.00	40.00	32.00
Butter Dish			
☐ marigold	65.00	75.00	67.00
Cracker Jar			
☐ marigold	70.00	80.00	72.00
Tumbler			
☐ marigold	80.00	90.00	82.00

DIAMOND FLUTES
U.S. Glass

	Current Price Range		Prior Year Average
Sundae			
☐ marigold	35.00	45.00	37.00

DIAMOND FOUNTAIN
Higbee

An intricate overall pattern decorates these pieces. The central motif is a beadwork fan in a wide panel. It is surrounded by an arched ridge just below the tightly lined neck of the cruet. The handle is curiously plain compared to the rest of the ornate piece. The color is iridescent and slightly transparent.

	Current Price Range		Prior Year Average
Cruet			
☐ marigold	1000.00	1100.00	1050.00

DIAMOND LACE
Imperial

A stained-glass window is what this pattern is reminiscent of, with its long diagonal frameworks containing a starburst. The pattern never ceases, with filler work of tiny beads and stippling. The only colors seem to be marigold, purple, and white.

Diamond Lace

	Current Price Range		Prior Year Average
Berry Bowl, diameter 5½″			
☐ marigold	15.00	20.00	16.00
☐ purple	20.00	25.00	22.00
Berry Bowl, diameter 9″			
☐ marigold	30.00	45.00	32.00
☐ purple	65.00	75.00	70.00
Fruit Bowl, diameter 10½″			
☐ marigold	35.00	70.00	38.00
☐ purple	65.00	85.00	70.00
Pitcher			
☐ purple	160.00	250.00	200.00

	Current Price Range		Prior Year Average
Tumbler			
☐ marigold	30.00	38.00	32.00
☐ purple	50.00	60.00	55.00
☐ white...	50.00	60.00	55.00

DIAMOND OVALS
Sowerby

The ovals make up more than the pattern; they influence the shape of the body. They frame a honeycomb-like design and the connecting piece on the upper rim is a fan made of ridges. The edge is nicely scalloped and the color is an iridescent marigold.

Creamer			
☐ marigold	25.00	30.00	26.00
Open Sugar			
☐ marigold	35.00	—	—

DIAMOND PINWHEEL
Davisons of Gateshead

The geometric swirls of gentle ridges complement the upper pattern of diamond trelliswork. The color is clear but iridescent, and the mold work is excellent.

Bowl, covered			
☐ marigold	30.00	35.00	32.00
Compote			
☐ marigold	45.00	—	—

DIAMOND POINT BASKETS

The basket is of an odd shape, the handles reaching out of the sides with a heavy triangularly fluted rim. The pattern is diamond-shaped trelliswork with a fill-in pattern of large beadwork. The colors are purple, cobalt, and blue.

	Current Price Range		Prior Year Average

Basket

☐ marigold	270.00	290.00	275.00
☐ purple	325.00	375.00	330.00
☐ cobalt blue....................................	325.00	375.00	330.00

DIAMOND POINT COLUMNS
Imperial/Fenton

The columns are made of rows of diamond-shaped checkerboard alternating with plain panels. It is a classically simple design, well balanced and pleasing to the eye. The pattern is known in a wide range of shapes.

Butter Dish

☐ marigold	55.00	75.00	60.00

Compote

☐ marigold	14.00	17.00	16.00

Creamer

☐ marigold	20.00	25.00	22.00

Plate

☐ marigold	22.00	28.00	24.00

Spooner

☐ marigold	27.00	34.00	30.00

Sugar Bowl

☐ marigold	27.00	34.00	30.00

Vase

☐ marigold	22.00	28.00	24.00
☐ purple	35.00	—	—
☐ green	40.00	—	—
☐ white...	40.00	—	—

DIAMOND POINT VASE
Northwood

The pattern is an all-over geometric design of stretched diamonds reaching in an arch toward a triangularly fluted rim. It is found in the full realm of Northwood colors.

Diamond Point Vase

	Current Price Range		Prior Year Average
Vase, height 11″			
☐ marigold	25.00	33.00	26.00
☐ purple	17.00	22.00	18.00
☐ blue..	17.00	22.00	18.00
☐ green...	17.00	22.00	18.00
☐ peach..	25.00	30.00	26.00
☐ white...	30.00	35.00	32.00
☐ aqua opalescent	450.00	—	—
☐ ice blue	200.00	—	—
☐ ice green	250.00	—	—

DIAMOND PRISMS

A standard geometric design on a wide, deep compote marks this English pattern. The arched panels contain faceted sunbursts in a diamond shape. It is usually seen in marigold.

	Current Price Range		Prior Year Average
Compote			
☐ marigold	45.00	50.00	47.00

DIAMOND RING
Imperial

This design is highlighted by swirling ribbons surrounding diamond prisms in an all-over pattern. The interior is smooth, glossy iridescent glass reaching out in a widely ruffled rim. The color are smoke and marigold.

Berry Bowl, diameter 4½″			
☐ marigold	15.00	20.00	16.00
☐ smoke	20.00	30.00	22.00
Berry Bowl, diameter 9″			
☐ marigold	25.00	28.00	26.00
☐ smoke	32.00	40.00	34.00
Fruit Bowl, diameter 8½″			
☐ marigold	23.00	29.00	24.00
☐ smoke	55.00	60.00	58.00

DIAMOND STAR

Mug			
☐ marigold	80.00	90.00	82.00
Vase			
☐ marigold	60.00	—	—

DIAMOND TOP
English Manufacturer

Creamer			
☐ marigold	25.00	35.00	27.00
Spooner			
☐ marigold	25.00	35.00	27.00

DIAMOND VANE
English Manufacturer

Creamer			
☐ marigold	30.00	40.00	32.00

DIAMONDS
Millersburg

Stretched-out diamonds in an all-over pattern take up most of the exterior space on pieces with this style. The shapes are outlined in beadwork, and the upper rim is resolved by gentle scalloping. The colors are deeply iridescent and come in marigold, purple, and green.

Diamonds

	Current Price Range		Prior Year Average
Pitcher			
☐ purple	500.00	700.00	550.00
☐ green	500.00	700.00	550.00
☐ amethyst	500.00	700.00	550.00
☐ marigold	150.00	—	—
Punch Bowl and Base			
☐ marigold	2000.00	—	—
☐ purple	1800.00	—	—
☐ green	1800.00	—	—
Tumbler			
☐ marigold	27.00	35.00	30.00
☐ purple	33.00	40.00	35.00
☐ green	33.00	40.00	35.00

DIVING DOLPHINS
Sowerby

This interesting pattern carries two motifs. The interior is a stippled scroll design, flowing in curves that resemble the exterior pattern of graceful dolphins. The colors are commonly green, blue, amethyst, and marigold.

	Current Price Range		Prior Year Average
Bowl, footed, diameter 7″			
☐ marigold	120.00	135.00	125.00
☐ green	200.00	225.00	210.00
☐ blue	200.00	225.00	210.00
☐ amethyst	200.00	225.00	210.00

DOGWOOD SPRAYS
Dugan

The circular wreath of dogwood blossoms and foliage gracefully decorates the interior of these wide bowls with ruffled edges. The rest of the piece is glossy smooth glass found in purple and peach.

Banana Bowl			
☐ purple	80.00	100.00	90.00
☐ green	80.00	100.00	90.00
☐ blue	80.00	100.00	90.00
☐ peach	100.00	125.00	100.00
Bowl, footed, diameter 9″			
☐ marigold	30.00	40.00	35.00
☐ purple	40.00	50.00	45.00
☐ aqua opalescent	140.00	—	—
☐ peach opalescent	40.00	50.00	45.00
Compote			
☐ marigold	18.00	23.00	20.00
☐ peach opalescent	60.00	—	—

DOLPHINS COMPOTE
Millersburg

Very playful dolphins pause on the exterior of this stately compote, forming the pedestal feet. They seem to be smiling, perhaps because they support one of the finest crafted bowls in Carnival glass. The interior, with the Rosalind pattern, is molded beautifully with stippled glass alternating in arches with smooth, glossy glass. The edge is gently scalloped.

	Current Price Range		Prior Year Average

Compote

☐ marigold	400.00	500.00	425.00
☐ purple	450.00	550.00	475.00
☐ green	450.00	550.00	475.00
☐ blue	800.00	1000.00	850.00
☐ amethyst	450.00	550.00	475.00

DORSEY AND FUNKENSTEIN
Northwood

Advertising Plate

☐ amethyst	230.00	240.00	232.00

DOTTED DAISIES

Plate

☐ marigold	60.00	70.00	62.00

DOUBLE DOLPHIN
Fenton

Large expanses of smooth, almost opaque glass, shimmeringly iridescent, make up this pattern. The decoration is the scaled dolphins flipping their tails in high relief off the side of the glass. It is a simple but effective pattern, an addition to any collection.

Bowl, diameter 8″

☐ pink	55.00	—	—
☐ ice blue	70.00	90.00	72.00
☐ ice green	70.00	90.00	72.00

Cake Plate

☐ pink	27.00	—	—
☐ ice blue	35.00	45.00	37.00
☐ ice green	35.00	45.00	37.00

Candlesticks, pair

☐ ice blue	45.00	55.00	48.00
☐ ice green	45.00	55.00	48.00
☐ white	45.00	55.00	48.00
☐ pink	45.00	55.00	48.00

Compote

☐ ice blue	55.00	60.00	58.00
☐ ice green	55.00	60.00	58.00
☐ topaz	55.00	60.00	58.00
☐ tangerine	55.00	60.00	58.00

	Current Price Range		Prior Year Average

Fan Vase

☐ ice blue	60.00	—	—
☐ ice green	60.00	—	—
☐ topaz	60.00	—	—
☐ tangerine	60.00	—	—
☐ pink	60.00	—	—
☐ white	60.00	—	—

DOUBLE DUTCH
Imperial

A lovely, well perspected scene graces the wide plate. The huge oak in the foreground gives way to water and a windmill in the rear. The rim is ridged and resolves in a gently fluted edge. Commonly in marigold, also in amethyst, green and smoke.

Bowl, diameter 9″, footed

☐ marigold	22.00	28.00	24.00
☐ purple	36.00	44.00	38.00
☐ green	36.00	44.00	38.00
☐ smoke	36.00	44.00	38.00
☐ amethyst	36.00	44.00	38.00

DOUBLE FAN

Fan motifs made up of cut glass ridges form an all over design on this beautiful tumbler. The glass is heavy and clear, the iridescence is excellent.

Tumbler

☐ marigold	85.00	100.00	90.00

DOUBLE LOOP
Northwood

A fine simple pattern of straight-sided arches with a slightly bulging waist adorn these creamers and sugars. The colors are green, purple, aqua opalescent, and cobalt.

Creamer

☐ marigold	30.00	37.00	32.00
☐ purple	45.00	50.00	47.00
☐ green	45.00	50.00	47.00
☐ blue	45.00	50.00	47.00
☐ aqua opalescent	170.00	200.00	175.00

	Current Price Range		Prior Year Average

Sugar Bowl

☐ marigold	17.00	25.00	20.00
☐ purple	28.00	40.00	30.00
☐ green	28.00	40.00	30.00
☐ blue	28.00	40.00	30.00
☐ aqua opalescent	125.00	175.00	130.00

DOUBLE SCROLL
Imperial

A spindled design, with scrolls of glass attached on the side, make this otherwise plain pattern distinctive. The glass is heavy and the iridescence is mirror-like and refractory. The colors are green, smoke, amethyst, and marigold.

Bowl, dome foot

☐ marigold	22.00	25.00	23.00
☐ purple	35.00	40.00	37.00
☐ green	35.00	40.00	37.00
☐ smoke	35.00	40.00	37.00
☐ red	185.00	—	—

Bowl, oval

☐ marigold	17.00	22.00	18.00
☐ purple	32.00	38.00	33.00
☐ green	32.00	38.00	33.00

Candlestick

☐ marigold	17.00	22.00	18.00
☐ purple	32.00	38.00	33.00
☐ green	32.00	38.00	33.00
☐ red	200.00	—	—

DOUBLE STAR

An excellent, well-balanced geometrical design is formed by various motifs working well together. The central design is a small radiating star with whirling etchings framed with deep slashes in a broken arch. The bottom band is reminiscent of Egyptian markings, with a rising sun and small stars surrounding. The colors are marigold, amethyst, and most commonly, green.

	Current Price Range		Prior Year Average
Pitcher			
☐ marigold	325.00	400.00	330.00
☐ purple	250.00	325.00	275.00
☐ green	250.00	325.00	275.00
Tumbler			
☐ marigold	45.00	60.00	47.00
☐ purple	40.00	55.00	42.00
☐ green	40.00	55.00	42.00

DOUBLE STEM ROSE
Dugan

The fully bloomed rose is the center point of this pattern, in high relief surrounded by petals. The midband is made up of a half dozen small roses and the rest of the piece remains smooth and clear. The colors are lavender, blue, green, amethyst, and marigold.

Bowl			
☐ marigold	27.00	34.00	28.00
☐ purple	40.00	50.00	42.00
☐ green	40.00	50.00	42.00
☐ blue	40.00	50.00	42.00
☐ peach opalescent	85.00	95.00	90.00
Plate, dome foot			
☐ peach opalescent	130.00	140.00	135.00

DOUGHNUT BRIDLE

Rosette			
☐ purple	75.00	—	—

DRAGON AND LOTUS
Fenton

Another busy, overall pattern with a distinctly oriental flair. The center point resembles a dragonfly, while the outer wide bands contain alternating portraits of winged dragons and beautiful lotus blossoms. All of the colors are represented in this prolific pattern by Fenton.

	Current Price Range		Prior Year Average

Bowl, flat or footed
☐ marigold	40.00	50.00	45.00
☐ purple	50.00	60.00	55.00
☐ green	50.00	60.00	55.00
☐ blue	50.00	60.00	55.00
☐ peach opalescent	220.00	280.00	225.00
☐ red	700.00	—	—

Plate
☐ marigold	180.00	230.00	185.00
☐ purple	260.00	350.00	270.00
☐ green	260.00	350.00	270.00
☐ blue	260.00	350.00	270.00
☐ amethyst	260.00	350.00	270.00

DRAGON AND STRAWBERRY

Stylized dragons with wings in attack position alternate with groups of three innocent strawberries. The oriental influence is evident especially in the central starburst which contains the dragon on a bed of the berries.

Bowl, flat, diameter 9″
☐ marigold	160.00	190.00	170.00
☐ green	235.00	310.00	240.00
☐ blue	235.00	310.00	240.00

Bowl, footed, diameter 9″
☐ marigold	130.00	160.00	140.00
☐ green	190.00	230.00	200.00
☐ amethyst	190.00	230.00	200.00

Dragonfly Lamp Shade
☐ white	48.00	—	—

DRAGON'S TONGUE
Fenton

Flickers of fire seem to adorn these pieces in an all-over pattern radiating from the center blossom. The flames are created by sharply molded ridgework, and the rim is made up of shallow fluting that mimics the ridging. The most common color is bright marigold.

Bowl, footed, diameter 11″
☐ marigold	275.00	—	—

Shade
☐ peach opalescent	75.00	—	—

DRAPERY
Northwood

The lines are graceful and full-bodied, reminding one of the draperies in a Renaissance painting. It is an all-over design, and the shape is a flowing swirl itself. The colors come in the widest range of Carnival tints.

	Current Price Range		Prior Year Average
Candy Dish			
☐ marigold	22.00	28.00	24.00
☐ purple	30.00	40.00	32.00
☐ green	30.00	40.00	32.00
☐ amethyst	30.00	40.00	32.00
☐ white	42.00	55.00	44.00
☐ ice blue	42.00	55.00	44.00
☐ ice green	42.00	55.00	44.00
☐ aqua opalescent	200.00	—	—
Rose Bowl			
☐ marigold	35.00	45.00	27.00
☐ purple	80.00	100.00	90.00
☐ green	46.00	54.00	48.00
☐ blue	46.00	54.00	48.00
☐ amethyst	46.00	54.00	48.00
☐ white	70.00	85.00	72.00
☐ ice blue	70.00	85.00	72.00
☐ ice green	70.00	85.00	72.00
☐ aqua opalescent	175.00	220.00	180.00
Vase			
☐ marigold	18.00	24.00	20.00
☐ purple	35.00	42.00	37.00
☐ green	35.00	42.00	37.00
☐ blue	35.00	42.00	37.00
☐ white	38.00	45.00	40.00
☐ ice blue	38.00	45.00	40.00
☐ ice green	38.00	45.00	40.00

DRAPERY VARIANT
Fenton

	Current Price Range		Prior Year Average
Pitcher			
☐ marigold	470.00	490.00	475.00
Tumbler			
☐ marigold	65.00	75.00	67.00

DREIBUS PARFAIT SWEETS
Northwood

	Current Price Range		Prior Year Average
Plate, 6"			
☐ amethyst......................................	170.00	180.00	172.00

DUGAN FAN
Dugan

Gravy Boat			
☐ marigold	45.00	55.00	47.00
☐ amethyst......................................	55.00	65.00	57.00
☐ peach opalescent...........................	80.00	90.00	82.00
☐ white...	85.00	95.00	87.00
Sauce			
☐ marigold	30.00	40.00	32.00
☐ amethyst......................................	40.00	50.00	42.00

DUNCAN
National Glass

Cruet			
☐ marigold	390.00	420.00	395.00

DUTCH MILL

Ashtray			
☐ marigold	30.00	40.00	32.00
Plate, 8"			
☐ marigold	30.00	40.00	32.00

DUTCH PLATE

Plate, 8"			
☐ marigold	35.00	45.00	38.00

DUTCH TWINS

Ashtray			
☐ marigold	35.00	45.00	37.00

EAGLE FURNITURE
Northwood

Plate			
☐ amethyst......................................	170.00	180.00	172.00

EBON

	Current Price Range		Prior Year Average
Vase			
☐ black amethyst	85.00	95.00	87.00

ELEGANCE

Bowl			
☐ amethyst	85.00	95.00	87.00

ELKS
Fenton

An Elks Club souvenir from three years, 1910, 1911, and 1914, the pattern is dominated by an inscribed ribbon. The outer band is of stippled stars with three tiered flutes to follow the design. The color is spectacular with a rich cobalt and green with a radium luster.

Bowl, Detroit			
☐ green	325.00	375.00	330.00
☐ blue	325.00	375.00	330.00
☐ marigold	1000.00	—	—
Plate, Parkersburg			
☐ green	350.00	425.00	360.00
☐ blue	350.00	425.00	360.00

ELKS
Millersburg

A highly decorated plate made for the Elks in 1910, the pattern is dominated by a huge elk's head. Atop his antlers rests a clock pointing to noon. The surrounding design is starlike flowers and foliage. The color is radized amethyst.

Bell, 1911			
☐ blue	850.00	—	—
Bell, 1914			
☐ blue	850.00	—	—
Bowl, diameter 8″			
☐ purple	450.00	550.00	475.00
☐ amethyst	450.00	550.00	475.00
☐ blue	400.00	—	—
Nappy			
☐ purple	650.00	750.00	675.00
☐ amethyst	650.00	750.00	675.00

	Current Price Range		Prior Year Average
Paperweight			
☐ purple	800.00	1000.00	825.00
☐ green	800.00	1000.00	825.00
☐ amethyst.......................................	800.00	1000.00	825.00
Plate			
☐ green	900.00	—	—
☐ blue	700.00	—	—

EMBROIDERED MUMS
Northwood

The central medallion is a giant multipetaled mum framed by a thin band of wreathed foliage. The design continues out with a number of various-sized flowers and a lot of branches and leaves. It is an overall pattern, reaching out to its sawtoothed rim. Known in many Northwood colors.

Bowl, diameter 9″			
☐ marigold	45.00	55.00	50.00
☐ purple	70.00	80.00	75.00
☐ green	36.00	46.00	37.00
☐ blue	36.00	46.00	37.00
☐ amethyst.......................................	36.00	46.00	37.00
☐ white..	60.00	75.00	62.00
☐ ice blue	60.00	75.00	62.00
☐ ice green	60.00	75.00	62.00
☐ aqua opalescent	200.00	250.00	225.00
Plate			
☐ marigold	50.00	65.00	52.00
☐ purple	85.00	110.00	90.00
☐ blue	85.00	110.00	90.00
☐ amethyst.......................................	85.00	110.00	90.00
☐ white..	70.00	90.00	72.00
☐ ice blue	70.00	90.00	72.00
☐ ice green	70.00	90.00	72.00

EMU
Australian Manufacturer

A large bird resembling an ostrich is the centerpiece on this octagonal plate. His background is simply smooth glossy glass, but the upper band of wreathed foliage busies the surface until the rim. The colors are purple, amber, and marigold.

Bowl			
☐ marigold :.....................................	70.00	85.00	72.00

ENGLISH BUTTON AND BAND

	Current Price Range		Prior Year Average

Creamer
| ☐ marigold | 35.00 | — | — |

Sugar
| ☐ marigold | 35.00 | — | — |

ENGLISH HOB AND BUTTON

Bowl
☐ marigold	60.00	—	—
☐ purple	70.00	—	—
☐ green	90.00	—	—
☐ blue	60.00	—	—

Epergne
| ☐ marigold | 100.00 | — | — |
| ☐ blue | 110.00 | — | — |

ENGRAVED FLORAL
Fenton

Tumbler
| ☐ green | 80.00 | — | — |

ENGRAVED GRAPES

Juice Glass
| ☐ marigold | 40.00 | 50.00 | 45.00 |

Tumbler
| ☐ marigold | 22.00 | 28.00 | 24.00 |

Water Pitcher
| ☐ marigold | 110.00 | 140.00 | 115.00 |

ESTATE
Westmoreland

Creamer
☐ marigold	40.00	50.00	42.00
☐ blue	80.00	90.00	82.00
☐ aqua opalescent	115.00	130.00	117.00
☐ peach opalescent	70.00	—	—

Mug
| ☐ marigold | 80.00 | 90.00 | 82.00 |
| ☐ ices | 90.00 | 100.00 | 92.00 |

Perfume
| ☐ aqua | 105.00 | 115.00 | 108.00 |

	Current Price Range		Prior Year Average

Sugar
☐ marigold	40.00	50.00	42.00
☐ ices	80.00	90.00	82.00
☐ aqua opalescent	115.00	130.00	117.00
☐ peach opalescent	70.00	—	—

Vase, bud, 6″
☐ marigold	35.00	45.00	37.00
☐ ice	70.00	80.00	72.00

ESTATE, STIPPLED
Westmoreland

Vase
☐ peach opalescent	80.00	90.00	82.00
☐ ices	90.00	100.00	92.00

EXCHANGE BANK
Northwood

Eye Cup
☐ marigold	50.00	—	—

Plate
☐ purple	200.00	—	—

FAMOUS

Puff Box
☐ marigold	75.00	—	—

FAN
Dugan

A classic design and a restrained, tasteful pattern makes these pieces quite distinctive. The bottom decoration is a tightly scrolled and flowered relief design; the rest of the body remains smooth and glossy. The upper rim is gently and widely ruffled, mimicking the tiny waves of scrolls that rise occasionally off the edge. Peach, purple, and marigold are existing colors.

Sauce Dish
☐ marigold	18.00	22.00	20.00
☐ purple	32.00	38.00	36.00
☐ green	32.00	38.00	36.00
☐ blue	32.00	38.00	36.00
☐ amethyst	32.00	38.00	36.00
☐ peach	32.00	38.00	36.00

FAN-TAILS
Fenton

Motion is the key to what this pattern attempts to achieve by radiating six well-detailed peacock feathers out from the center. The mold work is good, and the rest of the body is glossy and smooth. Colors are white, green, cobalt, and marigold.

	Current Price Range		Prior Year Average
Bowl, diameter 5″			
☐ marigold	20.00	25.00	22.00
☐ cobalt	31.00	34.00	32.00
☐ white	31.00	34.00	32.00
Bowl, diameter 9″			
☐ marigold	50.00	57.00	52.00
☐ cobalt	63.00	67.00	65.00
☐ white	63.00	67.00	65.00
Compote			
☐ marigold	32.00	35.00	34.00
☐ cobalt	42.00	47.00	43.00

FANCIFUL
Dugan

The basketweave exterior pattern complements the busy, overall design of the interior. Many motifs are used, dominated by foliage and beadwork. The colors are peach, white, purple, and marigold.

Fanciful

	Current Price Range		Prior Year Average
Bowl, diameter 7½″			
☐ marigold	40.00	50.00	42.00
☐ purple	60.00	75.00	62.00
☐ amethyst	60.00	75.00	62.00
☐ white	80.00	110.00	82.00
Bowl, diameter 8½″			
☐ marigold	25.00	32.00	21.00
☐ purple	40.00	55.00	42.00
☐ amethyst	40.00	55.00	42.00
☐ white	57.50	70.00	60.00
☐ peach opalescent	47.50	60.00	50.00
Plate, ruffled			
☐ marigold	80.00	100.00	82.00
☐ purple	100.00	130.00	110.00
☐ blue	100.00	130.00	110.00
☐ amethyst	100.00	130.00	110.00
☐ peach opalescent	175.00	—	—
☐ white	125.00	—	—
Plate, diameter 9″			
☐ marigold	70.00	85.00	72.00
☐ purple	90.00	110.00	95.00
☐ blue	90.00	110.00	95.00
☐ amethyst	90.00	110.00	95.00
☐ white	160.00	190.00	165.00
☐ peach opalescent	250.00	—	—

FANCY CUT

Miniature Pitcher

☐ marigold	120.00	130.00	122.00

FANCY FLOWERS
Imperial

Compote

☐ marigold	50.00	60.00	55.00
☐ green	75.00	100.00	160.00

FANS
Davisons of Gateshead

The fan shape is used here, overlapping the prisms in continuous motion around the piece. The shape is simple, the handle and spout restrained. Seen in marigold.

	Current Price Range		Prior Year Average

Milk Pitcher
| ☐ marigold | 62.00 | 70.00 | 65.00 |

FARMYARD

Two large roosters are placed back to back in a symmetrical way. The mold work is sharp, and the detail on the chickens is excellent and in high relief. Known to be one of the ten wonders of Carnival, these pieces rarely trade hands, and when they do, the price is sky high. Green, purple, peach opalescent, and amethyst are the colors.

Bowl, circular, diameter 10″
☐ green	2000.00	3000.00	2200.00
☐ purple	1500.00	2500.00	1775.00
☐ peach	7500.00	8200.00	7800.00
☐ amethyst	8200.00	8500.00	8400.00

Bowl, squared, diameter 10″
| ☐ purple | 2200.00 | 3000.00 | 2300.00 |
| ☐ amethyst | 8200.00 | 8500.00 | 8400.00 |

FASHION
Imperial

A common and prolific pattern, pieces with design were mass-produced throughout the Carnival era. It's an overall style, with diamonds, jewels, sunbursts and beadwork swirls filled in with stippling. The colors are green, purple, smoke, and marigold.

Compote
| ☐ smoke | 150.00 | — | — |

Creamer
☐ marigold	32.00	38.00	33.00
☐ purple	85.00	110.00	90.00
☐ green	85.00	110.00	90.00
☐ smoke	85.00	110.00	90.00
☐ amethyst	85.00	110.00	90.00

Pitcher
☐ marigold	85.00	110.00	90.00
☐ purple	600.00	700.00	650.00
☐ green	650.00	850.00	675.00
☐ amethyst	650.00	850.00	675.00
☐ smoke	500.00	—	—

	Current Price Range		Prior Year Average
Punch Bowl			
☐ marigold	90.00	110.00	100.00
☐ purple	500.00	600.00	525.00
☐ amethyst	500.00	600.00	525.00
Punch Cup			
☐ marigold	14.00	17.00	15.00
☐ purple	40.00	50.00	42.00
☐ amethyst	40.00	50.00	42.00
☐ marigold	32.00	38.00	34.00
☐ purple	85.00	110.00	87.00
☐ green	85.00	110.00	87.00
☐ blue	85.00	110.00	87.00
☐ amethyst	85.00	110.00	87.00
Rose Bowl			
☐ marigold	300.00	—	—
☐ amethyst	600.00	—	—
☐ green	500.00	—	—
Sugar Bowl			
☐ marigold	32.00	38.00	34.00
☐ purple	85.00	110.00	87.00
☐ green	85.00	110.00	87.00
☐ smoke	85.00	110.00	87.00
☐ amethyst	85.00	110.00	87.00
Tumbler			
☐ marigold	18.00	23.00	17.00
☐ purple	100.00	145.00	110.00
☐ green	100.00	145.00	110.00
☐ smoke	100.00	145.00	110.00
☐ amethyst	100.00	145.00	110.00

FEATHER AND HEART
Millersburg

An overall geometrical pattern, Feather and Heart is busy but well balanced. The bottom motif is a modified diamond frame containing sunbursts of various sizes. The upper design contrasts with a ridged, vertical feather design. The edge is gently scalloped. The glass is clear and colors are green, amethyst, and marigold.

Tumbler			
☐ marigold	100.00	130.00	110.00
☐ purple	140.00	170.00	145.00
☐ green	140.00	170.00	145.00
☐ amethyst	140.00	170.00	150.00

	Current Price Range		Prior Year Average

Water Pitcher

☐ marigold	450.00	525.00	460.00
☐ purple	600.00	800.00	650.00
☐ green	600.00	800.00	650.00
☐ amethyst	600.00	800.00	650.00

FEATHERED ARROW

Bowl

☐ marigold	35.00	45.00	37.00

FEATHERED SERPENT
Fenton

The interior design is a twirl of feathered scrolls in a wide upper band. The central medallion is four plumes radiating out from the connection in the middle. Blue, green, marigold, and amethyst are the existing colors.

Berry Bowl, diameter 9″

☐ marigold	45.00	60.00	55.00
☐ purple	50.00	60.00	52.00
☐ green	50.00	60.00	52.00
☐ blue	50.00	60.00	52.00
☐ amethyst	50.00	60.00	52.00

Bowl, 5″, footed

☐ marigold	25.00	—	—
☐ purple	30.00	—	—
☐ green	30.00	—	—
☐ blue	30.00	—	—

Fruit Bowl, diameter 10½″

☐ marigold	26.00	34.00	27.00
☐ purple	40.00	50.00	42.00
☐ green	40.00	50.00	42.00
☐ blue	40.00	50.00	42.00
☐ amethyst	40.00	50.00	42.00

FEATHERS
Northwood

The long vertical plumes decorate the side panels, resolving at the upper rim in widely ruffled flutes. Other than these geometrically ridged feathers, the body is smooth and glossy. The colors are purple, green, marigold, and the pastels.

	Current Price Range		Prior Year Average
Vase, height 7″			
☐ marigold	14.00	18.00	15.00
☐ purple	25.00	32.00	27.00
☐ green	25.00	32.00	27.00
☐ blue	25.00	32.00	27.00
☐ amethyst	25.00	32.00	27.00
☐ white	32.00	28.00	34.00
☐ ice blue	32.00	38.00	34.00
☐ ice green	32.00	38.00	34.00

FEATHER STITCH
Fenton

An overall pattern of rounds created by a light, plaited ridging in a wreath shape. The circles are arranged in concentric bands in ever-increasing sizes. The existent colors are blue, green, amethyst, and marigold.

Bowl, diameter 8½″			
☐ marigold	50.00	—	—
☐ purple	75.00	—	—
☐ green	65.00	—	—
☐ blue	60.00	—	—
☐ aqua	60.00	—	—

FEATHER SWIRL
U.S. Glass

Butter Dish			
☐ marigold	100.00	115.00	105.00
Vase			
☐ marigold	45.00	55.00	47.00

FELDMAN BROTHERS
Northwood

Bowl			
☐ amethyst	145.00	155.00	147.00

FENTONIA
Fenton

A pleasing diamond on the diagonal pattern, Fentonia is made up of bead-work frames surrounding scales and stitchery. Marigold, amethyst, green, and blue are the standard colors.

	Current Price Range		Prior Year Average

Bowl, 5″, footed
☐ marigold	25.00	—	—
☐ purple	30.00	—	—
☐ green	30.00	—	—
☐ blue	30.00	—	—

Berry Bowl, diameter 9″
☐ marigold	32.00	37.00	34.00
☐ purple	60.00	75.00	62.00
☐ green	60.00	75.00	62.00
☐ blue	60.00	75.00	62.00
☐ amethyst	60.00	75.00	62.00

Bowl, footed, diameter 7½″
☐ marigold	30.00	38.00	32.00
☐ purple	58.00	70.00	60.00
☐ green	58.00	70.00	60.00
☐ blue	58.00	70.00	60.00
☐ amethyst	58.00	70.00	60.00

Butter Dish, lidded
☐ marigold	100.00	125.00	110.00
☐ blue	135.00	170.00	140.00

Creamer
☐ marigold	60.00	80.00	70.00
☐ blue	75.00	100.00	80.00
☐ amethyst	75.00	100.00	80.00

Pitcher
☐ marigold	325.00	375.00	330.00
☐ blue	450.00	550.00	460.00

Spooner
☐ marigold	40.00	50.00	42.00
☐ purple	75.00	100.00	80.00
☐ blue	75.00	100.00	80.00
☐ amethyst	75.00	100.00	80.00

Sugar Bowl
☐ marigold	40.00	50.00	42.00
☐ purple	75.00	100.00	78.00
☐ blue	75.00	100.00	78.00
☐ amethyst	75.00	100.00	78.00

Tumbler
☐ marigold	80.00	110.00	82.00
☐ blue	120.00	150.00	125.00

FENTONIA FRUIT
Fenton

	Current Price Range		Prior Year Average
Bowl, 6"			
☐ marigold	40.00	50.00	42.00
☐ blue	50.00	60.00	52.00
Bowl, 10"			
☐ marigold	90.00	110.00	95.00
☐ blue	140.00	160.00	145.00
Pitcher			
☐ marigold	370.00	380.00	372.00
☐ blue	660.00	680.00	665.00
Tumbler			
☐ marigold	110.00	125.00	115.00
☐ blue	140.00	160.00	145.00

FENTON'S ARCHED FLUTE
Fenton

	Current Price Range		Prior Year Average
Toothpick Holder			
☐ marigold	70.00	80.00	72.00
☐ green	90.00	100.00	92.00
☐ ices	125.00	135.00	127.00

FENTON'S BASKET
Fenton

This pattern comes in a wide variety of sizes and shapes and is characterized by an openwork edge consisting of two or three rows. The body of the basket is in a basketweave pattern, and the colors used are marigold, green, blue, red, and various pastels.

	Current Price Range		Prior Year Average
Basket			
☐ marigold	30.00	40.00	32.00
☐ blue	35.00	45.00	37.00
☐ green	35.00	40.00	37.00
☐ ices	55.00	65.00	57.00
☐ red	260.00	280.00	270.00

FERN
Fenton

	Current Price Range		Prior Year Average
Bowl, 7"–9"			
☐ blue	800.00	—	—

FERN
Northwood

An interior pattern consisting of a series of ferns alternating with delicate branches growing out of the center. The rest of the interior body is clear of decoration, although usually the exterior contains some pattern. The colors are sharp and iridescent, and range widely.

	Current Price Range		Prior Year Average
Bowl, diameter 7″			
☐ marigold	22.00	28.00	24.00
☐ purple	35.00	44.00	37.00
☐ green	35.00	44.00	37.00
☐ blue	35.00	44.00	37.00
☐ amethyst	35.00	44.00	37.00
Bowl, diameter 8¼″			
☐ marigold	18.00	22.00	20.00
☐ purple	26.00	35.00	27.00
☐ green	26.00	35.00	27.00
☐ blue	26.00	35.00	27.00
☐ amethyst	26.00	35.00	27.00
☐ white	40.00	50.00	42.00
☐ ice blue	40.00	50.00	42.00
☐ ice green	40.00	50.00	42.00
Compote			
☐ marigold	14.00	17.00	15.00
☐ purple	18.00	23.00	19.00
☐ green	18.00	23.00	19.00
☐ blue	18.00	23.00	19.00
☐ amethyst	18.00	23.00	19.00
Hat			
☐ marigold	10.00	14.00	11.00
☐ purple	14.00	18.00	15.00
☐ green	14.00	18.00	15.00
☐ blue	14.00	18.00	15.00
☐ amethyst	14.00	18.00	15.00
☐ white	22.00	30.00	23.00
☐ ice blue	22.00	30.00	23.00
☐ ice green	22.00	30.00	23.00

FERN CHOCOLATES
Northwood

Plate			
☐ amethyst	170.00	180.00	172.00

FERN PANELS
Fenton

Wide delicate ferns decorate the interior sides of a hat-shaped bowl. The individual leaves grow wider as they reach the wide ruffled rim. Blue, green, red, and marigold are the usual colors.

	Current Price Range		Prior Year Average
Hat Shape			
☐ marigold	20.00	24.00	22.00
☐ blue	30.00	32.00	31.00
☐ green	30.00	32.00	31.00
☐ red...	115.00	135.00	120.00

FIELD FLOWER
Imperial

An overall pattern of incredible intricacy is achieved by a simple spray of stylized flowers with feathered foliage, framed by classical, architectural arches and filled in with a flat stippling. The colors are purple, green, and marigold.

Field Flower

	Current Price Range		Prior Year Average
Milk Pitcher			
☐ marigold	60.00	85.00	62.00
☐ purple	110.00	145.00	115.00
☐ green	110.00	145.00	115.00
☐ clambroth	200.00	—	—
☐ amethyst	110.00	145.00	115.00
Tumbler			
☐ marigold	22.00	28.00	24.00
☐ purple	42.00	52.00	44.00
☐ green	42.00	52.00	44.00
☐ blue	42.00	52.00	44.00
☐ amethyst	42.00	52.00	44.00
☐ amber	50.00	—	—
Water Pitcher			
☐ marigold	160.00	190.00	165.00
☐ purple	175.00	215.00	180.00
☐ green	175.00	215.00	180.00
☐ blue	175.00	215.00	180.00
☐ amethyst	175.00	215.00	180.00
☐ amber	350.00	—	—

FIELD THISTLE
U.S. Glass

An intaglio design of an overall pattern is created by swirling foliage radiating out to daisies and blooms with an impressionistic aura. The center medallion is a clear glass daisy, the color picked up with the circular foliage band. Marigold and green are the usual colors, and ice blue is known.

	Current Price Range		Prior Year Average
Butter Dish, lidded			
☐ marigold	65.00	85.00	70.00
Creamer			
☐ marigold	26.00	34.00	27.00
Plate, 6″			
☐ marigold	150.00	—	—
Plate, diameter 9″			
☐ marigold	150.00	200.00	175.00
Pitcher			
☐ marigold	175.00	225.00	180.00
Spooner			
☐ marigold	55.00	65.00	60.00
Sugar Bowl			
☐ marigold	26.00	34.00	28.00
Tumbler			
☐ marigold	40.00	50.00	42.00

FILE
Imperial

A delightful pattern formed by a series of rounded panels decorated by ridged files. The central band divides the two wide rows of files, consisting of pyramid-shaped jewels. The iridescence is excellent and golden; the colors are green, smoke, amethyst, and marigold.

	Current Price Range		Prior Year Average
Bowl, diameter 9″			
☐ marigold	18.00	23.00	20.00
☐ purple	25.00	35.00	27.00
☐ amethyst	25.00	35.00	27.00
Butter			
☐ marigold	195.00	—	—
Compote			
☐ marigold	18.00	23.00	20.00
☐ purple	25.00	35.00	27.00
☐ amethyst	25.00	35.00	27.00
Creamer			
☐ marigold	100.00	—	—
Spooner			
☐ marigold	100.00	—	—
Sugar			
☐ marigold	120.00	—	—
Tumbler			
☐ marigold	175.00	—	—
Vase			
☐ marigold	80.00	—	—
Water Pitcher			
☐ marigold	275.00	—	—

FILE AND FAN
Westmoreland

	Current Price Range		Prior Year Average
Bowl, 6″			
☐ marigold	35.00	45.00	37.00
☐ peach opalescent	50.00	60.00	52.00
Compote			
☐ aqua opalescent	95.00	105.00	97.00
☐ peach opalescent	180.00	—	—

FINE CUT AND ROSES
Northwood

A pleasing rose pattern with foliage in high relief is underscored with an interesting, diamond-etched band swirling up the sides in a reverse arc. The rose bowl is footed with clear stumpy glass, and the inwardly fluted rim resolves with opaque color. All the Northwood colors are represented.

	Current Price Range		Prior Year Average
Candy Dish, footed			
☐ marigold	28.00	36.00	50.00
☐ purple	60.00	80.00	70.00
☐ green	55.00	75.00	60.00
☐ blue	40.00	50.00	42.00
☐ amethyst	40.00	50.00	42.00
☐ white	130.00	160.00	145.00
☐ ice blue	50.00	65.00	54.00
Rose Bowl			
☐ marigold	45.00	65.00	50.00
☐ purple	60.00	80.00	70.00
☐ green	50.00	65.00	52.00
☐ blue	50.00	65.00	52.00
☐ amethyst	65.00	80.00	70.00
☐ white	90.00	115.00	95.00
☐ ice blue	90.00	115.00	95.00
☐ ice green	90.00	115.00	95.00
☐ aqua opalescent	500.00	600.00	550.00

FINE CUT FLOWER AND VARIANT, Pennsylvania Pattern
U.S. Glass

Compote			
☐ marigold	45.00	55.00	47.00
Goblet			
☐ marigold	45.00	55.00	47.00

FINECUT RINGS
Guggenheim, Ltd.

A prolific pattern on many shapes, the design is balanced and tasteful. A wide band of large rings rims these pieces just under the gently scalloped edge. They are of heavy ridges with a series of beadwork rows contained inside the rings. The rest of the body is decorated with a vertical pattern of alternate plain panels and beaded rows. Marigold is the only color produced.

	Current Price Range		Prior Year Average
Bowl, oval			
☐ marigold	30.00	35.00	32.00
Bowl, round			
☐ marigold	36.00	42.00	38.00
Butter Dish, covered			
☐ marigold	60.00	75.00	64.00
Cake Stand			
☐ marigold	50.00	60.00	52.00
Celery Dish			
☐ marigold	42.00	46.00	44.00
Creamer			
☐ marigold	60.00	62.00	61.00
Jam Jar			
☐ marigold	41.00	46.00	42.00
Sugar Bowl, lidded			
☐ marigold	42.00	48.00	43.00
Vase			
☐ marigold	45.00	60.00	46.00

FINE PRISMS AND DIAMONDS
English Manufacturer

A low wide band of elongated diamond trelliswork adorns the piece along the bottom near the base. The rest of the body is finely ridged with delicate prisms. The glass is heavy and the iridescence is good.

Vase, height 13½″			
☐ marigold	16.00	20.00	18.00
☐ purple	22.00	28.00	24.00
☐ blue	22.00	28.00	24.00
☐ green	22.00	28.00	24.00

FINE RIB
Northwood

A simple ribbed design of vertical ridges covers the exterior of these pieces, influencing the interior shape. The iridescence is excellent because the ripples refract the light. The colors are marigold, purple, and less commonly, green. Fenton also made a variation of this pattern, primarily in vases. The red vases are Fenton.

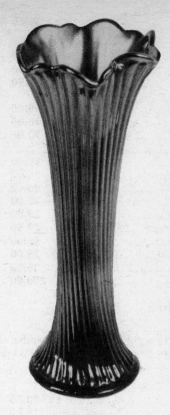

Fine Rib

	Current Price Range		Prior Year Average
Banana Dish			
☐ peach opalescent............................	60.00	75.00	62.00
Bowl, diameter 5″			
☐ purple, 5″	23.00	29.00	24.00
☐ green	23.00	29.00	24.00
☐ blue	23.00	29.00	24.00
☐ amethyst...	23.00	29.00	24.00
Bowl, diameter 10″			
☐ purple	45.00	65.00	48.00
☐ green	45.00	65.00	48.00
☐ blue	45.00	65.00	48.00
☐ amethyst...	45.00	65.00	48.00

	Current Price Range		Prior Year Average
Plate, diameter 8″			
☐ marigold	14.00	17.00	15.00
☐ purple	22.00	28.00	23.00
☐ amethyst	22.00	28.00	23.00
Plate, diameter 9″			
☐ marigold	55.00	65.00	56.00
☐ purple	70.00	95.00	72.00
☐ amethyst	70.00	95.00	72.00
Vase			
☐ marigold	16.00	20.00	18.00
☐ purple	25.00	34.00	26.00
☐ green	25.00	45.00	40.00
☐ blue	25.00	34.00	26.00
☐ amethyst	25.00	34.00	26.00
☐ aqua peach opalescent	27.50	37.00	30.00
☐ white	35.00	42.00	37.00
☐ ice blue	35.00	42.00	37.00
☐ ice green	35.00	42.00	37.00
☐ red	200.00	—	—

FISHERMAN'S MUG
Dugan

A fish rests in flowing water atop a lily pad on this classically shaped mug. The common colors are amethyst, marigold and purple, unusual in blue and peach opalescent.

	Current Price Range		Prior Year Average
Bowl			
☐ marigold	23.00	28.00	24.00
☐ purple	18.00	20.00	19.00
☐ amethyst	18.00	20.00	19.00
☐ peach opalescent	50.00	—	
☐ white	50.00	—	
Fisherman's Mug			
☐ marigold	180.00	220.00	185.00
☐ purple	90.00	120.00	95.00
☐ blue	90.00	120.00	95.00
☐ amethyst	90.00	120.00	95.00
☐ peach opalescent	650.00	850.00	675.00
Plate, diameter 7″			
☐ marigold	22.00	28.00	24.00
☐ purple	40.00	50.00	42.00
☐ white	80.00	—	—
☐ amethyst	40.00	50.00	42.00
☐ peach opalescent	60.00	75.00	65.00

FISH NET
Dugan

	Current Price Range		Prior Year Average
Epergne			
☐ purple	275.00	—	—
☐ peach opalescent...........................	325.00	—	—

FISH VASE

As intaglio design of wide panel ovals containing the fleur-de-lis, a stylized lily shape, adorns the long sides of these vases. The design is deeply engraved into the thick glass; the shape is concave. The colors are marigold and green.

	Current Price Range		Prior Year Average
Vase			
☐ marigold	90.00	100.00	95.00
☐ green	110.00	120.00	115.00
☐ amethyst......................................	110.00	120.00	115.00

FIVE HEARTS
Dugan

Stylized hearts are formed by swirling scrolls and filled in by stippling. Geometric fan shapes and diamonds form the outside band and dancing poppies are in the center of the hearts. The bottom of the connecting shapes form the central motif, a wide-petaled flower. Often seen in peach opalescent.

	Current Price Range		Prior Year Average
Bowl, domed, footed			
☐ purple	44.00	52.00	46.00
☐ marigold	40.00	—	—
☐ amethyst......................................	44.00	52.00	46.00
☐ peach opalescent...........................	50.00	65.00	52.00

FIVE LILY

	Current Price Range		Prior Year Average
Epergne			
☐ marigold	175.00	—	—
☐ purple	250.00	—	—

FLANNEL FLOWER
Crystal

	Current Price Range		Prior Year Average
Cake Plate, footed			
☐ marigold	110.00	130.00	115.00
☐ amethyst......................................	170.00	180.00	172.00

	Current Price Range		Prior Year Average

Compote
☐ marigold	85.00	95.00	87.00
☐ amethyst	135.00	145.00	137.00

FLEUR DE LIS
Jenkins

An excellent design of a fish swimming down the long side of the vase in a spiral. The fish is intricately molded with scales in high relief. The surrounding panels are frosted glass, an unusual technique on Carnival glass. The colors are marigold, green, and amethyst.

Vase
☐ green	180.00	200.00	190.00
☐ marigold	195.00	—	—

FLEUR DE LIS
Millersburg

The formal interior design of carefully placed fleur de lis is well balanced with alternating blossoms. The ridges are fluted in a sawtooth pattern, both the upper edge and on the base. It is seen in a wide range of colors.

Bowl, flat
☐ marigold	45.00	55.00	47.00
☐ purple	70.00	80.00	72.00
☐ green	70.00	80.00	72.00
☐ amethyst	70.00	80.00	72.00

Bowl, footed
☐ marigold	50.00	60.00	55.00
☐ purple	85.00	110.00	90.00
☐ green	85.00	110.00	90.00
☐ amethyst	200.00	300.00	250.00

FLORA

Bowl, shallow
☐ blue	80.00	90.00	82.00

FLORAL AND GRAPE
Dugan

A mass-produced design seen on many pieces, the pattern is an overall style of grapes and different blooms, all in high relief. The top band is a diagonally ridged bracelet broken here and there by blossoms. Colors are amethyst, marigold, cobalt, green, and rarely white. The Fenton version is called Floral and Grape Variant. The outer cords on the ribbon band are not as pronounced and the ridges run opposite of those on the Dugan version.

Floral and Grape

	Current Price Range		Prior Year Average
Pitcher			
☐ marigold	85.00	110.00	90.00
☐ purple	175.00	225.00	180.00
☐ blue	175.00	225.00	180.00
☐ amethyst	175.00	225.00	180.00
☐ white	300.00	400.00	350.00
Tumbler			
☐ marigold	22.00	28.00	24.00
☐ purple	20.00	30.00	25.00
☐ blue	32.00	40.00	34.00
☐ amethyst	32.00	40.00	34.00
☐ white	40.00	50.00	45.00

FLORAL AND GRAPE VARIANT
Fenton

	Current Price Range		Prior Year Average
Pitcher, two types			
☐ marigold	90.00	100.00	92.00
☐ blue	165.00	175.00	167.00
☐ amethyst	180.00	190.00	182.00
☐ green	185.00	195.00	187.00
Tumbler			
☐ marigold	25.00	35.00	27.00
☐ blue	25.00	35.00	28.00
☐ amethyst	30.00	40.00	32.00
☐ green	35.00	45.00	37.00

FLORAL AND OPTIC
Imperial

A simple design of wide panels topped with a band of curving branches and blossoms adorns these heavy glassed pieces. The colors range widely in almost all tints of Carnival glass.

	Current Price Range		Prior Year Average
Bowl, flat or footed			
☐ marigold	22.00	30.00	26.00
☐ celeste blue	30.00	—	—
☐ white	30.00	—	—
☐ smoke	30.00	—	—
☐ peach opalescent	165.00	—	—
☐ red	175.00	225.00	180.00
Cake Plate, footed			
☐ marigold	20.00	25.00	22.00
☐ celeste blue	28.00	—	—
☐ smoke	28.00	—	—
☐ red	28.00	—	—

FLORAL OVAL

	Current Price Range		Prior Year Average
Bowl, diameter 7½″			
☐ marigold	18.00	22.00	20.00
Creamer			
☐ marigold	40.00	50.00	42.00
Plate, diameter 7″			
☐ marigold	30.00	40.00	32.00
Sugar Bowl			
☐ marigold	30.00	40.00	32.00

FLORAL AND WHEAT
Dugan

	Current Price Range		Prior Year Average
Compote			
☐ marigold	14.00	16.00	15.00
☐ purple	22.00	27.00	23.00
☐ blue	22.00	27.00	23.00
☐ amethyst	22.00	27.00	23.00
☐ white	32.00	40.00	33.00
☐ peach opalescent	70.00	85.00	74.00

FLORENTINE
Fenton

	Current Price Range		Prior Year Average
Candlesticks, pair			
☐ marigold	75.00	85.00	78.00
☐ blue	110.00	120.00	112.00
☐ ices	130.00	140.00	132.00
☐ red	190.00	200.00	192.00

FLORENTINE
Imperial

	Current Price Range		Prior Year Average
Hat			
☐ ices	80.00	90.00	82.00

FLOWER AND BEADS

	Current Price Range		Prior Year Average
Plate, six-sided, 7½″			
☐ peach opalescent	100.00	—	—
☐ marigold	90.00	100.00	92.00
☐ amethyst	105.00	115.00	107.00
Plate, 8½″			
☐ marigold	70.00	80.00	72.00
☐ peach opalescent	90.00	—	—

FLOWER BASKET

	Current Price Range		Prior Year Average
Basket			
☐ marigold	45.00	55.00	47.00

FLOWER POT
Fenton

	Current Price Range		Prior Year Average
Container and Underplate			
☐ marigold	40.00	50.00	42.00

FLOWERING DILL
Fenton

Made in the hat shape, this exterior pattern is delicate and alive with blossoms in line art. It is an all over design, swirling and curving over the body to the wide fluted rim.

Hat Shape			
☐ marigold	14.00	18.00	16.00
☐ green	18.00	25.00	19.00
☐ blue	18.00	25.00	19.00
☐ red	250.00	—	—

FLOWERING VINE
Millersburg

An entangled vine of grape leaves and blooms covers the interior of these pieces until the rim ruffles out widely. The glass is radized and heavy. Colors are amethyst and green.

Compote			
☐ purple	325.00	375.00	340.00
☐ green	325.00	375.00	340.00
☐ amethyst	325.00	375.00	340.00

FLOWERS AND FRAMES
Dugan

The frames in question are arches of stippled glass, containing tall daisy-like flowers, also stippled. The upper rim is worked out into a squared ruffle and the base is plain. Colors are purple, green, marigold, and most commonly, peach opalescent.

Flowers and Frames

	Current Price Range		Prior Year Average
Bowl			
☐ marigold	20.00	30.00	24.00
☐ purple	40.00	50.00	42.00
☐ green	40.00	50.00	42.00
☐ peach opalescent	70.00	—	—
☐ white	85.00	—	—
☐ amethyst	40.00	50.00	42.00

FLOWERS AND SPADES
Dugan

	Current Price Range		Prior Year Average
Bowl, 5″			
☐ marigold	25.00	35.00	27.00
☐ amethyst	25.00	35.00	29.00
☐ green	30.00	40.00	32.00
☐ peach opalescent	30.00	40.00	34.00

	Current Price Range		Prior Year Average

Bowl, 10″

☐ marigold	40.00	50.00	42.00
☐ amethyst	75.00	85.00	78.00
☐ green	80.00	90.00	82.00
☐ peach opalescent	90.00	100.00	92.00

FLUFFY PEACOCK
Fenton

The high iridescence is the main feature on these pieces. They have a gold rainbow quality no matter what colors they are in. The design is long peacock feathers alternating with the figure of the birds prancing on the side. Colors are marigold, green, amethyst, and cobalt.

Pitcher

☐ marigold	375.00	450.00	400.00
☐ purple	425.00	500.00	450.00
☐ green	425.00	500.00	450.00
☐ blue	850.00	1000.00	875.00
☐ amethyst	425.00	500.00	450.00

Tumbler

☐ marigold	28.00	35.00	30.00
☐ purple	35.00	42.00	37.00
☐ green	35.00	42.00	37.00
☐ blue	70.00	90.00	72.00
☐ amethyst	35.00	42.00	37.00

FLUTE
English Manufacturer

A rather triangular series of flutes, wide at the top just below the plain rim and tapering toward the stem and pedestal base. The foot mimicks the panels with thumbprints. Color is marigold with a clear iridescence.

Compote

☐ marigold	37.50	40.00	39.00

FLUTE #3
Imperial

Wide fluted panels, similar to the Millersburg pattern make up the body of these pieces. The base is resolved by angular out sweeps mounted on a plain circular base. The glass is very heavy and the rim looks lipped, slightly pouting.

	Current Price Range		Prior Year Average
Bowl, diameter 5″			
☐ purple	62.00	72.00	65.00
☐ marigold	30.00	—	—
☐ amethyst	62.00	72.00	65.00
Bowl, diameter 10″			
☐ purple	190.00	225.00	200.00
☐ amethyst	190.00	225.00	200.00
Butter Dish, covered			
☐ marigold	170.00	200.00	190.00
☐ purple	195.00	225.00	200.00
☐ green	195.00	225.00	200.00
☐ amethyst	195.00	225.00	200.00
Celery Dish			
☐ purple	200.00	250.00	210.00
☐ amethyst	200.00	250.00	210.00
Creamer			
☐ marigold	80.00	90.00	85.00
☐ purple	90.00	100.00	95.00
☐ green	90.00	100.00	95.00
☐ amethyst	90.00	100.00	95.00
Pitcher			
☐ marigold	200.00	250.00	210.00
☐ purple	500.00	—	—
Punch Bowl, base			
☐ marigold	250.00	275.00	240.00
☐ purple	450.00	550.00	475.00
☐ green	450.00	550.00	475.00
☐ amethyst	450.00	550.00	475.00
Punch Cup			
☐ marigold	25.00	32.00	30.00
☐ purple	32.00	36.00	34.00
☐ green	32.00	36.00	34.00
☐ amethyst	32.00	36.00	34.00
Toothpick Holder, handled			
☐ marigold	50.00	70.00	52.00
☐ smoke	80.00	—	—
Toothpick Holder, unhandled			
☐ marigold	45.00	55.00	47.00
☐ purple	50.00	65.00	52.00
☐ green	50.00	65.00	52.00
☐ blue	50.00	65.00	52.00
☐ amethyst	50.00	65.00	52.00
☐ aqua	95.00	—	—

	Current Price Range		Prior Year Average
Tumbler			
☐ marigold	40.00	60.00	42.00
☐ purple	75.00	95.00	77.00
☐ green	75.00	95.00	77.00
☐ blue	75.00	95.00	77.00
☐ amethyst..	75.00	95.00	77.00

FLUTE

A series of thin flutes form sixteen panels on these pieces, resolved by creating the fluted upper edge. The glass is well colored, deep, and iridescent. It comes in a wide range of Millersburg colors.

	Current Price Range		Prior Year Average
Berry Bowl, diameter 10″			
☐ marigold	100.00	125.00	110.00
Berry Sauce Dish, diameter 5″			
☐ marigold	15.00	17.50	16.00
Bowl, diameter 4″			
☐ purple	38.00	42.00	40.00
☐ green	38.00	42.00	40.00
☐ blue	38.00	42.00	40.00
Creamer			
☐ marigold	45.00	55.00	48.00
☐ purple	65.00	85.00	40.00
☐ green	65.00	85.00	40.00
☐ blue	65.00	85.00	40.00
Punch Bowl			
☐ marigold	150.00	200.00	160.00
☐ purple	210.00	225.00	240.00
☐ green	210.00	225.00	240.00
☐ blue	210.00	225.00	240.00
☐ amethyst..	210.00	225.00	240.00
Punch Cup			
☐ marigold	17.00	22.00	18.00
☐ purple	23.00	28.00	24.00
☐ green	23.00	28.00	24.00
☐ blue	23.00	28.00	24.00
☐ amethyst..	23.00	28.00	24.00
Sugar Bowl, covered			
☐ marigold	45.00	65.00	50.00
☐ purple	70.00	75.00	72.00
☐ green	70.00	75.00	72.00
☐ blue	70.00	75.00	72.00
☐ amethyst..	70.00	75.00	72.00

FLUTE
Northwood

A prolific design on many pieces, the wide panels are made up of ridged flutes or arched designs. It is simple but effective because of the way the slightly concave panels refract the iridescence. It comes in the complete range of Northwood colors.

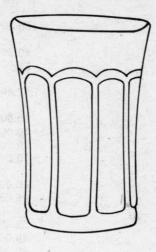

Flute

	Current Price Range		Prior Year Average
Bowl, diameter 5″			
☐ purple	30.00	38.00	32.00
☐ green	30.00	38.00	32.00
☐ marigold	30.00	38.00	32.00
☐ amethyst	30.00	38.00	32.00
Bowl, diameter 10″			
☐ purple	55.00	62.00	57.00
☐ green	55.00	62.00	57.00
☐ marigold	55.00	62.00	57.00
☐ amethyst	55.00	62.00	57.00
Butter Dish			
☐ marigold	120.00	—	—
☐ green	175.00	—	—

	Current Price Range		Prior Year Average

Creamer
☐ marigold	30.00	40.00	32.00
☐ green	70.00	85.00	75.00
☐ amethyst	70.00	85.00	75.00

Pitcher
☐ marigold	350.00	400.00	375.00
☐ purple	475.00	525.00	400.00
☐ green	475.00	525.00	400.00
☐ amethyst	475.00	525.00	400.00

Ring Tree
☐ marigold	150.00	165.00	160.00

Salt Dip, footed
☐ marigold	30.00	40.00	34.00
☐ vaseline	55.00	70.00	—

Sherbet
☐ marigold	17.00	38.00	18.00

Spooner
☐ marigold	30.00	40.00	32.00
☐ purple	70.00	85.00	74.00
☐ green	70.00	85.00	74.00
☐ amethyst	70.00	85.00	74.00

Sugar Bowl
☐ marigold	40.00	50.00	42.00
☐ green	85.00	95.00	90.00

Tumbler
☐ marigold	22.00	28.00	23.00
☐ purple	40.00	50.00	42.00
☐ amethyst	40.00	50.00	42.00

FLUTE AND CANE
Imperial

Goblet
☐ marigold	30.00	40.00	32.00

Milk Pitcher
☐ marigold	80.00	110.00	90.00

Wine Glass
☐ marigold	22.00	28.00	27.00

FLUTED SCROLL
Dugan

Rose Bowl
☐ amethyst	900.00	1000.00	925.00

FLYING BAT

	Current Price Range		Prior Year Average

Hat pin

☐ marigold	35.00	—	—
☐ purple	55.00	—	—
☐ green	55.00	—	—

FOLDING FAN

Compote

☐ purple	30.00	38.00	35.00
☐ peach opalescent	120.00	—	—
☐ aqua opalescent	200.00	—	—
☐ blue	30.00	38.00	35.00
☐ amethyst	30.00	38.00	35.00

FOOTED DRAPE
Westmoreland

Vase

☐ marigold	35.00	45.00	37.00
☐ pearl ice	45.00	55.00	47.00

FOOTED PRISMS
Sowerly

Spear-like prisms are filled with cut glass flowers and alternate with smooth, glossy inverted panels. The upper rim is triangle flutes, tall and sharp. The bottom base is clear paneled, following the glass panels. The color is marigold with a clear iridescence.

Vase

☐ marigold	32.50	45.00	34.00
☐ blue	85.00	—	—
☐ green	75.00	—	—

FOOTED SHELL
Westmoreland

Sweeping flutes ridging the entire body of this shell motif resolve in a feathery rim. The body is footed. Iridescence gleams on the inside sweep. The colors are green, blue, marigold, and amethyst.

Shell Shape, large

☐ marigold	20.00	26.00	22.00
☐ green	20.00	26.00	22.00
☐ blue	20.00	26.00	22.00
☐ amethyst	20.00	26.00	22.00
☐ peach opalescent	100.00	—	—

	Current Price Range		Prior Year Average

Shell Shape, miniature

☐ marigold	45.00	52.00	47.00
☐ green	45.00	52.00	47.00
☐ blue	45.00	52.00	47.00
☐ amethyst	45.00	52.00	47.00
☐ amber	70.00	—	—

FORKS
Cambridge

A grass rake is a closer description for this geometric pattern resembling cut glass. The molding is excellent, with the outward sweep of the V-form cuts deeply into the design. A band of star medallions creates the middle motif and continues down to the base. The colors are green, amethyst, and marigold.

Jar

☐ green	400.00	—	—

FORMAL
Dugan

The pattern is a chain alternating with a beadwork panel ending with a horizontal band of circles in high relief. The base is etched with a geometric design and the body has a flower-shaped rim. The colors are purple, marigold, and other pastels.

Jack in the Pulpit Vase

☐ marigold	40.00	50.00	42.00
☐ purple	52.00	65.00	55.00
☐ white	150.00	—	—

Hatpin Holder

☐ marigold	175.00	—	—
☐ purple	160.00	—	—

FORTY NINER
Imperial

Decanter

☐ marigold	120.00	130.00	122.00

Pitcher

☐ marigold	245.00	255.00	247.00

Tumbler

☐ marigold	70.00	80.00	72.00

Wine Goblet

☐ marigold	45.00	55.00	47.00

FOSTORIA #600

	Current Price Range		Prior Year Average
Napkin Ring			
☐ marigold	70.00	80.00	72.00

FOSTORIA #1231
Fostoria

Rose Bowl			
☐ white.............................	95.00	110.00	98.00

FOSTORIA #1299
Fostoria

Tumbler			
☐ marigold	70.00	80.00	72.00

FOUR FLOWERS
Dugan

Bowl, 6¼″			
☐ purple	35.00	—	—
☐ green	45.00	—	—
☐ blue	65.00	—	—
☐ peach opalescent...........................	60.00	—	—
Bowl, 10″			
☐ purple	65.00	—	—
☐ green	70.00	—	—
☐ blue	90.00	—	—
☐ peach opalescent...........................	85.00	—	—
Chop Plate			
☐ purple	700.00	—	—
☐ green	250.00	—	—
☐ peach opalescent...........................	475.00	—	—
Plate, 6½″			
☐ purple	70.00	—	—
☐ peach opalescent...........................	90.00	—	—
Plate, 10½″			
☐ green	650.00	—	—

FOUR FLOWERS VARIANT
Westmoreland

	Current Price Range		Prior Year Average
Bowl, footed, 8½"			
☐ amethyst......................................	65.00	75.00	67.00
☐ green	70.00	80.00	72.00
☐ teal...	95.00	110.00	97.00
Bowl, 9"			
☐ marigold	40.00	50.00	42.00
☐ amethyst......................................	55.00	65.00	57.00
☐ green	60.00	70.00	62.00
☐ peach opalescent..........................	65.00	75.00	67.00
☐ teal...	85.00	95.00	87.00
Bowl, 11"			
☐ marigold	40.00	50.00	42.00
☐ amethyst......................................	55.00	65.00	57.00
☐ green	60.00	70.00	62.00
☐ peach opalescent..........................	65.00	75.00	67.00
☐ teal...	85.00	95.00	87.00
Plate, 10½"			
☐ peach opalescent..........................	390.00	410.00	395.00
☐ smoke...	390.00	410.00	395.00
☐ amethyst......................................	640.00	675.00	645.00
☐ green	650.00	—	—

FOUR SEVENTY-FOUR
Imperial

The pattern covers the surface of the piece, the central motif is a large stately flower on a heavy stalk with willowy leaves. It is framed by heavy broken arches that interlock, forming spears that contain sunbursts and flowers. The colors are green, marigold, and amethyst.

Four Seventy-four

	Current Price Range		Prior Year Average
Butter Dish			
☐ marigold	85.00	110.00	90.00
☐ purple	160.00	200.00	170.00
☐ green	160.00	200.00	170.00
☐ amethyst	160.00	200.00	170.00
Milk Pitcher			
☐ marigold	85.00	110.00	90.00
☐ purple	325.00	400.00	350.00
☐ green	325.00	400.00	350.00
☐ amethyst	325.00	400.00	350.00
Pitcher			
☐ marigold	140.00	170.00	145.00
☐ purple	420.00	500.00	450.00
☐ green	420.00	500.00	450.00
☐ amethyst	420.00	500.00	450.00

	Current Price Range		Prior Year Average
Punch Bowl, two pieces			
☐ marigold	110.00	140.00	115.00
☐ purple	400.00	500.00	450.00
☐ green	400.00	500.00	450.00
☐ amethyst	400.00	500.00	450.00
Punch Cup			
☐ marigold	14.00	17.00	16.00
☐ purple	22.00	28.00	24.00
☐ green	22.00	28.00	24.00
☐ amethyst	22.00	28.00	24.00
Tumbler			
☐ marigold	32.00	38.00	34.00
☐ purple	70.00	100.00	75.00
☐ green	70.00	100.00	75.00
☐ amethyst	70.00	100.00	75.00

FRENCH KNOTS
Fenton

The overall design of flowers and foliage is spread out nicely, the background a shiny smooth glass. The hat shape of a tall straight base and wide ruffled rim is typically Fenton. The colors are marigold and blue.

	Current Price Range		Prior Year Average
Hat Shape			
☐ marigold	12.50	17.00	15.00
☐ blue	18.00	25.00	19.00
☐ purple	35.00	—	—

FROLICKING BEARS

A sought-after pattern for good reason. Roly-poly bears play on a field with fir trees in the background and mountains in the distance. An upper band of grapes and berries adorns the rim of the piece as well as around the base. The iridescence is unsurpassed, the color is dark, deep green, the price commanded higher than any other piece of Carnival glass.

	Current Price Range		Prior Year Average
Pitcher			
☐ green	7500.00	8200.00	7800.00
Tumbler			
☐ green	4000.00	6500.00	4200.00

FROSTED BLOCK
Imperial

An excellent paneled pattern of stippled glass separated into panels by beadwork columns. It comes in a wide realm of shapes and the colors are marigold and a lovely, pearly clambroth.

	Current Price Range		Prior Year Average

Bowl, diameter 8″
| ☐ marigold | 12.00 | 17.00 | 13.00 |
| ☐ clambroth | 32.00 | — | — |

Butter Dish, lidded
| ☐ marigold | 40.00 | 50.00 | 42.00 |
| ☐ clambroth | 45.00 | — | — |

Creamer
| ☐ marigold | 18.00 | 23.00 | 19.00 |

Plate, diameter 9″
| ☐ marigold | 22.00 | 28.00 | 24.00 |

Rose Bowl
| ☐ marigold | 32.00 | 40.00 | 33.00 |

Spooner
| ☐ marigold | 18.00 | 23.00 | 20.00 |

FROSTED BUTTONS

Bowl, large footed
| ☐ white | 100.00 | 150.00 | 110.00 |

FROSTED RIBBON

Pitcher
| ☐ marigold | 50.00 | 70.00 | 52.00 |

Tumbler
| ☐ marigold | 12.00 | 18.00 | 14.00 |

FRUIT AND BERRIES
English

Casserole, covered
| ☐ marigold | 240.00 | 260.00 | 245.00 |
| ☐ blue | 265.00 | 285.00 | 270.00 |

FRUIT BASKET
Millersburg

Compote, with handle
| ☐ amethyst | 990.00 | 1100.00 | 995.00 |

FRUIT LUSTER

Pitcher
| ☐ marigold | 55.00 | 75.00 | 60.00 |

Tumbler
| ☐ marigold | 12.00 | 17.00 | 14.00 |

FRUIT SALAD
Westmoreland

This pattern adorns a punch bowl set on a regal, massive pedestal and cups of the same style. Pineapples, grapes, apples, and other fruits are spaced in an overall design in high relief and great detail. A connecting band of vines intertwines the motifs and unifies the design. The colors are amethyst, marigold and peach opalescent.

	Current Price Range		Prior Year Average
Punch Bowl, with base			
☐ marigold	450.00	535.00	460.00
☐ purple	475.00	575.00	500.00
☐ peach opalescent...........................	2500.00	—	—
☐ amethyst.......................................	475.00	575.00	500.00
Punch Cup			
☐ marigold	20.00	30.00	25.00
☐ purple	27.50	35.00	30.00
☐ amethyst.......................................	27.50	35.00	30.00
☐ peach opalescent...........................	40.00	—	—

FRUITS AND FLOWERS
Northwood

An overall pattern of fruit, including grapes and berries, is interspersed among blossoms, with well-detailed foliage. The pattern covers the interior, with a basketweave exterior. The rim is modified sawtooth. Several Northwood colors are represented.

Berry Bowl, diameter 9″			
☐ marigold	40.00	50.00	42.00
☐ purple	35.00	47.00	37.00
☐ green	35.00	47.00	37.00
☐ blue	35.00	47.00	37.00
☐ amethyst.......................................	35.00	47.00	37.00
☐ white..	50.00	70.00	55.00
☐ ice blue	50.00	70.00	55.00
☐ ice green	50.00	70.00	55.00
Bowl, footed, diameter 10″			
☐ marigold	22.00	28.00	24.00
☐ purple	32.00	40.00	36.00
☐ amethyst.......................................	32.00	40.00	36.00
☐ aqua opalescent	90.00	125.00	95.00

	Current Price Range		Prior Year Average
Plate, diameter 7″			
☐ marigold	30.00	38.00	32.00
☐ purple	55.00	70.00	58.00
☐ green	55.00	70.00	58.00
☐ blue	55.00	70.00	58.00
☐ amethyst	55.00	70.00	84.00
☐ white	80.00	115.00	84.00
Plate, diameter 8″			
☐ marigold	40.00	50.00	42.00
☐ purple	75.00	100.00	80.00
☐ green	75.00	100.00	80.00
☐ blue	75.00	100.00	80.00
☐ amethyst	75.00	100.00	80.00
☐ white	100.00	130.00	110.00
☐ ice blue	100.00	130.00	110.00
☐ ice green	100.00	130.00	110.00
Plate, diameter 9″			
☐ marigold	50.00	70.00	55.00
☐ purple	65.00	85.00	70.00
☐ green	65.00	85.00	70.00
☐ blue	65.00	85.00	70.00
☐ amethyst	65.00	85.00	70.00

GARDEN MUMS

Bowl, diameter 5″			
☐ marigold	20.00	30.00	25.00
☐ purple	35.00	40.00	37.00
☐ green	35.00	40.00	37.00
☐ blue	35.00	40.00	37.00
☐ amethyst	35.00	40.00	37.00
Bowl, diameter 9″			
☐ marigold	20.00	30.00	25.00
☐ purple	35.00	40.00	37.00
☐ green	35.00	40.00	37.00
☐ blue	35.00	40.00	37.00
☐ amethyst	35.00	40.00	37.00
Plate, diameter 7″			
☐ marigold	40.00	50.00	42.00
☐ purple	65.00	85.00	67.00
☐ green	65.00	85.00	67.00
☐ blue	65.00	85.00	67.00
☐ amethyst	65.00	85.00	67.00

GARDEN PATH

A medieval star with six kite-shaped rays forms the central medallion and is mimicked by the rest of the intricate overall pattern. Made of ridging and beadwork, the large heraldic rays are arranged in a wide band from the center to the rim. The mold work is excellent, the glass heavy. The rare variant is one of the most expensive pieces in Carnival glass.

	Current Price Range		Prior Year Average
Bowl, diameter 9″			
☐ marigold	30.00	40.00	35.00
☐ purple	50.00	65.00	55.00
☐ white	85.00	—	—
☐ amethyst	50.00	65.00	55.00
☐ white	85.00	—	—
Compote			
☐ marigold	22.00	28.00	24.00
☐ purple	40.00	50.00	42.00
☐ amethyst	40.00	50.00	42.00
☐ white	60.00	75.00	62.00

GARDEN PATH VARIANT
Dugan

	Current Price Range		Prior Year Average
Bowl, 9″			
☐ peach opalescent	60.00	70.00	62.00
Bowl, 10″			
☐ amethyst	350.00	375.00	355.00
☐ peach opalescent	390.00	400.00	395.00
Plate, 11″			
☐ amethyst	65.00	75.00	67.00
☐ peach opalescent	3000.00	—	—
Variant Chop Plate, diameter 11″			
☐ purple	1350.00	1650.00	1450.00

GARLAND
Fenton

The overriding pattern is a filler of oval knobs almost resembling maile on armor. The garland is comprised of foliage and flowers and is twisted into a wreath. The colors are green, marigold, and amethyst.

	Current Price Range		Prior Year Average
Rose Bowl			
☐ marigold	32.00	40.00	34.00
☐ purple	50.00	60.00	52.00
☐ amethyst	50.00	60.00	52.00

GAY 90s
Millersburg

Considered to be among the most finely crafted water sets ever made, Gay 90s has a well-balanced geometrical pattern and a wonderfully detailed finish. The design resembles a dropping curtain, covering the body from the snug waist to just above the base. The rest of the glass is smooth and glossy, showing off the incredible iridescence achieved in spite of its transparency.

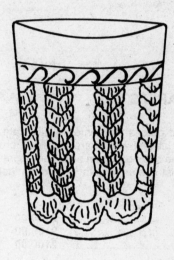

Gay 90s

	Current Price Range		Prior Year Average
Pitcher			
☐ purple	4000.00	6000.00	4100.00
☐ green	4000.00	6000.00	4100.00
☐ amethyst	4000.00	6000.00	4100.00
Tumbler			
☐ marigold	450.00	550.00	460.00
☐ purple	425.00	525.00	450.00
☐ amethyst	425.00	525.00	450.00

GEORGIA BELLE
Dugan

	Current Price Range		Prior Year Average
Compote			
☐ marigold	32.00	40.00	36.00
☐ purple	40.00	52.00	42.00
☐ green	40.00	52.00	42.00
☐ peach opalescent........................	80.00	—	—
☐ amethyst...................................	40.00	52.00	42.00

GOD AND HOME
Dugan

Pitcher			
☐ blue	1000.00	1300.00	1050.00

GODDESS OF HARVEST
Fenton

The lovely lady that graces the center of this plate has hair made up of flowers, foliage, and leaves. Her sharply molded profile is framed with a serpentine chain of fine ridging with an occasional spray of flowers to balance the design. Colors exist in blue, amethyst, and marigold.

Bowl			
☐ purple	2100.00	3000.00	2200.00
☐ green	2100.00	3000.00	2200.00
☐ blue	2100.00	3000.00	2200.00

GOLDEN CUPID
Australian Manufacturer

The well-detailed little cupid floats in the center of these small dishes. His clothes are draped in an utterly artistic way and his wings are intricately scaled. The outer rim is a stretched out triangle chain and the edge is gently scalloped. The clear glass has an excellent iridescence.

Plate, diameter 5¼″			
☐ clear with gold.............................	40.00	60.00	45.00
Plate, diameter 9″			
☐ clear with gold.............................	80.00	90.00	82.00

GOLDEN FLOWERS

Vase			
☐ marigold	30.00	40.00	34.00

GOLDEN GRAPE
Dugan

A well molded pattern of alternating leaves and grapes, both large and equally dominant. The band is playfully framed by a meandering vine. The rest of the body is smooth but the pattern is followed by the long flutes on the rim.

	Current Price Range		Prior Year Average
Bowl, diameter 7"			
☐ marigold	24.00	32.00	26.00
☐ purple	28.00	36.00	30.00
☐ green	28.00	36.00	30.00
☐ amethyst	28.00	36.00	30.00
Rose Bowl			
☐ marigold	30.00	50.00	40.00
☐ white	45.00	55.00	47.00
☐ ice blue	45.00	55.00	47.00
☐ ice green	45.00	55.00	47.00

GOLDEN HARVEST
U.S. Glass

An overall pattern of a stylized wheat sheaf, starts out naturalistically and emanates into a fountain of geometrical shapes. This alternates with bunches of grapes in high relief.

Wine Decanter			
☐ marigold	90.00	120.00	100.00
☐ purple	220.00	280.00	225.00
☐ amethyst	220.00	280.00	225.00
Wine Glass, stemmed			
☐ marigold	27.00	37.00	30.00
☐ purple	32.00	38.00	35.00
☐ amethyst	32.00	38.00	35.00

GOLDEN HONEYCOMB
Imperial

Reminiscent of the coin dot pattern, this design covers the piece with row after row of squared off circles resembling a honeycomb. The large central medallion is a starburst that covers the base. It is a deep marigold and the iridescence is successfully refracted by the honeycombs.

	Current Price Range		Prior Year Average

Bon Bon, diameter 5″
☐ marigold 42.00   50.00   44.00

Bowl, diameter 5″
☐ marigold 12.50   17.00   13.00

Compote
☐ marigold 17.00   20.00   19.00

Creamer
☐ marigold 27.00   32.00   30.00

Plate, diameter 7″
☐ marigold 22.50   30.00   28.00

Sugar Bowl
☐ marigold 27.00   32.00   28.00

GOLDEN OXEN

Mug
☐ marigold 40.00   50.00   42.00

GOLDEN WEDDING

Bottle
☐ marigold 15.00   20.00   16.00

GOOD LUCK
Northwood

The dominant theme on this piece is the inscription with the horseshoe-shaped with stippled glass. Surrounding this central medallion is a wreath of flowers and foliage that meanders toward the rim which is ruffled sharply. The pattern is prolific and comes in the full range of Carnival glass colors.

Bowl, diameter 9″
☐ marigold 60.00   75.00   65.00
☐ purple 100.00   130.00   110.00
☐ green 100.00   130.00   110.00
☐ blue 100.00   130.00   110.00
☐ amethyst... 100.00   130.00   110.00
☐ ice blue 400.00   500.00   425.00
☐ aqua opalescent 475.00   575.00   500.00
☐ white.. 600.00   —   —
☐ ice green .... 750.00   —   —

	Current Price Range		Prior Year Average

Plate, diameter 9″
☐ marigold	110.00	140.00	115.00
☐ purple	165.00	200.00	175.00
☐ green	165.00	200.00	175.00
☐ blue	165.00	200.00	175.00
☐ amethyst	165.00	200.00	175.00
☐ white	220.00	275.00	225.00
☐ ice blue	220.00	275.00	225.00
☐ ice green	220.00	275.00	225.00

GOOD LUCK VARIANT
Northwood

Bowl, 9″
☐ marigold	225.00	—	—
☐ purple	275.00	—	—
☐ green	275.00	—	—

GOOSEBERRY SPRAY
U.S. Glass

Berry Bowl, diameter 5″
| ☐ marigold | 22.00 | 28.00 | 24.00 |
| ☐ white | 42.00 | 55.00 | 44.00 |

Berry Bowl, diameter 9″
| ☐ marigold | 26.00 | 32.00 | 28.00 |
| ☐ white | 46.00 | 52.00 | 47.00 |

Compote
| ☐ white | 130.00 | 140.00 | 125.00 |

GRACEFUL
Northwood

This is a simple, classic pattern of a wide central band of ridges, running around the waist of the piece terminating on the gently paneled base. The rim begins at the top of the ridging, swooping out in a wide ruffle. The colors most often seen are emerald green and deep purple.

Vase
☐ marigold	45.00	55.00	47.00
☐ green	80.00	95.00	85.00
☐ purple	80.00	95.00	85.00
☐ white	85.00	90.00	85.00

GRAND THISTLE
Sweden

	Current Price Range		Prior Year Average
Pitcher			
☐ blue	1700.00	1900.00	1750.00
Tumbler			
☐ blue	540.00	560.00	545.00
Berry Bowl, diameter 5″			
☐ marigold	11.00	14.00	12.00
☐ purple	22.00	30.00	23.00
☐ green	22.00	30.00	23.00
☐ smoke	22.00	30.00	23.00

GRAPE
Imperial

	Current Price Range		Prior Year Average
Berry Bowl, diameter 10″			
☐ marigold	22.00	30.00	23.00
☐ purple	36.00	40.00	37.00
☐ green	36.00	40.00	37.00
☐ smoke	36.00	40.00	37.00
Compote			
☐ marigold	22.00	26.00	24.00
☐ green	32.00	36.00	35.00
☐ purple	32.00	36.00	35.00
☐ amethyst.......................................	32.00	36.00	35.00
Cup and Saucer			
☐ marigold	50.00	60.00	52.00
☐ green	70.00	75.00	72.00
☐ smoke	60.00	—	—
Cuspidor			
☐ marigold	600.00	750.00	620.00
☐ green	600.00	750.00	620.00
Goblet			
☐ marigold	25.00	35.00	30.00
☐ amber	70.00	—	—
☐ smoke	70.00	—	—
☐ green	58.00	65.00	60.00
☐ purple	58.00	65.00	60.00
☐ amethyst.......................................	58.00	65.00	60.00
Pitcher			
☐ marigold	100.00	120.00	110.00
☐ purple	225.00	260.00	230.00
☐ green	225.00	260.00	230.00
☐ amethyst.......................................	225.00	260.00	230.00
☐ smoke	335.00	370.00	340.00

	Current Price Range		Prior Year Average
Punch Bowl			
☐ marigold	135.00	150.00	145.00
☐ purple	185.00	220.00	200.00
☐ green	185.00	220.00	200.00
☐ smoke	185.00	—	—
☐ amber	400.00	—	—
☐ amethyst	185.00	220.00	200.00
Punch Cup			
☐ marigold	17.00	20.00	19.00
☐ purple	20.00	24.00	22.00
☐ green	20.00	24.00	22.00
☐ amber	35.00	—	—
☐ amethyst	20.00	24.00	22.00
☐ smoke	20.00	24.00	22.00
Shade			
☐ marigold	35.00	40.00	37.00
Tumbler			
☐ marigold	16.00	20.00	18.00
☐ purple	45.00	52.00	47.00
☐ green	45.00	52.00	47.00
☐ amber	60.00	—	—
☐ smoke	50.00	—	—
☐ amethyst	45.00	52.00	47.00
Water Bottle			
☐ marigold	90.00	110.00	95.00
☐ purple	125.00	140.00	130.00
☐ green	170.00	—	—
☐ clambroth	200.00	—	—
Wine Decanter			
☐ marigold	38.00	46.00	40.00
☐ purple	85.00	96.00	90.00
☐ green	85.00	96.00	90.00
☐ amethyst	85.00	96.00	90.00
Wine Glass			
☐ marigold	20.00	24.00	22.00
☐ purple	26.00	30.00	28.00
☐ green	26.00	30.00	28.00
☐ amethyst	26.00	30.00	28.00

GRAPE AND CABLE
Fenton

The cable is a reverse diagonal series of ridges, curving up and down just below the rim, and is intertwined with delicate grapevines. Attached to this vining is vertical bunches of heavy grapes alternating with big-veined leaves.

The upper edge follows the meandering vine. Colors come in amethyst, marigold, green, blue, and red.

Grape and Cable (Fenton)

	Current Price Range		Prior Year Average
Bowl, diameter 7″			
☐ marigold	50.00	60.00	55.00
☐ purple	35.00	45.00	36.00
☐ green	35.00	45.00	36.00
☐ blue	35.00	45.00	36.00
☐ amethyst	35.00	45.00	36.00
☐ red	350.00	400.00	375.00
Bowl, flat or footed			
☐ marigold	120.00	150.00	125.00
☐ purple	170.00	215.00	175.00
☐ green	170.00	215.00	175.00
☐ blue	170.00	215.00	175.00
☐ amethyst	170.00	215.00	175.00
☐ aqua opalescent	800.00	—	—
☐ red	450.00	—	—
Orange Bowl			
☐ marigold	85.00	110.00	90.00
☐ purple	130.00	170.00	135.00
☐ green	130.00	170.00	135.00
☐ blue	130.00	170.00	135.00
☐ amethyst	130.00	170.00	135.00

	Current Price Range		Prior Year Average
Plate, footed			
☐ marigold	50.00	65.00	55.00
☐ purple	65.00	85.00	70.00
☐ green	65.00	85.00	70.00
☐ blue	65.00	85.00	70.00
☐ amethyst......................................	65.00	85.00	70.00
☐ red..	300.00	400.00	310.00

GRAPE AND CABLE
Northwood

The moldwork is superior in high relief. Bunches of grapes form the center, raised so that almost three-quarters of their round little bodies are exposed. The surrounding leaves are sharp and detailed with veins. The base band is formed by concave coin dots alternating with teardrop shapes. The edges, when fluted, are in a sawtooth pattern. The colors range in all of the Northwood tints.

Grape and Cable (Northwood)

	Current Price Range		Prior Year Average

Banana Boat, footed, diameter 12″

☐ marigold	100.00	150.00	125.00
☐ purple	250.00	300.00	275.00
☐ green	250.00	300.00	275.00
☐ blue	250.00	300.00	275.00
☐ amethyst	225.00	275.00	250.00
☐ white	300.00	400.00	370.00
☐ ice blue	300.00	400.00	370.00
☐ ice green	300.00	400.00	370.00

Berry Bowl, diameter 5″

☐ marigold	14.00	18.00	15.00
☐ purple	22.00	28.00	24.00
☐ green	22.00	28.00	24.00
☐ amethyst	22.00	28.00	24.00
☐ white	40.00	50.00	42.00
☐ ice blue	40.00	50.00	42.00
☐ ice green	40.00	50.00	42.00

Berry Bowl, diameter 10″

☐ marigold	70.00	100.00	85.00
☐ purple	55.00	75.00	60.00
☐ green	55.00	75.00	60.00
☐ blue	55.00	75.00	60.00
☐ amethyst	55.00	75.00	60.00
☐ white	90.00	110.00	95.00
☐ ice blue	90.00	110.00	95.00
☐ ice green	90.00	110.00	95.00

Bowl, scalloped edge, diameter 7″

☐ marigold	35.00	45.00	37.00
☐ purple	62.00	80.00	65.00
☐ green	62.00	80.00	65.00
☐ blue	62.00	80.00	65.00
☐ amethyst	62.00	80.00	65.00
☐ white	75.00	95.00	80.00
☐ ice blue	75.00	95.00	80.00
☐ ice green	75.00	95.00	80.00

Bowl, footed, diameter 8¼″

☐ marigold	45.00	65.00	50.00
☐ purple	42.00	49.00	45.00
☐ green	42.00	49.00	45.00
☐ blue	42.00	49.00	45.00
☐ amethyst	42.00	49.00	45.00

Breakfast Set

☐ marigold	75.00	100.00	80.00
☐ purple	125.00	175.00	150.00

	Current Price Range		Prior Year Average
☐ green	90.00	140.00	95.00
☐ amethyst	90.00	140.00	95.00
Butter Dish			
☐ marigold	140.00	175.00	150.00
☐ purple	100.00	130.00	115.00
☐ green	140.00	185.00	145.00
☐ amethyst	140.00	185.00	145.00
☐ white	200.00	250.00	210.00
☐ ice blue	200.00	250.00	210.00
☐ ice green	200.00	250.00	210.00
Candle Lamp			
☐ marigold	80.00	110.00	85.00
☐ purple	120.00	155.00	130.00
☐ green	120.00	155.00	130.00
☐ amethyst	120.00	155.00	130.00
Candlesticks, pair			
☐ marigold	150.00	190.00	160.00
☐ purple	230.00	290.00	240.00
☐ green	230.00	290.00	240.00
☐ amethyst	230.00	290.00	240.00
Centerpiece, footed			
☐ marigold	250.00	325.00	260.00
☐ purple	340.00	420.00	350.00
☐ green	340.00	420.00	350.00
☐ amethyst	340.00	420.00	350.00
☐ white	450.00	550.00	460.00
☐ ice blue	450.00	550.00	460.00
☐ ice green	450.00	550.00	460.00
Compote, large, lidded			
☐ marigold	1800.00	2250.00	1900.00
☐ purple	300.00	400.00	310.00
☐ amethyst	475.00	525.00	500.00
Compote, large, unlidded			
☐ marigold	400.00	500.00	425.00
☐ purple	320.00	375.00	340.00
☐ blue	320.00	375.00	340.00
☐ amethyst	320.00	375.00	340.00
☐ white	550.00	650.00	575.00
☐ ice blue	550.00	650.00	575.00
☐ ice green	550.00	650.00	575.00
Cookie Jar			
☐ marigold	175.00	220.00	190.00
☐ purple	150.00	200.00	175.00

	Current Price Range		Prior Year Average
☐ green	220.00	280.00	225.00
☐ blue	220.00	280.00	225.00
☐ amethyst	220.00	280.00	225.00
☐ white	500.00	600.00	525.00
☐ ice blue	500.00	600.00	525.00
☐ ice green	500.00	600.00	525.00
☐ aqua opalescent	2500.00	3000.00	2750.00
Creamer			
☐ marigold	50.00	60.00	55.00
☐ purple	70.00	85.00	75.00
☐ green	70.00	85.00	75.00
☐ blue	70.00	85.00	75.00
☐ amethyst	225.00	275.00	250.00
☐ white	110.00	140.00	115.00
☐ ice blue	110.00	140.00	115.00
☐ ice green	110.00	140.00	115.00
Cup And Saucer			
☐ marigold	130.00	170.00	140.00
☐ purple	135.00	175.00	150.00
☐ ice blue	245.00	—	—
☐ ice green	220.00	—	—
☐ amethyst	135.00	175.00	150.00
Cuspidor (same as a spitoon)			
☐ marigold	1800.00	2800.00	1900.00
☐ purple	1800.00	2800.00	1900.00
☐ green	1800.00	2800.00	1900.00
☐ amethyst	1800.00	2800.00	1900.00
Dresser Tray			
☐ marigold	120.00	160.00	125.00
☐ purple	160.00	215.00	175.00
☐ green	160.00	215.00	175.00
☐ amethyst	160.00	215.00	175.00
☐ white	250.00	320.00	275.00
☐ ice blue	250.00	320.00	275.00
☐ ice green	250.00	320.00	275.00
Fernery, footed			
☐ marigold	1200.00	1500.00	1400.00
☐ purple	700.00	900.00	750.00
☐ green	700.00	900.00	750.00
☐ amethyst	700.00	900.00	750.00
☐ ice blue	2200.00	2875.00	2250.00
☐ white	500.00	—	—
☐ ice green	1200.00	—	—

	Current Price Range		Prior Year Average
Hatpin holder			
☐ marigold	110.00	125.00	115.00
☐ purple	100.00	200.00	150.00
☐ green	160.00	200.00	150.00
☐ blue	160.00	200.00	170.00
☐ amethyst	160.00	200.00	170.00
☐ white	150.00	200.00	175.00
☐ ice blue	265.00	335.00	275.00
☐ ice green	265.00	335.00	275.00
☐ aqua opalescent	1800.00	2300.00	2000.00
Ice Cream Bowl, diameter 4″			
☐ marigold	25.00	30.00	28.00
☐ purple	32.00	36.00	30.00
☐ green	32.00	36.00	30.00
☐ blue	32.00	36.00	30.00
☐ amethyst	32.00	36.00	30.00
☐ white	75.00	90.00	80.00
☐ ice blue	75.00	90.00	80.00
☐ ice green	75.00	90.00	80.00
Ice Cream Bowl, diameter 11″			
☐ marigold	80.00	100.00	85.00
☐ purple	160.00	200.00	170.00
☐ green	160.00	200.00	170.00
☐ blue	160.00	200.00	170.00
☐ amethyst	160.00	200.00	170.00
☐ white	220.00	270.00	225.00
☐ ice blue	220.00	270.00	225.00
☐ ice green	220.00	270.00	225.00
Lampshade			
☐ marigold	160.00	220.00	180.00
☐ purple	140.00	180.00	160.00
☐ green	140.00	180.00	160.00
☐ amethyst	140.00	180.00	160.00
Nappy			
☐ marigold	55.00	75.00	65.00
☐ purple	75.00	90.00	80.00
☐ green	75.00	90.00	80.00
☐ blue	75.00	90.00	80.00
☐ amethyst	75.00	90.00	80.00
☐ white	110.00	140.00	115.00
☐ ice blue	60.00	75.00	65.00
☐ ice green	60.00	75.00	65.00
Orange Bowl, footed			
☐ marigold	110.00	140.00	115.00
☐ purple	145.00	175.00	160.00

	Current Price Range		Prior Year Average
☐ green	155.00	185.00	160.00
☐ blue	155.00	185.00	160.00
☐ amethyst	155.00	185.00	160.00
☐ ice green	1200.00	1500.00	1300.00
☐ aqua opalescent	2400.00	2875.00	2600.00
Pin Tray			
☐ marigold	100.00	125.00	125.00
☐ purple	130.00	180.00	135.00
☐ green	130.00	180.00	135.00
☐ amethyst	130.00	180.00	135.00
☐ white	200.00	275.00	225.00
☐ ice blue	200.00	275.00	225.00
☐ ice green	200.00	275.00	225.00
Plate, diameter 7½″			
☐ marigold	60.00	75.00	62.00
☐ purple	70.00	85.00	75.00
☐ green	70.00	85.00	75.00
☐ blue	70.00	85.00	75.00
☐ amethyst	70.00	85.00	75.00
☐ white	100.00	120.00	110.00
☐ ice green	100.00	120.00	110.00
☐ ice blue	100.00	120.00	110.00
☐ aqua opalescent	375.00	450.00	400.00
Plate, footed			
☐ marigold	70.00	85.00	75.00
☐ purple	80.00	100.00	88.00
☐ green	80.00	100.00	88.00
☐ blue	80.00	100.00	88.00
☐ amethyst	80.00	100.00	88.00
☐ white	115.00	165.00	120.00
☐ ice blue	115.00	165.00	120.00
☐ ice green	115.00	165.00	120.00
Powder Jar, lidded			
☐ marigold	65.00	85.00	75.00
☐ purple	60.00	75.00	65.00
☐ green	75.00	95.00	85.00
☐ blue	60.00	75.00	65.00
☐ amethyst	75.00	95.00	85.00
☐ aqua opalescent	270.00	335.00	280.00
☐ ice blue	200.00	—	—
Punch Bowl, small, with base			
☐ marigold	250.00	350.00	275.00
☐ purple	360.00	450.00	275.00
☐ green	360.00	450.00	275.00

	Current Price Range		Prior Year Average

Punch Bowl, middle size

☐ marigold	370.00	—	—
☐ purple	500.00	—	—
☐ green	550.00	—	—
☐ white	1100.00	—	—
☐ ice blue	1500.00	—	—
☐ ice green	1500.00	—	—

Punch Bowl, banquet size, with base

☐ marigold	1275.00	1750.00	1400.00
☐ purple	1850.00	2350.00	2000.00
☐ aqua opalescent	7000.00	9000.00	7500.00
☐ white	3400.00	4000.00	3800.00
☐ ice blue	3400.00	4000.00	3800.00
☐ ice green	3400.00	4000.00	3800.00
☐ blue	3400.00	—	—
☐ green	2200.00	—	—

Punch Cup

☐ marigold	12.00	17.00	15.00
☐ purple	22.00	28.00	24.00
☐ green	22.00	28.00	24.00
☐ blue	22.00	28.00	24.00
☐ amethyst	22.00	28.00	24.00
☐ white	35.00	45.00	37.00
☐ ice blue	35.00	45.00	37.00
☐ ice green	35.00	45.00	180.00
☐ aqua opalescent	170.00	225.00	150.00

Shot Glass

☐ marigold	140.00	170.00	170.00
☐ purple	160.00	210.00	170.00
☐ amethyst	160.00	210.00	170.00

Spooner

☐ marigold	60.00	70.00	65.00
☐ purple	120.00	165.00	125.00
☐ green	130.00	170.00	140.00
☐ amethyst	120.00	165.00	125.00
☐ ice blue	170.00	210.00	180.00
☐ ice green	170.00	210.00	180.00

Sugar Bowl, lidded

☐ marigold	70.00	85.00	75.00
☐ purple	140.00	185.00	145.00
☐ green	80.00	120.00	95.00
☐ amethyst	140.00	185.00	145.00
☐ ice blue	210.00	275.00	220.00
☐ ice green	210.00	275.00	220.00

	Current Price Range		Prior Year Average
Sugar Bowl, unlidded			
☐ marigold	50.00	60.00	55.00
☐ purple	70.00	85.00	75.00
☐ green	70.00	85.00	75.00
☐ blue	70.00	85.00	75.00
☐ amethyst	70.00	85.00	75.00
☐ white	110.00	140.00	115.00
☐ ice blue	110.00	140.00	115.00
☐ ice green	110.00	140.00	115.00
Sweetmeat Dish, unlidded			
☐ marigold	380.00	460.00	390.00
☐ purple	225.00	275.00	240.00
☐ green	225.00	275.00	240.00
☐ blue	225.00	275.00	240.00
☐ amethyst	225.00	275.00	240.00
Sweetmeat Compote, lidded			
☐ marigold	600.00	700.00	610.00
☐ purple	150.00	190.00	170.00
☐ amethyst	150.00	190.00	170.00
Tobacco Jar, lidded			
☐ marigold	350.00	420.00	375.00
☐ purple	375.00	430.00	400.00
☐ blue	375.00	430.00	400.00
☐ amethyst	375.00	430.00	400.00
Tankard Pitcher			
☐ marigold	800.00	975.00	810.00
☐ purple	725.00	850.00	760.00
☐ green	725.00	850.00	760.00
☐ amethyst	725.00	850.00	760.00
☐ ice green	2500.00	3000.00	2775.00
Tumbler, small			
☐ marigold	45.00	70.00	60.00
☐ purple	30.00	50.00	40.00
☐ green	40.00	60.00	50.00
☐ amethyst	30.00	50.00	40.00
☐ ice green	65.00	80.00	67.00
Tumbler, large			
☐ marigold	45.00	55.00	47.00
☐ purple	65.00	80.00	69.00
☐ green	65.00	80.00	69.00
☐ amethyst	65.00	80.00	69.00
☐ ice green	85.00	110.00	88.00

	Current Price Range		Prior Year Average
Water Pitcher			
☐ marigold	250.00	320.00	260.00
☐ purple	350.00	420.00	375.00
☐ green	350.00	420.00	375.00
☐ amethyst......................................	350.00	420.00	375.00
Whiskey Decanter			
☐ marigold	800.00	950.00	850.00
☐ purple	900.00	1100.00	950.00
☐ green	900.00	1100.00	950.00
☐ blue	900.00	1100.00	950.00
☐ amethyst......................................	900.00	1100.00	1000.00

GRAPE AND CHERRY
Sowerby

An intaglio design, achieved from the exterior, grape bunches alternate with cherries attached to their branches with leaves. Separating the two large motifs is a design of a flaming torch rising out of scrolls. Colors are clearly iridescent and come in cobalt and marigold.

Bowl, large			
☐ marigold	65.00	70.00	67.50
☐ blue	145.00	160.00	150.00

GRAPE AND GOTHIC ARCHES
Northwood

The architectural background resembles a picket fence—the panels are separated by reliefed ridges and run the length of the side, terminating in a triangular arch. The grape bunches interrupt this pattern, more geometrical than most grape designs with leaves flanking.

Grape and Gothic Arches

	Current Price Range		Prior Year Average
Berry Bowl, large			
☐ marigold	30.00	42.00	32.00
☐ purple	50.00	65.00	52.00
☐ green	50.00	65.00	52.00
☐ blue	50.00	65.00	52.00
☐ amethyst	50.00	65.00	52.00
Bowl, diameter 5″			
☐ marigold	20.00	25.00	22.00
☐ purple	35.00	42.00	37.00
☐ green	35.00	42.00	37.00
☐ blue	35.00	42.00	37.00
☐ amethyst	35.00	42.00	37.00
Butter Dish, lidded			
☐ marigold	65.00	85.00	67.00
☐ purple	85.00	110.00	87.00
☐ green	85.00	110.00	87.00
☐ blue	85.00	110.00	87.00
☐ amethyst	85.00	110.00	87.00
☐ pearl	250.00	—	—

	Current Price Range		Prior Year Average
Creamer			
☐ marigold	35.00	45.00	37.00
☐ purple	50.00	60.00	52.00
☐ green	50.00	60.00	52.00
☐ blue	50.00	60.00	52.00
☐ amethyst	50.00	60.00	52.00
☐ pearl	120.00	—	—
Spooner			
☐ marigold	35.00	45.00	37.00
☐ purple	50.00	60.00	52.00
☐ green	50.00	60.00	52.00
☐ blue	50.00	60.00	52.00
☐ amethyst	50.00	60.00	52.00
☐ pearl	120.00	—	—
Sugar Bowl, lidded			
☐ marigold	45.00	55.00	47.00
☐ purple	60.00	75.00	62.00
☐ green	60.00	75.00	62.00
☐ blue	60.00	75.00	62.00
☐ amethyst	60.00	75.00	62.00
☐ pearl	120.00	—	—
Tumbler			
☐ marigold	22.00	30.00	25.00
☐ purple	30.00	42.00	32.00
☐ green	30.00	42.00	32.00
☐ blue	30.00	42.00	32.00
☐ amethyst	30.00	42.00	32.00
☐ pearl	150.00	—	—
Water Pitcher			
☐ marigold	170.00	210.00	175.00
☐ purple	260.00	330.00	275.00
☐ green	260.00	330.00	275.00
☐ blue	260.00	330.00	275.00
☐ amethyst	260.00	330.00	275.00
☐ pearl	500.00	—	—

GRAPE ARBOR
Northwood

A large basketweave is the background for this pattern, the grapes super-imposed on the design with foliage all around. The colors available are white, ice blue and green, and marigold.

	Current Price Range		Prior Year Average
Tankard Pitcher			
☐ marigold	170.00	220.00	175.00
☐ purple	450.00	550.00	475.00
☐ white...................................	700.00	900.00	750.00
☐ blue	450.00	550.00	475.00
☐ amethyst...............................	450.00	550.00	475.00
☐ ice green	2250.00	2800.00	2300.00
☐ ice blue	1100.00	—	—
Tumbler			
☐ marigold	30.00	40.00	32.00
☐ purple	55.00	67.50	58.00
☐ blue	55.00	67.50	58.00
☐ ice green	100.00	145.00	110.00
☐ white...................................	125.00	—	—
☐ ice blue	150.00	—	—

GRAPE DELIGHT
Dugan

Grape bunches in relief high enough to resemble marbles are superimposed on intricately detailed leaves. The viny branches wind around the body. There is no filler pattern. The shapes are usually small bowls with the unique six footed base. The colors range widely.

	Current Price Range		Prior Year Average
Nut Bowl			
☐ purple	60.00	75.00	62.00
☐ marigold	45.00	—	—
☐ blue	60.00	—	—
☐ white...................................	80.00	—	—
Rose Bowl			
☐ marigold	40.00	50.00	42.00
☐ purple	50.00	65.00	52.00
☐ blue	50.00	65.00	52.00
☐ amethyst...............................	50.00	65.00	52.00
☐ white...................................	60.00	75.00	62.00

GRAPE LEAVES
Millersburg

	Current Price Range		Prior Year Average
Bowl			
☐ marigold	57.50	70.00	60.00
☐ purple	80.00	110.00	82.00
☐ green	80.00	110.00	82.00
☐ amethyst...............................	80.00	110.00	82.00
☐ vaseline...............................	700.00	—	—

GRAPE LEAVES
Northwood

The iridescence and the coloring are the distinctive features on these lovely pieces. The design is sparse, grapes and foliage mingling in the center; the rest of the piece is smooth, slightly mottled glass. The pieces catch the light and reflect all the rainbow colors Carnival glass is cherished for.

	Current Price Range		Prior Year Average
Bowl, diameter 7½"			
☐ marigold	40.00	50.00	42.00
☐ purple	55.00	75.00	58.00
☐ green	55.00	75.00	58.00
☐ amethyst	55.00	75.00	58.00
☐ ice blue	110.00	135.00	115.00
Bride's Basket			
☐ purple	200.00	225.00	210.00
☐ amethyst	200.00	225.00	210.00

GRAPE VINE LATTICE
Dugan

An overall pattern of a barked trellis without further decoration dominates the interior on these pieces. Although the design is not intricate, it manages to be busy because of the diamond pattern created by the vines.

Bowl, diameter 7½"			
☐ marigold	20.00	27.00	22.00
☐ purple	35.00	43.00	37.00
☐ green	35.00	43.00	37.00
☐ blue	35.00	43.00	37.00
☐ amethyst	35.00	43.00	37.00
☐ white	45.00	55.00	47.00
Plate, diameter 7½"			
☐ marigold	35.00	45.00	37.00
☐ purple	55.00	67.50	57.00
☐ blue	55.00	67.50	57.00
☐ amethyst	55.00	67.50	57.00
☐ white	60.00	75.00	62.00

GRAPE WREATH
Millersburg

The iridescence is excellent on these pieces, going from almost opaque to golden mirror on the interior rim. The eight-point star that serves as the central medallion is formed by a triangular series of ridges. It is surrounded at the midpoint of the body by a wreath of grapes and stippled leaves.

	Current Price Range		Prior Year Average
Bowl			
☐ marigold	35.00	45.00	37.00
☐ purple	45.00	55.00	47.00
☐ green	45.00	55.00	47.00
☐ amethyst	45.00	55.00	47.00
Bowl, diameter 10"			
☐ marigold	40.00	50.00	42.00
☐ green	52.00	60.00	55.00
☐ amethyst	52.00	60.00	55.00
Spittoon			
☐ marigold	500.00	700.00	525.00

GREEK KEY
Northwood

A pattern repeated often in architecture, mold work, jewelry, and other decorative arts, the Greek key works well on these glass pieces. The central band is made up of the maze-like design, surrounding a starburst of fine rays and framed by a delicate row of beadwork. This pattern was used often and the colors vary widely.

Greek Key

	Current Price Range		Prior Year Average
Bowl, flat, diameter 9″			
☐ marigold	40.00	50.00	45.00
☐ purple	55.00	60.00	58.00
☐ green	55.00	60.00	58.00
Bowl, dome footed, diameter 9″			
☐ marigold	40.00	47.00	42.00
☐ purple	55.00	60.00	58.00
☐ green	55.00	60.00	58.00
Pitcher			
☐ marigold	450.00	500.00	475.00
☐ purple	225.00	250.00	230.00
☐ green	225.00	250.00	230.00
Plate			
☐ marigold	110.00	135.00	115.00
☐ purple	230.00	240.00	235.00
☑ blue	230.00	245.00	235.00
☐ green	260.00	300.00	270.00
Tumbler			
☐ marigold	40.00	60.00	42.00
☐ purple	85.00	100.00	92.00
☐ green	80.00	100.00	90.00

GREENGARD FURNITURE
Millersburg

Bowl

☐ amethyst	290.00	315.00	295.00

HAMMERED BELL

A lamp shade of iridescent glass with a metal-like appearance, the design resembles pewter hammered with large stiples. Along the waist of the piece is a heavy raised ridge, separating the two planes. The bell shape is slightly angular. White is the only known color.

Bell

☐ white metallic	120.00	130.00	125.00

HARVEST FLOWER

A sheaf of wheat surrounds the entire body of these pieces, with an intricately detailed petaled flower superimposed on two sides of the panel. The upper rim is a plain band but the base terminates the wheat design under the piece.

	Current Price Range		Prior Year Average

Pitcher
☐ marigold	1250.00	—	—

Tumbler
☐ amethyst	40.00	55.00	42.00
☐ marigold	120.00	—	—
☐ green	400.00	—	—

HARVEST POPPY

Compote
☐ marigold	30.00	40.00	35.00
☐ amethyst	45.00	55.00	47.00
☐ peach opalescent	55.00	65.00	57.00
☐ white	65.00	75.00	67.00

HATCHET
U.S. Glass

☐ marigold	145.00	—	—

HATTIE
Imperial

An extremely busy pattern, an all-over design of various motifs decorates these pieces. The central medallion is a plainly petaled flower resembling a daisy surrounded by the rest of the design made up of flowers in triangular ridges. The colors are marigold, green, amethyst, and smoke.

Bowl, diameter 9″
☐ marigold	30.00	50.00	32.00
☐ green	45.00	60.00	47.00
☐ amethyst	45.00	60.00	47.00
☐ smoke	62.00	70.00	64.00

Plate, diameter 9″
☐ marigold	72.00	80.00	75.00
☐ green	123.00	133.00	128.00
☐ amethyst	123.00	133.00	128.00
☐ smoke	136.00	145.00	140.00
☐ amber	1000.00	—	—

Rose Bowl
☐ marigold	58.00	65.00	60.00

HAWAIIAN LEI
Higbee

Creamer
☐ marigold	60.00	70.00	62.00

	Current Price Range		Prior Year Average

Sugar

☐ marigold	60.00	70.00	62.00

HEADDRESS
Imperial/England

A busy overall pattern of high-relief feathers composed of radiating ridges in an arched design. The center is a lobed petal flower, each feather radiating out of a section of the bloom. The colors vary widely.

Bowl, diameter 9″

☐ marigold	16.00	18.00	17.00
☐ green	25.00	30.00	28.00
☐ blue	25.00	30.00	28.00
☐ vaseline..	38.00	42.00	40.00
☐ clambroth	38.00	42.00	40.00

HEART AND HORSESHOE
Fenton

The outer design is large sweeps of foliage vines containing raised relief hearts. This wreath surrounds the central motif of the horseshoe of a smooth, thick ridge and the inscription "Good luck." The colors are green and marigold.

Bowl, diameter 9″

☐ marigold	25.00	40.00	26.00
☐ green	46.00	50.00	47.00

Plate, diameter 9″

☐ marigold	80.00	95.00	82.00
☐ green	125.00	145.00	130.00

HEART AND VINE
Fenton

Heart shapes grow as if naturally out of a large spread-out wreath of foliage and vine. The center is clear of decoration other than the lower leaves that dip toward the middle. The glass is heavy, the iridescence good, the colors green, blue, white, amethyst, and marigold.

Bowl, diameter 9″

☐ marigold	25.00	28.00	26.00
☐ green	40.00	45.00	42.00
☐ blue	40.00	45.00	42.00
☐ amethyst..	40.00	45.00	42.00
☐ white..	60.00	80.00	62.00

	Current Price Range		Prior Year Average

Plate, diameter 8″
☐ marigold	80.00	95.00	82.00
☐ green	130.00	135.00	132.00
☐ blue	130.00	135.00	132.00
☐ amethyst	130.00	135.00	132.00

HEART BAND SOUVENIR
McKee

Mug
☐ marigold	80.00	90.00	82.00
☐ green	90.00	100.00	92.00
☐ aqua	105.00	115.00	107.00

Mug, large
☐ marigold	85.00	95.00	87.00
☐ green	100.00	120.00	107.00
☐ aqua	115.00	125.00	117.00

Tumbler
☐ marigold	75.00	—	—

HEARTS AND FLOWERS
Northwood

A detailed overall design of heart-shaped scrolls surrounding petaled leaves form the pattern of these pieces. The center is defined by a diamond-work band framing the central medallion. The colors and shapes run the gamut of Northwood productions.

Bowl, diameter 9″
☐ marigold	35.00	45.00	37.00
☐ purple	60.00	75.00	62.00
☐ green	60.00	75.00	62.00
☐ blue	60.00	75.00	62.00
☐ amethyst	60.00	75.00	62.00
☐ white	70.00	90.00	72.00
☐ ice blue	70.00	90.00	72.00
☐ ice green	70.00	90.00	72.00

Compote
☐ marigold	40.00	50.00	70.00
☐ purple	70.00	90.00	80.00
☐ green	65.00	87.50	70.00
☐ blue	65.00	87.50	70.00
☐ amethyst	65.00	87.50	70.00
☐ white	80.00	100.00	82.00
☐ ice blue	175.00	225.00	200.00

	Current Price Range		Prior Year Average
☐ ice green	260.00	300.00	270.00
☐ aqua opalescent	160.00	220.00	180.00
☐ peach opalescent	650.00	—	—
Plate, diameter 9½"			
☐ marigold	110.00	140.00	115.00
☐ purple	220.00	280.00	225.00
☐ green	220.00	280.00	225.00
☐ blue	220.00	280.00	225.00
☐ amethyst	220.00	280.00	225.00
☐ white	250.00	320.00	275.00
☐ ice blue	250.00	320.00	275.00
☐ ice green	250.00	320.00	275.00
☐ aqua opalescent	600.00	—	—

HEARTS AND TREES
Fenton

Large knobby stipples serve as the ground for this many motifed pattern. Beadwork, hearts of triple ridges and trees growing out of a chain-link band adorn the pieces in an all-over design. The colors are green, marigold, blue, and amethyst.

Bowl, diameter 8"			
☐ marigold	130.00	150.00	140.00
☐ green	145.00	155.00	150.00
☐ blue	145.00	155.00	150.00

HEAVY BANDED DIAMONDS
Australian Manufacturer

The wonderful iridescence is highlighted by the high relief bands of diamonds chiseled out of the sides in a pyramid pattern. The upper rim is accented by a triple ridge formed into angular panels around the top. The glass is heavy and thick.

Berry Bowl			
☐ marigold	50.00	65.00	52.00
☐ purple	65.00	75.00	67.00

HEAVY DIAMOND
Imperial

The diamond trellis that adorns these pieces from top to bottom is made of intaglio ridges of faceted glass. The background is otherwise smooth, the glass transparent. Smoke and marigold are the existing colors.

	Current Price Range		Prior Year Average
Bowl			
☐ marigold	14.00	18.00	16.00
Creamer			
☐ marigold	13.00	16.00	14.00
Sugar Bowl			
☐ marigold	13.00	16.00	14.00

HEAVY GRAPE
Imperial

The central decoration is the thick, high-relief grape bunch surrounded by foliage and backgrounded with stippling. The rest of the piece is smooth but notched in huge thumbprints which pick up the light and shows off the incredible iridescence. The colors are green, purple, amber, blue, marigold, and amethyst.

Berry Bowl, diameter 5″			
☐ marigold	20.00	25.00	22.00
☐ green	25.00	30.00	27.00
☐ purple	25.00	30.00	27.00
☐ blue	25.00	30.00	27.00
☐ amethyst...	25.00	30.00	27.00
☐ amber	45.00	60.00	47.00
Berry Bowl, diameter 9″			
☐ marigold	40.00	60.00	42.00
☐ green	72.00	80.00	75.00
☐ purple	72.00	80.00	75.00
☐ amethyst...	72.00	80.00	75.00
☐ amber	72.00	80.00	75.00
Chop Plate, diameter 12″			
☐ marigold	180.00	210.00	185.00
☐ green	300.00	325.00	310.00
☐ purple	300.00	325.00	310.00
☐ amethyst...	300.00	325.00	310.00
☐ amber	360.00	400.00	275.00
Plate, diameter 7″			
☐ marigold	40.00	60.00	42.00
☐ green	65.00	80.00	67.00
☐ purple	65.00	80.00	67.00
☐ amethyst...	65.00	80.00	67.00
☐ amber	85.00	90.00	87.00

HEAVY GRAPE
Dugan

The design is sharply molded, almost resembling cut or engraved glass. The grape bunches in high relief alternate with oak leaves, connected with narrow branches and surrounding the central medallion of leaf over grapes. The pattern has a golden iridescence; colors are varied.

	Current Price Range		Prior Year Average
Bowl, 5″			
☐ marigold	45.00	55.00	70.00
☐ purple	45.00	55.00	70.00
☐ amethyst	45.00	55.00	70.00
Bowl, diameter 10″			
☐ marigold	75.00	90.00	80.00
☐ purple	110.00	155.00	115.00
☐ peach opalescent	500.00	—	—
☐ amethyst	110.00	155.00	120.00

HEAVY HEART
Higbee

Tumbler			
☐ marigold	70.00	80.00	72.00

HEAVY HOBNAIL
Fenton

The sculptured hobnail is made up of row after row of marble-like knobs, the symmetry broken by a ballooned effect around the waist. The ground is smooth. The glass is opaque but iridescent; the only reported colors are white and purple.

Vase			
☐ purple	90.00	110.00	95.00
☐ white	120.00	135.00	125.00

HEAVY IRIS
Dugan

The detail is in such high relief it appears to be sculptured. The design is stylized blooms on long stems with foliage and flora. The upper rim is fluted in a wide ruffle on the pitcher, the tumbler has a wide ridged band of smooth glass atop the design. The colors are marigold, white, and a desirable purple.

Pitcher			
☐ marigold	400.00	500.00	425.00
☐ purple	700.00	825.00	725.00

	Current Price Range		Prior Year Average
☐ peach opalescent............................	1000.00	—	—
☐ amethyst..	700.00	825.00	725.00
☐ white..	750.00	875.00	760.00
Tumbler			
☐ marigold	40.00	50.00	42.00
☐ purple	55.00	67.50	60.00
☐ green	55.00	67.50	60.00
☐ blue	55.00	67.50	60.00
☐ amethyst..	55.00	67.50	60.00
☐ white..	75.00	95.00	80.00

HEAVY PINEAPPLE
Fenton

This is an elegant pattern of dancing pineapples on ridged branches. The center piece is a contrasting geometric sunburst pointing to the four square fruit filled panels. The shape of the plate suggests a dogwood bloom with its four petals gracefully pointed. The colors are white iridescent and cobalt.

Bowl			
☐ cobalt blue.....................................	425.00	500.00	450.00
☐ white..	425.00	500.00	450.00

HEAVY PRISMS
Davisons of Gateshead

This is a tasteful design of balanced bands, lozenge style on the upper and lower portions of the body. The middle ground is heavily paneled with chunky prisms in high relief. The upper rim is a beaded strip; the base is decidedly plain. The colors are blue, marigold, and amethyst.

Celery Vase			
☐ marigold	75.00	—	—
☐ purple	90.00	—	—
☐ blue	85.00	—	—

HEAVY SHELL
Dugan

The pattern here refers to the modern stylized shell shape, heavily ruffled like nautical fingers. The iridescence is sharply delineated by the almost transparent glass.

Bowl, 8″			
☐ white..	150.00	—	—
Shell			
☐ white..	90.00	100.00	95.00

HEAVY VINE

	Current Price Range		Prior Year Average
Lamp			
☐ marigold	160.00	—	—
Perfume Bottle			
☐ marigold	60.00	70.00	62.00

HEAVY WEB
Dugan

These pieces, again, resemble a conch shell, because the richly opalescent peach color, combined with the draped ridges of the web pattern, has the look of the sea. The iridescent glass is rainbow-like, the colors peach, green, and purple.

Bowl, diameter 10″			
☐ peach opalescent	100.00	150.00	110.00
Plate, diameter 12″			
☐ peach opalescent	225.00	300.00	275.00

HEINZ

Bottle			
☐ white	35.00	—	—

HEISEY

Breakfast Set			
☐ pastel	185.00	—	—
Cartwheel Compote			
☐ clambroth	65.00	—	—
Creamer, Tray			
☐ marigold	75.00	—	—
☐ ice blue	165.00	—	—
☐ clambroth	165.00	—	—
Floral Spray, Candy, with lid			
☐ ice blue	70.00	—	—
Flute, Punch Cup			
☐ marigold	25.00	—	—
Priscilla Toothpick			
☐ marigold	95.00	—	—
☐ clambroth	95.00	—	—
Tumbler			
☐ marigold	40.00	—	—
#357, Water Bottle			
☐ marigold	75.00	—	—

HERON
Dugan

This is a straightforward design, realistically portrayed of a husky heron standing proudly among the marsh growth. The frame on the upper and lower rim is a corded band of diagonal ridges. The pattern decorates only one side, the rest of the mug is of smooth glossy iridescence. Colors are marigold and amethyst.

Heron

	Current Price Range		Prior Year Average
Mug			
☐ marigold	70.00	90.00	72.00
☐ amethyst..	100.00	120.00	110.00

HEXAGON AND CANE
Imperial

Covered Sugar			
☐ marigold	65.00	—	—

HICKMAN

Caster Set, four-piece			
☐ marigold	300.00	—	—

HOBNAIL
Millersburg

Often seen in other types of glass, iridized Carnival glass takes to this pattern well. The glossy knobs are perfectly suited to refracting the rainbows on these deeply colored, almost opaque pieces. The shapes and colors vary widely.

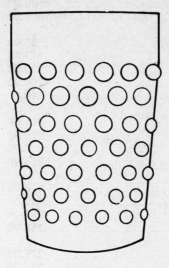

Hobnail

	Current Price Range		Prior Year Average
Bowl			
☐ cherries, marigold	550.00	675.00	560.00
☐ purple	460.00	550.00	475.00
☐ green	460.00	550.00	475.00
☐ blue	850.00	1000.00	875.00
☐ amethyst	460.00	550.00	475.00
Butter Dish			
☐ purple	225.00	275.00	240.00
☐ green	225.00	275.00	240.00
☐ blue	450.00	550.00	475.00
☐ amethyst	225.00	275.00	240.00
Creamer			
☐ purple	110.00	150.00	115.00
☐ green	110.00	150.00	115.00
☐ amethyst	225.00	300.00	240.00
☐ amethyst	110.00	150.00	115.00

	Current Price Range		Prior Year Average
Pitcher			
☐ marigold	1250.00	1700.00	1400.00
☐ purple	1800.00	2200.00	1950.00
☐ green	1800.00	2200.00	1950.00
☐ blue	3500.00	5000.00	3750.00
☐ amethyst	1800.00	2200.00	1950.00
Rose Bowl			
☐ marigold	85.00	110.00	90.00
☐ purple	110.00	130.00	115.00
☐ green	110.00	130.00	115.00
☐ blue	200.00	275.00	225.00
☐ amethyst	110.00	130.00	115.00
Spittoon			
☐ marigold	225.00	275.00	250.00
☐ purple	275.00	325.00	300.00
☐ green	275.00	325.00	300.00
☐ amethyst	275.00	325.00	300.00
Spooner			
☐ purple	110.00	150.00	115.00
☐ green	110.00	150.00	115.00
☐ blue	225.00	300.00	230.00
☐ amethyst	110.00	150.00	115.00
Tumbler			
☐ marigold	275.00	325.00	300.00
☐ purple	325.00	375.00	340.00
☐ green	325.00	375.00	340.00
☐ blue	650.00	850.00	675.00
☐ amethyst	325.00	375.00	340.00
Vase			
☐ green	110.00	155.00	115.00
☐ amethyst	110.00	155.00	115.00

HOBNAIL SODA
Imperial

A low-relief hobnail, the knobs almost suggested rather than standing, gives these pieces a milky iridescence. Only found on a angular, paneled spittoon with a wide skirted rim, the pattern is simple and utilitarian. The colors are marigold, green, and amber.

Spittoon			
☐ marigold	30.00	37.00	32.00
☐ green	42.00	50.00	45.00
☐ amber	42.00	50.00	45.00

HOBNAIL VARIANT
Millersburg

	Current Price Range		Prior Year Average
Jardiniere			
☐ amethyst...	850.00	950.00	875.00
☐ blue	950.00	1050.00	975.00
Rose Bowl			
☐ marigold	800.00	900.00	825.00
Vase			
☐ marigold	800.00	900.00	825.00
☐ amethyst...	800.00	900.00	825.00
☐ green	800.00	900.00	825.00

HOBSTAR
Imperial

It looks like cut glass; the pattern is geometrical and faceted. The diamond banding surrounds a mum-like central motif, repeated around the piece. The design is overall, the background is filled in with fan-shaped ridges. The colors are marigold, purple, and green.

Hobstar

	Current Price Range		Prior Year Average
Bowl, 5″			
☐ marigold	20.00	—	—
☐ smoke	25.00	—	—
Bowl, 10″			
☐ marigold	35.00	—	—
☐ smoke	45.00	—	—
Bowls, ruffled, 6″–12″			
☐ marigold	30.00	—	—
☐ smoke	35.00	—	—
Butter Dish			
☐ marigold	60.00	75.00	62.00
☐ purple	160.00	200.00	165.00
☐ green	160.00	200.00	165.00
☐ amethyst..	160.00	200.00	165.00
Cracker Jar			
☐ marigold	60.00	75.00	62.00
Creamer			
☐ marigold	18.00	23.00	20.00
☐ purple	85.00	110.00	90.00
☐ green	85.00	110.00	90.00
☐ amethyst..	85.00	110.00	90.00
Fruit Bowl and Base			
☐ marigold	50.00	—	—
☐ purple	65.00	—	—
☐ green	65.00	—	—
Pickle Castor			
☐ marigold	300.00	375.00	325.00
Spooner			
☐ marigold	18.00	23.00	20.00
☐ purple	85.00	110.00	90.00
☐ green	85.00	110.00	90.00
☐ amethyst..	85.00	110.00	90.00
Sugar Bowl			
☐ marigold	18.00	23.00	20.00
☐ purple	85.00	110.00	90.00
☐ green	85.00	110.00	90.00
☐ amethyst..	85.00	110.00	90.00

HOBSTAR AND ARCHES
Imperial

The hobstar flower, still the central design, is surrounded and almost obscured by a busy overall pattern. Beadwork arches, broken at the matrix and forming a tent-shaped form, sweep over the piece in continuous motion. The colors are marigold, amethyst, green, and smoke.

	Current Price Range		Prior Year Average

Bowl, diameter 9"
☐ marigold	32.00	36.00	34.00
☐ amethyst	42.00	46.00	43.00
☐ green	42.00	46.00	43.00
☐ smoke	52.00	66.00	54.00

Fruit Bowl, two-piece
☐ marigold	70.00	85.00	73.00
☐ amethyst	90.00	100.00	94.00
☐ green	90.00	100.00	94.00
☐ smoke	110.00	120.00	115.00

HOBSTAR AND CUT TRIANGLES
English Manufacturer

This is a bizarre pattern of sharp counterpoints. Lozenged triangles, slightly convex but very angular and geometrical, are spaced between flat planes of iridescent glass. The effect is good because it is so different. The shapes are varied, the colors are marigold, green, and amethyst.

Bowl
☐ marigold	45.00	65.00	47.00
☐ green	65.00	80.00	67.00
☐ amethyst	65.00	80.00	67.00

Compote
☐ marigold	45.00	65.00	47.00
☐ green	65.00	80.00	67.00
☐ amethyst	65.00	80.00	67.00

Plate
☐ marigold	45.00	65.00	50.00
☐ green	60.00	80.00	65.00
☐ amethyst	60.00	80.00	65.00

Rose Bowl
☐ marigold	45.00	65.00	50.00
☐ green	60.00	80.00	65.00
☐ amethyst	60.00	80.00	65.00

HOBSTAR AND FEATHER
Millersburg

A heavy, chunky pattern on thick glass distinguishes this style. The feathers are arranged around the hobstar which is deeply cut with a marble-like center. The rim is bullet-edged and scalloped, the bottom base is banded with a lozenge motif. The pedestals edge is also bullet-rimmed. The shapes vary widely and the colors are green, marigold, and amethyst.

	Current Price Range		Prior Year Average
Bowl, square, 10"			
☐ purple	1600.00	—	—
Butter			
☐ marigold	1200.00	—	—
☐ purple	1500.00	—	—
☐ green	1500.00	—	—
Creamer			
☐ marigold	700.00	—	—
☐ purple	800.00	—	—
☐ green	800.00	—	—
Punch Bowl			
☐ marigold	1600.00	2000.00	1800.00
☐ purple	2500.00	3000.00	2600.00
☐ green	2500.00	3000.00	2600.00
☐ amethyst	2500.00	3000.00	2600.00
Punch Cup			
☐ marigold	100.00	200.00	125.00
☐ purple	110.00	240.00	150.00
☐ green	110.00	240.00	150.00
☐ blue	160.00	240.00	200.00
☐ amethyst	110.00	240.00	150.00
Rose Bowl			
☐ marigold	2000.00	—	—
☐ purple	1500.00	—	—
☐ green	1800.00	—	—
Spooner			
☐ marigold	700.00	—	—
☐ purple	700.00	—	—
☐ green	800.00	—	—
Sugar			
☐ marigold	800.00	—	—
☐ purple	900.00	—	—
☐ green	900.00	—	—
Vase			
☐ purple	1500.00	1900.00	1600.00
☐ green	1500.00	1900.00	1600.00
☐ amethyst	1500.00	1900.00	1600.00

HOBSTAR AND FRUIT
Westmoreland

The central medallion on this piece is a stylized hobstar made up of curvy ridges interspersed with beadwork. The outer rim pattern is simpler, a wide band of various fruits sectioned off by heavy beaded bands. The colors are often unusual, such as peach opalescent, ice blue, and aqua opalescent.

	Current Price Range		Prior Year Average
Bowl			
☐ ice blue	45.00	55.00	47.00
☐ peach opalescent	45.00	55.00	47.00
☐ aqua opalescent	125.00	150.00	130.00
☐ marigold	35.00	—	—

HOBSTAR BAND
Imperial

This interesting pattern is made up of elongated petals, on the lower half containing vertical rows of beadwork; the upper pointed ovals contain the hobstar. The clear glass has a diamond-like iridescence shown off in marigold.

Bowl			
☐ marigold	55.00	—	—
Celery			
☐ marigold	55.00	—	—
Compote			
☐ marigold	75.00	—	—
Pitcher			
☐ marigold	190.00	210.00	195.00
Tumbler			
☐ marigold	40.00	45.00	42.00

HOBSTAR FLOWER
Northwood

This is a pleasing pattern of fruit and flower, spaced by triangular cuts framed by beaded strips. The flower or hobstar that forms the central motif is a sunlike shape of proportionately large size. It is found in marigold and amethyst.

Compote			
☐ marigold	55.00	65.00	57.00
☐ purple	70.00	85.00	72.00
☐ green	70.00	85.00	72.00
☐ blue	70.00	85.00	72.00
☐ amethyst	70.00	85.00	72.00

HOBSTAR PANELS

Creamer			
☐ marigold	40.00	50.00	42.00
Sugar			
☐ marigold	40.00	50.00	42.00

HOBSTAR REVERSED
Davisons of Gateshead

This is a similar pattern to Hobstar panels, but the elongated panels which contain a simple light sided hobstar have a gentler curve, a pointed oval shape. The glass is transparent but the colors are good in amethyst, marigold, and blue.

	Current Price Range		Prior Year Average
Butter Dish			
☐ marigold	45.00	55.00	47.00
☐ blue	50.00	65.00	52.00
☐ amethyst	50.00	65.00	52.00
Frog, with base			
☐ marigold	45.00	60.00	47.00
Spooner			
☐ marigold	40.00	60.00	42.00

HOBSTAR WHIRL

The hobstar is employed alone this time on a simple pattern consisting of a wide horizontal band of the faceted sunburst. The rest of the ground is glossy and smooth, which shows off the iridescent finish in cobalt blue.

Compote			
☐ cobalt blue	25.00	40.00	28.00

HOLIDAY
Northwood

This is a formal, stylized pattern resembling the Greek key without the maze. The perspective is excellent—the angles and geometry having a three dimensional look. The outer band is a simple line of eight-sided stars. The glass is heavy and the color is marigold.

Tray, diameter 11″			
☐ marigold	165.00	210.00	170.00

HOLLY
Fenton

This is an overall foliage pattern in high relief. The vines and leaves are presented delicately radiating out from the center in a broad circular pattern. The pattern is prolific, used on almost all the shapes and comes in all of the Fenton colors including amethyst and variations, different shades of marigold, green, blue and their icy counterparts, red, white, and vaseline.

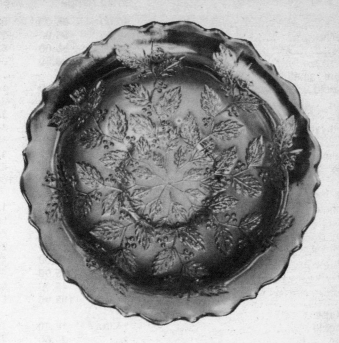

Holly

	Current Price Range		Prior Year Average
Bowl, diameter 7¼″			
☐ marigold	16.00	20.00	18.00
☐ green	32.00	40.00	36.00
☐ blue	32.00	40.00	36.00
☐ amethyst	32.00	40.00	36.00
☐ ice blue	50.00	65.00	52.00
☐ ice green	50.00	65.00	52.00
☐ vaseline	50.00	65.00	52.00
☐ white	50.00	65.00	52.00
☐ red	575.00	600.00	580.00
☐ peach opalescent	750.00	—	—
Bowl, diameter 10″			
☐ marigold	16.00	20.00	18.00
☐ green	32.00	40.00	34.00
☐ blue	32.00	40.00	34.00
☐ amethyst	32.00	40.00	34.00

	Current Price Range		Prior Year Average
☐ ices	50.00	65.00	52.00
☐ vaseline	50.00	65.00	52.00
☐ white	50.00	65.00	52.00
☐ red	575.00	600.00	580.00
Compote, small			
☐ marigold	12.00	18.00	14.00
☐ green	32.00	36.00	34.00
☐ blue	32.00	36.00	34.00
☐ amethyst	32.00	36.00	34.00
☐ ices	40.00	50.00	42.00
☐ vaseline	40.00	50.00	42.00
☐ white	40.00	50.00	42.00
☐ red	150.00	200.00	160.00
Goblet			
☐ marigold	16.00	19.00	17.00
☐ green	25.00	30.00	26.00
☐ blue	25.00	30.00	26.00
☐ amethyst	25.00	30.00	26.00
☐ ices	40.00	45.00	42.00
☐ vaseline	40.00	45.00	42.00
☐ white	40.00	45.00	42.00
☐ red	160.00	185.00	165.00
Hat Shape			
☐ marigold	14.00	16.00	16.00
☐ green	20.00	25.00	22.00
☐ blue	20.00	25.00	22.00
☐ amethyst	20.00	25.00	22.00
☐ ices	40.00	44.00	42.00
☐ vaseline	40.00	44.00	42.00
☐ white	40.00	44.00	42.00
☐ red	250.00	350.00	300.00
Plate			
☐ marigold	50.00	55.00	52.00
☐ green	65.00	72.00	67.00
☐ blue	65.00	72.00	67.00
☐ amethyst	65.00	72.00	67.00
☐ ices	100.00	120.00	110.00
☐ vaseline	100.00	120.00	110.00
☐ white	130.00	150.00	140.00
☐ red	600.00	750.00	625.00

HOLLY AND BERRY
Dugan

The central medallion is a sprig of holly and berries, sharply and delicately molded. The design then continues around the interior in a wide band of foliage and fruits. The colors are purple, blue, green, marigold, and peach opalescent.

	Current Price Range		Prior Year Average
Bowl			
☐ marigold	30.00	40.00	34.00
☐ purple	45.00	55.00	46.00
☐ green	45.00	55.00	46.00
☐ blue	45.00	55.00	46.00
☐ amethyst	45.00	55.00	46.00
☐ peach opalescent	60.00	75.00	62.00
Nappy, handled			
☐ marigold	40.00	50.00	42.00
☐ purple	60.00	75.00	62.00
☐ green	60.00	75.00	62.00
☐ blue	60.00	75.00	62.00
☐ amethyst	60.00	75.00	62.00
☐ peach opalescent	75.00	95.00	77.00

HOLLY SPRIG
Millersburg

This is a basic holly pattern, with the sharply pointed leaves twisting in a wreath shape around the waist, interspersed with berries. The rim is ruffled irregularly in an indented pattern. Colors are marigold, amethyst, and green.

Bowl			
☐ marigold	35.00	45.00	37.00
☐ purple	55.00	65.00	57.00
☐ green	55.00	65.00	57.00
☐ amethyst	55.00	65.00	57.00
Nappy			
☐ marigold	35.00	45.00	37.00
☐ purple	45.00	55.00	47.00
☐ green	45.00	55.00	47.00
☐ amethyst	45.00	55.00	47.00
Sauce Dish			
☐ marigold	110.00	150.00	115.00

HONEYCOMB AND CLOVER
Fenton

	Current Price Range		Prior Year Average
Bon Bon			
☐ marigold	30.00	40.00	32.00
☐ blue	40.00	50.00	42.00
☐ amethyst..	45.00	55.00	47.00
☐ green	50.00	60.00	52.00
☐ amber	65.00	75.00	70.00

HONEYCOMB AND CLOVER
Imperial

	Current Price Range		Prior Year Average
Compote			
☐ marigold	25.00	—	—
☐ purple	50.00	—	—
☐ green	65.00	—	—
☐ blue	50.00	—	—
Spooner			
☐ marigold	90.00	—	—

HONEYCOMB AND HOBSTAR
Millersburg

This is an interesting twist using the hobstar motif, the center raised in such high relief it resembles a marble. The petals are tiny ridges contrasting a glossy smoothness of iridescence. The gloss is heavy, the molding is good, the color is amethyst or deep blue.

	Current Price Range		Prior Year Average
Vase			
☐ amethyst..	1100.00	1200.00	1150.00
☐ blue	1100.00	1200.00	1150.00

HONEYCOMB ROSEBOWL
Dugan

High relief ridges make up this straightforward pattern. The sextagonal shape appears almost intaglio because the heightened ridges are over the piece in its entirety. The shape of the piece is simply rounded, altogether an effective design. Colors are marigold and peach.

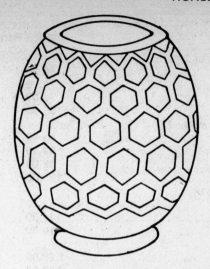

Honeycomb Rosebowl

	Current Price Range		Prior Year Average
Rose Bowl			
☐ marigold	100.00	125.00	115.00
☐ peach opalescent	150.00	175.00	160.00

HORN OF PLENTY

Bottle			
☐ marigold	50.00	60.00	52.00

HORSE SHOE

Jigger			
☐ marigold	35.00	45.00	37.00

HORSE'S HEAD
Fenton

  Beadwork ovals frame the heads of spirited horses encircling the interior of pieces with this pattern. The ground between these cameos is scale-like, covering the majority of the bowl. The colors are blue, green, white, vaseline, aqua, and marigold.

	Current Price Range		Prior Year Average
Bowl, flat, diameter 7″			
☐ marigold	50.00	60.00	52.00
☐ blue	72.00	80.00	75.00
☐ green	72.00	80.00	75.00
☐ vaseline	125.00	130.00	126.00
Bowl, footed, diameter 7″			
☐ marigold	58.00	62.00	60.00
☐ blue	58.00	62.00	60.00
☐ green	62.00	70.00	64.00
☐ vaseline	125.00	150.00	130.00
Plate, diameter 6½″			
☐ marigold	82.00	95.00	65.00
☐ green	110.00	130.00	115.00
☐ blue	110.00	130.00	115.00
Rose Bowl			
☐ marigold	90.00	95.00	92.00
☐ green	100.00	110.00	105.00
☐ blue	100.00	110.00	105.00
☐ vaseline	185.00	200.00	190.00

HOT SPRINGS VASE

An early Carnival piece of delicate triangular patterns terminating at a knob and pedestal. The upper rim is gently fluted and the finish is faceted. The glass is clear and beautifully iridescent and amber.

Vase			
☐ marigold	110.00	120.00	115.00

HYACINTH

Lamp			
☐ marigold	1900.00	—	—

ICE CRYSTALS

Bowl			
☐ ices	80.00	90.00	82.00
Candlesticks, pair			
☐ ices	155.00	165.00	157.00
Salt			
☐ ices	60.00	70.00	62.00

IDYLL
Fenton

	Current Price Range		Prior Year Average
Vase			
☐ blue	345.00	355.00	347.00
☐ amethyst.............................	370.00	380.00	372.00

ILLINOIS DAISY
Davisons of Gateshead

The daisies that ramble over the surface of these pieces are rounded and plump. The center is a marble circle in high relief. The framework that separates each flower is scroll-like, twisting and turning, interconnected. The glass is heavy, resembling cut glass; the color is marigold.

Bon Bon			
☐ marigold	42.00	530.00	45.00
Bowl			
☐ marigold	60.00	75.00	62.00
Cookie Jar			
☐ marigold	55.00	—	—

ILLUSION
Fenton

The pattern is an interesting combination of straightforward flora and foliage and a central medallion of bizarre Escher-like shapes. The connection between the blooms and the geometrics creates quite a different perspective. The colors are marigold and blue.

Bon Bon			
☐ marigold	42.00	50.00	45.00
☐ blue	62.00	80.00	65.00
Bowl			
☐ marigold	62.00	80.00	65.00
☐ blue	82.00	100.00	85.00

IMPERIAL BASKET

The distinguishing features on these baskets are the iridescence or, more properly, the lack of it. The color here is flat except for glowing rainbows suggested on the rim. The shade is smoke with a marigold blush.

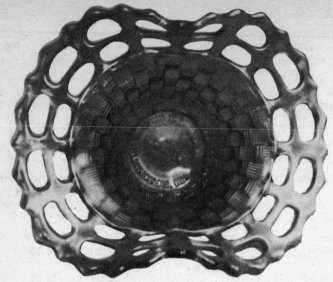

Imperial Basket

	Current Price Range		Prior Year Average
Basket			
☐ marigold	40.00	60.00	42.00
☐ smoke	70.00	—	—

IMPERIAL CANDLE HOLDER

A gentle candlestick, voluptuous and rounded, these rare pieces are decorated only by the bright iridescence. The glass is thick and smooth with no etched or molded design.

Candleholder, height 7″
| ☐ red... | 125.00 | 150.00 | 130.00 |

IMPERIAL DAISY

Shade
| ☐ marigold .... | 45.00 | — | — |

IMPERIAL GRAPE

Shade
| ☐ marigold .... | 65.00 | — | — |

IMPERIAL PAPERWEIGHT

This was probably a giveaway from the factory, inscribed with the names of the company and a representation of all its trademarks. It is a solid, heavy oval with a dish of iridescent amethyst on the top.

	Current Price Range		Prior Year Average
Paperweight			
☐ amethyst..	700.00	900.00	750.00

INCA VASE

This does resemble the angular etching on an archeological vase. Triangular ridges and vertical draping combine in a balanced pattern. It is modernistic, darkly iridescent in marigold.

Vase			
☐ marigold	700.00	800.00	725.00

INDIANA STATE HOUSE
Fenton

This is a souvenir plate with the state capitol building of Indiana featured in the center. The rest of the pattern is devoid of decoration but is richly iridized. The rim is an irregular scallop with a bullet edge. The colors are marigold and blue.

Plate			
☐ marigold	2500.00	3000.00	2700.00
☐ blue	2800.00	3200.00	2900.00

INTAGLIO DAISY
Sowerby

Horizontal and vertical panels of angular ridges frame deep-cut branches and intricately lined flowers. This combination of geometry and tradition makes a neat intaglio pattern. The color is marigold.

Bowl, diameter 4″			
☐ marigold	20.00	25.00	22.00
Bowl, diameter 7¾″			
☐ marigold	40.00	50.00	45.00
Rose Bowl			
☐ marigold	45.00	—	—

INTAGLIO FEATHERS

	Current Price Range		Prior Year Average
Cup			
☐ marigold	20.00	30.00	22.00

INTAGLIO OVALS
U.S. Glass

	Current Price Range		Prior Year Average
Bowl			
☐ white	60.00	70.00	62.00
Plate			
☐ white	75.00	85.00	77.00

INTERIOR PANELS

Mug			
☐ marigold	70.00	80.00	72.00

INTERIOR POINSETTIA
Northwood

Tumbler			
☐ marigold	460.00	470.00	462.00

INTERIOR RAYS
Westmoreland

Butter Dish, covered			
☐ marigold	60.00	70.00	62.00
Creamer			
☐ marigold	35.00	45.00	37.00
Jam Jar			
☐ marigold	35.00	45.00	37.00
Sugar Bowl			
☐ marigold	35.00	45.00	37.00

INVERTED COIN DOT
Fenton

Again, the pattern is mottled, showing through the darkly transparent glass from the interior. The coin dot motif is used, enlarged in smooth craters over the piece in its entirety. The iridescence is good, colors are amethyst, blue, and marigold.

	Current Price Range		Prior Year Average
Pitcher			
☐ marigold	220.00	230.00	222.00
☐ blue	390.00	420.00	395.00
☐ amethyst	440.00	460.00	445.00
Tumbler			
☐ marigold	70.00	80.00	72.00
☐ blue	80.00	90.00	82.00
☐ amethyst	90.00	100.00	92.00

INVERTED FEATHER
Cambridge

This is an elaborate, formal pattern of scrolls, hobstars, and heavy ridged frames. The main motif is a floral design surrounded by deep grooves in a triangular shape. The overall pattern is filled in with diagonal ridges and draped beadwork. The colors are green, blue, marigold, and amethyst.

	Current Price Range		Prior Year Average
Butter Dish, with cover			
☐ marigold	210.00	225.00	230.00
☐ amethyst	230.00	250.00	240.00
Compote			
☐ marigold	45.00	—	—
Cracker Jar, with cover			
☐ green	280.00	290.00	282.00
Creamer			
☐ marigold	180.00	200.00	182.00
☐ amethyst	210.00	230.00	215.00
Milk Pitcher			
☐ marigold	195.00	210.00	200.00
Parfait			
☐ marigold	55.00	—	—
Pitcher			
☐ marigold	3000.00	3500.00	3100.00
☐ green	3000.00	3500.00	3100.00
Punch Bowl			
☐ marigold	1700.00	2000.00	1750.00
Punch Cup			
☐ marigold	50.00	—	—
☐ green	65.00	—	—
Tumbler			
☐ marigold	490.00	520.00	495.00
☐ green	590.00	620.00	595.00
Wine			
☐ marigold	85.00	—	—

INVERTED STRAWBERRY
Cambridge

This is a lovely intaglio pattern of stylized fruit and foliage, dancing in motion over the piece. The strawberries are made up of tiny fretwork rows of diamonds, dainty and sharply cut. The branches and leaves are understated, showing of a glossy, smooth background. The colors are marigold, amethyst, green, blue, and purple.

	Current Price Range		Prior Year Average
Berry Bowl, diameter 5″			
☐ marigold	30.00	37.00	32.00
☐ amethyst	50.00	60.00	52.00
☐ green	50.00	60.00	52.00
☐ blue	50.00	60.00	52.00
Berry Bowl, diameter 9″			
☐ marigold	60.00	70.00	62.00
☐ amethyst	90.00	100.00	93.00
☐ green	80.00	90.00	82.00
Butter Dish, with cover			
☐ marigold	200.00	225.00	210.00
☐ amethyst	275.00	310.00	300.00
☐ green	275.00	310.00	300.00
Candlesticks, pair			
☐ marigold	245.00	255.00	247.00
☐ amethyst	320.00	330.00	322.00
☐ green	295.00	310.00	297.00
Celery			
☐ amethyst	275.00	—	—
☐ blue	350.00	—	—
Compote, large			
☐ marigold	245.00	255.00	247.00
☐ amethyst	390.00	410.00	395.00
☐ green	340.00	360.00	345.00
Creamer			
☐ marigold	70.00	90.00	72.00
☐ amethyst	95.00	115.00	100.00
☐ green	95.00	115.00	100.00
☐ purple	275.00	—	—
Cuspidor			
☐ marigold	900.00	1100.00	950.00
☐ amethyst	900.00	1100.00	950.00
☐ green	900.00	1100.00	950.00
☐ blue	900.00	1100.00	950.00
Honey Dip			
☐ marigold	75.00	—	—

	Current Price Range		Prior Year Average
Milk Pitcher			
☐ amethyst...........................	1200.00	1400.00	1250.00
Pitcher			
☐ marigold	575.00	700.00	600.00
☐ amethyst...........................	850.00	1000.00	860.00
☐ green	850.00	1000.00	860.00
Powder Jar			
☐ marigold	90.00	110.00	95.00
☐ green	110.00	120.00	115.00
Spooner			
☐ marigold	90.00	—	—
☐ green	100.00	—	—
☐ purple	140.00	—	—
Stemmed Sugar			
☐ purple	275.00	—	—
Sugar			
☐ marigold	90.00	—	—
☐ green	100.00	—	—
☐ purple	140.00	—	—
Tumbler			
☐ marigold	320.00	330.00	322.00
☐ amethyst...........................	260.00	270.00	262.00
☐ green	370.00	380.00	372.00
☐ blue	370.00	380.00	372.00

INVERTED THISTLE
Cambridge

This design is tasteful and classic. The flowers of the thistle are made up of the same fretwork as Inverted Strawberry, the branches and leaves are stylized into scrolls, the upper hat of the bloom suggests a crown. The colors are marigold, amethyst, green, and less commonly, blue.

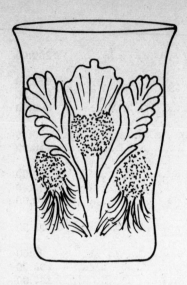

Inverted Thistle

	Current Price Range		Prior Year Average
Butter Dish, with cover			
□ marigold	320.00	335.00	325.00
□ amethyst	425.00	475.00	450.00
□ green	425.00	475.00	450.00
Creamer			
□ marigold	345.00	355.00	347.00
□ amethyst	375.00	385.00	377.00
□ green	375.00	385.00	377.00
Pitcher			
□ marigold	2500.00	3000.00	2600.00
□ amethyst	2500.00	3000.00	2600.00
Spooner			
□ marigold	345.00	355.00	347.00
□ amethyst	375.00	385.00	377.00
□ green	375.00	385.00	377.00
Sugar Bowl			
□ marigold	345.00	355.00	347.00
□ amethyst	375.00	385.00	377.00
□ green	375.00	385.00	377.00
Tumbler			
□ marigold	420.00	430.00	422.00
□ amethyst	345.00	355.00	347.00

IOWA

	Current Price Range		Prior Year Average
Mug			
☐ marigold	80.00	90.00	82.00

IRIS
Fenton

Simplicity is the distinguishing feature here. The desire to fill all of the available space on the piece has been squelched. From a central medallion, sprays of curvy iris blooms wind up and over the interior. The ground is smooth and glossy, the colors are green, marigold, amethyst, and less commonly, white.

Buttermilk Goblet			
☐ marigold	45.00	55.00	47.00
☐ amethyst	60.00	70.00	62.00
☐ green	60.00	70.00	62.00
Compote			
☐ marigold	40.00	50.00	42.00
☐ green	50.00	60.00	52.00
☐ blue	60.00	80.00	62.00
☐ amethyst	55.00	65.00	57.00
☐ white	275.00	—	—

ISAAC BENESCH BOWL
Millersburg

This is an advertising piece bearing the inscription "The Great House of Isaac Benesch and Sons, Wilkesbarre, PA, Baltimore, MD, Annapolis, MD." This is done in a ribbon motif, almost resembling the tail of a kite. The central motif is framed in flowers but the background is smooth. The iridescence is pearly, the color is marigold

Bowl			
☐ amethyst	130.00	150.00	135.00

I.W. HARPER

Decanter, with stopper			
☐ marigold	70.00	80.00	72.00

JACK-IN-THE-PULPIT
Northwood

Many companies made vases in this shape, which features a lily-like bloom. This Northwood pattern is simple and well balanced, the stem gently ribbed, the top of the bloom forms the rim. The edge is lightly fluted in flat scallops. The iridescence is golden, the colors vary widely.

	Current Price Range		Prior Year Average
Vase, amber lip, talon-footed			
☐ amberina swirl	175.00	220.00	180.00
☐ blue opalescent	45.00	57.00	46.00
☐ opaline	85.00	110.00	90.00
☐ yellow and white	50.00	60.00	52.00

JACKMAN WHISKEY

A strongly iridescent body made for commercial consumption but rare today, this whiskey body is of the traditional shape with a light stippled decoration over all. The central motif is a portrait of a ram's head on a heraldic shield. Color is marigold.

Bottle			
☐ marigold	30.00	35.00	32.00

JACOB'S LADDER

Perfume Bottle			
☐ marigold	25.00	35.00	27.00

JACOB'S LADDER VARIANT
U.S. Glass

Rose Bowl			
☐ marigold	45.00	55.00	47.00

JACOBEAN RANGER

Bowl, small			
☐ marigold	25.00	35.00	27.00
Decanter, with stopper			
☐ marigold	145.00	155.00	147.00
Juice Tumbler			
☐ marigold	65.00	75.00	67.00
Miniature Tumbler			
☐ marigold	60.00	70.00	62.00
Pitcher			
☐ marigold	245.00	255.00	247.00
Tumbler			
☐ marigold	70.00	80.00	72.00
Wine Goblet			
☐ marigold	20.00	30.00	22.00

JELLY JAR
Imperial

   This is an interesting conception in design. The pattern is on the interior, a series of triangularly terminated prisms bending under the base. The lid has a starburst, and when tipped over on its top, the design is formed in the jelly. The glass is close to transparent, the iridescence wonderful, the colors vary.

	Current Price Range		Prior Year Average
Jar, with lid			
☐ marigold	55.00	65.00	57.00

JEWELED HEART
Dugan

   The heart is made up of scrolls facing each other in a kiss, the background of the voluptuous heart is stippled, giving a gem-like appearance. In the center of each panel is a football shape, suggesting an oval jewel. The upper rim is beaded. The colors are marigold, purple, and peach.

Jeweled Heart

Berry Bowl, diameter 5″			
☐ peach opalescent	60.00	70.00	62.00
☐ purple	40.00	—	—

	Current Price Range		Prior Year Average
Berry Bowl, diameter 10″			
☐ peach opalescent..........................	130.00	140.00	132.00
☐ purple	95.00	—	—
Pitcher			
☐ marigold	770.00	780.00	777.00
Tumbler			
☐ marigold	70.00	100.00	72.00
☐ white..	570.00	590.00	577.00

JEWELS
Imperial

	Current Price Range		Prior Year Average
Candlestick			
☐ ices..	30.00	40.00	32.00
☐ red...	100.00	110.00	105.00
Creamer			
☐ ices..	65.00	75.00	67.00
☐ red...	130.00	140.00	132.00
Hat			
☐ ices..	80.00	90.00	82.00
☐ red...	185.00	195.00	187.00
Sugar Bowl			
☐ ices..	65.00	75.00	67.00
☐ red...	130.00	140.00	132.00
Vase			
☐ marigold	85.00	95.00	87.00
☐ ices..	65.00	75.00	67.00
☐ red...	165.00	175.00	167.00

JOCKEY CLUB
Northwood

The interior of the bowl is inscribed "Jockey Club" in elongated cursive, winding around a horseshoe. The floral pattern below is a neat bloom on foliage and stem, with a tiny duplicate right above the inscription. The iridescence is lavish, the color amethyst and other dark tints.

	Current Price Range		Prior Year Average
Bowl			
☐ purple	110.00	140.00	115.00
☐ amethyst....................................	140.00	150.00	142.00

KANGAROO
Crystal Glass Factory

The hopping animal in the center is well molded and shows motion. The rest of the pattern is subordinate to this central motif, the background that covers the rest of the piece is delicate foliage sparsely strewn, revealing a lot of smooth, glossy glass. The iridescence is fine; colors are marigold and purple.

	Current Price Range		Prior Year Average
Bowl, diameter 9″			
☐ marigold	65.00	75.00	67.00
☐ purple	90.00	100.00	92.00

KINGFISHER
Australian Manufacturer

The bird is perched proudly in the center sitting on delicate branches surrounded with a wreath of foliage. The central medallion is stippled, the rest of the glass smooth. A variant adds berries to the foliage. The color is purple or marigold.

Kingfisher

Bowl, diameter 9″			
☐ marigold	120.00	130.00	125.00
☐ purple	160.00	180.00	170.00

KITTENS
Fenton

Originally children's glass, this pattern is found on many bowls and other shapes and is a favorite with collectors. It shows a series of kittens falling over each other to drink from a long oval bowl. The rest of the glass is smooth and the iridescence magnificent. The colors are vaseline, marigold, cobalt, and purple.

	Current Price Range		Prior Year Average
Bowl, diameter 4″			
☐ marigold	115.00	125.00	117.00
☐ cobalt blue	190.00	200.00	192.00
☐ vaseline	240.00	250.00	242.00
☐ purple	250.00	—	—
Bowl, upswept sides			
☐ marigold	110.00	120.00	115.00
☐ cobalt blue	200.00	220.00	205.00
☐ purple	100.00	—	—
Cereal Bowl			
☐ marigold	125.00	135.00	127.00
☐ cobalt blue	160.00	170.00	162.00
Cup and Saucer			
☐ marigold	250.00	260.00	252.00
☐ cobalt blue	600.00	650.00	625.00
Plate, 4½″			
☐ marigold	130.00	—	—
☐ blue	170.00	—	—
Saucer			
☐ purple	190.00	—	—
Spittoon			
☐ marigold	3000.00	—	—
☐ blue	3500.00	—	—
Spooner			
☐ marigold	100.00	150.00	125.00
☐ cobalt blue	260.00	270.00	262.00
☐ vaseline	200.00	220.00	205.00
Vase, height 3¼″			
☐ marigold	155.00	165.00	162.00
☐ cobalt blue	205.00	220.00	210.00
☐ vaseline	225.00	235.00	228.00

KIWI
Australian Manufacturer

This is an interesting pattern of the New Zealand birds in the foreground, a mountain range in good perspective in the background. This scene makes up the central medallion; the rest of the piece is covered with delicate, etched ferns. The colors are dark marigold and purple.

Bowl, diameter 10″			
☐ marigold	130.00	140.00	132.00
☐ amethyst	170.00	180.00	172.00

KNOTTED BEADS
Fenton

This is a modernistic pattern consisting of stretched beads grouped in oval shapes and connected in big bows. The pattern is not directly vertical; it twists diagonally from the base to the upper rim which is ruffled irregularly. The colors are blue, green, white, vaseline, marigold, purple, and amber.

	Current Price Range		Prior Year Average
Vase			
☐ marigold	25.00	35.00	27.00
☐ blue	35.00	45.00	36.00
☐ green	35.00	45.00	37.00
☐ vaseline	80.00	90.00	82.00
☐ white	70.00	80.00	72.00
☐ purple	35.00	—	—
☐ amber	80.00	—	—

KOKOMO
English

Rose Bowl			
☐ marigold	40.00	50.00	42.00

KOOKABURRA
Australian Manufacturer

Looking like the Kingfisher, the little Australian bird is perched in the center on a thick horizontal branch. The outer pattern which rims the interior is a busy, varied design of different blooms and stylized foliage. As with the Kingfisher, there is a variant which is distinguished by a large stippled medallion.

Bowl, 5″			
☐ marigold	40.00	—	—
☐ purple	45.00	—	—
Bowl, 10″			
☐ marigold	80.00	—	—
☐ purple	95.00	—	—

KNIGHT TEMPLAR
Northwood

Mug			
☐ marigold	550.00	610.00	560.00
☐ ices	700.00	770.00	720.00

LACY DEWDROP
Phoenix

This overall pattern of elongated triangles and stippling, rounded out with beadwork and football jewels, is elegant and well balanced. Made in a variety of shapes, it is made in one Carnival color only—white opalescent.

	Current Price Range		Prior Year Average
Banana Dish			
☐ pearl	130.00	145.00	140.00
Berry Bowl, with cover			
☐ pearl	120.00	130.00	125.00
Compote, with cover			
☐ pearl	125.00	140.00	130.00
Creamer			
☐ pearl	90.00	—	—
Sugar			
☐ pearl	90.00	—	—
Tumbler			
☐ pearl	250.00	—	—
Water Pitcher			
☐ pearl	575.00	—	—

LATTICE
Dugan

Bowl			
☐ marigold	55.00	—	—
☐ purple	65.00	—	—

LATTICE AND DAISY
Dugan

The lattice is a wide-banded lozenge just under the smooth rim. Just below is a diagonally angled daisy on detailed foliage. The glass is nearly opaque, the iridescence is rainbow-like, and the colors are marigold, cobalt, and purple.

Lattice and Daisy

	Current Price Range		Prior Year Average
Berry Bowl, diameter 9″			
☐ marigold	55.00	65.00	58.00
Tankard Pitcher			
☐ marigold	130.00	140.00	132.00
☐ cobalt blue	180.00	190.00	182.00
☐ purple	200.00	—	—

LATTICE AND GRAPE
Fenton

Great bunches of grapes dangle down the sides in vertical panels, hanging from a zig zag latticework. The geometric band is made up of ridges in high relief, decorated with spaced knobs. The bottom band is a large diamond lozenge with the knobs in the middle of each. The colors are blue, green, white, marigold, amethyst, and peach opalescent.

Tankard Pitcher			
☐ marigold	155.00	165.00	157.00
☐ blue	300.00	325.00	315.00
☐ white	630.00	660.00	640.00
Tumbler			
☐ marigold	30.00	40.00	32.00
☐ blue	35.00	45.00	37.00
☐ white	190.00	210.00	195.00

LATTICE AND LEAVES

	Current Price Range		Prior Year Average
Vase			
☐ marigold	45.00	55.00	47.00
☐ blue	65.00	—	—

LATTICE AND POINTS
Dugan

	Current Price Range		Prior Year Average
Vase			
☐ marigold	30.00	40.00	32.00
☐ amethyst	35.00	45.00	37.00
☐ white	50.00	60.00	52.00

LATTICE AND PRISMS

Perfume Bottle			
☐ marigold	50.00	60.00	52.00

LATTICE AND SPRAYS

Vase, 10″			
☐ marigold	35.00	45.00	37.00

LATTICE HEART
English

Bowl, 5″			
☐ marigold	25.00	35.00	27.00
☐ blue	35.00	45.00	37.00
Bowl, 10″			
☐ marigold	45.00	55.00	47.00
☐ blue	65.00	75.00	67.00
☐ amethyst	70.00	80.00	72.00
Compote			
☐ marigold	55.00	65.00	60.00
☐ blue	80.00	90.00	82.00
☐ amethyst	85.00	95.00	87.00

LAUREL BAND

Tumbler			
☐ marigold	40.00	50.00	42.00

LAUREL LEAVES
Imperial

Plate			
☐ marigold	40.00	50.00	42.00

	Current Price Range		Prior Year Average
☐ amethyst..	**50.00**	**60.00**	**52.00**
☐ smoke	**55.00**	**65.00**	**57.00**

LEA
Sowerby

This is a simple, tasteful design made up of stippled bands horizontally alternating with vertical ridging. The interior is smooth but reflects the exterior design in an interesting effect. The colors are amethyst and marigold.

Bowl, oval, footed
☐ marigold	**35.00**	**45.00**	**37.00**
☐ amethyst..	**38.00**	**40.00**	**39.00**

Bowl, round, footed
☐ marigold	**35.00**	**45.00**	**37.00**
☐ amethyst..	**45.00**	**55.00**	**47.00**

Creamer, footed
☐ marigold	**35.00**	**45.00**	**37.00**
☐ amethyst..	**45.00**	**55.00**	**47.00**

LEAF AND BEADS
Northwood

This prolific pattern is found on many shapes in various types of glass. In Carnival, it has a wonderful iridescence on opaque color. The design is a row of leaves growing out of the base, terminating a quarter of the way up in a bead band that continues to the rim. The background is smooth and shows the rainbow effect. The colors available are the wide range of Northwood tints.

Leaf and Beads

	Current Price Range		Prior Year Average

Candy Bowl

☐ marigold	35.00	43.00	37.00
☐ purple	50.00	60.00	52.00
☐ green	50.00	60.00	52.00
☐ blue	50.00	60.00	52.00
☐ amethyst	50.00	60.00	52.00
☐ white	80.00	120.00	85.00
☐ ice green	80.00	120.00	85.00
☐ ice blue	80.00	120.00	85.00
☐ aqua opalescent	160.00	210.00	175.00

Rose Bowl, footed

☐ marigold	40.00	50.00	42.00
☐ purple	60.00	90.00	70.00
☐ green	57.50	72.50	60.00
☐ blue	57.50	72.50	60.00
☐ amethyst	57.50	72.50	60.00
☐ white	85.00	110.00	87.00
☐ ice green	85.00	110.00	87.00
☐ ice blue	85.00	110.00	87.00
☐ aqua opalescent	180.00	235.00	187.00
☐ aqua	300.00	—	—
☐ peach opalescent	345.00	—	—

LEAF AND LITTLE FLOWERS
Millersburg

Compote, miniature

☐ marigold	300.00	340.00	320.00
☐ purple	300.00	340.00	320.00
☐ green	375.00	400.00	380.00
☐ amethyst	440.00	460.00	445.00

LEAF CHAIN
Fenton

This overall design is common on many types of articles. It is made up of a snowflake medallion taking up the center in an intricate scrolled design. This motif is continued around the edge in panels surrounded by a scale background and curvy scrolls. Colors run the gamut available to Carnival glass.

	Current Price Range		Prior Year Average
Bon Bon			
☐ marigold	30.00	40.00	32.00
☐ purple	45.00	55.00	47.00
☐ green	50.00	60.00	52.00
☐ blue	40.00	50.00	42.00
☐ amethyst...	40.00	50.00	42.00
Bowl			
☐ marigold	35.00	45.00	37.00
☐ purple	45.00	55.00	47.00
☐ green	50.00	60.00	55.00
☐ blue	40.00	50.00	42.00
☐ amethyst...	40.00	50.00	42.00
☐ red...	375.00	—	—
☐ white..	65.00	—	—
☐ aqua opalescent	1000.00	—	—
Plate, 7″			
☐ marigold	310.00	—	—
☐ blue	90.00	—	—
Plate, 9″			
☐ marigold	60.00	70.00	62.00
☐ green	95.00	110.00	97.00
☐ blue	80.00	90.00	82.00
☐ purple	70.00	80.00	72.00
☐ amethyst...	90.00	100.00	92.00
☐ white..	100.00	110.00	105.00
☐ aqua opalescent	2000.00	2200.00	2050.00
☐ red...	295.00	—	—

LEAF COLUMN
Northwood

This is a stately pattern, a series of vertical bands made up of fern-like leaves. They curve around the vase framed with a reversed arch rather resembling twigs or branches. The iridescence is nice; the colors range widely.

Lamp Shade			
☐ white..	80.00	110.00	85.00
Vase			
☐ marigold	30.00	40.00	32.00
☐ purple	30.00	40.00	32.00
☐ green	35.00	45.00	37.00
☐ blue	35.00	45.00	37.00
☐ amethyst...	40.00	50.00	42.00
☐ white..	45.00	55.00	47.00

	Current Price Range		Prior Year Average
☐ ice green	45.00	55.00	47.00
☐ ice blue	45.00	55.00	47.00
☐ peach opalescent	50.00	60.00	52.00

LEAF RAYS
Dugan

The central medallion is rather geometrical, compared to the rest of the pattern. The rosette or starburst in the middle is smooth glass; the wide band of leaves that radiate out are stippled. The rest of the piece is smooth and glossy. The nearly opaque colors are blue, white, green, amethyst, marigold, and peach opalescent.

Nappy

☐ marigold	20.00	30.00	22.00
☐ amethyst	30.00	40.00	32.00
☐ white	35.00	45.00	37.00
☐ peach opalescent	35.00	45.00	37.00

LEAF SWIRL
Westmoreland

Again geometry combines with naturalistic design to create an overall pattern. Leaves grow out of the pedestal base, each framed with a diagonally curved panel that continues up the side, terminating at the widely ruffled rim. The colors are excellent and range widely.

Compote

☐ marigold	35.00	45.00	37.00
☐ purple	38.00	47.50	39.00
☐ teal	65.00	85.00	67.00
☐ amethyst	45.00	55.00	42.00
☐ white	50.00	60.00	52.00
☐ amber	55.00	65.00	57.00
☐ vaseline	55.00	65.00	57.00

LEAF SWIRL AND FLOWER
Fenton

The pattern is etched into the piece, not quite intaglio but in low relief. It is a lovely, delicate design of flowers and foliage, and it covers the piece sparingly. The colors available are marigold and other pastels.

	Current Price Range		Prior Year Average

Vase
☐ marigold	40.00	50.00	42.00
☐ white..	60.00	70.00	62.00

LEAF TIERS
Fenton

The leaves are set in rows overlapping around the piece, creating an interesting perspective. It is a straightforward, overall pattern that shows off the iridescence nicely. The most common color is marigold, then purple, green, and blue.

Berry Bowl, diameter 5½"
☐ marigold	25.00	35.00	27.00

Berry Bowl, diameter 9"
☐ marigold	50.00	60.00	52.00

Butter Dish
☐ marigold	170.00	180.00	172.00

Creamer
☐ marigold	75.00	85.00	77.00

Spooner
☐ marigold	75.00	85.00	77.00

Sugar Bowl
☐ marigold	80.00	90.00	85.00

Tumbler
☐ marigold	70.00	80.00	72.00
☐ blue	90.00	100.00	92.00

Water Pitcher
☐ marigold	450.00	470.00	455.00
☐ blue	680.00	690.00	682.00

LILY OF THE VALLEY
Fenton

This is a lovely, well-balanced pattern of flowers, neatly geometrical leaf work and beaded bands. Three motifs are used, horizontally rounding the pieces in wide bands. All of the bands contain tiny bell-like flowers. The iridescence is the finest, found in marigold and cobalt.

Pitcher
☐ marigold	1500.00	1700.00	1550.00
☐ cobalt...	4400.00	4600.00	4500.00

	Current Price Range		Prior Year Average
Tumbler			
☐ marigold	590.00	610.00	595.00
☐ cobalt.............................	440.00	460.00	445.00

LINED LATTICE
Dugan

This is an offbeat pattern of elongated diamond work curving asymmetrically around the piece. Each shape is filled in by vertical ridge which refract the light to a great degree. Colors come in marigold, amethyst, peach opalescent, blue, white, and green.

Vase			
☐ marigold	30.00	40.00	32.00
☐ blue	40.00	50.00	42.00
☐ green	40.00	50.00	42.00
☐ amethyst...........................	40.00	50.00	42.00
☐ white...............................	55.00	65.00	57.00
☐ peach opalescent..................	55.00	65.00	57.00

LION
Fenton

A series of four panels, each made up of a full-figured lion in a roaring gallop, round the wide middle of these pieces. The lions seem to be chasing each other head to tail. They are framed with natural looking trees topped with foliage, growing out of the central medallion of misplaced flowers. The colors are marigold and blue.

Lion

	Current Price Range		Prior Year Average
Bowl, diameter 7"			
☐ marigold	80.00	90.00	82.00
☐ blue	140.00	160.00	142.00
Plate, diameter 7½"			
☐ marigold	300.00	330.00	310.00
☐ blue	400.00	440.00	415.00

LITTLE BARREL
Imperial

These were probably giveaways or advertisers, containing liquid at one time. It is the straightforward shape and pattern of a pickle barrel, with slats and bands and a distinctive little hat-shaped top. They are found in marigold and amethyst, green, and smoke.

Barrel			
☐ marigold	70.00	80.00	72.00
☐ green	90.00	100.00	92.00
☐ amethyst.......................................	90.00	100.00	92.00
☐ smoke	100.00	120.00	105.00

LITTLE BEADS

Bowl, 8"			
☐ marigold	10.00	20.00	15.00
☐ peach opalescent...........................	40.00	50.00	42.00
Compote			
☐ marigold	20.00	30.00	22.00
☐ peach opalescent...........................	40.00	50.00	42.00

LITTLE DAISIES
Fenton

The central medallion is interesting, resembling a mantra flamed with jewel-like beadwork. The rest of the pattern is an overall design of daisies spaced throughout with sparse foliage. The color is marigold.

	Current Price Range		Prior Year Average

Bowl, diameter 8″
☐ marigold 180.00 190.00 185.00
Bowl, diameter 9″
☐ marigold 180.00 190.00 185.00

LITTLE DARLING

Bottle
☐ marigold 45.00 55.00 47.00

LITTLE FISHES
Fenton

The fishes are swimming around, practically obscured by a busy combination of geometry and natural designs. There are berries, flowers, leaves, and vines interspersed among diamonds and, most distinctively, X-shapes. The colors run the gamut.

Bowl, 5½″
☐ marigold 35.00 45.00 37.00
☐ purple 90.00 110.00 92.00
☐ green 50.00 60.00 52.00
☐ blue 65.00 75.00 67.00
☐ amethyst.. 90.00 110.00 92.00
Bowl, 10″
☐ marigold 75.00 85.00 77.00
☐ green 85.00 95.00 87.00
☐ blue 155.00 165.00 157.00
☐ white... 840.00 860.00 845.00

LITTLE FLOWERS
Fenton

The center is a big flower, widely petaled around a stippled center. The interior band which frames the center is a row of smaller flowers of a different variety; the background is smooth. The colors are green, blue, red, amber, aqua, vaseline, marigold, and amethyst.

Little Flowers

	Current Price Range		Prior Year Average
Berry Bowl, diameter 5″			
☐ marigold	25.00	28.00	26.00
☐ green	28.00	32.00	27.00
☐ blue	30.00	40.00	32.00
☐ amethyst	30.00	40.00	35.00
☐ amber	90.00	100.00	95.00
☐ vaseline	45.00	55.00	47.00
Berry Bowl, diameter 9″			
☐ marigold	40.00	50.00	42.00
☐ green	60.00	70.00	65.00
☐ blue	80.00	90.00	82.00
☐ amethyst	85.00	95.00	87.00
☐ amber	85.00	95.00	87.00
☐ red	1200.00	1300.00	1250.00
Plate, diameter 10″			
☐ marigold	180.00	190.00	182.00
Plate, 7″			
☐ marigold	75.00	—	—

LITTLE MERMAID

	Current Price Range		Prior Year Average

Figural

	Current Price Range		Prior Year Average
☐ white	75.00	—	—

LITTLE OWL

Fruit Bowl and Base

☐ marigold	125.00	—	—

Hatpin

☐ marigold	115.00	—	—
☐ green	150.00	—	—
☐ blue	165.00	—	—
☐ white	175.00	—	—

LITTLE STARS
Millersburg

The main motif is a huge-petaled flower, interestingly containing a spray of leafy foliage within each petal. The widest band is made up of a row of six-pointed faceted stars with a stippled ground. The colors are green, amethyst, and marigold.

Bowl, diameter 7–10½″

☐ marigold	60.00	70.00	62.00
☐ green	85.00	95.00	87.00
☐ amethyst	65.00	75.00	67.00

LOGANBERRY
Imperial

This pattern is considered to be one of the greatest in Carnival glass. The mold work is exceptional, tiny berries and foliage in high relief decorating the entire body of the piece, terminating in smooth, arched panels which resolve the neck. The iridescence is as glowing and as rainbow as any piece in Carnival. Colors are purple, green, amber, smoke, and marigold.

Vase

☐ marigold	120.00	130.00	122.00
☐ purple	180.00	190.00	182.00
☐ green	170.00	180.00	172.00
☐ amber	190.00	210.00	195.00
☐ smoke	190.00	210.00	195.00

LONG HOBSTAR
Imperial

The hobstar, molded in high relief, is stretched out of shape on these pieces. The overall pattern is busy, intricate, and decidedly geometric. The effect is one of cut glass, achieved by superior moldwork.

	Current Price Range		Prior Year Average
Bowl, diameter 8"			
□ marigold	40.00	50.00	42.00
Bowl, diameter 10"			
□ marigold	50.00	60.00	52.00
Compote			
□ marigold	60.00	70.00	62.00

LONG HORN

Wine Goblet			
□ marigold	30.00	40.00	32.00

LONG LEAF
Dugan

Bowl			
□ peach opalescent	50.00	60.00	52.00

LONG THUMBPRINT
Dugan

This is a simple design of rows of concave ovals in various sizes, eventually stretched out to an airy thinness. The glass is nearly transparent; the colors are blue, green, and amethyst.

Bowl			
□ marigold	25.00	35.00	27.00
□ amethyst	35.00	45.00	37.00
Compote			
□ marigold	30.00	40.00	32.00
□ green	35.00	45.00	37.00
□ amethyst	35.00	45.00	37.00
Creamer			
□ marigold	35.00	45.00	37.00
□ green	35.00	45.00	37.00
□ amethyst	35.00	45.00	37.00

	Current Price Range		Prior Year Average

Sugar Bowl
| ☐ marigold | 30.00 | 40.00 | 35.00 |
| ☐ green | 30.00 | 40.00 | 35.00 |

LOTUS AND GRAPE
Fenton

This pattern is distinctive because of the well-molded relief flowers and grapes which are raised nicely but flattened across the surface. The design is all encompassing, covering all of the available space. The colors are green, blue, red, white, amethyst, and marigold.

Bon Bon
☐ marigold	30.00	40.00	35.00
☐ green	35.00	45.00	37.00
☐ blue	35.00	45.00	37.00
☐ amethyst	35.00	45.00	37.00
☐ red	640.00	660.00	645.00
☐ vaseline	85.00	—	—

Bowl
☐ marigold	40.00	50.00	42.00
☐ green	45.00	55.00	47.00
☐ blue	45.00	55.00	47.00
☐ amethyst	45.00	55.00	47.00

Plate
☐ marigold	70.00	80.00	72.00
☐ green	570.00	580.00	572.00
☐ blue	480.00	520.00	485.00
☐ amethyst	440.00	460.00	445.00

LOTUS LAND
Northwood

Bon Bon Dish
| ☐ amethyst | 75.00 | 85.00 | 77.00 |

LOUISA
Westmoreland

Round panels of sparsely decorated flora are made up of vines and leaves. The rest of the ground is filled in with tiny leaves that resemble scales in the way they overlap. The colors are marigold, green, blue, and amethyst.

	Current Price Range		Prior Year Average
Candy Dish			
☐ marigold	40.00	50.00	42.00
☐ green	60.00	70.00	62.00
☐ amethyst	55.00	65.00	57.00
Rose Bowl			
☐ marigold	45.00	55.00	47.00
☐ amethyst	60.00	70.00	62.00
☐ green	65.00	75.00	67.00
☐ blue	60.00	70.00	62.00
☐ amber	90.00	—	—
☐ aqua	90.00	—	—

LOVEBIRDS

Bottle, with stopper

☐ marigold	135.00	145.00	136.00

LOVELY
Northwood

The iridescence, which is bright and golden, is the distinctive feature on these pieces. It is an interesting, vertically oriented pattern of beaded foliage growing from the center and out. The design terminates at the waist with three-pointed leaves; the rest of the piece smooth and glossy. The colors are purple and marigold.

Bowl

☐ marigold	50.00	65.00	52.00
☐ purple	135.00	—	—

LUCKY BELL

Bowl

☐ marigold	60.00	70.00	62.00

LUSTRE AND CLEAR
Imperial

A simple pattern of pillars resolved at the rim by matching flutes shows off the glowing iridescence. As the name implies, the glass is rather transparent and the color is marigold.

Bowl, 5"

☐ marigold	15.00	22.00	18.00
Butter Dish			
☐ marigold	60.00	70.00	62.00
Creamer			
☐ marigold	30.00	40.00	32.00

	Current Price Range		Prior Year Average
Nappy			
☐ marigold	30.00	40.00	32.00
Pitcher			
☐ marigold	190.00	200.00	192.00
Rose Bowl			
☐ marigold	50.00	—	—
Sugar Bowl			
☐ marigold	30.00	40.00	32.00
Tumbler			
☐ marigold	35.00	45.00	37.00

LUSTRE FLUTE
Northwood

A plain pattern of pillars topped by a lozenge band adorns these pieces. It was made in many shapes and a variety of colors.

Lustre Flute

	Current Price Range		Prior Year Average
Bowl			
☐ marigold	30.00	40.00	32.00
☐ purple	50.00	60.00	52.00
☐ green	50.00	60.00	52.00
☐ amethyst...	50.00	60.00	52.00
Compote			
☐ purple	30.00	40.00	32.00
☐ green	40.00	50.00	42.00
☐ amethyst...	40.00	50.00	42.00
Creamer			
☐ marigold	30.00	40.00	32.00
☐ purple	50.00	60.00	55.00
☐ green	50.00	60.00	55.00
☐ amethyst...	50.00	60.00	55.00

	Current Price Range		Prior Year Average
Nappy			
☐ marigold	25.00	35.00	27.00
☐ green	35.00	45.00	37.00
☐ amethyst.......................................	35.00	45.00	37.00
Punch Bowl, with base			
☐ marigold	150.00	180.00	160.00
☐ green	150.00	180.00	160.00
Sugar Bowl			
☐ marigold	30.00	38.00	32.00
☐ purple	35.00	45.00	37.00
☐ green	35.00	45.00	37.00
☐ amethyst.......................................	50.00	60.00	52.00

LUSTRE ROSE
Imperial

Another favorite among collectors, Lustre Rose was one of Imperial's first patterns. The quality is excellent, the moldwork sharp, and the iridescence, of course, wonderful. The design is an intricate band of roses among foliage and thorns. The pattern was made in many shapes, and the colors are green, purple, amber, smoke, clambroth, marigold, and red.

Lustre Rose

	Current Price Range		Prior Year Average
Berry Bowl, diameter 5″			
☐ marigold	15.00	25.00	17.00
☐ green	20.00	30.00	22.00
☐ purple	20.00	30.00	22.00
Berry Bowl, diameter 9″			
☐ marigold	30.00	40.00	32.00
☐ green	40.00	50.00	42.00
☐ purple	35.00	45.00	38.00
Bowl, flat			
☐ marigold	30.00	40.00	32.00
☐ green	40.00	50.00	45.00
☐ purple	40.00	50.00	42.00
☐ amber	55.00	65.00	57.00
☐ smoke	55.00	65.00	57.00
☐ clambroth	55.00	65.00	57.00
Bowl, footed			
☐ marigold	30.00	40.00	32.00
☐ green	50.00	60.00	52.00
☐ purple	50.00	60.00	52.00
☐ amber	70.00	80.00	72.00
☐ smoke	70.00	80.00	72.00
☐ clambroth	70.00	80.00	72.00
☐ red	1350.00	—	—
Fernery			
☐ marigold	35.00	45.00	37.00
☐ green	60.00	70.00	62.00
☐ purple	55.00	65.00	57.00
☐ amber	90.00	100.00	92.00
☐ smoke	90.00	100.00	92.00
☐ clambroth	90.00	100.00	92.00
Tumbler			
☐ marigold	20.00	40.00	30.00
☐ green	20.00	30.00	25.00
☐ purple	30.00	35.00	32.00
☐ amber	45.00	55.00	47.00
☐ smoke	45.00	55.00	47.00
☐ clambroth	45.00	55.00	47.00
Water Pitcher			
☐ marigold	80.00	90.00	82.00
☐ green	90.00	100.00	92.00
☐ purple	90.00	100.00	92.00
☐ amber	150.00	170.00	155.00
☐ smoke	150.00	170.00	155.00
☐ clambroth	150.00	170.00	155.00

LUTZ
McKee

	Current Price Range		Prior Year Average
Mug			
☐ marigold	40.00	50.00	42.00

MAGPIE
Australian Manufacturer

The singing bird warbles in the center, perched on diagonally placed branches. The background on this central medallion is stippled, the rest of the ground is smooth. The bird is framed by a row of angularly petaled flowers.

Bowl			
☐ marigold	40.00	50.00	42.00

MAIZE
Libbey

Celery Vase			
☐ clear ice	180.00	200.00	182.00
Syrup Pitcher			
☐ clear ice	230.00	250.00	232.00

MALAGA
Dugan

It's a new twist on the many grape patterns that exist. The central motif is one big bunch of grapes nestled on leaves like a fruit salad on lettuce. It is framed by a series of rectangular panels, set off at an angle and terminating into a stippled background. The colors are marigold, purple, and green.

Bowl, diameter 9″			
☐ marigold	65.00	75.00	67.00
☐ purple	85.00	95.00	87.00
☐ green	85.00	95.00	87.00

MANY FRUITS
Dugan

As the name implies, the overall pattern consists of a great variety of fruits and foliage. The distinctive quality is the sharp moldwork combined with the achievement of wonderful iridescent coloring that makes these pieces a treasure. The luminescent colors are green, blue, purple, marigold, and white.

	Current Price Range		Prior Year Average
Punch Bowl, with base			
☐ marigold	175.00	200.00	195.00
☐ purple	400.00	500.00	450.00
☐ blue	275.00	325.00	300.00
☐ amethyst	275.00	325.00	300.00
☐ white	900.00	1100.00	925.00
Punch Cup			
☐ purple	23.00	29.00	25.00
☐ blue	30.00	40.00	32.00
☐ amethyst	25.00	35.00	27.00
☐ white	35.00	45.00	37.00
☐ marigold	25.00	—	—

MANY PRISMS

	Current Price Range		Prior Year Average
Perfume Bottle			
☐ marigold	60.00	70.00	62.00

MANY STARS
Millersburg

Also seen on the Bernheimer bowl, this pattern employs an all-over star design culminating with a five-point star central medallion. This is framed by a beadwork circle and has one beaded jewel in the center. The ground is smooth in contrast to the stippled stars. The colors are green, blue, amethyst, marigold, and purple.

	Current Price Range		Prior Year Average
Bowl, fluted edge, diameter 9″			
☐ marigold	320.00	340.00	322.00
☐ purple	300.00	330.00	315.00
☐ green	300.00	330.00	315.00
☐ blue	780.00	820.00	790.00
☐ amethyst	290.00	310.00	295.00

	Current Price Range		Prior Year Average
Bowl, round			
☐ marigold	340.00	360.00	345.00
☐ purple	320.00	340.00	322.00
☐ green	340.00	360.00	345.00
☐ blue	320.00	340.00	322.00
☐ amethyst	320.00	340.00	322.00

MAPLE LEAF
Dugan

This is an interesting pattern. The geometric mosaic shapes are formed by ridges in high relief and are the background for maple leaf panels that are on the same surface as the ridging. This gives the background an appearance of intaglio design while the panels show in relief. The combination works well as the iridescence is highlighted by these illusions. The colors are blue, amethyst, purple, and marigold.

Maple Leaf

	Current Price Range		Prior Year Average
Butter Dish, with cover			
☐ marigold	95.00	105.00	97.00
☐ purple	110.00	120.00	112.00
☐ blue	110.00	120.00	112.00
☐ amethyst	120.00	130.00	122.00
Creamer			
☐ marigold	50.00	60.00	52.00
☐ purple	55.00	65.00	57.00
☐ blue	55.00	65.00	57.00
☐ amethyst	60.00	70.00	62.00
Ice Cream Bowl, stemmed			
☐ marigold	65.00	75.00	67.00
☐ purple	85.00	95.00	87.00
☐ blue	85.00	95.00	87.00
☐ amethyst	100.00	125.00	115.00
Pitcher			
☐ marigold	140.00	160.00	145.00
☐ purple	190.00	240.00	210.00
☐ blue	290.00	320.00	295.00
☐ amethyst	300.00	330.00	310.00
Spooner			
☐ marigold	50.00	60.00	52.00
☐ purple	55.00	65.00	57.00
☐ blue	55.00	65.00	57.00
☐ amethyst	60.00	70.00	62.00
Sugar Bowl, with lid			
☐ marigold	60.00	70.00	62.00
☐ purple	60.00	75.00	62.00
☐ blue	60.00	75.00	62.00
☐ amethyst	70.00	80.00	72.00
Tumbler			
☐ marigold	25.00	35.00	27.00
☐ purple	35.00	43.00	37.00
☐ blue	35.00	43.00	37.00
☐ amethyst	40.00	50.00	42.00

MARILYN
Millersburg

The pattern is a combination of rosettes and fanned ridges framed by X shapes and double arches. The background is smooth, the design balanced and tasteful. The glass is very heavy, well radiated, and the colors are almost opaque in the darker colors.

Marilyn

	Current Price Range		Prior Year Average
Pitcher			
☐ marigold	480.00	520.00	490.00
☐ green	1200.00	1400.00	1250.00
☐ amethyst..	700.00	800.00	725.00
Tumbler			
☐ marigold	115.00	125.00	117.00
☐ green	370.00	380.00	372.00
☐ amethyst..	135.00	145.00	137.00

MARY ANN
Dugan

A loving cup shape, with three shallow handles made up of beadwork jewels, is decorated with a sparse design of foliage and flowers in low relief. The overall effect is delicate and elegant. The iridescence is golden and reflects the highest at the rim.

Vase, three handled			
☐ marigold	240.00	260.00	245.00

MAY BASKETS
Davisons of Gateshead

This is an extremely delicate shape, with a wide shallow bowl and a thin airy handle stretching across the width. The pattern is alternating diamonds with the stylized lily, the fleur-de-lis. The color is marigold.

	Current Price Range		Prior Year Average
Basket			
☐ marigold	40.00	50.00	42.00

MAYAN
Millersburg

A unique pattern consisting of a large feathery flower bloom over three quarters of the surface. It is surrounded by a beaded band which is framed by panels of gentle flutes. The glass is very heavy, iridescence good.

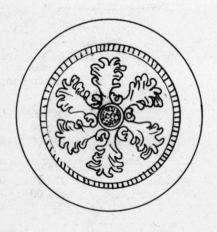

Mayan

	Current Price Range		Prior Year Average
Bowl			
☐ green	40.00	47.50	42.00
Plate			
☐ purple	350.00	400.00	375.00
☐ green	350.00	400.00	375.00
☐ blue	375.00	400.00	390.00
☐ amethyst...........................	375.00	400.00	390.00

MAYFLOWER
Imperial

	Current Price Range		Prior Year Average
Bowl			
☐ marigold	20.00	30.00	22.00
☐ amethyst	35.00	45.00	37.00
☐ smoke	45.00	55.00	47.00
☐ peach opalescent	50.00	60.00	52.00
Compote			
☐ marigold	30.00	40.00	35.00
☐ amethyst	45.00	55.00	47.00
☐ smoke	55.00	65.00	57.00
Hat			
☐ marigold	25.00	35.00	27.00
☐ amethyst	30.00	40.00	32.00
☐ smoke	55.00	65.00	57.00
Lamp Shade			
☐ marigold	30.00	—	—
☐ purple	35.00	—	—
☐ green	25.00	—	—
☐ smoke	15.00	—	—

MAYPOLE

	Current Price Range		Prior Year Average
Vase			
☐ marigold	35.00	45.00	37.00
☐ amethyst	45.00	55.00	50.00
☐ green	50.00	60.00	52.00

MELON RIB
Imperial

	Current Price Range		Prior Year Average
Candy Jar			
☐ marigold	25.00	35.00	27.00
Puff Box			
☐ marigold	30.00	40.00	32.00
Salt and Pepper Shakers, pair			
☐ marigold	45.00	55.00	47.00

MEMPHIS
Northwood

	Current Price Range		Prior Year Average
Berry Bowl			
marigold	50.00	70.00	55.00
purple	75.00	100.00	80.00
green	75.00	100.00	80.00
amethyst	75.00	100.00	80.00
Fruit Bowl, with base			
marigold	125.00	135.00	127.00
purple	235.00	245.00	237.00
green	280.00	290.00	282.00
blue	1200.00	1300.00	1225.00
amethyst	235.00	245.00	237.00
ice blue	1100.00	1250.00	1150.00
white	1100.00	1250.00	1150.00
ice green	1100.00	1250.00	1150.00
Punch Bowl, with base			
marigold	190.00	200.00	192.00
purple	340.00	360.00	345.00
green	340.00	360.00	345.00
blue	340.00	360.00	345.00
amethyst	285.00	295.00	287.00
ice green	1900.00	2100.00	1950.00
ice blue	1900.00	2100.00	1950.00
white	1900.00	2100.00	1950.00
Punch Cup			
marigold	25.00	35.00	27.00
purple	30.00	36.00	32.00
green	35.00	45.00	37.00
blue	30.00	36.00	32.00
amethyst	30.00	40.00	32.00
ice blue	37.00	45.00	40.00
white	37.00	45.00	40.00
ice green	37.00	45.00	40.00

MIKADO
Fenton

The central motif is a multi-rayed star terminated by a scarab of rosettes and scrolled ovals. The base is decorated with smooth medallions of cherries, over a roughly stippled background. The colors are blue, green, marigold, purple, and white.

	Current Price Range		Prior Year Average

Compote

☐ marigold	90.00	110.00	92.00
☐ blue	275.00	300.00	278.00
☐ green	530.00	550.00	535.00
☐ purple	275.00	—	—
☐ white..	450.00	—	—

MILADY
Fenton

This is a complex overall design of flowers and foliage, detailed and sharply molded. The vertical panels give the shape of the long sides some character as they divide up the pattern. The colors are marigold, green, blue, amethyst, and purple.

Pitcher

☐ marigold	450.00	500.00	470.00
☐ green	500.00	600.00	525.00
☐ blue	475.00	525.00	490.00
☐ purple	650.00	—	—

Tumbler

☐ marigold	90.00	100.00	95.00
☐ green	115.00	130.00	122.00
☐ blue	90.00	105.00	97.00
☐ amethyst...	130.00	150.00	135.00

MINIATURE BELL

Paperweight

☐ marigold	40.00	50.00	42.00

MINIATURE FLOWER BASKET
Westmoreland

Basket

☐ marigold	55.00	65.00	57.00

MINIATURE INTAGLIO

Goblet

☐ marigold	440.00	460.00	445.00

MINIATURE SHELL

Candleholder

☐ clear	70.00	80.00	72.00

MIRRORED LOTUS

The central medallion is plain smooth glass, surrounded by the first of many radiating panels, each one of pine cone-like foliage. A geometric panel follows and then a repeat of the foliage in reverse. The colors are green, blue, and marigold.

	Current Price Range		Prior Year Average
Bon Bon			
☐ marigold	45.00	55.00	47.00
☐ green	55.00	65.00	57.00
☐ blue	50.00	60.00	52.00
Bowl, diameter 8″			
☐ marigold	40.00	50.00	42.00
☐ green	50.00	60.00	52.00
☐ blue	45.00	55.00	47.00
Plate, diameter 7″			
☐ marigold	140.00	150.00	142.00
☐ blue	180.00	—	—
☐ celeste blue	1200.00	—	—
Rose Bowl			
☐ marigold	85.00	95.00	87.00
☐ blue	140.00	150.00	145.00
☐ white	730.00	760.00	745.00

MIRRORED PEACOCKS

Tumbler

	Current Price Range		Prior Year Average
☐ marigold	85.00	95.00	87.00

MITERED DIAMONDS AND PLEATS

The pattern borders on architecture like an upward look at a dome in a Byzantine church. This exterior pattern is a series of pleats or ridges in close rows, alternating with a diamond lozenge. The central medallion is composed of honeycombs of these diamonds. The colors are blue, smoke, and marigold.

Bowl

	Current Price Range		Prior Year Average
☐ marigold	15.00	25.00	17.00
☐ blue	85.00	100.00	90.00

MITERED OVALS
Imperial

This pattern is an overall design of elongated ovals, resembling tree knots or tear drops. These cover the piece entirely, varying in size to fit the proportions. The neck has the only variant theme, a ring of grapes in fat bunches, accentuating the rim. The colors are marigold, amethyst, and green.

	Current Price Range		Prior Year Average
Vase			
☐ marigold	2000.00	2200.00	2075.00
☐ amethyst	1700.00	1900.00	1750.00
☐ green	1700.00	1900.00	1750.00

MOONPRINT
Sowerly

This is a tasteful, well-balanced pattern, simply conceived of orbs in intaglio alternating with four-pointed stars. These geometric panels cover the body of the piece, the rim is smooth and gently scalloped. The pedestal base has a starburst motif. The color is marigold—transparent and beautifully iridescent.

Banana Boat			
☐ marigold	130.00	140.00	132.00
Bowl, diameter 8″			
☐ marigold	40.00	50.00	42.00
Butter Dish			
☐ marigold	90.00	110.00	97.00
Covered Jar			
☐ marigold	55.00	65.00	57.00
Creamer			
☐ marigold	40.00	50.00	42.00
Milk Pitcher			
☐ marigold	90.00	110.00	95.00
Sugar Bowl			
☐ marigold	45.00	55.00	47.00
Vase			
☐ marigold	45.00	55.00	47.00

MORNING GLORY
Millersburg

	Current Price Range		Prior Year Average
Pitcher			
☐ marigold	5000.00	7000.00	5500.00
☐ green	8000.00	9000.00	8500.00
☐ amethyst	6000.00	8000.00	6500.00
Tumbler			
☐ marigold	900.00	1000.00	925.00
☐ purple	425.00	525.00	440.00
☐ green	850.00	950.00	875.00
☐ amethyst	800.00	900.00	850.00

MOXIE BOTTLE

A commercial product, a popular soft drink from the 1920s, was bottled in these pieces. It has an overall diamond trellis background with stippling. The color is white opaque with an excellent iridescence.

Bottle			
☐ white opalescent	75.00	80.00	77.00

MT. GAMBIER MUG
Australian Manufacturer

This is a souvenir mug, inscribed with "Greetings From Mt. Gambier." It is a straightforward pattern of paneled flutes in an architectural design on smooth, heavy glass. The color is transparent and marigold.

Mug			
☐ marigold	80.00	90.00	85.00
☐ white	90.00	110.00	95.00

MULTI FRUITS AND FLOWERS
Millersburg

Many motifs have been used together in this pattern and although it is an overall design, it is not busy. The relief is high and sharply molded, the glass is heavy and almost opaque.

Dessert Dish			
☐ purple	650.00	750.00	675.00
☐ green	650.00	750.00	675.00
☐ amethyst	650.00	750.00	675.00

	Current Price Range		Prior Year Average
Pitcher			
☐ marigold	7000.00	8000.00	7300.00
☐ purple	5500.00	6500.00	5700.00
☐ green	6000.00	7000.00	6500.00
☐ amethyst	5500.00	6500.00	5700.00
Punch Bowl			
☐ marigold	900.00	1100.00	950.00
☐ green	1500.00	1700.00	1550.00
☐ blue	2900.00	3100.00	2950.00
☐ amethyst	1000.00	1200.00	1050.00
Punch Cup			
☐ marigold	35.00	45.00	37.00
☐ green	45.00	50.00	47.00
☐ blue	75.00	85.00	77.00
☐ amethyst	40.00	50.00	47.00

MY LADY'S POWDER BOX
Davisons of Gateshead

This is a simply conceived design of high quality and craftsmanship. The heavy glass is molded in slightly convex panels on the body; the fitted top has two panels for each one on the base. The lid is topped with a sculptured lady serving as a handle. The iridescence is marvelous and the color is marigold.

Jar

☐ marigold	80.00	90.00	82.00

NARCISSUS AND RIBBON
Fenton

Wine Bottle, with stopper

☐ marigold	480.00	500.00	482.00

NAUTILUS
Northwood/Dugan

This is an artistic pattern of curving ridges radiating out of the middle of the rim in outward sweeps. The ridges are rounded and have suggestions of knobs spaced around.

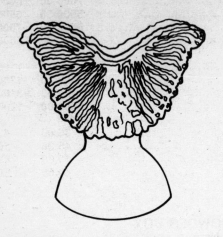

Nautilus

	Current Price Range		Prior Year Average
Dish			
☐ purple	160.00	225.00	175.00
Oblong Bowl			
☐ marigold	1000.00	—	—
☐ amethyst.............................	160.00	225.00	175.00
☐ peach opalescent...........................	135.00	170.00	145.00

NEAR CUT
Northwood

The hobstar motif is treated this time with a teardrop shaped frame in a wide band across the middle. There are triangular shapes of lozenges, placed together to form a diamond. The rest of the glass is smooth, highly iridescent and the colors are purple and marigold.

Near Cut

	Current Price Range		Prior Year Average
Compote			
☐ purple	80.00	100.00	90.00
☐ marigold	85.00	—	—
Goblet			
☐ marigold	70.00	90.00	72.00
☐ purple	100.00	125.00	110.00
Pitcher			
☐ marigold	1200.00	1600.00	1400.00

NEAR CUT DECANTER
Cambridge

This medallion panel motif is as sharply molded as cut glass. The long sides of the piece are decorated with hobstars and stippled flowers appearing in line, framed by heavy diamond ridging, alternating in rows of beadwork creating a jeweled effect. The decanter is in a cruet style, the smooth paneling on the neck and base are gently modeled in panels. The glass is opaque, the colors marigold or green.

Carafe			
☐ green	2000.00	2400.00	2100.00
☐ marigold	1100.00	1700.00	1600.00

NEAR CUT SOUVENIR
Cambridge

	Current Price Range		Prior Year Average
Mug			
☐ marigold	175.00	—	—
Tumbler			
☐ marigold	210.00	—	—

NEIL
Higbee

Mug			
☐ marigold	65.00	—	—

NELL
Higbee

Mug			
☐ marigold	60.00	70.00	62.00

NESTING SWAN
Millersburg

The big bird is graceful and beautiful, defining the uniqueness of the swan. He floats on a glossy pond in good perspective and is surrounded by diagonally placed sprays of foliage and flowers. The rim is resolved in fan-like ridges that form the scalloped edge. The colors are marigold, green, amber, blue, and amethyst.

Bowl, 10"			
☐ marigold	160.00	170.00	162.00
☐ green	230.00	240.00	232.00
☐ blue	2000.00	2800.00	2500.00
☐ amethyst	190.00	200.00	192.00
☐ vaseline	2500.00	3000.00	2600.00
Rose Bowl			
☐ marigold	1750.00	—	—
Spittoon			
☐ green	3500.00	4000.00	3700.00

NEW ORLEANS CHAMPAGNE
U.S. Glass

A souvenir from the Mardi Gras in 1910, this piece is an excellent representation of the essence of Carnival glass. Besides the clear glass and high iridescence, the design of a bearded king with a well-detailed crown in high relief is typical to this era. The funny face is flanked by molded alligators attached vertically to the side of body.

	Current Price Range		Prior Year Average

Glass
| ☐ clear iridescent | 85.00 | 95.00 | 87.00 |

NIGHT STARS
Millersburg

The central medallion is a big faceted star, surrounded by a band of similar shapes, smaller and separated by tear drops. The background is all stippled. The rim of the bowl is gently fluted and waved in and out. The finish is fine and radiated.

Bon Bon
☐ purple	225.00	250.00	230.00
☐ green	225.00	250.00	230.00
☐ amethyst	400.00	500.00	425.00

Card Tray
☐ purple	300.00	340.00	325.00
☐ vaseline	425.00	440.00	430.00
☐ amethyst	570.00	590.00	577.00

NIPPON
Northwood

Bowl, 9″
☐ marigold	45.00	—	—
☐ purple	55.00	—	—
☐ green	55.00	—	—
☐ blue	60.00	—	—
☐ white	125.00	—	—
☐ aqua opalescent	475.00	—	—
☐ ice blue	175.00	—	—

Plate, 9″
☐ marigold	300.00	—	—
☐ purple	375.00	—	—
☐ green	375.00	—	—
☐ blue	350.00	—	—
☐ white	600.00	—	—

NORTHERN STAR
Fenton

The pattern is a large medallion containing the five point star in high ridging, repeated in a wide panel around the piece. The radium finish is glossy and rainbow like, the color is marigold.

	Current Price Range		Prior Year Average
Bowl			
☐ marigold	20.00	30.00	22.00
Plate			
☐ marigold	65.00	75.00	67.00

NU-ART CHRYSANTHEMUM
Imperial

Plate, 10″			
☐ marigold	600.00	—	—
☐ purple	900.00	—	—
☐ green	950.00	—	—
☐ amber	950.00	—	—
☐ white...................................	950.00	—	—

NU-ART HOMESTEAD
Imperial

Plate, 10″			
☐ marigold	400.00	—	—
☐ purple	600.00	—	—
☐ green	625.00	—	—
☐ blue	700.00	—	—
☐ smoke	600.00	—	—
☐ clambroth	400.00	—	—
☐ amber	500.00	—	—
☐ white...................................	500.00	—	—

NUMBER 4
Imperial

This is a simple pattern, actually suggested rather than apparent, of diamond bands rowed vertically from rim to base. The upper rim is bullet-edged and waved. The colors are marigold and smoke.

Bowl			
☐ marigold	20.00	30.00	22.00
☐ smoke	30.00	40.00	32.00
Compote			
☐ marigold	25.00	35.00	27.00

NUMBER 5
Imperial

Bundles of curvy ridges are tied together in the middle of the sheaf, form a pattern that resembles Siamese fans. The exterior design is in low relief, the glass is clear, the color amber or marigold.

	Current Price Range		Prior Year Average
Bowl			
☐ amber	50.00	60.00	52.00
☐ marigold	40.00	50.00	42.00

NUMBER 9
Imperial

This geometric pattern suggests stylized grape bunches, arranged in ice cream cone shapes around broken arches. The central medallion is a rayed star. The colors are smoke, marigold and green. The pattern is also known as Tulip and Cane or Pecorah.

Bowl			
☐ marigold	25.00	35.00	27.00
☐ smoke	40.00	50.00	42.00
☐ green	50.00	60.00	52.00

NUMBER 270
Westmoreland

The shape creates this pattern, a series of molded flutes wave over the body of these pieces. The glass is otherwise devoid of decoration, smooth and glossy with good iridescence. The colors are aqua and peach.

Compote			
☐ aqua opalescence	30.00	40.00	32.00
☐ peach opalescence	40.00	50.00	42.00
☐ purple	70.00	—	—
☐ green	100.00	—	—
☐ blue	70.00	—	—
☐ aqua	115.00	—	—

OCTAGON
Imperial

A prolific pattern made in many shapes, this geometric design was very popular. It is a variation on a theme used in many types of glass—light, near-cut panels of vertical stars, diamonds, lozenge, and beadwork. The panels alternate in a broken arch and cathedral shape with concave sides. Colors are marigold and, rarely, purple and other dark colors.

Octagon

	Current Price Range		Prior Year Average
Butter Dish, with cover			
☐ marigold	80.00	90.00	82.00
☐ green	120.00	130.00	124.00
☐ purple	120.00	—	—
Cordial			
☐ marigold	105.00	—	—
☐ white..	150.00	—	—
Creamer			
☐ marigold	40.00	50.00	42.00
☐ green	60.00	70.00	62.00
☐ purple	60.00	—	—
Goblet			
☐ marigold	60.00	70.00	62.00
☐ purple	80.00	—	—
Spooner			
☐ marigold	40.00	50.00	42.00
☐ green	60.00	70.00	62.00
☐ purple	60.00	—	—

	Current Price Range		Prior Year Average
Sugar Bowl, with cover			
☐ marigold	50.00	60.00	52.00
☐ green	70.00	80.00	72.00
☐ purple	70.00	—	—
Toothpick			
☐ marigold	100.00	120.00	105.00
Tumbler			
☐ marigold	25.00	30.00	28.00
☐ amethyst..	45.00	55.00	47.00
☐ aqua	100.00	—	—
☐ green	90.00	—	—
☐ smoke	110.00	—	—
Water Pitcher			
☐ marigold	115.00	125.00	117.00
☐ amethyst..	200.00	250.00	210.00
☐ green	300.00	—	—
Wine Decanter			
☐ marigold	80.00	110.00	85.00
☐ purple	225.00	275.00	240.00
☐ aqua	90.00	—	—
☐ white...	100.00	—	—
Wine Glass			
☐ marigold	20.00	30.00	22.00
☐ purple	45.00	55.00	47.00

OCTET
Northwood

A tasteful, simply conceived pattern of intaglio marbles indented in a row, radiating from the central medallion. This is composed of a faceted petaled flower, deep cut and well molded. the shape of the body mimics the bloom shape with a gently scalloped rim. The colors are purple, green, ice green, and white.

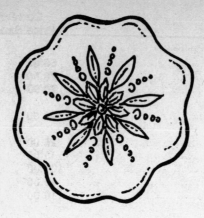

Octet

	Current Price Range		Prior Year Average
Bowl, footed, diameter 9″			
☐ marigold	35.00	43.00	37.00
☐ purple	50.00	60.00	52.00
☐ green	50.00	60.00	52.00
☐ amethyst	50.00	60.00	52.00
☐ white	60.00	75.00	62.00

OHIO STAR

Compote			
☐ marigold	750.00	—	—
Vase			
☐ marigold	650.00	—	—
☐ purple	750.00	—	—
☐ green	800.00	—	—
☐ aqua opalescent	10,000.00	—	—
☐ blue	1500.00	—	—
☐ white	1200.00	—	—
Vase Whimsy			
☐ purple	1500.00	—	—
☐ green	1500.00	—	—
☐ aqua opalescent	10,000.00	—	—

OKLAHOMA
Imperial

Pitcher			
☐ marigold	475.00	500.00	480.00

	Current Price Range		Prior Year Average

Tumble Up
| ☐ marigold | 170.00 | 180.00 | 172.00 |

Tumbler
| ☐ marigold | 1100.00 | 1250.00 | 1150.00 |

OLYMPIC
Millersburg

Compote
☐ purple	425.00	525.00	450.00
☐ green	900.00	1100.00	950.00
☐ amethyst	900.00	1100.00	950.00

OPEN FLOWER
Dugan

Bowl, 7″
☐ marigold	20.00	30.00	25.00
☐ amethyst	30.00	40.00	32.00
☐ green	30.00	40.00	34.00
☐ peach opalescent	40.00	50.00	42.00

OPEN ROSE

Berry Bowl, 5″
☐ marigold	20.00	—	—
☐ purple	25.00	—	—
☐ green	25.00	—	—
☐ clambroth	30.00	—	—

Berry Bowl, 9″
☐ marigold	35.00	—	—
☐ purple	40.00	—	—
☐ green	40.00	—	—
☐ clambroth	60.00	—	—

Bowl, footed, 9–12″
☐ marigold	40.00	—	—
☐ purple	45.00	—	—
☐ green	45.00	—	—
☐ clambroth	65.00	—	—
☐ smoke	75.00	—	—
☐ blue	45.00	—	—

Fruit Bowl, 7″–10″
☐ marigold	35.00	—	—
☐ purple	65.00	—	—
☐ green	65.00	—	—
☐ clambroth	60.00	—	—
☐ amber	55.00	—	—

	Current Price Range		Prior Year Average

Plate, diameter 9"
☐ marigold	65.00	75.00	67.00
☐ green	80.00	90.00	82.00
☐ amethyst	85.00	95.00	87.00
☐ clambroth	90.00	100.00	92.00
☐ amber	90.00	100.00	92.00

OPTIC AND BUTTONS
Imperial

This is a straightforward design of long, plain, vertical panels taking up most of the space, resolved with a beaded band. This is repeated around the base. The glass is smooth and glossy, the color is marigold.

Bowl, diameter 6"
| ☐ marigold | 20.00 | 30.00 | 22.00 |

Bowl, diameter 10"
| ☐ marigold | 20.00 | 30.00 | 22.00 |

Bowl, handled, diameter 12"
| ☐ marigold | 35.00 | 45.00 | 37.00 |

Cup and Saucer
| ☐ marigold | 185.00 | — | — |

Goblet
| ☐ marigold | 50.00 | 60.00 | 52.00 |

Plate, diameter 7"
| ☐ marigold | 25.00 | 35.00 | 27.00 |

OPTIC FLUTE
Imperial

Bowl, diameter 5"
| ☐ marigold | 20.00 | 30.00 | 22.00 |
| ☐ smoke | 25.00 | 35.00 | 27.00 |

Bowl, diameter 10"
| ☐ marigold | 35.00 | 45.00 | 37.00 |
| ☐ smoke | 40.00 | 50.00 | 42.00 |

Compote
| ☐ marigold | 25.00 | — | — |

OPTIC 66
Fostoria

Goblet
| ☐ marigold | 40.00 | 50.00 | 42.00 |

ORANGE PEEL
Westmoreland

This is an interesting pattern of smooth stippling, orange peel like, shaped into large petals that make up the sides. The color is marigold.

	Current Price Range		Prior Year Average
Fruit Bowl			
☐ aqua	150.00	—	—
Fruit Cup, footed			
☐ aqua	75.00	—	—
☐ purple	65.00	—	—
☐ marigold	35.00	—	—
Punch Bowl			
☐ marigold	120.00	130.00	122.00
☐ purple	145.00	—	—
☐ teal	145.00	—	—
Punch Cup			
☐ marigold	15.00	25.00	17.00
☐ teal	35.00	—	—
☐ purple	30.00	—	—

ORANGE TREE
Fenton

An extremely pleasing pattern, an asset to any collection. The fruit trees are wonderfully stylized, three branches on a thick trunk with a topping of funny orange blossoms with a stippled center. The upper band is a border of delicate ridges forming a bull horn–shaped chain. This is repeated on the base. The pattern was made in many shapes and colors.

Orange Tree

	Current Price Range		Prior Year Average
Berry Bowl, diameter 5″, footed			
☐ marigold	20.00	30.00	22.00
☐ green	25.00	35.00	27.00
☐ blue	25.00	35.00	27.00
☐ white	50.00	60.00	52.00
Berry Bowl, diameter 9″, footed			
☐ marigold	20.00	30.00	22.00
☐ green	35.00	45.00	37.00
☐ blue	35.00	45.00	37.00
☐ white	70.00	80.00	72.00
Bowl, flat			
☐ marigold	20.00	30.00	22.00
☐ amethyst	35.00	45.00	37.00
☐ purple	35.00	45.00	37.00
☐ green	35.00	45.00	37.00
☐ white	35.00	45.00	37.00
☐ red	590.00	610.00	592.00
☐ milk glass	125.00	175.00	130.00

	Current Price Range		Prior Year Average

Butter Dish, lidded

☐ marigold	130.00	140.00	132.00
☐ blue	140.00	160.00	145.00
☐ white	180.00	200.00	185.00
☐ ice green	245.00	310.00	250.00

Centerpiece, footed, diameter 12″

☐ marigold	650.00	700.00	685.00
☐ green	990.00	1050.00	995.00
☐ blue	2500.00	2700.00	2550.00

Creamer

☐ marigold	40.00	50.00	42.00
☐ blue	60.00	70.00	62.00
☐ white	100.00	115.00	105.00
☐ ice green	100.00	115.00	105.00

Hatpin Holder

☐ marigold	120.00	130.00	125.00
☐ green	180.00	200.00	185.00
☐ blue	160.00	170.00	162.00
☐ peach opalescent	2200.00	2400.00	2250.00
☐ white	275.00	—	—

Mug

☐ marigold	30.00	40.00	32.00
☐ purple	30.00	40.00	32.00
☐ green	55.00	65.00	57.00
☐ blue	35.00	45.00	37.00
☐ amethyst	40.00	50.00	42.00
☐ white	1000.00	1300.00	1150.00
☐ amber	175.00	—	—
☐ red	400.00	—	—
☐ aqua	150.00	—	—
☐ vaseline	150.00	—	—

Orange Bowl, footed

☐ marigold	70.00	80.00	72.00
☐ purple	70.00	80.00	72.00
☐ green	100.00	120.00	105.00
☐ blue	115.00	125.00	117.00
☐ amethyst	100.00	120.00	105.00
☐ white	120.00	135.00	125.00

Pitcher, footed

☐ marigold	200.00	220.00	205.00
☐ blue	260.00	280.00	265.00
☐ white	435.00	455.00	440.00

Plate, diameter 9″

☐ marigold	70.00	80.00	72.00
☐ purple	90.00	110.00	95.00

	Current Price Range		Prior Year Average
☐ green	90.00	110.00	95.00
☐ blue	90.00	110.00	95.00
☐ amethyst	90.00	110.00	95.00
☐ white	145.00	155.00	147.00
☒ peach opalescent	1000.00	—	—
Powder Jar, with cover			
☐ marigold	65.00	85.00	75.00
☐ purple	70.00	80.00	72.00
☐ white	120.00	—	—
☐ blue	80.00	90.00	82.00
☐ amethyst	70.00	80.00	72.00
Punch Bowl, with base			
☐ marigold	190.00	210.00	195.00
☐ purple	200.00	240.00	210.00
☐ blue	290.00	310.00	295.00
☐ white	315.00	325.00	320.00
☐ amethyst	200.00	240.00	210.00
☐ peach opalescent	900.00	1100.00	925.00
Punch Cup			
☐ marigold	20.00	30.00	22.00
☐ purple	25.00	35.00	27.00
☐ blue	25.00	35.00	27.00
☐ amethyst	30.00	40.00	32.00
☐ white	30.00	40.00	32.00
Shaving Mug			
☐ marigold	40.00	50.00	42.00
☐ purple	60.00	70.00	62.00
☐ green	60.00	70.00	62.00
☐ blue	60.00	70.00	62.00
☐ amethyst	60.00	70.00	62.00
Spooner			
☐ marigold	65.00	75.00	67.00
☐ blue	80.00	115.00	85.00
☐ white	120.00	150.00	125.00
☐ ice green	120.00	150.00	125.00
Sugar Bowl			
☐ marigold	65.00	75.00	67.00
☐ blue	80.00	115.00	85.00
☐ white	120.00	150.00	125.00
☐ ice green	120.00	150.00	125.00
Tumbler, footed			
☐ marigold	30.00	40.00	32.00
☐ blue	35.00	45.00	37.00
☐ white	70.00	80.00	72.00

	Current Price Range		Prior Year Average

Wine Glass

☐ marigold	20.00	30.00	22.00
☐ aqua	70.00	—	—

ORANGE TREE AND SCROLL
Fenton

This pattern is a work of art. The orange trees are more naturally repre-sented than in other patterns, but the fruit laden branches seem to be out of the Garden of Eden. The wide bottom band is scrollwork rows with a green iridescence that bring to mind the planted hills of Florida. The upper band is a series of eight serpentine scrolls catching and reflecting the radium finish. The colors are green, marigold, and amethyst.

Pitcher

☐ marigold	250.00	300.00	275.00
☐ green	350.00	450.00	360.00
☐ amethyst.......................................	350.00	450.00	360.00

Tumbler

☐ marigold	40.00	45.00	42.00
☐ green	55.00	65.00	57.00
☐ amethyst.......................................	55.00	65.00	57.00

ORANGE TREE ORCHARDS
Fenton

The orange grove that covers the body of these pieces is naturally repre-sented with the trunk molded in bark, the foliage is nicely detailed and the oranges are nestled within. A diagonally placed scrollwork band contrasts and separates the trees all around the bottom half. The colors are blue, green, white, amethyst, and marigold.

Pitcher

☐ marigold	150.00	200.00	160.00
☐ blue	200.00	250.00	210.00
☐ white..	350.00	450.00	370.00

Tumbler

☐ marigold	30.00	40.00	32.00
☐ blue	40.00	50.00	42.00
☐ white..	80.00	90.00	85.00

ORIENTAL POPPY
Northwood

This is a wonderful pattern with oriental influences. The long panels of poppies are sharply molded, decorated with deeply cut foliage and leaves, and framed with curvy beadwork. The bottom rim is a series of rounded horizontal ridging. The colors are green, purple, white, ice blue, green, and marigold.

	Current Price Range		Prior Year Average
Tankard Pitcher			
☐ marigold	380.00	420.00	390.00
☐ purple	500.00	600.00	550.00
☐ green	840.00	860.00	845.00
☐ blue	2400.00	2600.00	2450.00
☐ amethyst	580.00	620.00	590.00
☐ white	800.00	1000.00	850.00
☐ ice blue	800.00	1000.00	850.00
☐ ice green	1700.00	2000.00	1750.00
Tumbler			
☐ marigold	37.00	47.00	40.00
☐ purple	35.00	45.00	37.00
☐ green	45.00	60.00	50.00
☐ blue	250.00	270.00	255.00
☐ amethyst	35.00	45.00	37.00
☐ white	80.00	100.00	85.00
☐ ice green	80.00	100.00	85.00
☐ ice blue	180.00	200.00	185.00

OSTRICH CAKE PLATE
Australian Manufacturer

	Current Price Range		Prior Year Average
Cake Plate			
☐ purple	200.00	250.00	225.00
☐ marigold	160.00	—	—
☐ amethyst	200.00	250.00	225.00
Compote			
☐ purple	160.00	—	—
☐ marigold	125.00	—	—

OVAL AND ROUND
Imperial

	Current Price Range		Prior Year Average
Bowl, diameter 9″			
☐ marigold	25.00	35.00	27.00
☐ purple	30.00	35.00	32.00
☐ green	40.00	50.00	42.00
☐ blue	40.00	50.00	42.00
☐ amethyst	40.00	52.00	42.00

	Current Price Range		Prior Year Average

Plate, diameter 10″
☐ marigold	50.00	60.00	52.00
☐ purple	70.00	80.00	72.00
☐ green	70.00	80.00	72.00
☐ blue	65.00	75.00	67.00
☐ amethyst	65.00	75.00	67.00

OVAL STAR AND FAN
Jenkins

Rose Bowl
| ☐ marigold | 40.00 | 50.00 | 42.00 |
| ☐ amethyst | 50.00 | 60.00 | 52.00 |

OWL BANK

Owl
| ☐ marigold | 30.00 | 40.00 | 32.00 |

OWL BOTTLE

Bottle
| ☐ clear iridescent | 30.00 | 40.00 | 32.00 |

OXFORD

Mustard Pot, covered
| ☐ marigold | 45.00 | 55.00 | 47.00 |

PALM BEACH
U.S. Glass

Banana Bowl
| ☐ marigold | 100.00 | — | — |
| ☐ purple | 220.00 | — | — |

Bowl, 5″
| ☐ marigold | 30.00 | — | — |
| ☐ white | 50.00 | — | — |

Bowl, 9″
| ☐ marigold | 50.00 | — | — |
| ☐ white | 75.00 | — | — |

Butter
| ☐ marigold | 120.00 | — | — |
| ☐ white | 175.00 | — | — |

Creamer
| ☐ marigold | 75.00 | — | — |
| ☐ white | 120.00 | — | — |

	Current Price Range		Prior Year Average
Pitcher			
☐ marigold	450.00	—	—
☐ white	700.00	—	—
Plate, 9″			
☐ marigold	160.00	—	—
☐ purple	250.00	—	—
☐ white	225.00	—	—
Rose Bowl			
☐ marigold	85.00	—	—
☐ white	110.00	—	—
Spooner			
☐ marigold	75.00	—	—
☐ white	120.00	—	—
Sugar, lidded			
☐ marigold	75.00	—	—
☐ white	120.00	—	—
Tumbler			
☐ marigold	100.00	—	—
☐ white	165.00	—	—
Vase, Whimsy			
☐ marigold	85.00	—	—
☐ purple	120.00	—	—
☐ white	140.00	—	—

PANAMA
U.S. Glass

	Current Price Range		Prior Year Average
Goblet			
☐ marigold	115.00	125.00	118.00

PANELLED CRUET

Cruet			
☐ marigold	90.00	100.00	92.00

PANELED DANDELION
Fenton

Another work of art from Fenton, the iridescence is marvelous, the panels are sharply and beautifully molded. The design is a long branch with dandelion blossoms out of the top. The detail work is sharply etched and sometimes beaded. The panels are flat arches ending in a wide flat band rotating around the top under the rim. The colors are blue, green, marigold, and amethyst.

	Current Price Range		Prior Year Average

Pitcher

☐ marigold	380.00	400.00	385.00
☐ purple	480.00	520.00	485.00
☐ green	480.00	520.00	485.00
☐ blue	490.00	510.00	492.00

Tumbler

☐ marigold	45.00	55.00	47.00
☐ purple	50.00	60.00	52.00
☐ green	50.00	60.00	52.00
☐ blue	65.00	75.00	67.00

PANELED DIAMOND AND BOWS
Fenton

Vase, 7–14"

☐ marigold	25.00	—	—
☐ purple	35.00	—	—
☐ green	38.00	—	—
☐ blue	38.00	—	—
☐ white	60.00	—	—
☐ peach opalescent	55.00	—	—

PANELED HOBNAIL
Dugan

Vase

☐ marigold	45.00	—	—
☐ purple	65.00	—	—
☐ green	70.00	—	—
☐ peach opalescent	75.00	—	—
☐ white	90.00	—	—

PANELED HOLLY
Northwood

The panels that make up the shape of these pieces are given a different treatment—a combination of a teardrop shape and a diamond. These alternate across the body in an overall pattern, the diamonds on the lower half. The upper band is decorated with sprays of holly. The colors are amethyst, purple, and green.

Bowl

☐ purple	45.00	57.50	47.00
☐ green	45.00	57.50	47.00
☐ amethyst	45.00	57.50	47.00

Water Pitcher

☐ amethyst	1600.00	2000.00	1800.00

PANELED PALM
U.S. Glass

	Current Price Range		Prior Year Average
Mug			
☐ marigold	90.00	—	—

PANELED PRISM

Jam Jar, covered
☐ marigold	40.00	50.00	42.00

PANELED SMOCKING

Sugar
☐ marigold	40.00	50.00	42.00

PANELED SWIRL

Rose Bowl
☐ marigold	60.00	65.00	62.00

PANELED THISTLE
Higbee

☐ marigold	90.00	100.00	92.00

PANELED TREE TRUNK
Dugan

Vase, height 7″
☐ marigold	65.00	75.00	67.00
☐ amethyst	90.00	100.00	92.00
☐ green	100.00	120.00	110.00
☐ peach opalescent	140.00	160.00	142.00

PANELS AND BALL
Fenton

Bowl, diameter 11″
☐ marigold	40.00	50.00	42.00
☐ white	70.00	80.00	72.00

PANSY
Imperial

This lovely pattern has a stippled background that covers the piece to just below the rim providing a setting for a dancing bouquet of flowers. The wide detailed pansies are of smooth paneled glass and are arranged among branches and foliage. This combination of stippling and gloss provides an excellent showcase for the gleaming iridescence.

Pansy

	Current Price Range		Prior Year Average
Bowl			
☐ marigold	30.00	40.00	32.00
☐ amethyst	40.00	50.00	45.00
☐ green	45.00	—	—
☐ blue	45.00	—	—
Creamer			
☐ marigold	20.00	30.00	22.00
☐ amethyst	35.00	45.00	37.00
☐ green	35.00	—	—
☐ smoke	50.00	—	—
☐ amber	65.00	—	—

	Current Price Range		Prior Year Average

Dresser Tray
☐ marigold	50.00	60.00	52.00
☐ purple	80.00	100.00	85.00
☐ green	85.00	—	—
☐ smoke	110.00	—	—

Nappy
☐ marigold	18.00	—	—
☐ green	20.00	—	—

Relish Dish
☐ marigold	20.00	30.00	22.00
☐ amethyst	40.00	50.00	42.00
☐ green	45.00	—	—
☐ aqua opal	275.00	—	—
☐ smoke	60.00	—	—
☐ amber	65.00	—	—

PANTHER
Fenton

Berry Bowl, footed, diameter 5″
☐ marigold	50.00	60.00	52.00
☐ blue	85.00	95.00	87.00
☐ green	90.00	100.00	92.00
☐ amethyst	85.00	95.00	87.00
☐ red	540.00	560.00	545.00
☐ white	200.00	—	—

Berry Bowl, footed, diameter 9″
☐ marigold	90.00	100.00	92.00
☐ blue	145.00	155.00	147.00
☐ green	160.00	180.00	165.00
☐ amethyst	160.00	170.00	162.00
☐ white	960.00	980.00	970.00

PARLOR

Ashtray
☐ blue	90.00	100.00	92.00

PARLOR PANELS
Imperial

The design could not be simpler, yet the effect is one of the outstanding feats of Carnival glass. Is it draping or waves? The panels are made up of sweeping curves, convexly molding the body down to a thick reverse arch at the base. The upper rim is a wide ruffle, flowing around the top of the base. The colors are smoke, amethyst, and marigold.

	Current Price Range		Prior Year Average
Vase			
☐ marigold	35.00	—	—
☐ smoke	75.00	85.00	77.00
☐ amethyst	70.00	80.00	72.00

PASTEL HAT

☐ marigold	10.00	12.50	11.00
☐ smoky blue	15.00	17.50	16.00

PASTEL PANELS
Imperial

Creamer			
☐ ices	55.00	65.00	57.00
Mug, footed			
☐ ices	80.00	90.00	82.00
Pitcher			
☐ ices	300.00	325.00	310.00
Sugar Bowl			
☐ ices	55.00	65.00	57.00
Tumbler			
☐ ices	65.00	75.00	67.00

PEACH
Northwood

This is a pattern in high relief, expertly molded with lifelike representation. On each side of the piece a bunch of plump peaches hang suspended from leaf clusters, superimposed over panels of parallel ridges. The upper and lower horizontal framing is beadwork. The glass is heavy and glossy, the iridescence excellent. The colors are cobalt and white.

Peach

	Current Price Range		Prior Year Average
Berry Bowl, diameter 5″			
☐ white	55.00	65.00	57.00
Berry Bowl, diameter 9″			
☐ white	200.00	220.00	205.00
Butter Dish, with cover			
☐ white	215.00	230.00	217.00
Creamer			
☐ white	120.00	130.00	122.00
Pitcher			
☐ cobalt blue	575.00	595.00	585.00
☐ white	650.00	670.00	665.00
Spooner			
☐ white	120.00	130.00	122.00
Sugar Bowl			
☐ white	120.00	130.00	122.00
Tumbler			
☐ cobalt blue	70.00	90.00	75.00
☐ white	90.00	100.00	92.00

PEACH AND PEAR
Dugan

This delicate pattern is a well-balanced overall design of foliage and fruit. The fat pears and peaches ripen in the central medallion surrounded by a wreath of leaves. Sparsely covering the rest of the body are sprays of foliage growing outward toward the rim. The rim is ruffled with a gently bulleted edge. Colors are amethyst and marigold.

	Current Price Range		Prior Year Average
Banana Bowl			
☐ marigold	65.00	75.00	67.00
☐ amethyst	90.00	100.00	92.00

PEACH BLOSSOM

Bowl			
☐ marigold	50.00	60.00	52.00
☐ amethyst	65.00	75.00	67.00

PEACHES

Wine Bottle			
☐ marigold	30.00	40.00	32.00

PEACOCK
Millersburg

A regal pattern of great ambition, these designs are well executed and intricate. The peacock struts in a royal setting, with a Grecian pillar behind and a spray of ferns at his foot. The detail is magnificent, each feather molded in relief, the body of the bird roughly stippled. The scene is framed by a wreath of elegant foliage stopping before the wide glossy band that ruffles along the edge. The colors are marigold, amethyst, green, and vaseline.

Bowl, diameter 5″			
☐ marigold	35.00	45.00	37.00
☐ purple	45.00	55.00	47.00
☐ green	50.00	60.00	52.00
☐ amethyst	50.00	60.00	52.00
Bowl, diameter 7½″			
☐ marigold	400.00	430.00	410.00
☐ purple	360.00	380.00	365.00
☐ green	360.00	380.00	365.00
☐ amethyst	360.00	380.00	370.00
Bowl, diameter 9″			
☐ marigold	160.00	170.00	162.00
☐ purple	200.00	230.00	210.00
☐ green	280.00	300.00	285.00
☐ vaseline	2500.00	—	—
☐ amethyst	270.00	280.00	272.00

	Current Price Range		Prior Year Average
Chop Plate			
☐ marigold	800.00	1000.00	900.00
Ice Cream Bowl			
☐ marigold	350.00	—	—
☐ purple	500.00	—	—
☐ green	450.00	—	—
Plate, diameter 6″			
☐ purple	490.00	525.00	495.00
☐ marigold	500.00	—	—
☐ amethyst	370.00	380.00	372.00
Rose Bowl			
☐ purple	2000.00	—	—
☐ vaseline	3200.00	—	—

PEACOCK AND DAHLIA
Fenton

This interior pattern is one large medallion cut into eight sections of alternating flowers and peacocks in full regalia. It is simple but effective, the mold work excellent. The outside rim of the design is geometrically scalloped while the edge on the piece is bulleted and widely scalloped in a concave manner. The colors are blue, green, aqua, white, amethyst, and marigold.

Bowl, diameter 9″			
☐ marigold	45.00	55.00	47.00
☐ blue	90.00	100.00	92.00
☐ green	45.00	55.00	47.00
☐ amethyst	45.00	55.00	47.00
☐ white	70.00	90.00	72.00
☐ aqua	70.00	90.00	72.00
☐ vaseline	80.00	—	—
Plate, 8½″			
☐ marigold	200.00	—	—
☐ blue	225.00	—	—

PEACOCK AND GRAPES
Fenton

Similar to the Peacock and Dahlia in style but not execution, this pattern is busier and more encompassing. The medallion motif is used again, but this one resembles a huge flower, each section a petal. The alternating grapes and peacocks, again in full dress, rounds the middle section of the interior, surrounding a cobweb center. The colors are blue, green, aqua, white, red, peach opalescent, vaseline, marigold, and amethyst.

Peacock and Grapes

	Current Price Range		Prior Year Average
Bowl, footed			
☐ marigold	30.00	40.00	32.00
☐ blue	45.00	50.00	47.00
☐ green	45.00	50.00	47.00
☐ amethyst	45.00	50.00	47.00
☐ peach opalescent	280.00	300.00	285.00
Bowl, flat			
☐ marigold	30.00	40.00	32.00
☐ blue	45.00	50.00	47.00
☐ green	45.00	50.00	47.00
☐ amethyst	45.00	50.00	47.00
☐ peach opalescent	280.00	300.00	285.00
☐ red	560.00	580.00	565.00

	Current Price Range		Prior Year Average
Plate			
☐ marigold..	120.00	130.00	122.00
☐ blue..	200.00	250.00	210.00
☐ green..	225.00	275.00	250.00
☐ amethyst.......................................	205.00	260.00	230.00

PEACOCK AND URN
Fenton

	Current Price Range		Prior Year Average
Bowl			
☐ marigold..	45.00	55.00	47.00
☐ amethyst.......................................	65.00	75.00	67.00
☐ blue..	65.00	75.00	67.00
☐ green..	70.00	80.00	72.00
☐ peach opalescent..........................	900.00	1100.00	950.00
☐ red...	1500.00	1700.00	1550.00
Compote			
☐ marigold..	30.00	40.00	32.00
☐ blue..	35.00	45.00	37.00
☐ amethyst.......................................	40.00	50.00	42.00
☐ green..	45.00	55.00	47.00
☐ vaseline..	120.00	130.00	122.00
☐ red...	780.00	800.00	790.00
Goblet			
☐ marigold..	55.00	65.00	57.00
☐ blue..	70.00	80.00	72.00
☐ amethyst.......................................	80.00	90.00	82.00
☐ vaseline..	85.00	95.00	87.00
Plate			
☐ marigold..	100.00	120.00	105.00
☐ amethyst.......................................	155.00	165.00	157.00
☐ blue..	165.00	175.00	167.00
☐ white..	170.00	180.00	172.00
☐ green..	175.00	185.00	177.00

PEACOCK AND URN
Millersburg

The difference between this pattern and the Millersburg Peacock is the stylized bee in the bird's beak. Also, the ridgework on the urn is more rigid as opposed to the scrollwork on the one above. The quality workmanship is evident in both. Colors are green, amethyst, and marigold.

	Current Price Range		Prior Year Average
Bowl, diameter 9″			
☐ marigold	75.00	95.00	80.00
☐ purple	120.00	150.00	125.00
☐ green	225.00	275.00	250.00
☐ amethyst	120.00	150.00	125.00
Compote			
☐ marigold	45.00	55.00	47.50
☐ purple	45.00	55.00	47.50
☐ green	45.00	55.00	47.50
☐ amethyst	45.00	55.00	47.50
Spittoon			
☐ purple	1750.00	2250.00	1800.00
☐ marigold	1750.00	—	—
☐ amethyst	1750.00	2250.00	1800.00

PEACOCK AND URN
Northwood

Although this design is similar to Millersburg, there are apparent differences in the foliage wreath that makes it easy to tell them apart. The circle of leaves has less detail and has lots of glossy space between. The flowers appear only on the inside of the band, and the whole pattern stops well within the inside of the body. The colors run the gamut of Northwood tints.

Peacock and Urn

	Current Price Range		Prior Year Average
Bowl, diameter 5″			
☐ purple	30.00	40.00	32.00
☐ green	40.00	50.00	42.00
☐ blue	40.00	50.00	42.00
☐ amethyst	40.00	50.00	42.00
☐ ice blue	50.00	60.00	52.00
☐ ice green	50.00	60.00	52.00
☐ aqua opalescent	1800.00	—	—
Bowl, 9″			
☐ marigold	65.00	—	—
☐ purple	95.00	—	—
☐ green	100.00	—	—
Bowl, 10″, ice cream			
☐ marigold	175.00	—	—
☐ purple	240.00	—	—
☐ green	250.00	—	—
☐ blue	275.00	—	—
☐ aqua opalescent	3600.00	—	—
☐ aqua	3000.00	—	—
☐ white	750.00	—	—
☐ ice green	1500.00	—	—
☐ ice blue	1100.00	—	—
Chop Plate			
☐ marigold	1200.00	1300.00	1225.00
☐ ice green	1650.00	—	—
☐ amethyst	600.00	700.00	620.00
Ice Cream Bowl, diameter 6″			
☐ marigold	45.00	55.00	47.00
☐ purple	65.00	75.00	67.00
☐ green	65.00	75.00	67.00
☐ blue	70.00	80.00	72.00
☐ amethyst	40.00	50.00	42.00
☐ aqua opalescent	1600.00	—	—
☐ ice blue	300.00	—	—
☐ ice green	500.00	—	—
☐ white	250.00	—	—

PEACOCK AND URN VARIANTS
Millersburg

	Current Price Range		Prior Year Average
Bowl, diameter 6″			
☐ marigold	40.00	50.00	42.00
☐ amethyst	55.00	65.00	57.00
☐ green	130.00	140.00	132.00
☐ blue	440.00	460.00	445.00

	Current Price Range		Prior Year Average
Bowl, diameter 8½″			
☐ marigold	280.00	300.00	285.00
☐ amethyst	350.00	385.00	360.00
Bowl, diameter 9½″			
☐ marigold	90.00	100.00	92.00
☐ amethyst	140.00	150.00	142.00
☐ green	150.00	170.00	155.00
Bowl, diameter 10″			
☐ marigold	270.00	280.00	272.00
☐ amethyst	340.00	360.00	345.00
☐ green	420.00	440.00	422.00
☐ blue	1500.00	1800.00	1600.00
Compote, large			
☐ amethyst	875.00	900.00	880.00
☐ green	930.00	960.00	945.00
☐ marigold	950.00	1050.00	975.00
Plate, diameter 10½″			
☐ marigold	1800.00	2000.00	1850.00
☐ amethyst	4500.00	4700.00	4600.00

PEACOCK AT THE FOUNTAIN
Dugan

	Current Price Range		Prior Year Average
Pitcher			
☐ marigold	250.00	—	—
☐ purple	350.00	—	—
☐ blue	350.00	—	—
Tumbler			
☐ marigold	35.00	—	—
☐ purple	45.00	—	—
☐ blue	50.00	—	—

PEACOCK AT THE FOUNTAIN
Northwood

An elegant, almost surrealistic design, this is one of the collectors' favorites. The design consists of the big bird in marvelous detail with a wavy ridged tail and eight scales body feathers. He is standing on a brick pedestal with a single daisy growing out of the masonry. Behind him stands a stylized fruit tree with ray-like branches. There's a fountain with its flow represented by closely lined ridges and other details, all with an oriental flair. The colors and shapes vary widely.

Peacock at the Fountain (Northwood)

	Current Price Range		Prior Year Average
Berry Bowl, diameter 5″, 10″			
☐ marigold	25.00	35.00	27.00
☐ purple	40.00	50.00	42.00
☐ green	35.00	45.00	37.00
☐ blue	40.00	50.00	42.00
☐ amethyst	35.00	45.00	37.00
☐ white	50.00	60.00	52.00
☐ ice blue	50.00	60.00	52.00
☐ ice green	50.00	60.00	52.00
Butter Dish			
☐ marigold	120.00	130.00	122.00
☐ purple	170.00	180.00	172.00
☐ green	190.00	200.00	192.00
☐ blue	200.00	220.00	205.00
☐ amethyst	190.00	200.00	192.00
☐ white	250.00	270.00	255.00
☐ ice blue	250.00	270.00	255.00

	Current Price Range		Prior Year Average

Compote

☐ marigold	180.00	200.00	185.00
☐ purple	200.00	260.00	220.00
☐ green	200.00	260.00	220.00
☐ blue	200.00	260.00	220.00
☐ amethyst	200.00	265.00	220.00
☐ aqua opalescent	260.00	320.00	275.00
☐ white	310.00	330.00	315.00
☐ ice green	310.00	330.00	315.00
☐ ice blue	310.00	330.00	315.00

Creamer

☐ marigold	60.00	70.00	62.00
☐ purple	70.00	80.00	72.00
☐ green	80.00	90.00	82.00
☐ blue	80.00	90.00	82.00
☐ amethyst	70.00	80.00	72.00
☐ white	115.00	130.00	117.00
☐ ice blue	115.00	130.00	117.00

Orange Bowl

☐ marigold	145.00	155.00	147.00
☐ purple	155.00	195.00	160.00
☐ green	155.00	195.00	160.00
☐ blue	280.00	300.00	285.00
☐ amethyst	280.00	300.00	285.00
☐ white	550.00	570.00	555.00
☐ ice blue	550.00	570.00	555.00
☐ aqua opalescent	3200.00	—	—

Pitcher

☐ marigold	270.00	280.00	272.00
☐ purple	350.00	420.00	375.00
☐ white	500.00	600.00	525.00
☐ ice blue	740.00	760.00	745.00
☐ ice green	500.00	600.00	525.00
☐ blue	450.00	—	—
☐ green	1600.00	—	—

Punch Bowl, with base

☐ marigold	180.00	190.00	182.00
☐ purple	270.00	340.00	275.00
☐ green	270.00	340.00	275.00
☐ blue	270.00	340.00	275.00
☐ amethyst	270.00	340.00	275.00
☐ aqua opalescent	8500.00	10500.00	9000.00
☐ white	360.00	435.00	375.00
☐ ice blue	1900.00	2100.00	1950.00
☐ ice green	360.00	435.00	375.00

	Current Price Range		Prior Year Average
Punch Cup			
☐ marigold	16.00	20.00	18.00
☐ purple	23.00	30.00	25.00
☐ green	23.00	30.00	25.00
☐ blue	23.00	30.00	25.00
☐ amethyst	23.00	30.00	25.00
☐ aqua opalescent	135.00	165.00	140.00
☐ white	32.00	40.00	34.00
☐ ice blue	32.00	40.00	34.00
☐ ice green	32.00	40.00	34.00
Spooner			
☐ marigold	65.00	—	—
☐ purple	75.00	—	—
☐ green	85.00	—	—
☐ blue	90.00	—	—
☐ white	120.00	—	—
☐ ice blue	150.00	—	—
☐ ice green	200.00	—	—
Sugar			
☐ marigold	75.00	—	—
☐ purple	90.00	—	—
☐ green	95.00	—	—
☐ blue	110.00	—	—
☐ white	135.00	—	—
☐ ice blue	225.00	—	—
☐ ice green	250.00	—	—
Tumbler			
☐ marigold	35.00	—	—
☐ purple	45.00	—	—
☐ green	450.00	—	—
☐ blue	50.00	—	—
☐ white	150.00	—	—
☐ ice blue	250.00	—	—
☐ ice green	350.00	—	—

PEACOCK GARDEN VASE
Northwood/Fenton

This overall design consists of the peacock with his long sweeping tail swirling around the piece from bottom to top. He is perched on a dogwood branch which appears to have no trunk, stretching vinelike around the body. The moldwork is sharp and the color exceptional. This is a very rare piece with only a few known examples in existence.

		Current Price Range		Prior Year Average

Vase

	Current Price Range		Prior Year Average
☐ marigold	500.00	550.00	525.00
☐ amber opalescent...........................	1500.00	—	—

PEACOCK LAMP

The peacock is framed by his full plumed tail covering most of the body of the piece. The feathers are ridged in high relief terminating in oval eyes. The iridescence is excellent and covers the outside only. The colors are amethyst, marigold, smoke, and red.

Lamp

☐ marigold	225.00	230.00	227.00
☐ amethyst..	285.00	310.00	290.00
☐ smoke	300.00	400.00	320.00
☐ red...	550.00	700.00	560.00

PEACOCK TAIL
Fenton

The interior of the body is shaped in wavy flutes of peacock feathers, radiating out of the center from a star shaped medallion. The scroll work is excellent, arching around over and over, covering the available space. The colors come in marigold, amethyst, amber, blue, and green.

Peacock Tail

	Current Price Range		Prior Year Average
Bon Bon, handled			
☐ marigold	15.00	20.00	16.00
☐ purple	25.00	30.00	27.00
☐ green	25.00	30.00	27.00
☐ amethyst	25.00	30.00	27.00
☐ blue	35.00	—	—
Bowl, diameter 9″			
☐ marigold	20.00	30.00	22.00
☐ blue	30.00	40.00	32.00
☐ green	30.00	40.00	32.00
☐ amethyst	30.00	40.00	32.00

	Current Price Range		Prior Year Average
Compote			
☐ marigold	30.00	40.00	32.00
☐ blue	40.00	50.00	42.00
☐ green	50.00	60.00	52.00
☐ amethyst..	40.00	50.00	42.00
Hat Shape			
☐ marigold	25.00	35.00	27.00
☐ blue	30.00	40.00	32.00
☐ green	40.00	50.00	42.00
☐ amethyst..	30.00	40.00	32.00

PEACOCK TAIL
Millersburg

The central medallion is made up of ridged arches, stacked together in petal formation. Straightforward feathers radiate out to the rim spaced between each petal. There are stippled panels alternating with the plumes, creating the only other design on the outer rim. The colors are amethyst, green, and marigold.

Compote			
☐ marigold	20.00	25.00	22.00
☐ amethyst..	25.00	30.00	27.00
☐ green	25.00	30.00	27.00

PEACOCK VARIANT
Millersburg

Another peacock and urn scene with the distinctive feature being that the wreath is arranged in sprays of dogwoods and foliage rather than an all-over pattern. The peacock pecks a bee as in other patterns but the scrolly pillars have no bead working. The colors are green, amethyst, marigold, and possibly blue.

Compote			
☐ marigold	20.00	30.00	22.00
☐ amethyst..	30.00	40.00	32.00
☐ blue	30.00	40.00	32.00
☐ green	30.00	40.00	32.00

PEACOCKS
Northwood

Two peacocks flirt with each other, surrounded by flowers and foliage. The male is in full plume, the female stretches out on a basket, well detailed with lozenge patterns. The mold work is sharp, the coloring magnificent. The colors run the gamut of Northwood tints.

	Current Price Range		Prior Year Average
Plate, diameter 9″			
☐ marigold	180.00	200.00	185.00
☐ green	250.00	260.00	252.00
☐ blue	250.00	270.00	255.00
☐ amethyst	240.00	260.00	245.00
☐ aqua opalescent	740.00	760.00	745.00
☐ white	280.00	300.00	285.00
☐ ice blue	1900.00	—	—
☐ ice green	2500.00	—	—

PEARL AND JEWELS
Fenton

Basket			
☐ white	85.00	95.00	87.00

PEARL LADY
Northwood

Shade			
☐ white	50.00	60.00	52.00

PEBBLE AND FAN
English Manufacturer

This is a different pattern, consisting of oval panels of stippling resembling pebbles on a beach. The framework is made up of pulled ridging bundled into drapelike arches, tied in the middle by shell designed motifs. The glass is heavy, the iridescence is good, the colors cobalt, amber, and vaseline.

	Current Price Range		Prior Year Average

Vase
☐ cobalt..	440.00	460.00	445.00
☐ amber	440.00	460.00	445.00
☐ vaseline..	90.00	110.00	95.00

PENNY

Match Holder
☐ amethyst......................................	230.00	250.00	235.00

PEOPLE'S VASE
Millersburg

This delightful scene illustrates the incredible craftsmanship that the Millersburg Company was capable of. Children dance with glee, holding hands in a ring around the rosy. A happy adult beams in the background, the whole picture the representation of joy. The moldwork is sharp, the coloring fantastic, shades are cobalt, green, amethyst, and blue.

Vase
☐ marigold	7500.00	7800.00	7700.00
☐ purple	7800.00	8200.00	7900.00
☐ green	8400.00	8600.00	8500.00
☐ amethyst.......................................	6000.00	7500.00	6100.00
☐ blue	8100.00	—	—

PERFECTION
Millersburg

A large heavy piece, sharply molded with a distinctive pattern, shops off iridescence in true Carnival form. The design is ovals in a row, just under the neck of pitcher, made up of beadwork and lined with deep ridges. The bottom body is filled with featherlike columns, disappearing to airy nothingness by the base. These ovals are repeated in a delicate, elongated style up the neck, divided by maple leaves. The colors are marigold and the deep, vivid shades.

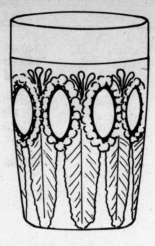

Perfection

	Current Price Range		Prior Year Average
Pitcher			
☐ marigold	3700.00	3900.00	3750.00
☐ purple	3700.00	3900.00	3750.00
☐ green	3700.00	3900.00	3750.00
☐ amethyst	3400.00	3600.00	3450.00
Tumbler			
☐ marigold	550.00	650.00	575.00
☐ purple	550.00	650.00	575.00
☐ green	640.00	660.00	645.00
☐ amethyst	550.00	650.00	575.00

PERSIAN GARDEN
Dugan

A joy of a geometric pattern. Row after row of interloping arches holding flowers and checkerboards emanate from the central starred medallion. These resolve with a band of fountains made of teardrops reaching toward the rim. The iridescence is special on these nearly opaque colors of marigold, amethyst, green, blue, white, ice blue, and green.

Berry Bowl, diameter 5″

☐ marigold	35.00	45.00	37.00
☐ purple	55.00	—	—
☐ white	60.00	—	—

	Current Price Range		Prior Year Average
Berry Bowl, diameter 10″			
☐ marigold	125.00	155.00	130.00
☐ purple	150.00	—	—
☐ white..	185.00	—	—
Fruit and Base			
☐ marigold	110.00	—	—
☐ peach opalescent..........................	400.00	—	—
☐ purple	275.00	—	—
☐ white..	225.00	—	—
Ice Cream Bowl, diameter 6″			
☐ marigold	55.00	65.00	57.00
☐ green..	75.00	85.00	77.00
☐ blue..	85.00	95.00	87.00
☐ purple	50.00	60.00	55.00
☐ white..	85.00	95.00	87.00
Ice Cream Bowl, diameter 11″			
☐ marigold	160.00	180.00	165.00
☐ green..	280.00	290.00	282.00
☐ blue..	285.00	300.00	287.00
☐ purple	160.00	180.00	165.00
☐ white..	200.00	210.00	205.00
☐ peach opalescent..........................	225.00	—	—
Plate, diameter 6″			
☐ marigold	50.00	60.00	52.00
☐ blue..	90.00	100.00	95.00
☐ purple	90.00	100.00	95.00
☐ white..	90.00	100.00	95.00
☐ peach opalescent..........................	180.00	—	—
Sandwich Plate, diameter 12″			
☐ peach opalescent..........................	4500.00	—	—
☐ purple	2000.00	2500.00	—
☐ white..	1600.00	1800.00	—

PERSIAN MEDALLION
Fenton

This is a prolific Fenton pattern consisting of flowery medallions with an offbeat oriental flair. The shapes vary widely but they all carry a band of these petaled circles containing teardrops and eggshapes formed by delicate ridges. The colors are marigold, green, amethyst, amber, red, white, and blue.

	Current Price Range		Prior Year Average

Bon Bon

☐ marigold	30.00	40.00	32.00
☐ green	45.00	55.00	47.00
☐ blue	45.00	55.00	47.00
☐ amethyst	40.00	50.00	42.00
☐ white	70.00	80.00	72.00
☐ amber	70.00	80.00	72.00
☐ red	500.00	—	—
☐ vaseline	65.00	—	—
☐ ice blue	400.00	—	—

Bowl, diameter 5″

☐ marigold	20.00	30.00	22.00
☐ green	30.00	40.00	32.00
☐ blue	25.00	35.00	27.00
☐ purple	30.00	—	—

Bowl, collar base, diameter 10″

☐ marigold	40.00	50.00	42.00
☐ green	60.00	70.00	62.00
☐ blue	50.00	60.00	52.00
☐ purple	60.00	—	—

Chop Plate, 10″

☐ blue	310.00	—	—

Compote

☐ marigold	35.00	45.00	37.00
☐ blue	60.00	70.00	62.00
☐ green	50.00	60.00	52.00
☐ purple	55.00	—	—
☐ white	300.00	—	—
☐ red	400.00	—	—

Plate, diameter 6″

☐ marigold	65.00	75.00	67.00
☐ blue	70.00	80.00	72.00
☐ green	65.00	75.00	67.00
☐ purple	80.00	—	—
☐ vaseline	95.00	—	—
☐ white	95.00	—	—

Plate, diameter 9″

☐ marigold	120.00	130.00	122.00
☐ blue	240.00	260.00	245.00
☐ green	240.00	280.00	260.00
☐ purple	150.00	—	—
☐ white	500.00	—	—

	Current Price Range		Prior Year Average

Rose Bowl

☐ marigold	55.00	65.00	57.00
☐ blue	55.00	65.00	57.00
☐ green	60.00	70.00	62.00
☐ amber	60.00	70.00	62.50
☐ white	100.00	120.00	110.00
☐ purple	75.00	—	—

PETAL AND FAN
Dugan

The fans are almost suggested rather than apparent, ghosts of low-relief in a shell design. They haunt the outside band, surrounding a stylized flower with long stippled petals that grace the center. The rims of these bowls are widely ruffled with a sawtooth edge. The colors vary widely.

Bowl, diameter 10″

☐ marigold	40.00	45.00	42.00
☐ purple	80.00	115.00	85.00
☐ amethyst	60.00	70.00	62.00
☐ peach opalescent	90.00	100.00	92.00
☐ white	100.00	130.00	110.00

Bowl, 5″

☐ marigold	30.00	—	—
☐ purple	40.00	—	—
☐ green	40.00	—	—
☐ peach opalescent	50.00	—	—
☐ white	60.00	—	—

Plate, 6″, ruffled

☐ marigold	50.00	—	—
☐ purple	85.00	—	—
☐ peach opalescent	150.00	—	—

PETALS
Dugan

Banana Bowl

☐ amethyst	85.00	95.00	87.00
☐ peach opalescent	100.00	120.00	105.00

Bowl, diameter 8½″

☐ marigold	35.00	45.00	37.00
☐ amethyst	45.00	55.00	47.00
☐ peach opalescent	60.00	—	—

	Current Price Range		Prior Year Average
Compote			
☐ marigold	40.00	50.00	42.00
☐ amethyst	55.00	65.00	57.00
☐ white	75.00	85.00	77.00

PETER RABBIT
Fenton

This pattern consists of a series of bands, alternating design with smooth, glossy glass. The center is clear, the next band made up of ridging that resembles pine needles separated with four shapes. The next larger band has Peter, a rotund rabbit hopping at a mad pace around the piece, divided by two leafy trees. The band which stretches the diameter of rim is a repeat of the first band. The colors are blue, green, amber, marigold, and amethyst.

Bowl			
☐ marigold	675.00	725.00	680.00
☐ blue	770.00	780.00	772.00
☐ green	840.00	860.00	845.00
Plate			
☐ marigold	1500.00	1700.00	1550.00
☐ blue	1800.00	2000.00	1850.00
☐ green	2000.00	2200.00	2100.00

PICKLE

Paperweight			
☐ amethyst	40.00	50.00	42.00

PIGEON

Paperweight			
☐ marigold	75.00	85.00	78.00

PILLOW AND SUNBURST
Westmoreland

This pattern appears often in crystal but in iridescence only in bowls. It consists of a series of egg shapes containing diamond lozenges surrounding a star burst and fans. It is a flowing design, the glass is heavy and well molded.

	Current Price Range		Prior Year Average

Bowl

☐ marigold	35.00	45.00	37.00
☐ purple	50.00	60.00	52.00
☐ peach opalescent.............	60.00	—	—
☐ blue opalescent	80.00	—	—
☐ teal.................................	60.00	—	—
☐ amber	60.00	—	—

PINEAPPLE
Sowerby

Six well-defined pineapples grace the corner panels on these pieces, creating an unusual fluted shape. The detail work is excellent, each fruit, made up of row after geometric row of triangular lozenges, separated by fan-like ridging. The colors are marigold, blue, and purple.

Bowl

☐ marigold	40.00	50.00	45.00
☐ purple	60.00	70.00	65.00
☐ blue.................................	60.00	70.00	65.00

Compote

☐ purple	60.00	70.00	65.00
☐ blue.................................	60.00	70.00	65.00

Creamer

☐ marigold	35.00	45.00	37.00
☐ purple	60.00	70.00	65.00
☐ blue.................................	60.00	70.00	65.00

PINECONE
Fenton

This pattern makes excellent use of texture, stippling and tiny beads which make up the design. The clump of pine cones dangle from long fern-like leaves, some with feather-like scrolls. The background is smooth, accentuating the low relief. Colors are marigold and dark shades.

Bowl

☐ marigold	30.00	35.00	32.50
☐ purple	35.00	40.00	37.00
☐ blue.................................	35.00	40.00	37.00
☐ green...............................	35.00	40.00	37.00
☐ amethyst..........................	35.00	40.00	37.00

Plate, diameter 8″

☐ blue.................................	90.00	100.00	92.00
☐ green...............................	90.00	100.00	92.00

	Current Price Range		Prior Year Average

Plate, diameter 6″
☐ marigold	40.00	50.00	42.00
☐ purple	50.00	60.00	52.00
☐ blue	50.00	60.00	52.00
☐ green	50.00	60.00	52.00
☐ amethyst..	30.00	40.00	32.00

PIN-UPS
Australian Manufacturer

This is a geometric pattern of sparse, well placed squares on stems, re-sembling road signs arranged in threes around the waist of the interior bowls. The glass is transparent, the color is purple or, less commonly, marigold.

Bowl
☐ purple	70.00	80.00	75.00
☐ marigold	85.00	95.00	87.00

PINWHEEL
English Manufacturer

A faceted, near cut pattern, this design is deeply molded and very effec-tive. The central panels consist of an eight point star of large proportion, surrounded by a broken oval, heraldic shields at either end. The top rim is raggedly bullet edged, the base resolves the geometric design. The colors are marigold, blue, and purple.

Vase, diameter 6½″
☐ marigold	35.00	45.00	37.00
☐ purple	50.00	75.00	55.00
☐ green	50.00	75.00	55.00
☐ blue	100.00	150.00	110.00
☐ amethyst..	80.00	90.00	82.00

PIPE HUMIDOR
Millersburg

The handle on the lid is made up of a pipe shape with a bowl and stem. The glass is smooth and glossy here, with a suggestion of a flower in low relief around the bowl of the pipe. The bottom design consists of elegant etching in the form of tree bark, under the floating branches with acorns. The colors are marigold, green, and amethyst.

	Current Price Range		Prior Year Average
Humidor			
☐ marigold	2900.00	3100.00	2950.00
☐ green	3100.00	3300.00	3150.00
☐ amethyst......................................	3400.00	3600.00	3450.00

PIPE MATCH HOLDER
U.S. Glass

☐ marigold	80.00	—	—
☐ purple	135.00	—	—

PLAID
Fenton

This is a neat pattern of ray-like ridges, closely spaced and emanating from the center point. There is a series of bands that circle the piece creating the plaid effect. The outer rim is ruffled and bullet edged. The colors are cobalt, purple, a rare red, and other colors.

Bowl			
☐ marigold	40.00	50.00	42.00
☐ green	40.00	50.00	45.00
☐ cobalt...	50.00	60.00	52.00
☐ red..	1250.00	—	—
☐ ice blue	480.00	—	—
Plate			
☐ marigold	120.00	130.00	122.00
☐ cobalt...	180.00	190.00	182.00

PLAIN JANE
Imperial

The design is simple but the glass has a clear iridescence that is attractive. The handle has a bark motif, the body is smooth except for ripples of fluting and has a scalloped edge. The colors are smoke and marigold.

Basket			
☐ marigold	60.00	—	—
Paperweight			
☐ marigold	75.00	85.00	78.00

PLAIN PETALS
Northwood

Nappy

☐ amethyst...	80.00	90.00	82.00
☐ green	85.00	95.00	87.00

PLEATS AND HEARTS

Shades

☐ ices..	65.00	75.00	67.00

PLUME PANELS
Fenton

This is an elegant design of long stretched panels with a feathery look. The upper panel is resolved by scrolls in arch shape, the bottom starts from under the base. The panels are separated by clear glass strips. The color is luminous, in marigold, amethyst, blue, and rare in red.

Vase

☐ marigold	35.00	45.00	37.00
☐ blue	40.00	50.00	42.00
☐ amethyst...	45.00	55.00	47.00
☐ red...	340.00	360.00	345.00
☐ green	50.00	—	—
☐ white..	100.00	—	—

POINSETTIA
Northwood

This is an entirely different approach to the same motif as the Imperial pattern. Here the flower is treated naturalistically, winding around the face of the piece of a basketweave or trellis background. The mold work is sharp, the iridescence marvelous, the colors green, purple, white, marigold, amethyst, and ice blue.

Poinsettia

	Current Price Range		Prior Year Average
Bowl			
☐ marigold	75.00	95.00	78.00
☐ purple	120.00	150.00	125.00
☐ blue	120.00	150.00	125.00
☐ amethyst	120.00	150.00	125.00
☐ white	200.00	—	—
☐ ice blue	400.00	—	—

POINSETTIA
Imperial

This is quite a spectacular design, a flower that is as alive as fireworks. The eight petalled flowers form the wide band at the top, the stem and branches comprise the bottom three-quarters of the body. The foliage is the focal point comprised of wonderful jewel-like beadwork in sweeping arches. The colors are marigold and smoke, less common in green and purple.

	Current Price Range		Prior Year Average

Milk Pitcher

☐ marigold	80.00	90.00	82.00
☐ green	240.00	260.00	245.00
☐ purple	140.00	200.00	150.00
☐ smoke	120.00	140.00	130.00

POINSETTIA
Northwood

A rarity in Carnival glass tumblers, this design appears on the inside, showing through a clear glass. The iridescence is good, the glass finely transparent. The color is marigold.

Tumbler

☐ marigold	275.00	325.00	300.00

POLO PONY
Dugan

A trusty steed graces the center of these cute pieces, in bridle with well defined features and mane. The Greek Key motif is elongated and used as an outside border. The colors are ice green, amethyst, and marigold.

Ash Tray

☐ marigold	35.00	45.00	37.00

POND LILY
Fenton

The central medallion is a scale medallion assembled like a mosaic in stippled glass. The panels of lilies surround this center divided by rippled bead work, stylizing light rays on a pond. The outer band is a complement to the center, the same fitted scales. The colors are blue, green, marigold, and white.

Bon Bon

☐ marigold	30.00	40.00	32.00
☐ blue	45.00	50.00	45.50
☐ green	45.00	50.00	45.50
☐ white	60.00	70.00	62.00

PONY
Dugan.

	Current Price Range		Prior Year Average
Bowl			
☐ marigold	50.00	75.00	55.00
☐ purple	120.00	160.00	125.00
☐ ice green	400.00	—	—
☐ aqua	475.00	—	—
☐ amethyst	120.00	160.00	125.00
Plate			
☐ purple	200.00	260.00	225.00
☐ marigold	300.00	—	—
☐ amethyst	200.00	260.00	225.00

POPPY
Millersburg

	Current Price Range		Prior Year Average
Compote			
☐ marigold	640.00	660.00	645.00
☐ purple	160.00	215.00	165.00
☐ green	390.00	410.00	395.00
☐ amethyst	540.00	560.00	545.00

POPPY
Northwood

Poppies are placed sparingly in low relief on a stippled background. The pattern starts out naturalistically, getting more elaborate as it reaches for the feathery scrolled border. The detail work is good, the design well executed, the colors are blue, purple, peach, white, and marigold.

	Current Price Range		Prior Year Average
Bowl			
☐ marigold	20.00	30.00	22.00
☐ purple	30.00	40.00	32.00
☐ blue	30.00	40.00	32.00
☐ amethyst	30.00	40.00	32.00
Relish Dish			
☐ marigold	45.00	55.00	47.00
☐ purple	52.00	67.50	53.00
☐ aqua opal	350.00	—	—
☐ blue	52.00	67.50	53.00
☐ amethyst	52.00	67.50	53.00
☐ white	65.00	85.00	67.00
☐ ice green	65.00	85.00	67.00
☐ ice blue	65.00	85.00	67.00

POPPY AND FISH NET
Imperial

	Current Price Range		Prior Year Average
Vase			
☐ red....................................	525.00	575.00	535.00

POPPY SHOW
Northwood

Three big, bold poppies are arranged together in a tight bunch, with slips of foliage in between. The mold work is sharp and the design is elegant and artistic. The distinctive feature here is a gently rayed wide rim, ruffled and straight edged. The iridescence is high powered, the colors available run the gamut.

Bowl			
☐ marigold	125.00	150.00	130.00
☐ purple	160.00	200.00	170.00
☐ blue..	230.00	245.00	235.00
☐ green......................................	240.00	260.00	245.00
☐ amethyst.................................	160.00	200.00	170.00
☐ ices..	140.00	180.00	150.00
☐ white......................................	230.00	240.00	232.00
Plate			
☐ marigold	200.00	240.00	210.00
☐ purple	300.00	350.00	320.00
☐ blue..	300.00	350.00	320.00
☐ green......................................	860.00	880.00	865.00
☐ amethyst.................................	300.00	350.00	280.00
☐ ices..	275.00	300.00	280.00
☐ white......................................	470.00	480.00	472.00
☐ aqua opalescent	4400.00	4600.00	4450.00

POPPY SHOW VASE
Imperial

Four vertical panels of poppies and foliage are molded in high relief almost forming the shape of the vase. The design stems from the base and continues to a band of gentle arches just below the rim. The wide-mouth edge is flatly scalloped. The colors are marigold, amethyst, purple, blue, green, and others.

	Current Price Range		Prior Year Average

Vase

☐ marigold	250.00	300.00	275.00
☐ purple	400.00	500.00	425.00
☐ blue	400.00	500.00	425.00
☐ green	400.00	500.00	425.00
☐ amethyst	400.00	500.00	425.00
☐ amber	750.00	—	—
☐ smoke	700.00	—	—

POTPOURRI
Millersburg

Milk Pitcher

☐ marigold	1000.00	1200.00	1050.00

PRAYER RUG
Fenton

Bon Bon

☐ peach opalescent	400.00	450.00	410.00
☐ milk glass	450.00	500.00	455.00

PREMIUM
Imperial

This is a pattern distinguished by shape rather than decoration. The iridescence is highlighted by the smooth glossy finish, clear in places and highly luminescent in others. The colors are purple, green, smoke, marigold, and clambroth.

Bowl

☐ marigold	40.00	50.00	42.00
☐ purple	90.00	110.00	95.00
☐ smoke	95.00	—	—
☐ clambroth	80.00	90.00	85.00

Candlesticks

☐ marigold	60.00	—	—
☐ smoke	110.00	—	—
☐ purple	95.00	—	—
☐ clambroth	110.00	—	—

PRETTY PANELS
Northwood

This is an enameled pattern on an iridescent background. The painted design is bunches of long stemmed cherries dangling off a straight branch with a leaf or two thrown in for good measure. The colors are ice green and marigold.

	Current Price Range		Prior Year Average
Pitcher			
☐ ice green	400.00	500.00	415.00
☐ marigold	120.00	—	—
Tumbler			
☐ ice green	60.00	70.00	65.00
☐ marigold	60.00	—	—

PRIMROSE
Millersburg

This is a simple pattern of flowers growing out a leafy center. Each spray consists of two six-petaled flowers with snakelike leaves stemming out of the branches. The iridescence is excellent, the colors, marigold, amethyst, purple, and a rare frosty blue.

Bowl			
☐ marigold	140.00	150.00	142.00
☐ purple	80.00	110.00	85.00
☐ green	80.00	110.00	85.00
☐ blue	2400.00	2600.00	2450.00
☐ amethyst	90.00	100.00	92.00

PRIMROSE AND FISHNET

This is an interesting design of one curvy primrose, looking suspiciously like a poppy, running down one side of the piece. The rest of the pattern is an all over scheme of fishnetting made up of X shapes in squares. They work well together, creating an interesting texture. The only reported color in Carnival glass is red.

Vase			
☐ red	540.00	560.00	545.00

PRINCELY PLUMES

Candleholder			
☐ amethyst	250.00	270.00	255.00

PRINCESS
U.S. Glass

	Current Price Range		Prior Year Average
Lamp			
☐ amethyst............................	1000.00	1300.00	1150.00

PRISM

Shakers, pair
☐ marigold	60.00	—	—
Tray			
☐ marigold	45.00	—	—

PRISM AND CANE
Sowerby

The prisms make up the wide band around the middle of these pieces, taking up two-thirds of the side. They are rounded and terminate on the base and at the rim in a sextagonal shape of deeply etched glass. The base motif is a multi-rayed sunburst with a lozenge band that circles the bottom.

Bowl
☐ marigold	40.00	60.00	45.00
☐ purple	60.00	90.00	65.00

PRISM AND DAISY

This is a simple design of light relieved ridges that take up most of the body, forming spear ended prisms. The top band is a delicate row of flowers with foliage in low relief. It can be found in a variety of shapes but only in marigold.

Vase
☐ marigold	20.00	30.00	22.00

PRISM BAND
Fenton

Pitcher, with decoration
☐ marigold	160.00	170.00	162.00
☐ white	320.00	340.00	325.00
☐ amethyst............................	330.00	350.00	335.00
☐ green	370.00	380.00	372.00
☐ blue	380.00	390.00	382.00

	Current Price Range		Prior Year Average

Tumbler, with decoration

☐ marigold	25.00	35.00	28.00
☐ white	55.00	65.00	57.00
☐ amethyst	65.00	75.00	67.00
☐ green	70.00	80.00	72.00
☐ blue	75.00	85.00	77.00

PRISMS
Westmoreland

An intaglio design of bead worked prisms, all in a row and over the entire space. They terminate on the fluted upper edge and appear from under the base. The bottom design is a huge multi-rayed star. The colors are amethyst, marigold, green, and others.

Compote

☐ marigold	50.00	60.00	55.00
☐ purple	65.00	85.00	60.00
☐ green	65.00	85.00	60.00
☐ blue	65.00	85.00	60.00
☐ amethyst	65.00	85.00	60.00
☐ aqua	90.00	115.00	95.00

PROPELLER
Imperial

From the starred base to the wide ruffled upper rim, this pattern is simple and elegant. It consists of a series of panels, each containing a multi-petaled star with triangular prisms dividing them down the middle.

Candy Dish

☐ marigold	25.00	35.00	27.00

Compote

☐ marigold	30.00	—	—
☐ green	35.00	—	—

PROUD PUSS
Cambridge

Bottle

☐ white	75.00	85.00	77.00

PULLED HUSK CORN VASE
Northwood

A geometrically designed corn cob, row after row of squared pellets, rests in the base of the vase with interesting husks pulled away in curvy scrolls. The base is smooth glass, the entire piece has a heavy, solid look. The iridescence is excellent, the colors purple and green.

	Current Price Range		Prior Year Average
Vase			
☐ purple	1800.00	2400.00	1900.00
☐ green	1800.00	2400.00	1900.00

PULLED LOOP
Dugan

Dugan also made this pattern. It is difficult to tell the difference, except for the red, which was only made by Fenton.

Vase			
☐ marigold	25.00	—	—
☐ purple	35.00	—	—
☐ green	35.00	—	—
☐ blue	30.00	—	—
☐ peach opalescent	50.00	—	—

PULLED LOOP
Fenton

The design is simple and elegant, smooth glass pulled into a series of thumbprinted panels, rotating slightly in a vertical manner. The upper rim is a rounded fluting, the base is plain. The colors are heavily luminized in blue, green, marigold, and amethyst.

Vase			
☐ marigold	25.00	35.00	27.00
☐ blue	25.00	35.00	27.00
☐ peach opalescent	45.00	—	—
☐ aqua opalescent	87.50	—	—
☐ aqua	75.00	—	—
☐ red	295.00	—	—
☐ amethyst	30.00	40.00	32.00

PUZZLE
Dugan

This is another interior design whose central feature is the stippled background. The scrolly designs that dot the piece intermittently resemble upside down lilies or bells. The colors vary widely including purple, blue, green, marigold, and peach opalescent.

	Current Price Range		Prior Year Average

Bon Bon, stemmed and two-handled

☐ marigold	35.00	—	—
☐ purple	48.00	—	—
☐ blue	48.00	—	—
☐ green	55.00	—	—
☐ peach opalescent	60.00	—	—
☐ white	65.00	—	—

Compote

☐ purple	45.00	—	—
☐ blue	45.00	—	—
☐ green	50.00	—	—
☐ peach opalescent	55.00	—	—
☐ white	60.00	—	—
☐ marigold	35.00	—	—

QUARTERED BLOCK

Butter Dish

☐ marigold	85.00	95.00	87.00

Creamer

☐ marigold	45.00	55.00	47.00

Sugar

☐ marigold	45.00	55.00	47.00

QUEEN'S LAMP

☐ green	1500.00	—	—

QUESTION MARKS
Dugan

This stippled pattern resembles a scrolly octopus more than a series of question marks, as there seems to be life in this design. The central motif is in high relief, surrounded by triple teardrops of smooth glass arranged in a band around the middle rim. The rest of the glass is heavy and smooth, the colors are marigold, purple, white, peach opalescent, and others.

	Current Price Range		Prior Year Average
Bon Bon			
☐ marigold	38.00	—	—
☐ purple	48.00	—	—
☐ peach opalescent	70.00	—	—
☐ ice blue	75.00	—	—
☐ ice green	75.00	—	—
Compote			
☐ marigold	35.00	45.00	37.00
☐ purple	35.00	45.00	37.00
☐ amethyst	45.00	55.00	47.00
☐ peach opalescent	70.00	80.00	72.00
☐ white	60.00	70.00	62.00

QUILL
Dugan

This low-relief pattern of fat feathers covering the lower half of the body has a wide neck band of imprinted ovals. The rest of the glass is smooth creating a simple effect that looks well balanced. The iridescence is excellent, the colors marigold, amethyst, and purple.

Pitcher			
☐ marigold	1200.00	1500.00	1300.00
☐ purple	2400.00	—	—
Tumbler			
☐ marigold	360.00	380.00	370.00
☐ amethyst	440.00	460.00	445.00

RAGGED ROBIN
Fenton

The outstanding feature on these pieces is the irregular "ragged" rim that takes up almost half the plate. The design, in low relief is a wreath of foliage surrounding a central medallion of a bird perched among the flora. The colors are marigold, purple, blue, green, and white.

	Current Price Range		Prior Year Average
Bowl			
☐ marigold	50.00	60.00	52.00
☐ purple	50.00	60.00	52.00
☐ blue	55.00	65.00	57.00
☐ green	70.00	80.00	72.00
☐ white	85.00	95.00	87.00

RAINDROPS
Dugan

This is a simple overall pattern of elongated ovals in a teardrop form, arranged in neat rows down to the center. The glass is smooth and heavy, the colors are the pastels and vivids, as well as peach opalescent.

Bowl, diameter 9″			
☐ purple	85.00	110.00	90.00
☐ peach opalescent	50.00	65.00	55.00

RAMBLER ROSE
Dugan

An overall foliage and flower design in low relief refracts the excellent iridescence on these pieces. The central motif is a well detailed rose nestled in leaves; this design is repeated on most of the available space. The colors are marigold, purple, green, blue, and amethyst.

Rambler Rose

	Current Price Range		Prior Year Average
Pitcher			
☐ marigold	115.00	130.00	117.00
☐ purple	115.00	130.00	117.00
☐ green	190.00	200.00	192.00
☐ blue	165.00	175.00	167.00
☐ amethyst	180.00	190.00	182.00
Tumbler			
☐ marigold	22.00	27.00	24.00
☐ purple	32.00	42.00	34.00
☐ green	32.00	42.00	34.00
☐ blue	32.00	42.00	34.00
☐ amethyst	40.00	60.00	50.00

RANGER
Imperial

A simple, tasteful geometric pattern adorns the entire piece, made up of concave checkerboards rising from under the base and terminating with a band of gentle arches just below the upper rim. The glass is smooth, the clarity and iridescence excellent, the color is marigold.

Creamer			
☐ marigold	35.00	45.00	37.00
Pitcher, milk			
☐ marigold	150.00	170.00	155.00
Tumbler			
☐ marigold	260.00	280.00	265.00

RANGER TOOTHPICK

	Current Price Range		Prior Year Average
Toothpick Holder			
☐ marigold	70.00	80.00	72.00

RASPBERRY
Northwood

The bottom wide panel has a basketweave pattern, ending a quarter of the way up in a beaded raspberry design. These circular berries appear in low relief but are well detailed. The colors are purple, marigold, ice blue, and green.

	Current Price Range		Prior Year Average
Berry Bowl, diameter 5½″			
☐ marigold	20.00	30.00	22.00
☐ purple	30.00	40.00	32.00
☐ green	30.00	40.00	32.00
Berry Bowl, diameter 9″			
☐ marigold	40.00	50.00	42.00
☐ purple	55.00	65.00	57.00
☐ green	60.00	70.00	62.00
Milk Pitcher			
☐ marigold	110.00	130.00	115.00
☐ purple	140.00	160.00	145.00
☐ green	150.00	170.00	155.00
☐ ice blue	1250.00	—	—
☐ white	1100.00	—	—
☐ ice green	1500.00	—	—
Occasional Bowl, footed			
☐ marigold	40.00	50.00	42.00
☐ purple	50.00	60.00	52.00
☐ green	50.00	60.00	52.00
☐ blue	160.00	—	—
Tumbler			
☐ marigold	30.00	35.00	32.00
☐ purple	35.00	40.00	37.00
☐ green	35.00	40.00	37.00
☐ ice blue	75.00	80.00	76.00
☐ white	250.00	—	—
☐ ice green	350.00	—	—
☐ blue	300.00	—	—

	Current Price Range		Prior Year Average

Water Pitcher

☐ marigold	90.00	110.00	95.00
☐ purple	200.00	225.00	215.00
☐ green	200.00	225.00	215.00
☐ ice blue	300.00	350.00	315.00
☐ blue	1600.00	—	—
☐ ice green	1800.00	—	—
☐ white	1500.00	—	—

RAYS AND RIBBONS
Millersburg

This is a neat pattern of alternating glossy spears and stippled rays emanating out of a central medallion of a starburst. The outer border is an interesting pattern of connected spades. The glass is heavy and iridescence good. The colors are marigold, green, vaseline, and amethyst.

Bowl

☐ marigold	40.00	50.00	42.00
☐ purple	50.00	75.00	60.00
☐ green	50.00	60.00	52.00
☐ amethyst	50.00	60.00	52.00

Plate, flat

☐ purple	160.00	190.00	180.00
☐ amethyst	160.00	190.00	175.00

REGAL IRIS
Consolidated

Gone With The Wind Lamp

☐ marigold	1800.00	2200.00	1900.00
☐ red	8000.00	10000.00	9000.00

REGAL SWIRL

Candlestick

☐ marigold	50.00	60.00	52.00

REX

Pitcher

☐ marigold	350.00	370.00	355.00

	Current Price Range		Prior Year Average

Tumbler
☐ marigold 50.00   60.00   52.00

RIB AND PANEL
Fenton

Spittoon
☐ marigold .... 90.00   —   —
Vase
☐ marigold 40.00   50.00   42.00

RIBBED ELIPSE

Mug
☐ clambroth 85.00   95.00   87.00

RIBBED SWIRL

Milk Pitcher
☐ marigold .... 35.00   —   —
Tumbler
☐ marigold 50.00   60.00   52.00
☐ green 65.00   75.00   67.00

RIBBON AND BLOCK

Lamp
☐ marigold 490.00   520.00   495.00

RIBBON AND LEAVES

Sugar Bowl
☐ marigold 40.00   50.00   42.00

RIBBON TIE
Fenton

The basic, underlying pattern is circular ridges covering the entire piece. They are boldly interrupted by curvy sprays of diagonally placed ridges creating a whirling comet effect. The colors are blue, red, green, amethyst, and marigold.

	Current Price Range		Prior Year Average
Bowl			
☐ marigold	40.00	50.00	42.00
☐ blue...	50.00	60.00	52.00
☐ green...	55.00	65.00	57.00
☐ amethyst......................................	55.00	65.00	57.00
☐ red..	1400.00	1600.00	1450.00
Plate			
☐ marigold	60.00	70.00	65.00
☐ blue...	70.00	80.00	75.00
☐ green...	70.00	80.00	75.00
☐ amethyst......................................	70.00	80.00	75.00
☐ red..	1850.00	—	—

RIPPLE
Imperial

This delicate vase is practically devoid of decoration because it is pulled to an airy thinness. Where the design remains, it appears as a suggested series of vertical ridges, rippling on the piece, showing off the iridescence. The colors are marigold, amethyst, clear iridescent, and very rarely, teal blue, as well as others. It comes in various heights from 10″ to 16″.

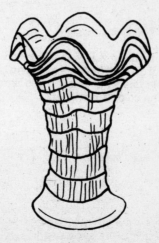

Ripple

	Current Price Range		Prior Year Average
Vase, height 14″			
☐ marigold	20.00	30.00	25.00
☐ amethyst	30.00	40.00	35.00
☐ green	35.00	—	—
☐ blue	36.00	—	—
☐ amber	40.00	—	—
☐ smoke	40.00	—	—
☐ red	200.00	—	—

RISING SUN

This is a busy, seemingly mismatched pattern. The upper half is the rising sun, half showing out of a geometrical draping pattern. The effect is achieved in a near-cut manner, the mold work is sharp. The colors are cobalt and marigold.

Pitcher			
☐ marigold	840.00	875.00	845.00
☐ cobalt	1700.00	1900.00	1750.00
Tumbler			
☐ marigold	380.00	410.00	385.00
☐ cobalt	740.00	760.00	745.00

ROBIN
Imperial

This delicate, elegant pattern was well conceived and remains one of the most popular in Carnival glass. It features a singing bird perched on a branch with foliage around. The design is detailed and sharply molded and covers the pieces tastefully. The color is marigold.

Robin

	Current Price Range		Prior Year Average
Mug			
☐ marigold	40.00	60.00	50.00
Pitcher			
☐ marigold	275.00	325.00	300.00

ROCK CRYSTAL
McKee

Punch Bowl and Base			
☐ amethyst..	500.00	600.00	525.00
Punch Cup			
☐ amethyst..	40.00	50.00	42.00

ROCOCO
Imperial

This old style pattern is made up of long heavy drapes covering the piece in thick ridges. All of the lines are curved or scrolled creating a feeling of movement. The vase's wide ruffled edge adds to this fluid feeling. The colors are marigold, smoke, and green.

Bowl			
☐ smoke..	35.00	45.00	38.00

	Current Price Range		Prior Year Average
Vase			
☐ marigold	30.00	35.00	32.50
☐ green	60.00	70.00	65.00
☐ smoke	50.00	70.00	52.50

ROLL

Cocktail Shaker			
☐ marigold	35.00	45.00	37.00
Pitcher			
☐ clear iridescent	250.00	280.00	265.00
Tumbler			
☐ marigold	30.00	40.00	32.00

ROMAN ROSETTE
U.S. Glass

Goblet			
☐ clear iridescent	85.00	95.00	87.00

ROOD'S CHOCOLATES
Northwood

Advertising Plate			
☐ amethyst	230.00	250.00	240.00

ROSALIND
Millersburg

Also known as Drape and Tie, this pattern consists of one huge rosette that covers the entire interior space. The burst has the look of a kaleidoscope alternating curvy arches with scale-like panels all radiating out of a well molded center. The colors vary widely.

Bowl, diameter 10″			
☐ marigold	140.00	160.00	142.00
☐ green	250.00	—	—
☐ amethyst	230.00	250.00	240.00
Compote, diameter 9″			
☐ green	1300.00	1500.00	1350.00
☐ purple	1300.00	1500.00	1350.00
☐ blue	1300.00	1500.00	1350.00
☐ marigold	1600.00	—	—

ROSE AND GREEK KEY

This one of a kind piece is lovingly detailed with a rose and foliage border and line after line of small Greek key in low relief, taking up most of the interior in horizontal banding. The pattern is busy and intricate, sharply molded in smoky amber.

	Current Price Range		Prior Year Average
Plate, square			
☐ amber	5400.00	5600.00	5500.00

ROSE BOUQUET

Creamer			
☐ marigold	50.00	60.00	52.00

ROSE COLUMNS
Millersburg

This is a very special pattern due to the very pronounced bas relief roses which are hollow on the inside. This presented difficulty in removing the pieces successfully from the molds. The iridescence is wonderful, the colors are blue, green, marigold, and amethyst.

Vase			
☐ marigold	1400.00	1600.00	1450.00
☐ blue	8000.00	9000.00	8200.00
☐ green	1200.00	1400.00	1250.00
☐ amethyst	1200.00	1300.00	1225.00

ROSE GARDEN
English Manufacturer

The roses alternate with geometric rosettes in panel around the exterior of these pieces. The interesting detail on the flowers is comprised of vertical ridging, a new twist to a widely used design. The effect of this all-intaglio design is a surprising combination of flora and geometry, traditional versus modern, executed beautifully in high iridescence and a variety of colors.

	Current Price Range		Prior Year Average
Butter Dish, with cover			
☐ marigold	120.00	125.00	130.00
☐ blue	250.00	275.00	260.00
☐ green	250.00	275.00	260.00
☐ amethyst	250.00	275.00	260.00
☐ purple	250.00	275.00	260.00
Creamer			
☐ marigold	40.00	50.00	45.00
☐ blue	80.00	90.00	85.00
☐ green	80.00	90.00	85.00
☐ amethyst	80.00	90.00	85.00
Milk Pitcher			
☐ marigold	300.00	400.00	315.00
☐ blue	500.00	600.00	515.00
☐ green	500.00	600.00	515.00
☐ purple	500.00	600.00	515.00
☐ amethyst	500.00	600.00	515.00
Spooner			
☐ marigold	40.00	50.00	42.00
☐ blue	80.00	90.00	84.00
☐ green	80.00	90.00	84.00
☐ purple	80.00	90.00	84.00
☐ amethyst	80.00	90.00	84.00
Sugar Bowl			
☐ marigold	40.00	50.00	42.00
☐ blue	80.00	90.00	84.00
☐ green	80.00	90.00	84.00
☐ purple	80.00	90.00	84.00
☐ amethyst	80.00	90.00	84.00
Vase			
☐ blue	170.00	200.00	175.00
☐ green	170.00	200.00	175.00
☐ purple	170.00	200.00	175.00
☐ amethyst	170.00	200.00	175.00

ROSE PANELS
Australian Manufacturer

Compote			
☐ marigold	110.00	130.00	115.00

ROSE PINWHEEL

	Current Price Range		Prior Year Average
Bowl			
☐ blue	880.00	920.00	890.00
☐ purple	800.00	—	—

ROSE SHOW
Northwood

The background for the bouquet of fully blooming roses is a quiet basket-weave, covering all of the interior. The moldwork is just excellent, the representation is very naturalistic. Each flower is nestled in foliage, pointed and detailed leaves in high relief. The colors were produced in a wide range.

Bowl, diameter 8″			
☐ marigold	125.00	150.00	130.00
☐ blue	190.00	200.00	192.00
☐ purple	150.00	175.00	160.00
☐ green	150.00	175.00	160.00
☐ amethyst	150.00	175.00	160.00
☐ ices	180.00	200.00	190.00
☐ white	180.00	200.00	190.00
☐ aqua opalescent	460.00	480.00	465.00
Plate			
☐ marigold	200.00	250.00	225.00
☐ blue	300.00	350.00	315.00
☐ purple	300.00	350.00	315.00
☐ green	300.00	350.00	315.00
☐ amethyst	300.00	350.00	315.00
☐ ices	325.00	375.00	330.00
☐ white	325.00	375.00	330.00
☐ milk glass	800.00	1000.00	850.00
☐ lime green opalescent	2100.00	—	—

ROSE SPRAY

This delicate, suggested pattern is faintly etched on the high side of the compote. The roses and a few leaves wind up the interior, the only decoration other than the wonderful color and iridescence. Seen in ice blue, ice green, and marigold.

Compote			
☐ ice blue	75.00	85.00	78.00
☐ ice green	75.00	85.00	78.00
☐ marigold	60.00	—	—

ROSE TIME

	Current Price Range		Prior Year Average

Vase
☐ marigold	60.00	—	—

ROSE TREE
Fenton

This intricate pattern, covering most of the space, manages to look elegant rather than busy. There are four wide panels of rose blooms and branches, lots of leaves in a graceful, symmetrical design. The center medallion is smooth, glossy glass with just the tips of the dangling leaves dipping toward the middle. The colors are marigold and cobalt blue.

Bowl, diameter 10″
☐ marigold	230.00	240.00	232.00
☐ cobalt blue..................................	290.00	300.00	292.00

ROSE WREATH
Northwood

This rare piece features an exterior basketweave pattern.

Bon Bon
☐ amethyst.....................................	220.00	250.00	230.00

ROSES AND FRUIT
Millersburg

☐ marigold	575.00	—	—
☐ purple	700.00	—	—
☐ green...	700.00	—	—
☐ blue..	1000.00	—	—

ROSES AND RUFFLES
Gone With the Wind Lamp

☐ marigold	1750.00	—	—
☐ red...	4500.00	—	—

ROSETTE
Northwood

The central medallion is a large rayed sunburst taking up most of the bottom of the interior. It is simply conceived of alternating smooth and stippled rays, surrounded by a band of flowery rosettes against a stippled background. The last band is simple vertical ridge work that reaches halfway to the wavy ruffled rim. Colors are marigold, amethyst, purple, and green.

Rosette

	Current Price Range		Prior Year Average
Bowl, flat			
☐ marigold	40.00	50.00	42.00
☐ amethyst	80.00	90.00	82.00
Bowl, footed			
☐ purple	95.00	—	—
☐ green	22.50	—	—

ROUND-UP
Dugan

Round because it whirls, the pattern is an overall design of movement and symmetry. The center medallion is a plump-petaled flower, with its fat parts made up of diagonally placed alternated of stipples and smooth. The wide band that surrounds the outer reaches of the interior is most interesting, two decorated panels separated by one plain, smooth one in a whirlpool design around the piece, creating motion as the eye sweeps over it. The colors vary widely.

Bowl

☐ marigold	50.00	60.00	52.00
☐ purple	70.00	80.00	72.00
☐ blue	75.00	85.00	77.00
☐ amethyst	70.00	80.00	72.00
☐ white	75.00	85.00	77.00

	Current Price Range		Prior Year Average

Plate

☐ marigold	120.00	130.00	122.00
☐ purple	100.00	120.00	110.00
☐ blue	170.00	180.00	172.00
☐ amethyst...	100.00	120.00	125.00
☐ white..	200.00	220.00	205.00
☐ peach opalescent............................	350.00	370.00	355.00

ROYALTY
Imperial

This pattern is made up of deep cut teardrop shapes over lozenge work, separated occasionally by large rosettes. The design is executed in a deep cut manner with excellent molding. The colors are marigold and smoke.

Fruit Bowl, with base

☐ marigold	90.00	110.00	95.00
☐ smoke..	130.00	140.00	132.00

Punch Cup

☐ marigold	20.00	25.00	25.00
☐ smoke..	20.00	25.00	25.00

RUFFLED RIB SPITTOON
Northwood

This is a simple pattern of rounded, interior ridges, vertically covering the body of the piece. They are made of smooth, glossy iridescence and terminate under the angularly ruffled rim. The colors are marigold and its height is 4 inches.

Bowl

☐ marigold	40.00	50.00	42.00
☐ green	55.00	65.00	57.00

RUFFLES, RINGS AND DAISY BAND
Northwood

Bowl

☐ amethyst.......................................	85.00	95.00	87.00

RUSTIC
Fenton

The elongated hobnail stretches to airy thinness by the waist of these tall vases. The design appears again at the upper rim, knobby in high relief under a triangularly fluted edge. The colors are blue, green, vaseline, amber, marigold, amethyst, peach opalescent, and red.

	Current Price Range		Prior Year Average

Vase
☐ marigold	25.00	30.00	27.00
☐ blue	50.00	60.00	52.00
☐ green	30.00	40.00	32.00
☐ amethyst	25.00	35.00	27.00
☐ amber	50.00	60.00	52.00
☐ vaseline	50.00	60.00	52.00
☐ peach opalescent	50.00	60.00	52.00
☐ red	470.00	490.00	472.00

S-BAND
Australian Manufacturer

Compote
| ☐ marigold | 45.00 | 55.00 | 47.00 |
| ☐ amethyst | 60.00 | 70.00 | 62.00 |

S-REPEAT
Dugan

A continuing row of serpentine scrolls in high relief and decorated with beadwork, covers the entire available exterior space on these pieces. The voluptuous swirls are molded beautifully, the design is utterly elegant. The colors in Carnival glass are marigold, amethyst, and purple.

S-Repeat

	Current Price Range		Prior Year Average
Creamer			
☐ marigold	55.00	65.00	57.00
Punch Bowl			
☐ amethyst.................................	1400.00	1600.00	1450.00
Punch Cup			
☐ marigold	30.00	40.00	35.00
Toothpick			
☐ purple	200.00	225.00	215.00

SACIC ASHTRAY
English Manufacturer

A Brazilian souvenir made in England, the inscription reads: "Naranja Sacic Pamelo." The design is devoid of decoration but the color is excellent and iridescent in marigold.

Ashtray			
☐ marigold	75.00	95.00	80.00

SAILBOATS
Fenton

Wide panels framed with ridged ribbons contain a floating sailboat on rippling water. This motif repeats around the piece, showing motion. It is a sparse and tasteful pattern with excellent iridescence. Colors are blue, green, amber, vaseline, marigold, red, and purple.

Bowl, diameter 6″			
☐ marigold	20.00	30.00	22.00
☐ blue	55.00	65.00	57.00
☐ green	70.00	80.00	72.00
☐ purple	80.00	—	—
☐ amber	70.00	80.00	72.00
☐ vaseline....................................	70.00	80.00	72.00
☐ red..	200.00	250.00	215.00
Goblet			
☐ marigold	25.00	35.00	27.00
☐ blue	35.00	45.00	37.00
☐ ices...	170.00	180.00	172.00
☐ green	225.00	—	—
☐ purple	350.00	—	—

	Current Price Range		Prior Year Average
Plate			
☐ marigold	180.00	200.00	185.00
☐ blue	250.00	270.00	255.00
Wine Glass			
☐ marigold	25.00	35.00	27.00
☐ blue	200.00	220.00	210.00

SAILING SHIP

Plate			
☐ marigold	35.00	45.00	37.00

SAINT
English Manufacturer

Plate			
☐ marigold	35.00	45.00	37.00

SCALE BAND
Fenton

The title of this pattern is aptly descriptive, two wide bands of ridged scales framed on both sides with fine diagonal etchings, emanate from the handle at its connection. The rest of the piece contrasts with a vertical paneling that covers the surface. The glass is transparent, the colors are marigold, amethyst, green and the opalescents, quite rare in red.

Bowl			
☐ marigold	20.00	30.00	22.00
Pitcher			
☐ marigold	100.00	120.00	105.00
Plate, footed			
☐ marigold	40.00	50.00	42.00
Tumbler			
☐ marigold	20.00	30.00	22.00
☐ green	175.00	—	—
☐ blue	30.00	40.00	32.00

SCALES
Westmoreland

This interior design is a simple overall effect of fish scales, radiating out of a central medallion made up of a rosette with scaly petals. It is sparsely decorated and the big scales resemble upside-down arches. The colors vary; the glass is transparent.

	Current Price Range		Prior Year Average
Bowl			
☐ marigold	20.00	22.00	22.00
☐ purple	25.00	28.00	27.00
☐ green	25.00	28.00	27.00
☐ amethyst	25.00	28.00	27.00
☐ white	30.00	35.00	32.00
☐ milk white	125.00	145.00	130.00
☐ peach opalescent	20.00	25.00	22.00
☐ aqua opalescent	175.00	225.00	180.00
Plate			
☐ marigold	20.00	25.00	22.00
☐ purple	30.00	35.00	32.00
☐ green	30.00	35.00	32.00
☐ amethyst	30.00	35.00	32.00
☐ white	45.00	60.00	47.00
☐ peach opalescent	60.00	70.00	65.00
☐ milk	125.00	170.00	130.00
☐ amber	65.00	—	—
☐ teal	65.00	—	—

SCOTCH THISTLE
Fenton

This interior pattern is beautifully executed, the barklike background is well defined, the thistles with their feathery caps in high relief. It is a well-balanced design that complements the widely and irregularly ruffled rim on the compote. The colors are amethyst, blue, marigold, and green.

Compote			
☐ marigold	40.00	50.00	42.00
☐ blue	40.00	50.00	42.00
☐ green	40.00	50.00	42.00
☐ amethyst	40.00	50.00	42.00

SCROLL
Westmoreland

Pin Tray			
☐ marigold	40.00	50.00	42.00

SCROLL AND FLOWERS PANELS
Imperial

Another intricate, elegant design reminiscent of Victorian drawing rooms, the scrollwork is the eye catcher. The swirling serpentines frame the feathery petaled flower which occupies the middle ground. Gentle arches terminate the pattern just under the bulleted rim. Colors are purple, green, and marigold.

Vase

☐ marigold	85.00	95.00	87.00
☐ purple	175.00	225.00	190.00

SCROLL EMBOSSED
Imperial

This marvelous pattern consists of a central series of circles in glossy ribbing, surrounded by four round panels arranged in a cross design. Alternating stippled glass with glossy lends to the sparkle on these grandly iridescent pieces. The colors are purple, marigold, green, and smoke.

Bowl

☐ marigold	30.00	40.00	32.00
☐ purple	40.00	50.00	42.00
☐ green	30.00	35.00	32.00
☐ smoke	30.00	35.00	32.00

Plate

☐ marigold	50.00	60.00	52.00
☐ purple	90.00	100.00	92.00
☐ green	70.00	80.00	75.00
☐ smoke	70.00	80.00	75.00

SEACOAST
Millersburg

This pattern has so many designs the eye can't take it all in at one time. The outer frame is a bold, scaled fish swimming toward the bottom. The rest of the frame is made up of nautical scrolls and seaweed representations. The center scene is a lighthouse and a rising sun, in the background of a rippling sea. The colors are green, purple, amethyst, and marigold.

Pin Tray

☐ marigold	280.00	300.00	285.00
☐ purple	260.00	300.00	275.00
☐ green	260.00	300.00	275.00
☐ amethyst	260.00	300.00	275.00

SEA GULLS

	Current Price Range		Prior Year Average
Bowl			
☐ marigold	65.00	—	—

SEA GULL VASE
English Manufacturer

The sea gulls are represented with wide wings and diving in an impressionistic manner. The wings are geometric wide ridges, the birds stalking body is made up of arched ribbing. The sky and clouds, as well as the earth below is almost surreal, very modernistic. The color is iridescent and marigold.

	Current Price Range		Prior Year Average
Vase			
☐ marigold	725.00	750.00	735.00

SEAWEED
Millersburg

Motion is evident on these pieces, serpentine scrolls representing wavy seaweed twirl from a center point. The background suggests the roaring sea. The iridescence is outstanding, especially picked up in the series of bubbly beads. The colors are marigold, green, and amethyst.

	Current Price Range		Prior Year Average
Bowl, diameter 5″			
☐ marigold	380.00	400.00	385.00
☐ green	440.00	460.00	445.00
Bowl, 9″			
☐ marigold	260.00	—	—
☐ green	350.00	—	—
Bowl, 10½″, ice cream			
☐ marigold	400.00	—	—
☐ purple	450.00	—	—
☐ green	450.00	—	—
Bowl, 10½″, ruffled			
☐ marigold	180.00	—	—
☐ purple	225.00	—	—
☐ green	195.00	—	—
Lamp			
☐ marigold	195.00	—	—
Plate, 10″			
☐ marigold	800.00	—	—
☐ green	900.00	—	—

SHARP

	Current Price Range		Prior Year Average
Jigger, 1 ounce			
☐ marigold	35.00	45.00	37.00
☐ smoke	40.00	50.00	42.00

SHELL
Imperial

A straightforward pattern, perfect for Carnival glass, this design is a band of eight ridged shells taking up most of the outer edge and surrounding a center motif that resembles a sand dollar. The long rays that make up the middle design are voluptuously rounded in high relief. The colors are green, purple, marigold, amber, and smoke.

Bowl			
☐ marigold	30.00	38.00	32.00
☐ green	40.00	45.00	42.00
☐ purple	40.00	45.00	42.00
☐ amethyst	40.00	45.00	42.00
☐ smoke	80.00	—	—
Plate			
☐ marigold	70.00	80.00	75.00
☐ green	120.00	140.00	125.00
☐ purple	120.00	140.00	125.00
☐ amethyst	120.00	140.00	125.00
☐ smoke	250.00	—	—

SHELL AND JEWEL
Westmoreland

The shells are massive arches fluted widely and centered by a nice, simple flower. The background which takes up most of the body is roughly stippled. The upper rim has an interesting drapework with beaded decoration. The colors are green, amethyst, and marigold. The tumbler illustrates pattern only. It is not found in Carnival glass.

Shell and Jewel

	Current Price Range		Prior Year Average
Creamer, lidded			
☐ marigold	40.00	50.00	42.00
☐ green	40.00	50.00	42.00
☐ amethyst	50.00	60.00	52.00
Sugar Bowl			
☐ marigold	40.00	50.00	42.00
☐ green	50.00	60.00	52.00
☐ amethyst	50.00	60.00	52.00

SHERATON
U.S. Glass

Butter			
☐ clambroth	120.00	—	—
Creamer			
☐ clambroth	65.00	—	—
Pitcher			
☐ clambroth	165.00	—	—
Spooner			
☐ clambroth	65.00	—	—
Sugar			
☐ clambroth	80.00	—	—
Tumbler			
☐ clambroth	40.00	—	—

SHIP AND STARS

	Current Price Range		Prior Year Average
Plate			
☐ marigold	25.00	35.00	27.00

SHRINE CHAMPAGNE
U.S. Glass

A series of three champagne glasses was made for premiums given away at conventions held by Shriners in 1909, 1910, and 1911. They vary in detail, but the workmanship is uniformly excellent. The stems are decorated by applied scrollwork, usually gilded.

Glass, stemmed			
☐ crystal	85.00	95.00	87.00

SHRINE TOOTHPICK

Toothpick Holder			
☐ purple flash	500.00	—	—

SIGNET
English Manufacturer

Sugar Bowl, covered			
☐ marigold	65.00	75.00	67.00

SILVER AND GOLD

Pitcher			
☐ marigold	95.00	110.00	97.00
Tumbler			
☐ marigold	20.00	30.00	22.00

SILVER QUEEN
Fenton

Pitcher			
☐ marigold	170.00	180.00	172.00
Tumbler			
☐ marigold	40.00	50.00	42.00

SINGING BIRDS
Northwood

	Current Price Range		Prior Year Average
Berry Bowl, diameter 4½″			
☐ green	35.00	45.00	37.00
☐ purple	25.00	35.00	27.50
☐ amethyst	30.00	40.00	32.00
Berry Bowl, diameter 9½″			
☐ green	70.00	80.00	72.00
☐ purple	70.00	80.00	72.00
☐ amethyst	55.00	65.00	57.00
Butter Dish, with cover			
☐ marigold	180.00	200.00	182.00
☐ green	300.00	325.00	310.00
☐ amethyst	280.00	300.00	285.00
☐ purple	300.00	325.00	310.00
Creamer			
☐ marigold	75.00	85.00	77.00
☐ green	110.00	120.00	115.00
☐ amethyst	95.00	105.00	97.00
☐ purple	95.00	105.00	97.00
Mug			
☐ marigold	190.00	200.00	192.00
☐ green	340.00	360.00	345.00
☐ blue	270.00	290.00	275.00
☐ amethyst	110.00	125.00	115.00
☐ ices	700.00	730.00	720.00
☐ aqua opalescent	1100.00	—	—
Pitcher			
☐ marigold	200.00	230.00	215.00
☐ green	280.00	300.00	285.00
☐ purple	250.00	275.00	255.00
☐ amethyst	250.00	275.00	255.00
Spooner			
☐ marigold	75.00	85.00	77.00
☐ green	110.00	130.00	115.00
☐ purple	95.00	105.00	97.00
☐ amethyst	95.00	105.00	97.00
Sugar Bowl			
☐ marigold	100.00	120.00	105.00
☐ green	140.00	160.00	145.00
☐ purple	140.00	160.00	145.00
☐ amethyst	135.00	145.00	137.00
Tumbler			
☐ marigold	40.00	50.00	42.00

	Current Price Range		Prior Year Average
☐ green	50.00	60.00	52.00
☐ purple	50.00	60.00	52.00
☐ amethyst	50.00	60.00	52.00

SINGLE FLOWER
Dugan

Banana Bowl

☐ peach opalescent	110.00	130.00	115.00

Bowl

☐ marigold	20.00	30.00	22.00
☐ amethyst	30.00	40.00	32.00
☐ green	30.00	40.00	32.00
☐ peach opalescent	45.00	55.00	47.00

SINGLE FLOWER FRAMED
Dugan

Bowl, diameter 9″

☐ marigold	45.00	—	—
☐ purple	80.00	—	—
☐ green	80.00	—	—
☐ peach opalescent	120.00	—	—

SIX PETALS
Dugan

The center medallion is a simple representation of a six-sided flower, quite small for the pattern that originates from it. Surrounding the middle and taking up most of the space is a wreath of feathery flowers and leaves, nicely molded and tastefully placed around the piece. The rest of the space is smooth with a high radium finish. The colors are purple, blue, green, and white and commonly seen in peach opalescent.

Bowl

☐ marigold	30.00	40.00	32.00
☐ purple	40.00	50.00	42.00
☐ green	40.00	50.00	42.00
☐ blue	45.00	55.00	47.00
☐ white	60.00	70.00	62.00
☐ peach opalescent	55.00	65.00	67.00

SIX-SIDED CANDLESTICK
Imperial

This tall, massive candlestick is quite beautiful, alternating a glossy finish with a thin vertical band of beadwork to make up the six panels. The center knob, just above the long stem, has a band of rosettes, deep cut and well molded. The color is fantastic in purple, marigold, smoke, and green.

	Current Price Range		Prior Year Average
Candlesticks, each			
☐ marigold	120.00	130.00	122.00
☐ purple	225.00	245.00	230.00
☐ green	225.00	245.00	230.00
☐ smoke	150.00	170.00	155.00

SKI STAR
Dugan

This star medallion is a variation on a theme that runs through Carnival glass. The eight sided star is made up of long curves and pointed edges, comprised of row after row of beadwork. The small center is a mimic of the larger one; the background is slightly mottled as if refracting light. The colors are blue, green, purple, and peach opalescent.

Basket, handled			
☐ peach opalescent........................	480.00	520.00	485.00
Berry Bowl, diameter 5″			
☐ purple	40.00	50.00	42.00
☐ peach opalescent........................	50.00	60.00	52.00
Berry Bowl, diameter 10″			
☐ purple	70.00	80.00	75.00
☐ peach opalescent........................	60.00	75.00	62.00

SMALL BLACKBERRY
Northwood

Compote			
☐ marigold	40.00	50.00	42.00
☐ green	50.00	60.00	52.00
☐ amethyst................................	50.00	60.00	52.00

SMALL RIB COMPOTE
Fenton

Another plainly conceived pattern that works, the piece is made up of gentle panels of rounded ribs, slightly concave into the side of the body. The upper rim is interesting with deep flutes sparsely spaced resembling cigarette holders on an ashtray. The base and pedestal is glossy smooth glass, the colors are amethyst, green, and marigold, and occasionally seen in color overlay.

	Current Price Range		Prior Year Average
Compote			
☐ marigold	30.00	40.00	32.00
☐ amethyst	35.00	45.00	37.00
☐ green	35.00	45.00	37.00
☐ amber	45.00	—	—
Rose Bowl			
☐ marigold	35.00	—	—
☐ purple	42.00	—	—
☐ green	42.00	—	—
☐ amber	48.00	—	—

SMALL THUMBPRINT

Creamer			
☐ marigold	55.00	65.00	57.00

SMOOTH PANELS

It is the lack of design or decoration that is the achievement here. The smooth, slightly convex panels ripple over the piece like a breath of wind. The effect is that the color and the iridescence are showcased, both are of superior craftsmanship. Colors are marigold, amethyst, green, smoke, purple, amber, and others.

Pitcher			
☐ marigold	80.00	90.00	82.00
☐ green	150.00	175.00	160.00
Tumbler			
☐ crystal clear	90.00	—	—
Vase			
☐ marigold	30.00	40.00	32.00
☐ green	45.00	50.00	47.00
☐ purple	45.00	50.00	47.00
☐ amethyst	45.00	50.00	47.00
☐ smoke	50.00	60.00	52.00
☐ amber	180.00	200.00	185.00
☐ peach opalescent	65.00	—	—

SMOOTH RAYS
Northwood

Bowl, diameter 6″			
☐ marigold	40.00	50.00	42.00
☐ amethyst	40.00	50.00	44.00
☐ peach opalescent	55.00	65.00	57.00

	Current Price Range		Prior Year Average
Compote			
☐ marigold	30.00	40.00	32.00
Plate, diameter 7"			
☐ marigold	55.00	65.00	57.00
Rose Bowl			
☐ marigold	35.00	45.00	37.00
☐ amethyst.......................................	50.00	60.00	52.00

SMOOTH RAYS
Westmoreland

Bowl, with base, diameter 5"			
☐ green...	45.00	55.00	47.00
☐ peach opalescent............................	65.00	75.00	67.00
☐ teal blue	70.00	80.00	72.00
Bowl, flat, diameter 9"			
☐ marigold	30.00	40.00	32.00
☐ green...	40.00	50.00	42.00
☐ peach opalescent............................	65.00	75.00	67.00

SNOW FANCY
McKee

This little-known manufacturer creates a near cut pattern of geometry and floral arrangements, coinciding on the same plane. The design is basically circular with arches, rosettes, and beadwork. The glass is transparent, the colors, green, marigold, and white.

Bowl			
☐ green...	35.00	45.00	37.00
☐ marigold	25.00	—	—
Creamer			
☐ marigold	40.00	50.00	42.00
Sugar Bowl			
☐ marigold	40.00	50.00	42.00

SODA GOLD
Imperial

Similar in conception to Imperial's Crackle, this pattern differs in execution. The stippled background lies far below the raised ridges that form the irregular design. The moldwork is excellent due to this contrast, the color and glass clear as a bell, in smoke or marigold.

	Current Price Range		Prior Year Average
Candlesticks, each			
☐ marigold	25.00	35.00	27.00
☐ smoke	35.00	40.00	37.00
Pitcher			
☐ marigold	190.00	220.00	195.00
☐ smoke	310.00	330.00	315.00
Salad Bowl			
☐ marigold	40.00	50.00	45.00
Tumbler			
☐ marigold	35.00	45.00	37.00
☐ smoke	70.00	80.00	72.00

SODA GOLD SPEARS
Dugan

	Current Price Range		Prior Year Average
Bowl, diameter 4½″			
☐ marigold	20.00	30.00	22.00
Bowl, diameter 8½″			
☐ marigold	30.00	40.00	32.00
Plate			
☐ marigold	45.00	55.00	47.00

SOLDIERS AND SAILORS
Fenton

Illinois' commemorative plate features the soldiers and sailors home in Quincy, Illinois as designated by the inscription. This interior pattern seems superimposed through the clear iridescence on the berry and leaf design that graces the exterior. The colors are blue, amethyst, and marigold.

	Current Price Range		Prior Year Average
Plate			
☐ marigold	550.00	575.00	560.00
☐ blue	730.00	750.00	735.00

SOUTACHE
Northwood

This neat pattern has the look of an oak worm biting his way in a maze of wood. The swirling ridged design surrounds a straightforward daisy medallion and is framed by a series of suggested fans on the outer rim. The glass is clear but iridized excellently in peach opalescent.

	Current Price Range		Prior Year Average

Bowl
☐ marigold 40.00 60.00 55.00
Plate
☐ peach opalescent 350.00 375.00 360.00

SOUTHERN IVY

Wine Goblet
☐ marigold 30.00 40.00 32.00

SOUVENIR BANDED

Mug
☐ marigold .... 70.00 — —

SPHINX PAPERWEIGHT
English Manufacturer

Paperweight
☐ amber 460.00 480.00 470.00

SPIDERWEB

Vase
☐ marigold 40.00 50.00 42.00

SPIDERWEB AND TREE BARK
Dugan

Vase
☐ white 55.00 65.00 57.00

SPIRAL CANDLE
Imperial

A classic design of a turned stem on a massive base distinguishes these candlesticks. The glass is quite heavy and the spiral cutting down to the base is sharply molded. The colors are smoke, marigold, and green.

Candlestick
☐ marigold 50.00 60.00 52.00
☐ green 70.00 80.00 72.00
☐ smoke 85.00 95.00 87.00

SPIRALEX
English Manufacturer

The iridescence is the distinguishing feature on these tall stretched vases. They have the appearance of turning from top to bottom, framed by pinched ridges. The glaze is mirrorlike; a rainbow of colors are refracted. The colors are amethyst, marigold, blue, and green.

	Current Price Range		Prior Year Average
Vase			
☐ marigold	40.00	50.00	42.00
☐ blue	50.00	60.00	55.00
☐ green	50.00	60.00	55.00
☐ amethyst..	50.00	60.00	55.00

SPLIT DIAMOND
Davisons of Gateshead

Long arches interconnect forming fanlike shapes made up of ridges. The effect produces alternating wheat sheafs and diamonds of smooth glass panels. The color is clear and iridescent and marigold.

Butter			
☐ marigold	65.00	75.00	67.00
Creamer			
☐ marigold	30.00	40.00	32.00
Sugar Bowl			
☐ marigold	35.00	40.00	37.00

SPRING BASKET
Imperial

Basket			
☐ marigold	35.00	45.00	37.00
☐ smoke	40.00	50.00	42.00

SPRING OPENING
Millersburg

Plate			
☐ amethyst..	250.00	270.00	255.00

SPRINGTIME
Northwood

Basketweave borders the bottom and top of these panelled pieces. The floral pattern in high relief that sits in the middle of the body is made up of daisy in chain, all stippled and nicely molded. The colors are rich and luminous, in the pastels as well as green, marigold, and amethyst.

Springtime

	Current Price Range		Prior Year Average
Berry Bowl, diameter 4½″			
☐ green	50.00	60.00	52.00
☐ amethyst	45.00	55.00	47.00
Berry Bowl, diameter 7½″			
☐ green	120.00	130.00	122.00
☐ amethyst	100.00	115.00	105.00
Butter Dish, with cover			
☐ marigold	160.00	180.00	170.00
☐ green	225.00	260.00	230.00
☐ amethyst	225.00	260.00	230.00
Creamer			
☐ marigold	120.00	130.00	122.00
☐ green	190.00	210.00	195.00
☐ amethyst	180.00	200.00	185.00

	Current Price Range		Prior Year Average
Pitcher			
☐ marigold	500.00	525.00	510.00
☐ green	940.00	960.00	945.00
☐ amethyst..	840.00	880.00	845.00
Spooner			
☐ marigold	110.00	130.00	115.00
☐ green	180.00	200.00	185.00
☐ amethyst..	180.00	200.00	185.00
Sugar Bowl			
☐ marigold	130.00	140.00	132.00
☐ green	210.00	230.00	215.00
☐ amethyst..	190.00	210.00	195.00
Tumbler			
☐ marigold	60.00	70.00	62.00
☐ green	110.00	130.00	115.00
☐ purple	110.00	—	—

SQUARE DAISY AND BUTTON
Imperial

Toothpick Holder			
☐ smoke...	100.00	130.00	110.00

SQUARE DIAMOND
English Manufacturer

Vase			
☐ blue...	110.00	130.00	115.00

STAG AND HOLLY
Fenton

Bowl, diameter 8–13″, footed			
☐ red...	1000.00	—	—
☐ marigold	80.00	90.00	82.00
☐ purple	150.00	170.00	160.00
☐ green	180.00	190.00	182.00
☐ blue	180.00	190.00	182.00
Plate, diameter 9″, footed			
☐ marigold	380.00	420.00	395.00
Plate, diameter 13″, footed			
☐ marigold	540.00	560.00	545.00
Rose Bowl			
☐ marigold	175.00	200.00	177.00
☐ blue...	300.00	—	—

STAR AND FAN
Imperial

This geometric pattern seems to stand out among the many others because of its simple symmetry and tasteful design. Stars of Bethlehem alternate up and down around the vase, separated by deep-cut fanned ridges. There is beadwork and lozenges to fill in the background and adding to the balance in an elegant way. Colors are clear in marigold and cobalt blue.

	Current Price Range		Prior Year Average
Vase			
☐ marigold	240.00	260.00	245.00
☐ cobalt blue	180.00	210.00	185.00

STAR AND FILE
Imperial

Another good geometric pattern, this is made up of a wide band of hobstars, separated by spears of filework, all beautifully balanced and sharply molded. The iridescence is golden, the glass heavy and near cut, the colors marigold, smoke, and others.

Bon Bon			
☐ marigold	30.00	—	—
Bowl			
☐ marigold	25.00	35.00	27.00
Celery Vase			
☐ marigold	25.00	35.00	27.00
☐ smoke	85.00	95.00	87.00
Creamer			
☐ marigold	20.00	30.00	22.00
Decanter			
☐ marigold	110.00	—	—
☐ wine	40.00	—	—
Pickle Dish			
☐ marigold	40.00	—	—
Plate, diameter 6″			
☐ marigold	50.00	—	—
Rose Bowl			
☐ marigold	65.00	—	—
☐ pastel green	100.00	—	—
Sherbet			
☐ marigold	30.00	—	—
Spooner			
☐ marigold	30.00	—	—
Sugar			
☐ marigold	20.00	30.00	22.00

	Current Price Range		Prior Year Average

Tumbler
| ☐ marigold | 65.00 | — | — |

Water Pitcher
| ☐ marigold | 200.00 | — | — |

STAR CENTER
Imperial

Bowl
☐ marigold	25.00	35.00	27.00
☐ amethyst	30.00	40.00	32.00
☐ smoke	35.00	45.00	37.00

Plate
☐ marigold	50.00	60.00	52.00
☐ amethyst	60.00	70.00	62.00
☐ smoke	85.00	95.00	87.00

STAR COASTER
English Manufacturer

Utility is the key to the distinctiveness of this pattern. It is a simple many-rayed central medallion imprinted into heavy glass and surrounded by a clear glass circle with a border of double beadwork, delicately executed. The color is clear in marigold.

Coaster, each
| ☐ marigold | 30.00 | 35.00 | 32.00 |

STAR FLOWER

This distinctly paneled design carries sprays of flowers on each spear that are naturalistically molded. The flowers stand tall with beadwork decoration on the foliage. The rounds in the middle of the ridged petals are also beaded. It is a lovely pattern, the iridescence something to behold, the colors marigold and blue. This is a true rarity.

Pitcher
| ☐ marigold | 1800.00 | 2200.00 | 1900.00 |
| ☐ blue | 1200.00 | 1400.00 | 1300.00 |

STAR MEDALLION
Imperial

This pattern makes use of contrasts—the sharply cut stars in a wide band around the piece are multi-rayed and splayed outward. The background is a neat vertical and horizontal row of heavy round knobs covering the piece. The overall effect is one of eyecatching balances. The glass is very heavy, the colors rich in marigold and smoke.

Star Medallion

	Current Price Range		Prior Year Average
Bowl, round, diameter 7″			
☐ marigold	20.00	30.00	22.00
☐ smoke	30.00	40.00	32.00
Bowl, square, diameter 7″			
☐ marigold	20.00	30.00	22.00
☐ smoke	30.00	40.00	32.00
Bowl, square, diameter 9″			
☐ marigold	20.00	30.00	22.00
☐ smoke	30.00	40.00	32.00
Butter Dish, with lid			
☐ marigold	80.00	90.00	82.00
Compote			
☐ marigold	30.00	40.00	32.00
Creamer			
☐ marigold	40.00	50.00	42.00

	Current Price Range		Prior Year Average
Goblet			
☐ marigold	40.00	50.00	42.00
Milk Pitcher			
☐ marigold	60.00	—	—
☐ clambroth	65.00	—	—
☐ smoke..	65.00	—	—
Pitcher			
☐ marigold	55.00	65.00	57.00
Punch Bowl			
☐ marigold	70.00	80.00	72.00
Punch Cup			
☐ marigold	10.00	20.00	11.00
Spooner			
☐ marigold	40.00	50.00	42.00
Sugar Bowl			
☐ marigold	40.00	50.00	42.00
Tumbler			
☐ marigold	25.00	35.00	27.00
☐ smoke..	50.00	—	—

STAR OF DAVID
Imperial

The Star of David is the centerpiece made up of braided ribbons with a smooth background. From the tips of these rays starts a busy many-rayed pattern that covers the rest of the piece. The ribbing that makes up the rays seems stretched in the motion of reflecting light. Under the vertical panels, on the exterior are contrasting horizontal arcs in a wave pattern. The glass is sharply molded, the colors green with silver finish, marigold, smoke, and purple.

Bowl			
☐ marigold	55.00	65.00	57.00
☐ purple	70.00	80.00	72.00
☐ green	70.00	80.00	72.00
☐ smoke..	90.00	100.00	95.00

STAR OF DAVID AND BOWS
Northwood

A simple Star of David creates the center motif, consisting of plaited bead-work in the five-point shape. There is a smoothly stippled background and the surrounding border is a neat band of bows with beaded ribbons and flowers. The colors are marigold, amethyst, and green.

	Current Price Range		Prior Year Average

Bowl
☐ marigold	40.00	50.00	42.00
☐ amethyst	55.00	65.00	57.00
☐ green	65.00	75.00	67.00

STAR SPRAY
Imperial

Bowl, diameter 7″
☐ marigold	20.00	30.00	22.00
☐ smoke	30.00	40.00	32.00

Plate, diameter 7½″
☐ marigold	45.00	55.00	47.00
☐ smoke	70.00	80.00	72.00

STARBRIGHT

Vase
☐ marigold	30.00	40.00	32.00
☐ blue	35.00	45.00	37.00
☐ amethyst	35.00	45.00	37.00

STARBURST

Cologne Bottle
☐ marigold	45.00	55.00	47.00

STARFISH
Dugan

The starfish nestles in the middle of a scrolly design, stippled roughly in a naturalistic way. The rest of the pattern resembles stylized flowers, lilies in voluptuous relief with some stippling as a divider. The colors are green, purple, marigold, and peach opalescent.

Compote
☐ marigold	35.00	45.00	37.00
☐ purple	45.00	55.00	47.00
☐ green	50.00	60.00	52.00
☐ peach opalescent	60.00	70.00	62.00

STARS AND BARS

Wine Goblet
☐ marigold	35.00	45.00	37.00

STARS AND STRIPES

	Current Price Range		Prior Year Average

Plate
| ☐ marigold .... | 90.00 | 100.00 | 92.00 |

STIPPLED DIAMOND SWAG
English Manufacturer

Stippled panels in a modified diamond shape alternate with lozenge work and draped ridges. It is a busy geometric design covering all of the available space. The pedestal is neatly ridged to under the base. The colors are marigold, blue, and green.

Compote
☐ marigold	45.00	65.00	50.00
☐ blue	65.00	75.00	70.00
☐ green	65.00	75.00	70.00

STIPPLED FLOWER
Dugan

Bowl
| ☐ peach opalescent .... | 55.00 | 65.00 | 57.00 |

STIPPLED PETALS
Dugan

Bowl, diameter 9″
| ☐ peach opalescent .... | 50.00 | 60.00 | 52.00 |
| ☐ purple .... | 80.00 | — | — |

STIPPLED RAMBLER ROSE

A pretty rambler rose is the eye-catching motif on these pieces, lovingly detailed in high relief. The background is stippled and surrounding the flower is foliage and scrolls. The distinguishing feature on the nut bowl is the three knobby feet. The glass is heavy, iridescent on the inside and out. Colors are marigold and blue.

Nut Bowl
| ☐ marigold .... | 55.00 | 65.00 | 57.00 |
| ☐ blue .... | 70.00 | 80.00 | 72.00 |

STIPPLED RAYS
Fenton

Alternating rays of glossy smooth glass and stippled spears are used once again, this time on an interior pattern. It is a simple, effective design, especially suited to iridescent Carnival glass. The central medallion is a thousand-rayed star in deep cut. The colors are marigold, green, blue, amethyst, and rarely red.

Stippled Rays

	Current Price Range		Prior Year Average
Bon Bon			
☐ marigold	20.00	30.00	25.00
☐ green	35.00	45.00	37.00
☐ blue	35.00	45.00	37.00
☐ amethyst	35.00	45.00	37.00
☐ red	300.00	400.00	315.00

	Current Price Range		Prior Year Average

Bowl, diameter 5″–9″

☐ green	25.00	30.00	27.00
☐ blue	35.00	45.00	37.00
☐ amethyst	35.00	45.00	37.00
☐ red	270.00	300.00	275.00
☐ marigold	30.00	—	—
☐ white	60.00	—	—

Compote

☐ marigold	25.00	30.00	27.00
☐ green	35.00	45.00	37.00
☐ blue	35.00	45.00	37.00
☐ amethyst	35.00	45.00	37.00

Creamer

☐ marigold	20.00	30.00	22.00
☐ green	25.00	35.00	26.00
☐ blue	25.00	35.00	26.00
☐ amethyst	25.00	35.00	26.00
☐ red	280.00	320.00	285.00

Plate

☐ marigold	25.00	35.00	27.00
☐ green	40.00	50.00	42.00
☐ blue	40.00	50.00	42.00
☐ amethyst	40.00	50.00	42.00
☐ red	320.00	350.00	325.00

STIPPLED RAYS
Imperial

Again we have stippling versus smooth but the Imperial version has gently scalloped edges and the relief is low. The glass is clear, the iridescence is luminous, and the colors are helios green, smoke, and marigold.

Creamer, footed

☐ marigold	35.00	50.00	37.00
☐ green	35.00	50.00	37.00
☐ smoke	45.00	55.00	47.00

Sugar Bowl, footed

☐ marigold	35.00	50.00	37.00
☐ green	35.00	50.00	37.00
☐ smoke	45.00	55.00	47.00

STIPPLED RAYS
Northwood

Another interior pattern of mildly fluted panels, stipples and glossies decorate the whole of the piece. They radiate from a central medallion of tightly ridged rays. The colors are varied, as are the shapes.

	Current Price Range		Prior Year Average
Compote			
☐ marigold	45.00	—	—

STIPPLED STRAWBERRY
Jenkins

This sparsely decorated pattern consists of floral and foliage designs in high relief. The berries are well molded and stippled, dangling on the sides. The colors are mild and transparent, the iridescence good.

Spittoon			
☐ marigold	210.00	230.00	215.00
Tumbler			
☐ marigold	70.00	80.00	72.00

STORK ABC PLATE
Imperial

A children's plate with the ABCs on the outside band in low stippling, and the numbers one through ten frame a knobby design of a stork. The background is glossy and smooth, the iridescence high and the marigold is clear.

Plate, diameter 7"			
☐ marigold	60.00	70.00	62.00

STORK AND RUSHES
Dugan

Berry Bowl, diameter 4½"			
☐ marigold	20.00	30.00	22.00
☐ purple	20.00	30.00	22.00
☐ amethyst...........................	20.00	30.00	22.00

	Current Price Range		Prior Year Average
Berry Bowl, diameter 10″			
☐ marigold	40.00	50.00	42.00
☐ purple	45.00	55.00	42.00
☐ amethyst	45.00	55.00	42.00
Hat Shape			
☐ marigold	15.00	25.00	16.00
☐ blue	23.00	28.00	25.00
Mug			
☐ marigold	30.00	40.00	32.00
☐ purple	60.00	—	—
☐ blue	350.00	—	—
☐ aqua	400.00	—	—
Punch Bowl			
☐ marigold	140.00	170.00	156.00
☐ purple	210.00	225.00	220.00
☐ blue	210.00	225.00	220.00
☐ amethyst	210.00	225.00	220.00
Punch Cup			
☐ marigold	10.00	20.00	14.00
☐ blue	27.00	31.00	30.00
☐ amethyst	27.00	31.00	30.00
Tumbler			
☐ marigold	25.00	35.00	27.00
☐ blue	30.00	40.00	32.00
☐ amethyst	30.00	40.00	32.00
Water Pitcher			
☐ marigold	210.00	230.00	215.00
☐ blue	280.00	310.00	290.00
☐ amethyst	280.00	310.00	290.00

STORK VASE
Imperial

The finish is lightly stippled, showing off the iridescence in a lovely way. The stork struts on one side backed by cane, molded in low relief. The color is clear, marigold, and luminous.

Stork Vase

	Current Price Range		Prior Year Average
Vase			
□ marigold	40.00	50.00	42.00

STRAWBERRY
Millersburg

Perhaps this is a later pattern, as the workmanship and coloring seems to be at the peak of quality on these pieces. The design consists of foliage and strawberries, the fruit having a well-detailed stippling. The glass is heavy and glossy, highlighting the pattern's high relief. There is a multi-rayed star at the base that shines through, seeming to illuminate the foliage wreath.

	Current Price Range		Prior Year Average

Bon Bon
☐ marigold	25.00	30.00	28.00
☐ green	50.00	60.00	52.00
☐ cobalt blue	60.00	70.00	62.00
☐ amethyst	60.00	70.00	62.00
☐ amberina	210.00	220.00	215.00
☐ red	300.00	350.00	310.00
☐ vaseline	80.00	—	—
☐ vaseline opalescent	500.00	—	—

Bowl, diameter 8–10″
☐ marigold	110.00	—	—
☐ purple	175.00	—	—
☐ green	175.00	—	—

Compote
☐ purple	175.00	—	—
☐ green	190.00	—	—
☐ marigold	125.00	—	—

STRAWBERRY
Northwood

This deep pattern is a swirl of fruit and well detailed leaves on vines covering most of the body of the piece. There are two versions of the pattern, plain glossy background or stippled throughout. The colors are widely varied, as are the shapes.

Bowl, diameter 5″
☐ marigold	20.00	30.00	22.00
☐ purple	28.00	32.00	29.00
☐ green	28.00	32.00	29.00
☐ blue	28.00	32.00	29.00
☐ amethyst	28.00	32.00	29.00

Bowl, diameter 8½″
☐ marigold	40.00	50.00	42.00
☐ purple	55.00	65.00	56.00
☐ green	55.00	65.00	56.00
☐ blue	55.00	65.00	56.00
☐ amethyst	55.00	65.00	56.00
☐ ices	440.00	460.00	445.00
☐ aqua opalescent	1900.00	—	—

Plate, diameter 7″, handgrip
☐ marigold	70.00	80.00	72.00
☐ purple	85.00	100.00	86.00
☐ green	85.00	100.00	86.00
☐ amethyst	85.00	100.00	86.00

	Current Price Range		Prior Year Average

Plate, diameter 9″
☐ marigold	80.00	90.00	82.00
☐ purple	90.00	110.00	92.00
☐ blue	90.00	110.00	92.00
☐ green	90.00	110.00	92.00
☐ amethyst	90.00	110.00	92.00
☐ white	150.00	180.00	160.00

STRAWBERRY EPERGNE
Northwood/Dugan

Epergne Set
☐ purple	300.00	400.00	325.00
☐ amethyst	300.00	400.00	325.00

STRAWBERRY INTAGLIO
Northwood

The design is under the thick glass, swirling beneath the surface in fruit and foliage.

Bowl, diameter 5″
☐ marigold	20.00	30.00	22.00

Bowl, diameter 9½″
☐ marigold	45.00	55.00	47.00

STRAWBERRY SCROLL
Fenton

Bordering on art glass, this is one of Fenton's outstanding achievements. It consists of three wide horizontal bands. The bottom, which covers almost half of the piece, is a lovely floral design of reeds and flowers. The middle band is ridged on both sides and contains scrolls and feathers. The upper band, just under the plain rim, has the strawberries in high relief. The outstanding feature is the golden iridescence, and colors are marigold and purple.

Pitcher
☐ marigold	1700.00	1900.00	1750.00
☐ blue	1500.00	1700.00	1550.00

Tumbler
☐ marigold	360.00	380.00	365.00
☐ blue	280.00	320.00	290.00

STREAM OF HEARTS
Fenton

	Current Price Range		Prior Year Average
Bowl, diameter 9½"			
☐ marigold	60.00	80.00	62.00
☐ blue	80.00	100.00	82.00
☐ amethyst	80.00	100.00	82.00
Compote			
☐ marigold	45.00	60.00	47.00
☐ white	65.00	75.00	68.00

STRETCHED DIAMOND
Northwood's Near Cut

Tumbler			
☐ marigold	270.00	300.00	275.00

STRUTTING PEACOCK
Westmoreland

Once again we have a truly elegant pattern, perhaps because the peacock prances so proudly, truly a regal bird. On the body of the piece there is no need for any other decoration, just a roughly stippled background to show off the high relief on the detail of the peacock. The upper rim has a jewelry appearance, draped with chains of beadwork as luminous as gold. Around this border, thick knobs anchor each chain, creating the fluted edge. The colors are amethyst and green.

Creamer			
☐ amethyst	60.00	70.00	62.00
☐ green	55.00	65.00	57.00
Sugar			
☐ amethyst	60.00	70.00	62.00
☐ green	55.00	65.00	57.00

STUDS
Imperial

Milk Pitcher			
☐ marigold	65.00	75.00	67.00
Tray			
☐ marigold	55.00	65.00	57.00

	Current Price Range		Prior Year Average
Tumbler			
☐ marigold	25.00	35.00	27.00

STYLE

Bowl			
☐ amethyst.........................	85.00	95.00	87.00

SUMMER DAYS
Dugan

Vase			
☐ marigold	40.00	—	—
☐ blue	60.00	—	—

SUNFLOWER
Millersburg

Pin Tray			
☐ marigold	325.00	—	—
☐ purple	295.00	—	—
☐ green	275.00	—	—

SUNFLOWER
Northwood

Bowl, diameter 8½″			
☐ marigold	45.00	—	—
☐ purple	65.00	—	—
☐ green	55.00	—	—
☐ blue	250.00	—	—
☐ ice blue	80.00	—	—
Plate, footed			
☐ marigold	150.00	—	—
☐ green	325.00	—	—

SUNFLOWER AND DIAMOND
English Manufacturer

Vase			
☐ marigold	65.00	—	—
☐ blue	90.00	—	—

SUNGOLD
Australian Manufacturer

	Current Price Range	Prior Year Average
Epergne		
☐ white	150.00	— —

SUNK DIAMOND BAND
U.S. Glass

Pitcher		
☐ marigold	145.00	— —
☐ white	215.00	— —
Tumbler		
☐ marigold	50.00	— —
☐ white	70.00	— —

SUNKEN DAISY
English Manufacturer

Sugar		
☐ marigold	25.00	— —
☐ blue	35.00	— —

SUNKEN HOLLYHOCK

Gone With the Wind Lamp		
☐ marigold	2500.00	— —
☐ red	96.00	— —

SUN PUNCH

Bottle		
☐ marigold	20.00	— —
☐ clambroth	25.00	— —

SUNRAY
Fenton

Compote		
☐ marigold	55.00	— —

SUPERB DRAPE
Northwood

Vase		
☐ aqua opalescent	900.00	— —

SWAN
Dugan

A swan shaped novelty in heavy glass, these pieces are nicely detailed and beautifully iridescent. The feathers are represented by low relief beads, the body is roughly stippled. The colors range widely.

	Current Price Range		Prior Year Average
Swan Shape			
☐ marigold	60.00	70.00	62.00
☐ green	90.00	100.00	92.00
☐ blue	90.00	100.00	92.00
☐ amethyst...................................	90.00	100.00	92.00
☐ ices..	35.00	45.00	37.00
☐ peach opalescent..........................	140.00	150.00	142.00

SWEETHEART
Cambridge

Cookie Jar, lidded			
☐ marigold	1100.00	—	—
☐ green	700.00	—	—
Tumbler			
☐ marigold	600.00	—	—

SWIRL

Rather the same as the Imperial pattern, the important difference is the termination of the swirled panels in sharp spear-like forms. The glass is heavy, the colors amethyst, marigold, green, and others, often with enameled flowers applied.

Tumbler			
☐ marigold	40.00	50.00	42.00
☐ green	65.00	75.00	67.00
Vase			
☐ marigold	225.00	—	—
☐ purple	275.00	—	—
☐ green	250.00	—	—
☐ blue	400.00	—	—
Water Pitcher			
☐ marigold	150.00	—	—
☐ green	190.00	—	—

SWIRLED FLUTE
Fenton

	Current Price Range	Prior Year Average
Vase		
☐ marigold	25.00	— —
☐ purple	30.00	— —
☐ green	40.00	— —
☐ blue	30.00	— —
☐ white	40.00	— —
☐ red	350.00	— —

SWIRL HOBNAIL
Millersburg

Van Gogh is brought to mind by this delightful impressionistic pattern. The hobnails are in correct position and in between, wavy ridges curve in the background. The iridescence is mirror like, the mold work outstanding, the pattern bordering on art glass.

Rose Bowl			
☐ marigold	270.00	280.00	272.00
☐ purple	260.00	320.00	270.00
☐ green	500.00	530.00	515.00
☐ amethyst	260.00	320.00	270.00
Spittoon			
☐ marigold	360.00	430.00	370.00
☐ purple	420.00	480.00	425.00
☐ green	420.00	480.00	425.00
☐ amethyst	420.00	480.00	425.00

SWIRL VARIANT
Imperial

Bowl, diameter 7″			
☐ marigold	20.00	30.00	22.00
☐ smoke	30.00	40.00	32.00
☐ peach opalescent	40.00	50.00	42.00
Epergne			
☐ green	165.00	175.00	167.00
☐ peach opalescent	180.00	210.00	195.00
Pitcher			
☐ marigold	140.00	150.00	142.00
Plate			
☐ marigold	40.00	50.00	42.00
☐ green	45.00	55.00	47.00
☐ smoke	55.00	65.00	57.00
Vase			
☐ marigold	20.00	30.00	22.00

	Current Price Range		Prior Year Average
☐ green	35.00	45.00	37.00
☐ white	30.00	—	—

SWIRLED RIBS
Northwood

Pitcher
☐ marigold	160.00	170.00	162.00

Tumbler
☐ marigold	55.00	65.00	57.00

SWORD AND CIRCLE

Tumbler
☐ marigold	80.00	90.00	82.00

SYDNEY
Fostoria

Tumbler
☐ marigold	350.00	380.00	365.00

TAFFETA LUSTRE
Fostoria

A simple knobbed design on these chunky candlesticks is enhanced by the luxurious iridescent lustre. The finish is smooth and radiated, the colors are blue, green, amber, amethyst, and others.

Bowl, diameter 10″
☐ blue	145.00	155.00	147.00
☐ green	145.00	155.00	147.00
☐ amber	160.00	170.00	162.00
☐ amethyst	145.00	155.00	147.00

Candlesticks
☐ blue	280.00	320.00	290.00
☐ green	280.00	320.00	290.00
☐ amber	390.00	410.00	395.00
☐ amethyst	280.00	320.00	285.00

TARGET
Fenton

Vase, diameter 7″
☐ marigold	25.00	35.00	27.00
☐ amethyst	40.00	50.00	45.00
☐ white	40.00	50.00	45.00
☐ green	40.00	50.00	45.00
☐ peach opalescent	85.00	—	—

TEJAS HEADDRESS
Westmoreland

	Current Price Range		Prior Year Average
☐ Punch Cup.............................	35.00	45.00	37.00

TEN MUMS
Fenton

This pattern shows off mold work and coloring in a most tasteful and well balanced way. The central medallion is a multi-petalled mum resting between two fern-like branches. The surrounding wreath is interconnected leaves, showcasing the ten half mums that appear from the fluted edge. The glass is heavy, the colors are green, cobalt, marigold, peach opalescent, white, and others.

Ten Mums

Bowl, flat

☐ marigold..	70.00	80.00	75.00
☐ green..	90.00	100.00	95.00
☐ blue..	90.00	100.00	95.00
☐ white...	120.00	140.00	125.00
☐ purple	90.00	—	—
Pitcher			
☐ marigold..	400.00	425.00	405.00
☐ blue..	700.00	900.00	750.00
☐ white...	1100.00	1200.00	1150.00

	Current Price Range		Prior Year Average

Tumbler
☐ marigold	45.00	—	—
☐ white	250.00	—	—
☐ blue	80.00	—	—

THREE DIAMONDS
Dugan

Vase, height 6″
☐ marigold	25.00	35.00	27.00
☐ blue	40.00	50.00	42.00
☐ amethyst	40.00	50.00	42.00
☐ green	40.00	50.00	42.00
☐ white	45.00	55.00	47.00
☐ peach opalescent	70.00	80.00	72.00

THREE-IN-ONE
Imperial

Bowl, diameter 4″
☐ marigold	15.00	—	—
☐ purple	20.00	—	—
☐ green	20.00	—	—
☐ smoke	25.00	—	—

Bowl, diameter 9″
☐ marigold	25.00	—	—
☐ purple	35.00	—	—
☐ green	35.00	—	—
☐ smoke	40.00	—	—

Plate, diameter 6½″
☐ marigold	55.00	—	—
☐ smoke	80.00	—	—

Rose Bowl
☐ marigold	195.00	—	—

THREE FLOWERS
Imperial

Tray, with handle in center
☐ marigold	40.00	50.00	42.00
☐ smoke	45.00	55.00	47.00

THREE FRUITS
Northwood

This delicate overall pattern is well conceived as a series of branches, twining around the outside band, framing three fruits: a well molded pair of pears, a spray of cherries and double apples. The pattern is filled in with stippling, creating a very unified look. The colors are widely varied.

Three Fruits

	Current Price Range		Prior Year Average
Berry Bowl, diameter 5″			
☐ marigold	20.00	30.00	22.00
☐ purple	25.00	35.00	27.00
☐ blue...	25.00	35.00	27.00
☐ green	25.00	35.00	27.00
☐ amethyst.......................................	25.00	35.00	27.00
☐ aqua opalescent	100.00	125.00	110.00
☐ ices..	35.00	45.00	37.00
Berry Bowl, diameter 10″			
☐ marigold	30.00	40.00	32.00
☐ purple	45.00	55.00	47.00
☐ blue...	50.00	60.00	52.00
☐ green	50.00	60.00	52.00
☐ amethyst.......................................	45.00	55.00	47.00
☐ aqua opalescent	375.00	395.00	380.00
☐ ices..	65.00	75.00	67.00
Bon Bon			
☐ marigold	40.00	50.00	42.00
☐ purple	50.00	60.00	52.00
☐ blue...	60.00	70.00	62.00
☐ green	55.00	65.00	57.00
☐ amethyst.......................................	50.00	60.00	52.00
☐ aqua opalescent	440.00	460.00	465.00
☐ ices..	70.00	80.00	72.00
Plate			
☐ marigold	70.00	80.00	72.00
☐ blue...	130.00	140.00	132.00
☐ green	100.00	120.00	110.00
☐ amethyst.......................................	95.00	105.00	97.00
☐ aqua opalescent	740.00	760.00	745.00
☐ ices..	680.00	720.00	690.00

THREE FRUITS

The same theme is given a different treatment here, a central spray of cherries on a smooth background is framed by a wreath of foiliage and dangling fruit. The design is sparsely planted around the plate, showing off a golden iridescence. The colors vary.

	Current Price Range		Prior Year Average
Plate			
☐ marigold	75.00	85.00	77.00
☐ purple	110.00	120.00	115.00
☐ green	110.00	120.00	115.00
☐ blue	110.00	120.00	115.00
☐ amethyst...........................	110.00	120.00	115.00
☐ ices.................................	130.00	140.00	132.00

THREE ROW
Imperial

Vase			
☐ marigold	300.00	—	—
☐ purple	400.00	—	—

THUMBPRINT AND OVAL
Imperial

Vase			
☐ marigold	165.00	—	—
☐ purple	175.00	—	—

THUNDERBIRD
Australian Manufacturer

Bowl, diameter 5″			
☐ marigold	35.00	—	—
☐ purple	45.00	—	—
Bowl, diameter 9″			
☐ marigold	65.00	—	—
☐ purple	85.00	—	—

TIGER LILY
Imperial

Water Pitcher			
☐ marigold	130.00	—	—
☐ purple	250.00	—	—
☐ green	195.00	—	—
Tumbler			
☐ marigold	30.00	—	—
☐ purple	45.00	—	—
☐ green	35.00	—	—
☐ blue	100.00	—	—

TINY BERRY

	Current Price Range	Prior Year Average
Tumbler, 2¼"		
☐ blue	40.00	— —

TINY HOBNAIL

Lamp		
☐ marigold	95.00	— —

TOBACCO LEAF
U.S. Glass

Champagne		
☐ clear	90.00	— —

TOLTEC
McKee

Butter		
☐ ruby iridized	350.00	— —

TOMAHAWK
Cambridge

☐ blue	1350.00	— —

TORNADO
Northwood

Vase, plain		
☐ marigold	220.00	— —
☐ blue	750.00	— —
☐ purple	250.00	— —
☐ white	675.00	— —
Vase, ribbed		
☐ marigold	250.00	— —
☐ blue	90.00	— —
☐ purple	270.00	— —
☐ green	290.00	— —
☐ ice blue	1000.00	— —

TRACERY
Millersburg

Bon Bon		
☐ purple	500.00	— —
☐ green	500.00	— —

TREE BARK
Imperial

	Current Price Range	Prior Year Average	
Pitcher			
☐ marigold	60.00	—	—
Pitcher, with lid			
☐ marigold	70.00	—	—
Bowl			
☐ marigold	18.00	—	—
Candlesticks			
☐ marigold	40.00	—	—
Candy Jar			
☐ marigold	15.00	—	—
Pickle Jar			
☐ marigold	35.00	—	—
Tumbler			
☐ marigold	15.00	—	—

TREE OF LIFE
Imperial

	Current Price Range	Prior Year Average	
Bowl, diameter 5″			
☐ marigold	20.00	—	—
Hand Basket			
☐ marigold	30.00	—	—
Pitcher			
☐ marigold	60.00	—	—
Plate			
☐ marigold	20.00	—	—
Tumbler			
☐ marigold	22.00	—	—

TREE TRUNK
Northwood

	Current Price Range	Prior Year Average	
Funeral Vase			
☐ marigold	90.00	—	—
☐ purple	120.00	—	—
☐ green	115.00	—	—
☐ blue	135.00	—	—
☐ peach	700.00	—	—
☐ white	175.00	—	—
Jardiniere			
☐ marigold	190.00	—	—
☐ purple	300.00	—	—

	Current Price Range	Prior Year Average

Vase
☐ marigold	30.00	—	—
☐ purple	45.00	—	—
☐ green	40.00	—	—
☐ blue	50.00	—	—
☐ aqua opalescent	900.00	—	—
☐ ice blue	150.00	—	—

TRIANDS
English Manufacturer

Butter
| ☐ marigold | 60.00 | — | — |

Celery Vase
| ☐ marigold | 55.00 | — | — |

Creamer, Sugar, Spooner
| ☐ marigold (each) | 45.00 | — | — |

TRIPLETS

Bowl, 6″–8″
☐ marigold	25.00	—	—
☐ purple	35.00	—	—
☐ green	40.00	—	—
☐ peach	45.00	—	—

Hat Shape
☐ marigold	25.00	—	—
☐ purple	30.00	—	—
☐ amber	35.00	—	—

TROPICANA
English

Vase
| ☐ marigold | 1000.00 | — | — |

TROUT AND FLY
Millersburg

Bowl
☐ marigold	375.00	—	—
☐ purple	400.00	—	—
☐ green	400.00	—	—
☐ lavender	700.00	—	—

Plate
| ☐ purple | 5500.00 | — | — |

TULIP
Millersburg

	Current Price Range		Prior Year Average	
Compote, 9″				
☐ marigold	500.00	—	—	
☐ purple	800.00	—	—	
☐ green	800.00	—	—	

TULIP AND CANE
Imperial

	Current Price Range		Prior Year Average	
Claret				
☐ marigold	55.00	—	—	
☐ smoke	65.00	—	—	
Goblet				
☐ marigold	60.00	—	—	
☐ smoke	65.00	—	—	
Wine				
☐ marigold	45.00	—	—	
☐ smoke	55.00	—	—	

TULIP SCROLL
Millersburg

	Current Price Range		Prior Year Average	
Vase				
☐ marigold	150.00	—	—	
☐ purple	175.00	—	—	
☐ green	175.00	—	—	

TWINS
Imperial

This geometric, symmetrical pattern consists of vaguely pointed arches, made up of high relief ridges and separated by tear drop shaped rosettes arranged in a wide band wreath around a central sunburst. The color is clearly iridescent, the mold work is excellent.

Twins

	Current Price Range		Prior Year Average
Berry Bowl, diameter 4½″			
☐ marigold	20.00	30.00	22.00
☐ green	25.00	35.00	28.00
Berry Bowl, diameter 9″			
☐ marigold	30.00	40.00	32.00
☐ green	40.00	50.00	42.00
Bowl, diameter 7″–10″, footed			
☐ marigold	25.00	—	—
☐ purple	45.00	—	—
Bowl, diameter 8″			
☐ marigold	16.00	20.00	17.00
☐ smoke	35.00	50.00	40.00
Bride's Basket			
☐ marigold	60.00	70.00	62.00
Fruit Bowl, with base			
☐ marigold	50.00	60.00	52.00

Twins

	Current Price Range		Prior Year Average
Plate, diameter 9½″			
☐ marigold	225.00	—	—
Plate, 13″			
☐ marigold	365.00	—	—
☐ blue	400.00	—	—
☐ green	400.00	—	—
Punch Bowl, with base			
☐ marigold	35.00	40.00	37.00
Punch Cup			
☐ marigold	16.00	20.00	18.00

TWO FLOWERS
Fenton

An overall pattern nicely arranged from the rim to the floral center, contains foliage, waterlilies, and cattails. The background is smooth glossy glass, heavy molded, and the outer rim is a wavy scale band. The finish is radiated.

	Current Price Range		Prior Year Average

Bowl
☐ green	50.00	—	—
☐ blue	40.00	—	—
☐ white	375.00	—	—
☐ red	800.00	1600.00	—

Bowl, flat
☐ marigold	35.00	—	—
☐ purple	45.00	—	—
☐ green	45.00	—	—
☐ blue	45.00	—	—
☐ vaseline	55.00	—	—

Rose Bowl
☐ marigold	95.00	—	—
☐ blue	150.00	—	—
☐ purple	140.00	—	—

TWO FRUITS
Fenton

Bowl
☐ marigold	60.00	—	—
☐ blue	85.00	—	—
☐ purple	85.00	—	—
☐ green	100.00	—	—
☐ white	110.00	—	—

TWO FRUITS
Northwood

Spooner
☐ blue	450.00	—	—

Sugar
☐ blue	450.00	—	—

TWO ROW
Imperial

Vase
☐ purple	475.00	—	—

U.S. DIAMOND BLOCK
U.S. Glass

Compote
☐ marigold	55.00	—	—
☐ peach opalescent	75.00	—	—

	Current Price Range		Prior Year Average

Shakers
- ☐ marigold .... 60.00 — —

VALENTINE
Ring Tray

- ☐ marigold .... 75.00 — —

VALENTINE
Northwood

Bowl, diameter 10″
- ☐ marigold .... 150.00 — —

Bowl, diameter 5″
- ☐ marigold .... 75.00 — —
- ☐ purple .... 125.00 — —

VENETIAN
Cambridge

Butter
- ☐ marigold .... 600.00 — —
- ☐ clambroth .... 700.00 — —

Creamer
- ☐ marigold .... 400.00 — —
- ☐ clambroth .... 500.00 — —

Sugar
- ☐ marigold .... 400.00 — —
- ☐ clambroth .... 500.00 — —

Vase/Rose Bowl
- ☐ marigold .... 1100.00 — —
- ☐ green .... 900.00 — —

VICTORIAN
Dugan

Bowl, diameter 10″–12″
- ☐ purple .... 200.00 — —
- ☐ peach opalescent.. 1250.00 — —

VINEYARD
Dugan

Pitcher
- ☐ marigold 80.00 90.00 82.00
- ☐ amethyst.. 280.00 300.00 285.00

	Current Price Range		Prior Year Average

Tumbler
☐ marigold	15.00	25.00	17.00
☐ amethyst	40.00	50.00	42.00

VINING LEAF AND VARIANT
English Manufacturer

Rose Bowl
☐ marigold	250.00	270.00	255.00

Vase
☐ marigold	240.00	260.00	245.00

VINING TWIGS
Dugan

Bowl
☐ marigold	20.00	30.00	22.00
☐ amethyst	30.00	40.00	32.00
☐ green	30.00	40.00	34.00
☐ white	40.00	50.00	42.00

VINTAGE
Dugan

Dresser Tray
☐ marigold	70.00	80.00	72.00

Plate, 1″ dome, footed, diameter 9½″
☐ marigold	300.00	—	—
☐ purple	500.00	—	—

Powder Jar, covered
☐ marigold	50.00	60.00	52.00
☐ amethyst	140.00	160.00	145.00
☐ white	250.00	—	—

VINTAGE
Fenton

A straightforward, utilitarian pattern, Vintage is a grape-and-leaf design. The motif is sparsely sprinkled over the surface, the moldwork is in low relief.

Berry Bowl, diameter 4″
☐ marigold	20.00	30.00	22.00
☐ green	30.00	40.00	32.00
☐ blue	30.00	40.00	32.00
☐ purple	30.00	40.00	32.00
☐ amethyst	30.00	40.00	32.00
☐ amber	40.00	50.00	42.00

	Current Price Range		Prior Year Average
Berry Bowl, diameter 8″			
☐ marigold	30.00	40.00	32.00
☐ green	40.00	50.00	42.00
☐ blue	40.00	50.00	42.00
☐ purple	40.00	50.00	42.00
☐ amethyst	40.00	50.00	42.00
☐ amber	55.00	65.00	57.00
Bowl, flat, 8″–10″			
☐ marigold	15.00	18.00	16.00
☐ purple	24.00	28.00	26.00
☐ blue	24.00	28.00	26.00
☐ green	24.00	28.00	26.00
☐ amethyst	24.00	28.00	26.00
☐ amber	24.00	28.00	26.00
☐ red	700.00	1200.00	
☐ aqua opalescent	800.00	—	—
Bowl, footed, Fernery			
☐ marigold	25.00	—	—
☐ purple	45.00	—	—
☐ blue	50.00	—	—
☐ green	45.00	—	—
☐ amethyst	45.00	—	—
☐ amber	75.00	—	—
☐ red	500.00	—	—
Compote			
☐ marigold	32.00	42.00	35.00
☐ purple	36.00	40.00	37.00
☐ blue	35.00	45.00	37.00
☐ green	40.00	50.00	42.00
☐ amethyst	40.00	50.00	42.00
Epergne			
☐ marigold	90.00	100.00	92.00
☐ purple	125.00	135.00	127.00
☐ blue	125.00	135.00	127.00
☐ green	140.00	150.00	142.00
☐ amethyst	130.00	140.00	132.00
Nut Bowl, trifoot			
☐ marigold	20.00	30.00	25.00
☐ purple	38.00	45.00	39.00
☐ green	38.00	45.00	39.00
☐ blue	38.00	45.00	39.00
☐ amethyst	38.00	45.00	39.00
☐ amber	38.00	45.00	39.00

	Current Price Range		Prior Year Average
Nut Bowl, six-footed			
☐ marigold	35.00	40.00	37.00
☐ purple	70.00	80.00	72.00
☐ green...	70.00	80.00	72.00
☐ blue...	70.00	80.00	72.00
☐ amethyst.......................................	70.00	80.00	72.00
☐ amber	70.00	80.00	72.00
Orange Bowl, footed			
☐ marigold	60.00	70.00	62.00
☐ purple	80.00	100.00	82.00
☐ green...	80.00	100.00	82.00
☐ blue...	80.00	100.00	82.00
☐ amethyst.......................................	80.00	100.00	82.00
☐ amber	80.00	100.00	82.00
Plate, flat, 7″–7½″			
☐ purple	60.00	70.00	62.00
☐ blue...	60.00	70.00	62.00
☐ green...	60.00	70.00	62.00
☐ amethyst.......................................	60.00	70.00	62.00
Plate, diameter 9″			
☐ marigold	225.00	—	—
☐ blue...	700.00	—	—
Punch Bowl			
☐ marigold	185.00	195.00	187.00
☐ purple	370.00	380.00	372.00
☐ blue...	370.00	380.00	372.00
☐ green...	360.00	370.00	362.00
☐ blue...	370.00	380.00	372.00
☐ amber	360.00	370.00	362.00
Punch Cup			
☐ marigold	20.00	30.00	22.00
☐ purple	30.00	40.00	32.00
☐ blue...	30.00	40.00	32.00
☐ green...	30.00	40.00	32.00
☐ blue...	32.00	42.00	34.00
☐ amber	40.00	50.00	42.00
Rose Bowl			
☐ marigold	50.00	60.00	52.00
☐ purple	70.00	80.00	72.00
☐ green...	70.00	80.00	72.00
☐ blue...	70.00	80.00	72.00
☐ amethyst.......................................	70.00	80.00	72.00
☐ amber	70.00	80.00	72.00
☐ amberina	90.00	100.00	92.00

	Current Price Range		Prior Year Average
Sandwich			
☐ marigold	40.00	50.00	45.00
☐ amberina	60.00	70.00	62.00
Wine Glass			
☐ marigold	16.00	18.00	17.00
☐ purple	30.00	40.00	32.00
☐ amethyst	30.00	40.00	32.00

VINTAGE
Millersburg

Bowl, diameter 5″			
☐ purple	500.00	—	—
☐ green	500.00	—	—
☐ blue	500.00	—	—
Bowl, diameter 9″			
☐ marigold	500.00	—	—
☐ green	650.00	—	—
☐ blue	3000.00	—	—

VINTAGE BANDED
Dugan

Mug			
☐ marigold	30.00	—	—
☐ smoke	45.00	—	—
Pitcher			
☐ marigold	200.00	—	—
Tumbler			
☐ marigold	400.00	—	—

WAFFLE BLOCK
Imperial

Basket			
☐ marigold	40.00	50.00	42.00
Parfait Glass			
☐ marigold	25.00	35.00	27.00
☐ clambroth	35.00	45.00	37.00
Punch Bowl			
☐ marigold	175.00	—	—
☐ clambroth	150.00	—	—
☐ purple	250.00	—	—
☐ teal	220.00	—	—
Punch Cup			
☐ marigold	10.00	14.00	12.00

	Current Price Range		Prior Year Average
☐ purple	30.00	—	—
☐ clambroth	14.00	16.00	15.00
Rose Bowl			
☐ marigold	70.00	—	—
☐ clambroth	270.00	—	—
Tumbler			
☐ marigold	180.00	210.00	185.00
Vase, diameter 9″			
☐ marigold	35.00	45.00	38.00
☐ clambroth	50.00	60.00	52.00

WAR DANCE
English Manufacturer

Compote

☐ marigold	60.00	70.00	62.00

WASHBOARD

Creamer

☐ marigold	35.00	45.00	37.00

WATER LILY
Fenton

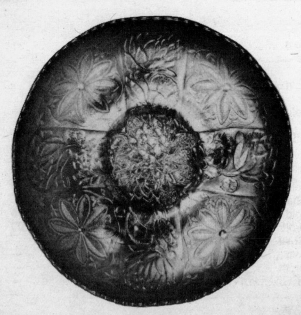

Water Lily

	Current Price Range		Prior Year Average
Bon Bon			
☐ marigold	30.00	40.00	32.00
☐ blue	40.00	50.00	42.00
☐ amethyst............................	40.00	50.00	42.00
☐ green	42.00	52.00	44.00
☐ ices.................................	45.00	55.00	47.00
Bowl, diameter 5″, footed			
☐ marigold	20.00	30.00	22.00
☐ blue	25.00	35.00	27.00
☐ amethyst............................	27.00	37.00	30.00
☐ green	30.00	40.00	32.00
☐ red.................................	340.00	360.00	347.00
Bowl, diameter 10″, footed			
☐ marigold	35.00	45.00	37.00
☐ green	40.00	50.00	42.00
☐ blue	40.00	50.00	42.00
☐ amethyst............................	45.00	55.00	47.00

WEEPING CHERRY
Dugan

Bowl, dome and flat base			
☐ marigold	45.00	—	—
☐ purple	65.00	—	—
☐ peach opalescent....................	195.00	—	—
☐ white...............................	85.00	—	—

WESTERN DAISY
Westmoreland

Bowl			
☐ marigold	35.00	—	—
☐ purple	45.00	—	—
☐ marigold over milk..................	165.00	—	—
Hat			
☐ marigold	30.00	—	—
☐ purple	45.00	—	—

WESTERN THISTLE

Tumbler			
☐ marigold	235.00	—	—

WHEAT
Northwood

	Current Price Range		Prior Year Average
Bowl, covered			
☐ amethyst...........................	1800.00	2200.00	1900.00

WHEELS
Imperial

Bowl, diameter 9″			
☐ marigold	40.00	50.00	42.00

WHIRLING HOBSTER
U.S. Glass

Cup			
☐ marigold	15.00	—	—
Pitcher			
☐ marigold	150.00	—	—
Punch Bowl/Base			
☐ marigold	90.00	—	—

WHIRLING LEAVES
Millersburg

Bowl, diameter 9″–11″			
☐ marigold	65.00	—	—
☐ purple	95.00	—	—
☐ green	95.00	—	—
☐ vaseline..........................	350.00	—	—

WHIRLING STAR
Imperial

Bowl			
☐ marigold	35.00	—	—
Compote			
☐ marigold	55.00	—	—
☐ green	60.00	—	—

	Current Price Range		Prior Year Average

Cup
☐ marigold .... 15.00 — —
Punch Bowl/Base
☐ marigold .... 130.00 — —

WHITE OAK
Fenton/Northwood

Compote, miniature
☐ ice blue .... — — —
☐ aqua opalescent .... 5500.00 — —
☐ blue .... 425.00 — —
Covered Candy
☐ marigold .... 30.00 — —
☐ purple .... 40.00 — —
☐ white .... 50.00 — —
☐ celeste blue .... 50.00 — —
☐ pink .... 50.00 — —
☐ vaseline.................................. 50.00 — —
Tumbler
☐ marigold .... 350.00 — —

WIDE PANEL
Imperial

A simple, elegant look in iridized glass catches the eye; these pieces use their iridescence to show off their style. The wide panels take up three quarters of the body, gently convex and terminated by a three rim band that horizontally rims the upper edge. The glass is almost opaque and heavy.

Compote
☐ marigold 30.00 40.00 32.00
Console Set
☐ marigold 85.00 95.00 87.00
☐ ice blue 105.00 115.00 107.00
☐ ice green 105.00 115.00 107.00
☐ vaseline.................................. 105.00 115.00 107.00
☐ pink 105.00 115.00 107.00
Epergne
☐ marigold 440.00 460.00 445.00
☐ purple 560.00 580.00 565.00
☐ white 840.00 860.00 845.00
Goblet, small
☐ marigold 30.00 40.00 32.00

	Current Price Range		Prior Year Average
Goblet, large			
☐ marigold	35.00	45.00	37.00
Lemonade Pitcher, handled			
☐ marigold	22.00	26.00	24.00
Plate, diameter 10″			
☐ marigold	25.00	30.00	27.00
☐ smoke	35.00	40.00	37.00
☐ clambroth	35.00	40.00	37.00
Punch Bowl			
☐ marigold	85.00	95.00	87.00
Punch Cup			
☐	15.00	25.00	17.00

WIDE PANEL VI
Northwood

Pitcher			
☐ marigold	150.00	—	—
☐ purple	200.00	—	—
☐ green	250.00	—	—

WIDE RIB
Dugan

Vase			
☐ marigold	35.00	—	—
☐ purple	40.00	—	—
☐ green	45.00	—	—
☐ blue	45.00	—	—
☐ peach opalescent	60.00	—	—
☐ aqua opalescent	85.00	—	—
☐ white...	65.00	—	—

WILD BERRY

Jar and Lid			
☐ marigold	75.00	—	—

WILD BLACKBERRY
Fenton

	Current Price Range	Prior Year Average
Bowl		
☐ marigold	45.00	— —
☐ purple	55.00	— —
☐ green	55.00	— —
Maday Advertising Bowl		
☐ green	750.00	— —
☐ purple	750.00	— —

WILD FERN
Australian Manufacturer

Compote		
☐ marigold	135.00	— —
☐ purple	165.00	— —

WILD FLOWER
Millersburg

Compote		
☐ marigold	900.00	— —
☐ purple	120.00	— —
☐ green	1500.00	— —

WILD LOGANBERRY
Westmoreland

Cider Pitcher		
☐ marigold over milk	450.00	— —
Covered Compote		
☐ marigold over milk	120.00	— —
Creamer		
☐ marigold over milk	90.00	— —
Goblet		
☐ marigold over milk	100.00	— —
Sugar		
☐ marigold over milk	90.00	— —
Wine		
☐ marigold	85.00	— —

WILD ROSE
Millersburg

	Current Price Range	Prior Year Average
Lamp, small		
☐ marigold	650.00	— —
☐ purple	750.00	— —
☐ green	700.00	— —
Lamp, midsize		
☐ marigold	600.00	— —
☐ purple	850.00	— —
☐ green	750.00	— —
Lamp, large		
☐ marigold	1500.00	— —
Lamp, ladies		
☐ marigold	1500.00	— —
☐ purple	1600.00	— —
☐ green	1600.00	— —

WILD ROSE
Northwood

This exterior pattern is a draped wreath of an eight petaled rose and holly-like leaves. The background is smooth and glossy, the glass is opaque, the iridescence is milky.

	Current Price Range		Prior Year Average
Bowl, flat, diameter 8″			
☐ marigold	30.00	40.00	32.00
☐ green	35.00	45.00	38.00
☐ amethyst	40.00	50.00	42.00
Bowl, open work edge, fluted, diameter 6″			
☐ marigold	25.00	35.00	27.00
☐ green	35.00	45.00	37.00
☐ amethyst	40.00	50.00	42.00
☐ ice blue	380.00	400.00	385.00

WILD ROSE
Westmoreland

Syrup		
☐ marigold	595.00	— —

WILD STRAWBERRY
Northwood

This is an interesting, swirling pattern, full of action and movement. The foliage wreath is arranged diagonally in a curve around the outer band, lightly detailed strawberries separate the sprays of foilage.

	Current Price Range		Prior Year Average
Bowl, flat, diameter 8½"			
☐ purple	60.00	70.00	65.00
☐ green	60.00	70.00	65.00
Plate, handgrip, diameter 7"			
☐ purple	60.00	70.00	65.00
☐ green	60.00	70.00	65.00
Plate, flat, diameter 8"			
☐ purple	120.00	130.00	125.00
☐ green	120.00	130.00	125.00

WINDFLOWER
Dugan

	Current Price Range		Prior Year Average
Bowl			
☐ marigold	35.00	—	—
☐ blue	40.00	—	—
Nappy			
☐ marigold	50.00	—	—
☐ peach opalescent	50.00	—	—
Plate			
☐ marigold	125.00	—	—
☐ blue	150.00	—	—

WINDMILL
Imperial

The windmill motif is treated with high relief, framed by popular trees and surrounded by a ridged oval, creating a picture effect. The rest of the body has blossoms raining down the stippled paneled sides. The color is glimmering, the glass almost opaque.

Windmill

	Current Price Range		Prior Year Average
Berry Bowl, diameter 4″			
☐ marigold	10.00	20.00	12.00
☐ green	20.00	30.00	22.00
☐ purple	20.00	30.00	22.00
Berry Bowl, diameter 8″			
☐ marigold	20.00	30.00	22.00
☐ green	32.00	42.00	35.00
☐ purple	32.00	42.00	35.00
Fruit Bowl			
☐ marigold	25.00	35.00	27.00
☐ green	35.00	45.00	37.00
☐ purple	35.00	45.00	37.00
Milk Pitcher			
☐ marigold	40.00	50.00	42.00
☐ purple	130.00	140.00	132.00
☐ green	90.00	100.00	92.00

	Current Price Range		Prior Year Average
Pickle Dish			
☐ marigold	15.00	25.00	17.00
☐ purple	30.00	40.00	32.00
☐ green	40.00	50.00	42.00
Pitcher			
☐ marigold	65.00	75.00	67.00
☐ purple	170.00	180.00	175.00
☐ green	140.00	160.00	145.00
Tray			
☐ marigold	35.00	45.00	37.00
☐ purple	60.00	70.00	62.00
☐ green	60.00	70.00	62.00
☐ smoke	75.00	—	—

WINE AND ROSES
Fenton

	Current Price Range		Prior Year Average
Cider Pitcher			
☐ marigold	300.00	—	—
Wine			
☐ marigold	40.00	—	—
☐ blue	80.00	—	—
☐ aqua	100.00	—	—
☐ vaseline	100.00	—	—

WISHBONE
Northwood

Wishbone

	Current Price Range		Prior Year Average
Bowl, flat			
☐ marigold	35.00	40.00	37.00
☐ purple	58.00	65.00	60.00
☐ green	58.00	65.00	60.00
☐ blue	58.00	65.00	60.00
☐ white...	500.00	—	—
☐ ices...	90.00	110.00	95.00
Bowl, footed			
☐ marigold	40.00	45.00	42.00
☐ purple	65.00	75.00	67.00
☐ green	65.00	75.00	67.00
☐ blue	65.00	75.00	67.00
☐ white...	120.00	130.00	125.00
☐ ices...	120.00	130.00	125.00
☐ aqua opalescent	1800.00	—	—

	Current Price Range		Prior Year Average
Epergne			
☐ marigold	160.00	180.00	165.00
☐ purple	255.00	275.00	260.00
☐ green..	260.00	290.00	270.00
☐ blue	190.00	200.00	195.00
☐ white..	300.00	400.00	310.00
☐ ice blue	300.00	400.00	310.00
Pitcher			
☐ purple	900.00	1100.00	950.00
☐ green..	860.00	875.00	865.00
☐ marigold	700.00	—	—
Plate, footed			
☐ purple	310.00	340.00	320.00
☐ green..	310.00	340.00	320.00
Plate, flat			
☐ purple	390.00	410.00	400.00
☐ green..	390.00	410.00	400.00
☐ marigold	300.00	—	—
Tumbler			
☐ marigold	70.00	80.00	72.00
☐ purple	125.00	140.00	145.00
☐ green..	125.00	140.00	145.00

WISHBONE AND SPADES

This well-ridged pattern is primarily centered in the middle of these pieces. A large voluptuous eight-sided bloom is the most striking motif, covering over three quarters of the body and framed by smart little blossoms that radiate out of the petals. The background is smooth but the detail is stippled, giving a contrasting texture.

Wishbone and Spades

	Current Price Range		Prior Year Average
Bowl, diameter 6″			
☐ purple	65.00	75.00	67.00
☐ green	65.00	75.00	67.00
☐ peach opalescent...........................	80.00	90.00	82.00
Plate, diameter 6″			
☐ purple	55.00	60.00	57.00
☐ green	55.00	60.00	57.00
☐ peach opalescent...........................	65.00	76.00	67.00
Plate, diameter 9″			
☐ purple	120.00	160.00	140.00
☐ green	270.00	300.00	275.00
Plate, diameter 11″			
☐ purple	750.00	—	—
☐ peach opalescent...........................	600.00	—	—

WISTERIA
Westmoreland

Bank			
☐ white..	800.00	—	—
Berry Bowl, oval			
☐ blue	290.00	—	—
Tumbler			
☐ white..	350.00	—	—
☐ ice blue	450.00	—	—
☐ ice green	750.00	—	—
Water Pitcher			
☐ white..	2500.00	—	—
☐ ice blue	3600.00	—	—

WREATHED CHERRY
Dugan

The cherries are not only molded in high relief, they are usually treated with a different and darker color. The result is an interesting pattern with an eye catching motif. The wreath is a slight band of draped ridges in gentle scallops and it frames the three cherry bunch.

Berry Bowl, diameter 4″, oval			
☐ marigold	14.00	18.00	15.00
☐ amethyst...	25.00	30.00	28.00
☐ purple	25.00	30.00	28.00
☐ white..	38.00	40.00	39.00

	Current Price Range		Prior Year Average

Berry Bowl, diameter 8″, oval
☐ marigold	60.00	70.00	62.00
☐ amethyst	120.00	125.00	122.00
☐ purple	120.00	125.00	122.00
☐ white	290.00	300.00	295.00

Butter Dish
☐ marigold	90.00	100.00	92.00
☐ amethyst	150.00	170.00	160.00
☐ purple	150.00	170.00	160.00
☐ white	180.00	200.00	185.00

Creamer
☐ marigold	60.00	70.00	62.00
☐ amethyst	90.00	100.00	92.00
☐ purple	90.00	100.00	92.00
☐ white	95.00	105.00	97.00

Pitcher
☐ marigold	190.00	210.00	195.00
☐ amethyst	400.00	430.00	415.00
☐ purple	400.00	430.00	415.00
☐ white	760.00	780.00	765.00

Spooner
☐ marigold	60.00	70.00	62.00
☐ amethyst	90.00	100.00	92.00
☐ purple	90.00	100.00	92.00
☐ white	95.00	105.00	97.00

Sugar Bowl
☐ marigold	70.00	80.00	72.00
☐ amethyst	95.00	105.00	97.00
☐ purple	95.00	105.00	97.00
☐ white	100.00	120.00	105.00

Toothpick
☐ amethyst	150.00	170.00	155.00

Tumbler
☐ marigold	30.00	40.00	32.00
☐ amethyst	50.00	60.00	52.00
☐ purple	50.00	60.00	52.00
☐ white	150.00	170.00	152.00

WREATHS OF ROSES
Fenton

Bon Bon, flat
☐ marigold	18.00	20.00	19.00
☐ green	30.00	35.00	32.00

	Current Price Range		Prior Year Average
☐ blue	30.00	35.00	32.00
☐ amethyst	30.00	35.00	32.00
☐ white	45.00	50.00	46.00
Bon Bon, footed			
☐ marigold	35.00	40.00	37.00
☐ green	45.00	55.00	47.00
☐ blue	45.00	55.00	47.00
☐ amethyst	45.00	55.00	47.00
☐ white	80.00	90.00	82.00
Compote			
☐ marigold	20.00	25.00	22.00
☐ green	35.00	40.00	37.00
☐ blue	35.00	40.00	37.00
☐ amethyst	35.00	40.00	37.00
Punch Bowl			
☐ marigold	210.00	225.00	215.00
☐ green	250.00	275.00	260.00
☐ blue	250.00	275.00	260.00
☐ amethyst	250.00	275.00	260.00
Punch Cup			
☐ marigold	13.00	16.00	14.00
☐ green	17.00	19.00	18.00
☐ blue	17.00	19.00	18.00
☐ amethyst	17.00	19.00	18.00
Rose Bowl			
☐ marigold	30.00	40.00	32.00
☐ amethyst	50.00	60.00	52.00

ZIG ZAG
Fenton

Pitcher, decorated			
☐ marigold	180.00	—	—
☐ purple	225.00	—	—
☐ green	325.00	—	—
☐ blue	250.00	—	—
Tumbler, decorated			
☐ marigold	30.00	—	—
☐ purple	35.00	—	—
☐ green	40.00	—	—
☐ blue	45.00	—	—

ZIG ZAG
Millersburg

Bowl
☐ marigold	240.00	—	—
☐ purple	325.00	—	—
☐ green	350.00	—	—

Card Tray
☐ green	750.00	—	—

ZIPPERED HEART

Bowl, diameter 5″
☐ marigold	35.00	—	—
☐ purple	40.00	—	—

Bowl, diameter 9″
☐ marigold	70.00	—	—
☐ purple	110.00	—	—

Queen's Vase
☐ marigold	1500.00	—	—
☐ purple	1200.00	—	—
☐ green	1500.00	—	—

ZIPPER LOOP
Imperial

Hand Lamp
☐ marigold	425.00	—	—
☐ smoke	475.00	—	—

Lamp, mid-size
☐ marigold	250.00	—	—
☐ smoke	275.00	—	—

Lamp, large
☐ marigold	300.00	—	—
☐ smoke	350.00	—	—

ZIPPER STITCH
English Manufacturer

Cordial set (decanter, tray, and cordials)
☐ marigold	750.00	—	—

BIBLIOGRAPHY

Often glass collectors are attracted to more than one type of glass. For this reason, the following bibliography lists a variety of books pertaining to glass.

Addis, Wily P., *What's Behind Old Carnival: A Study of Patterns Seldom Seen*, Lakewood, OH, privately printed, 1971.

Arwas, Victor, *Glass: Art Nouveau to Art Deco*, NY, Rizzoli International, 1977.

Avila, George C., *The Pairpont Glass Story*, Reynolds-DeWalt Printing, Inc., 1968.

Barret, Richard Carter, *A Collector's Handbook of Blown and Pressed American Glass*, Manchester, VT, Forward's Color Productions, Inc., 1967.

Barret, Richard Carter, *A Collector's Handbook of American Art Glass*, Manchester, VT, Forward's Color Productions, 1971.

Belknap, E.M., *Milk Glass*, Crown Publishers, NY.

Boggess, Bill and Louise, *American Brilliant Cut Glass*, Crown Publishers, Inc.,1977.

Bones, Frances, *The Book of Duncan Glass*, Wallace-Homestead Book Co., 1973.

Bount, Henry, and Blount, Berniece, *French Cameo Glass*, Des Moines, IA, Wallace-Homestead, 1968.

Brahmer, Bonnie J., *Custard Glass*, Springfield, MO, privately published, 1966.

Bridgeman, Harriet, and Elizabeth Drury, *The Encyclopedia of Victoriana*, Macmillan, Inc., 1975.

Brown, Clark W., *A Supplement to Salt Dishes*, Wallace-Homestead Book Co., 1970.

Butler, Joseph T., *American Antiques 1800–1900*, Odyssey Press, 1965.

Carved and Decorated European Glass, Charles E. Tuttle Co., Inc., 1970.

Cole, Ann Kilborn, *Golden Guide to American Antiques*, NY, Golden Press, 1967.

Contemporary Art Glass, Crown Publishers, Inc., 1975.

Cooke, Lawrence S., ed., *Lighting in America. From Colonial Rushlights to Victorian Chandeliers*, Antiques Magazine Library, NY, Main Street/Universe Books, 1977.

Cosentino, Geraldine, and Regina Stewart, *Carnival Glass, A Guide for the Beginning Collector,* Golden Press, 1976.

Daniel, Dorothy, *Cut and Engraved Glass 1771–1905*, NY, M. Barrows & Company, 1950.

Darr, Patrick, *A Guide to Art and Pattern Glass*, Pilgrim House Publishing Co., 1960.

Davidson, Marshall B., ed., *The American Heritage History of Colonial Antiques*, NY, American Heritage Publishing Company, 1967.

Davis, Derek C. and Keith Middlemas, *Colored Glass*, Clarkson N. Potter, Inc., Publisher, NY.

Davis, Frank, *Antique Glass and Glass Collecting*, London, Hamlyn, 1973.

Davis, Frank, *The Country Life Book of Glass*, Glasgow, The University Press, 1966.

DiBartolomeo, Robert E., ed., *American Glass From the Pages of Antiques*, Vol. II, Pressed and Cut, Princeton, The Pyne Press, 1974.

Drepperd, Carl W., *ABC's of Old Glass*, NY, Doubleday & Company, 1968.

Drepperd, Carl W., *A Dictionary of American Antiques*, NY, Doubleday & Company, 1968.

Edwards, Bill, *Fenton Carnival Glass, The Early Years*, Collector Books, 1981.

Edwards, Bill, *Imperial Carnival Glass, The Early Years*, Collector Books, 1980.

Edwards, Bill, *Millersburg, The Queen of Carnival Glass*, Collector Books, 1976.

Edwards, Bill, *Northwood, King of Carnival Glass*, Collector Books, 1980.

Edwards, Bill, *Rarities In Carnival Glass*, Collector Books, 1978.

Edwards, Bill, *The Standard Encyclopedia of Carnival Glass*, Collector Books, 1982.

Elville, E.M., *English and Irish Cut Glass*, Country Life Limited, 1953.

Ericson, Eric E., *A Guide To Colored Steuben Glass (1903–1933)*, two vols., Colorado, The Lithographic Press, 1963–65.

Florence, Gene, *Elegant Glassware of the Depression Era*, Paducah, KY, Collector Books, 1983.

Florence, Gene, *Kitchen Glassware of the Depression Years*, Paducah, KY, Collector Books, 1981.

Florence, Gene, *Pocket Guide to Depression Glass*, revised third edition, Paducah, KY, Collector Books, 1983.

Florence, Gene, *The Collector's Encyclopedia of Akro Agate Glassware*, Paducah, KY, Collector Books, 1982.

Florence, Gene, *The Collector's Encyclopedia of Depression Glass*, sixth edition, Paducah, KY, Collector Books, 1984.

Frazer, Margaret, *Colored Glass, Discovering Antiques*, vol. 8, NY, Greystone Press, 1973, pp. 904–907.

Gardner, Paul V., *The Glass of Frederick Carder*, NY, Crown Publishers, 1971.

Greguire, Helen, *Carnival in Lights*, 103 Trimmer Road, Hilton, NY 14468, privately published, 1975.

Grover, Ray and Grover, Lee, *Art Glass Nouveau*, Rutland, VT, Charles E. Tuttle Co., 1967.

Grover, Ray and Grover, Lee, *Carved & Decorated European Art Glass*, Rutland, VT, Charles E. Tuttle Co., 1967.

Hallam, Angela, *English-Made Carnival*, Wise Books, Reigate, England.

Hammond, Dorothy, *Confusing Collectibles*, IA, Mid-American Book Company, 1969.

Hammond, Dorothy, *More Confusing Collectibles*, KS, C.B.P. Publishing Company, 1972.

Hand, Sherman, *Colors in Carnival Glass*, Books 1–4, Wallace-Homestead Book Co., 1967–1974.

Hartley, Julia M., and Cobb, Mary M., *The States Series, Early American Pattern Glass*, privately published, 1976.

Hartung, Marion T., *Carnival Glass*, Books 1–10, 718 Constitution Street, Emporia, KS 66801, privately published, 1967–1973.

Hartung, Marion T., *Northwood Pattern Glass in Color*, privately published, 1969.

Haslam, Malcolm, *Marks and Monograms of the Modern Movement*, 1875–1930, NY, Charles Scribner's Sons, 1977.

Heacock, William, *Encyclopedia of Victorian Colored Pattern Glass, Book I, Toothpick Holders from A-Z*, Antique Publications, 1976.

Heacock, William, *Encyclopedia of Victorian Colored Pattern Glass, Book II, Opalescent Glass from A-Z*, Antique Publications, 1975.

Heacock, William, *Encyclopedia of Victorian Colored Pattern Glass, Book III, Syrups, Sugar Shakers & Cruets from A-Z*, Antique Publications, 1976.

Heacock, William, *Encyclopedia of Victorian Colored Pattern Glass, Book 4, Custard Glass from A-Z*, Antique Publications, 1976.

Heacock, William, *Encyclopedia of Victorian Colored Pattern Glass, Book 5, U.S. Glass from A-Z*, Antique Publications, 1978.

Heacock, William, *Fenton Glass: The First Twenty-Five Years*, O-Val Advertising Corporation, 1978.

Heacock, William, *Fenton Glass: The Second Twenty-Five Years*, O-Val Advertising Corporation, 1980.

Hinds, Maxine, *Smashed Glass Reclaimed and Restored*, Route 2, P.O. Box 540, Galt, CA 95632, privately printed, 1972.

Hollister, Paul, Jr., *The Encyclopedia of Glass Paperweights*, NY, Clarkson N. Potter, 1969.

Hotchkiss, John F., *Art Glass Handbook*, NY, Hawthorn Books, 1972.

Hunter, Frederick William, *Stiegel Glass*, NY, Dover Publications, 1950.

Innes, Lowell, *Pittsburgh Glass 1797–1891: A History and Guide for Collectors,* Houghton Mifflin Company, 1976.

Jenkins, Dorothy H., *A Fortune in the Junk Pile*, Crown Publishing, Inc., NY, 1963.

Kamm, Minnie Watson, *Two Hundred Pattern Glass Pitchers*, six volumes., Grosse Pointe Farms, MI, privately published.

Kamm, Minnie Watson, *A Second Two Hundred Pattern Glass Pitchers*, Kamm Publications, 1940.

Kamm, Minnie Watson, *A Fourth Pitcher Book*, Kamm Publications 1950.

Kamm, Minnie W., and Wood, Serry (editors), *Encyclopedia of Antique Pattern Glass I*, Kamm Publications, 1961.

Kamm, Minnie W., and Wood, Serry (editors), *Encyclopedia of Antique Pattern Glass II*, Kamm Publications, 1961.

Klamkin, Marion, *The Collector's Guide to Carnival Glass*, Hawthorn Books, Inc., 1976.

Klein, William Karl, *Repairing and Restoring China and Glass*, NY., Harper & Row, 1962.

Koch, Robert, *Louis C. Tiffany, Rebel in Glass*, NY., Crown Publishers, 1964.

Koch, Robert, *Louis C. Tiffany's Glass—Bronzes—Lamps*, Crown Publishers, Inc., NY.

Lagerberg, Theodore and Viola, *Collectible Glass*, vols. 1, 2, and 4, New Port Richey, FL, pivately published, 1963–1968.

Lee, Ruth Webb, *Early American Pressed Glass*, Wellesley Hills, MA, Lee Publications, 105 Suffolk Road, Wellesley Hills, MA 02181, 1933.

Lee, Ruth Webb, *Nineteenth Century Art Glass*, NY, M. Barrows and Company, 1952.

Lee, Ruth Webb, *Sandwich Glass*, Wellesley Hills, MA, Lee Publications, 1966.

Lee, Ruth Webb, *Victorian Glass Handbook*, Wellesley Hills, MA, Lee Publications, 1946.

Lee, Ruth Webb, and Rose, James H., *American Glass Cup Plates*, Wellesley Hills, MA, Lee Publications, 1948.

Libbey Glass, *A Tradition of 150 Years*, Toledo Museum of Art, 1968.

Lindsey, Bessie M., *American Historical Glass*, VT, Charles E. Tuttle, 1967.

Malone, Laurence Adams, *How to Mend Your Treasures: Porcelain—(China)—Pottery—Glass*, NY, Phaedra Publishers, 1972.

McClinton, Katharine M., *Collecting American Victorian Antiques*, Charles Scribner's Sons, 1966.

McKean, Hugh F., *The "Lost" Treasures of Louis Comfort Tiffany*, Garden City, NY, Doubleday, 1980.

McKearin, George and Helen, *American Glass*, NY, Crown Publishers, 1966.

Mebane, John, *Collecting Brides' Baskets and Other Glass Fancies*, Wallace-Homestead Book Co., 1976.

Metz, Alice Hulett, *Early American Pattern Glass*, Chicago, IL, privately published.

Metz, Alice Hulett, *More Early American Pattern Glass*, vol. II, Chicago, privately published, 1965.

Moore, Donald E., *The Shape of Things in Carnival Glass*, 2101 Shoreline Drive, Alameda, CA 94501, privately published, 1975.

New England Glass Co., 1818–1888, Toledo Museum of Art, 1963.

Newman, Harold, *An Illustrated Dictionary of Glass*, London, Thames and Hudson, 1977.

Notley, Ray, *Carnival Glass*, 7 Hills Books.

Oliver, Elizabeth, *American Antique Glass*, NY, Golden Press, 1977.

Owens, Richard E., *Carnival Glass Tumblers*, 2611 Brass Lantern Drive, La Habra, CA 90361, privately published, 1975.

Papert, Emma, *The Illustrated Guide to American Glass*, Hawthorn Books, Inc., 1972.

Pearson, J. Michael, *Encyclopedia of American Cut and Engraved Glass (1880–1917), Vol. I; Geometric Conceptions*, 402844 Ocean View Station, Miami Beach, FL 33140, privately printed, 1975.

Pearson, J. Michael, *Encyclopedia of American Cut and Engraved Glass (1880–1917), Vol. II: Realistic Patterns*, 402844 Ocean View Station, Miami Beach, FL 33140, privately printed, 1977.

Pearson, J. Michael and Dorothy T., *American Cut Glass for the Discriminating Collector*, Miami, FL, The Franklin Press, 1965.

Pennsylvania Glassware, 1870–1904, American Historical Catalog Collection, Princeton, The Pyne Press, 1972.

Peterson, Arthur G., *400 Trademarks on Glass*, Takoma Park, MD, Washington College Press, 1968.

Peterson, Arthur G., *Glass Salt Shakers: 1,000 Patterns*, Wallace-Homestead Book Company, Des Moines, IA.

Peterson, Arthur G., *Salt and Salt Shakers*, Washington College Press, Washington, D.C.

Peterson, Arthur G., *333 Glass Salt Shakers*, Washington College Press, Washington, D.C.

Polak, Ada, *Glass, Its Tradition and Its Makers*, G.P. Putnam's Sons, 1975.

Presznick, Rose M., *Carnival Glass*, Books 1–6, 7810 Avon Lake Road, Lodi, OH 44254, privately published, 1966.

Presznick, Rose M., *Encyclopedia of New Carnival Glass and Iridescent Glass*, 7810 Avon Lake Road, Lodi, OH 44254, privately published, 1974.

Rainwater, Dorothy T. and H. Ivan, *American Silverplate*, Thomas Nelson, Inc., Nashville, TN, and Everybody's Press, Hanover, Pa.

Rainwater, Dorothy T., and H. Ivan, *Sterling Silver Holloware*, Pyne Press, Princeton, NJ.

Revi, Albert Christian, *American Art Nouveau Glass*, TN, Thomas Nelson, 1968.

Revi, Albert C., *American Cut and Engraved Glass*, Thomas Nelson, Inc., 1970.

Revi, Albert C., *American Pressed Glass and Figure Bottles*, Thomas Nelson & Sons, 1964.

Revi, Albert Christian, *Nineteenth Century Glass*, NY, Galahad Books, 1967.

Revi, Albert Christian, (ed), *The Spinning Wheel's Complete Book of Antiques*, NY, Grosset & Dunlap, 1972.

Rose, James H., *The Story of American Pressed Glass of the Lacy Period, 1825–1850*, The Corning Museum of Glass, 1954.

Schrijver, Elka, *Glass and Crystal*, Universe Books, Inc., 1964.

Schwartz, Marvin D., *American Glass: Blown and Moulded*, NJ, The Pyne Press, 1974.

Schwartz, Marvin D., *Collector's Guide to Antique American Glass*, Doubleday & Company, Inc., 1969.

Shull, Thelma, *Victorian Antiques*, Charles E. Tuttle Company, Rutland, VT.

Springer, L. Elsinore, *The Collector's Book of Bells*, Crown Publishers, Inc., NY.

Stout, Sandra McPhee, *Depression Glass in Color*, Ephrata, WA, privately published.

Stout, Sandra M., *Depression Glass III*, Wallace-Homestead Book Co., 1976.

Swan, Frank H., *Portland Glass*, Wallace-Homestead Book Co.

Traub, Jules S., *The Glass of Desire Christian*, Chicago, The Art Glass Exchange, 1978.

Warren, Phelps, *Irish Glass*, Charles Scribner's Sons, 1970.

Watkins, Laura W., *Cambridge Glass, 1818–1888*, Bramhill House, 1930.

Weatherman, Hazel Marie, *Colored Glassware of the Depression Era*, revised and expanded edition, Springfield, MO, privately published.

Weatherman, Hazel Marie, *Colored Glassware of the Depression Era 2*, privately printed, 1970.

Weatherman, Hazel Marie, *Fostoria: Its First Fifty Years*, privately printed.

Weatherman, Hazel, Marie, *The Decorated Tumbler*, privately printed.

Webb, Jack Lawton, *A Guide to New Carnival Glass*, Joplin, MO, Imperial Publishing Company.

Webber, Norman W., *Collecting Glass*, NY, Arco, 1972.

Weiss, Gustav, *Books of Glass*, Praeger Publishers, Inc., 1971.

Whitlow, Harry H., *Art, Colored and Cameo Glass*, Riverview, MI, privately published, 1967.

Whitmyer, Margaret and Kenn, *Children's Dishes*, Paducah, KY, Collector Books, 1984.

Wiener, Herbert, and Freda Liplowitz, *Rarities in American Cut Glass*, The Collectors House of Books Publishing Co., 1975.

Wilson, Kenneth M., *New England Glass and Glassmaking*, Old Sturbridge, Inc., 1972.

Ziegfeld, Edwin, Faulkner, Ray, and Hill, Gerald, *Art Today*, NY, Holt, Rinehart and Winston, 1965.

THE INTERNATIONAL CARNIVAL GLASS ASSOCIATION
Invites Your Membership

Share Your Enjoyment of Collecting

☆ Yearly Convention

☆ Quarterly Bulletin
Showing Carnival in Color

☆ $10.00 per family per year

Write to:
LeRoy Markley, Secretary/OPG
R.R. 1, Box 14
Mentone, IN 46539

The HOUSE OF COLLECTIBLES Series

☐ Please send me the following price guides—
☐ I would like the most current edition of the books listed below.

THE OFFICIAL PRICE GUIDES TO:

☐ 753-3	American Folk Art (ID) 1st Ed.	$14.95
☐ 199-3	American Silver & Silver Plate 5th Ed.	11.95
☐ 513-1	Antique Clocks 3rd Ed.	10.95
☐ 283-3	Antique & Modern Dolls 3rd Ed.	10.95
☐ 287-6	Antique & Modern Firearms 6th Ed.	11.95
☐ 755-X	Antiques & Collectibles 9th Ed.	11.95
☐ 289-2	Antique Jewelry 5th Ed.	11.95
☐ 362-7	Art Deco (ID) 1st Ed.	14.95
☐ 447-X	Arts and Crafts: American Decorative Arts, 1894–1923 (ID) 1st Ed.	12.95
☐ 539-5	Beer Cans & Collectibles 4th Ed.	7.95
☐ 521-2	Bottles Old & New 10th Ed.	10.95
☐ 532-8	Carnival Glass 2nd Ed.	10.95
☐ 295-7	Collectible Cameras 2nd Ed.	10.95
☐ 548-4	Collectibles of the '50s & '60s 1st Ed.	9.95
☐ 740-1	Collectible Toys 4th Ed.	10.95
☐ 531-X	Collector Cars 7th Ed.	12.95
☐ 538-7	Collector Handguns 4th Ed.	14.95
☐ 748-7	Collector Knives 9th Ed.	12.95
☐ 361-9	Collector Plates 5th Ed.	11.95
☐ 296-5	Collector Prints 7th Ed.	12.95
☐ 001-6	Depression Glass 2nd Ed.	9.95
☐ 589-1	Fine Art 1st Ed.	19.95
☐ 311-2	Glassware 3rd Ed.	10.95
☐ 243-4	Hummel Figurines & Plates 6th Ed.	10.95
☐ 523-9	Kitchen Collectibles 2nd Ed.	10.95
☐ 080-6	Memorabilia of Elvis Presley and The Beatles 1st Ed.	10.95
☐ 291-4	Military Collectibles 5th Ed.	11.95
☐ 525-5	Music Collectibles 6th Ed.	11.95
☐ 313-9	Old Books & Autographs 7th Ed.	11.95
☐ 298-1	Oriental Collectibles 3rd Ed.	11.95
☐ 761-4	Overstreet Comic Book 18th Ed.	12.95
☐ 522-0	Paperbacks & Magazines 1st Ed.	10.95
☐ 297-3	Paper Collectibles 5th Ed.	10.95
☐ 744-4	Political Memorabilia 1st Ed.	10.95
☐ 529-8	Pottery & Porcelain 6th Ed.	11.95
☐ 524-7	Radio, TV & Movie Memorabilia 3rd Ed.	11.95
☐ 081-4	Records 8th Ed.	16.95
☐ 763-0	Royal Doulton 6th Ed.	12.95
☐ 280-9	Science Fiction & Fantasy Collectibles 2nd Ed.	10.95
☐ 747-9	Sewing Collectibles 1st Ed.	8.95
☐ 358-9	Star Trek/Star Wars Collectibles 2nd Ed.	8.95
☐ 086-5	Watches 8th Ed.	12.95
☐ 248-5	Wicker 3rd Ed.	10.95

THE OFFICIAL:

☐ 760-6	Directory to U.S. Flea Markets 2nd Ed.	5.95
☐ 365-1	Encyclopedia of Antiques 1st Ed.	9.95
☐ 369-4	Guide to Buying and Selling Antiques 1st Ed.	9.95
☐ 414-3	Identification Guide to Early American Furniture 1st Ed.	9.95
☐ 413-5	Identification Guide to Glassware 1st Ed.	9.95
☐ 412-7	Identification Guide to Pottery & Porcelain 1st Ed.	$9.95
☐ 415-1	Identification Guide to Victorian Furniture 1st Ed.	9.95

THE OFFICIAL (SMALL SIZE) PRICE GUIDES TO:

☐ 309-0	Antiques & Flea Markets 4th Ed.	4.95
☐ 269-8	Antique Jewelry 3rd Ed.	4.95
☐ 085-7	Baseball Cards 8th Ed.	4.95
☐ 647-2	Bottles 3rd Ed.	4.95
☐ 544-1	Cars & Trucks 3rd Ed.	5.95
☐ 519-0	Collectible Americana 2nd Ed.	4.95
☐ 294-9	Collectible Records 3rd Ed.	4.95
☐ 306-6	Dolls 4th Ed.	4.95
☐ 762-2	Football Cards 8th Ed.	4.95
☐ 540-9	Glassware 3rd Ed.	4.95
☐ 526-3	Hummels 4th Ed.	4.95
☐ 279-5	Military Collectibles 3rd Ed.	4.95
☐ 764-9	Overstreet Comic Book Companion 2nd Ed.	4.95
☐ 278-7	Pocket Knives 3rd Ed.	4.95
☐ 527-1	Scouting Collectibles 4th Ed.	4.95
☐ 494-1	Star Trek/Star Wars Collectibles 3rd Ed.	3.95
☐ 088-1	Toys 5th Ed.	4.95

THE OFFICIAL BLACKBOOK PRICE GUIDES OF:

☐ 092-X	U.S. Coins 27th Ed.	4.95
☐ 095-4	U.S. Paper Money 21st Ed.	4.95
☐ 098-9	U.S. Postage Stamps 11th Ed.	4.95

THE OFFICIAL INVESTORS GUIDE TO BUYING & SELLING:

☐ 534-4	Gold, Silver & Diamonds 2nd Ed.	12.95
☐ 535-2	Gold Coins 2nd Ed.	12.95
☐ 536-0	Silver Coins 2nd Ed.	12.95
☐ 537-9	Silver Dollars 2nd Ed.	12.95

THE OFFICIAL NUMISMATIC GUIDE SERIES:

☐ 254-X	The Official Guide to Detecting Counterfeit Money 2nd Ed.	7.95
☐ 257-4	The Official Guide to Mint Errors 4th Ed.	7.95

SPECIAL INTEREST SERIES:

☐ 506-9	From Hearth to Cookstove 3rd Ed.	17.95
☐ 504-2	On Method Acting 8th Printing	6.95

	TOTAL	

SEE REVERSE SIDE FOR ORDERING INSTRUCTIONS

FOR IMMEDIATE DELIVERY

VISA & MASTER CARD CUSTOMERS

ORDER TOLL FREE!
1-800-638-6460

This number is for orders only; it is not tied into the customer service or business office. Customers not using charge cards must use mail for ordering since payment is required with the order—sorry, no C.O.D.'s.

OR SEND ORDERS TO

THE HOUSE OF COLLECTIBLES
201 East 50th Street
New York, New York 10022

POSTAGE & HANDLING RATES

First Book $1.00
Each Additional Copy or Title $0.50

Total from columns on order form. Quantity_____$_____

☐ Check or money order enclosed $_____ (include postage and handling)

☐ Please charge $_____to my: ☐ MASTERCARD ☐ VISA

Charge Card Customers Not Using Our Toll Free Number Please Fill Out The Information Below

Account No. _____ Expiration Date_____
(all digits)
Signature_____

NAME (please print)_____PHONE_____

ADDRESS_____APT. #_____

CITY_____STATE_____ZIP_____